The Problem of Democracy in Postwar Europe

The current perception of democratic crisis in Western Europe gives a renewed urgency to a new perspective on the way democracy was reconstructed after World War II and the principles that underpinned its postwar transformation. This study accounts for the formation of the postwar democratic order in Western Europe by studying how the main political actors in France, West Germany, and Italy conceptualized democracy and strove over its meaning. Based upon a wide range of librarian and archival sources from these countries, it tracks changing conceptions of democracy among leading politicians, political parties, and leaders of social movements and unveils how they were deeply divided over key principles of postwar democracy—such as the political party, the free market economy, representation, and civic participation. By comparing three national debates on the question what democracy meant and how it should be institutionalized and practiced, this study argues that only in the 1970s, conceptions of democracy converged, and key political actors accepted each other as democrats with similar conceptions of democracy. This study thereby deconstructs the myth of the quick emergence of one consensual Western European model of democracy after 1945, demonstrates that its formation was a long and contentious process in which national differences were often of crucial importance, and contributes to an enhanced understanding of the historical roots of the current sentiment of democratic crisis.

Pepijn Corduwener is an assistant professor in history at Utrecht University.

Routledge Studies in Modern European History

For a full list of titles in this series, please visit www.routledge.com

25 Violence, Memory, and History
   Western Perceptions of Kristallnacht
   Edited by Colin McCullough and Nathan Wilson

26 Turkey and the Rescue of European Jews
   I. Izzet Bahar

27 Antifascism After Hitler
   East German Youth and Socialist Memory, 1949–1989
   Catherine Plum

28 Fascism and Ideology
   Italy, Britain, and Norway
   Salvatore Garau

29 Hitler's Brudervolk
   The Dutch and the Colonization of Occupied Eastern Europe, 1939–1945
   Geraldien von Frijtag Drabbe Künzel

30 Alan S. Milward and Contemporary European History
   Collected Academic Reviews
   Edited by Fernando Guirao and Frances M.B. Lynch

31 Ireland's Great Famine and Popular Politics
   Edited by Enda Delaney and Breandán Mac Suibhne

32 Legacies of Violence in Contemporary Spain
   Exhuming the Past, Understanding the Present
   Edited by Ofelia Ferrán and Lisa Hilbink

33 The Problem of Democracy in Postwar Europe
   Political Actors and the Formation of the Postwar Model of Democracy in France, West Germany and Italy
   Pepijn Corduwener

The Problem of Democracy in Postwar Europe

Political Actors and the Formation of the Postwar Model of Democracy in France, West Germany, and Italy

Pepijn Corduwener

NEW YORK AND LONDON

First published 2017
by Routledge
711 Third Avenue, New York, NY 10017

and by Routledge
2 Park Square, Milton Park, Abingdon, Oxon OX14 4RN

First issued in paperback 2018

Routledge is an imprint of the Taylor & Francis Group, an informa business

© 2017 Taylor & Francis

The right of Pepijn Corduwener to be identified as author of this work has been asserted in accordance with sections 77 and 78 of the Copyright, Designs and Patents Act 1988.

All rights reserved. No part of this book may be reprinted or reproduced or utilised in any form or by any electronic, mechanical, or other means, now known or hereafter invented, including photocopying and recording, or in any information storage or retrieval system, without permission in writing from the publishers.

Trademark notice: Product or corporate names may be trademarks or registered trademarks, and are used only for identification and explanation without intent to infringe.

Library of Congress Cataloging-in-Publication Data
Names: Corduwener, Pepijn, author.
Title: The problem of democracy in postwar Europe : political actors and the formation of the postwar model of democracy in France, West Germany and Italy / by Pepijn Corduwener.
Description: New York : Routledge, [2017] | Series: Routledge studies in modern European history ; 33 | Includes bibliographical references and index.
Identifiers: LCCN 2016019400 (print) | LCCN 2016031675 (ebook) | ISBN 9781138690639 (hbk) | ISBN 9781315536835 (ebk) | ISBN 9781315536835 ()
Subjects: LCSH: Europe—Politics and government—1945–1989. | Democracy—Europe—History—20th century. | France—Politics and government—1945– | Democracy—France—History—20th century. | Germany (West)—Politics and government—1945–1990. | Democracy—Germany (West)—History. | Italy—Politics and government—1945–1976. | Democracy—Italy—History—20th century.
Classification: LCC JN12 .C67 2017 (print) | LCC JN12 (ebook) | DDC 320.9409/044—dc23
LC record available at https://lccn.loc.gov/2016019400

ISBN 13: 978-1-138-32972-0 (pbk)
ISBN 13: 978-1-138-69063-9 (hbk)

Typeset in Sabon
by Apex CoVantage, LLC

To Jo

Contents

List of Abbreviations ix
Acknowledgements xi

Introduction 1
1 Transforming Democracy After the Second World War 11
2 Contesting Democratic Legitimacy During the Cold War 39
3 Converging Conceptions of Democracy at the Turn of the 1960s 65
4 Political Elites and the Challenge to the Parliamentary Model 94
5 Democracy Between Crisis and Consensus After the 1973 Oil Crisis 124
Conclusion 160

References 169
Index 197

Abbreviations

CDU	Christlich Demokratische Union
CLN	Comitato di Liberazione Nazionale
CSU	Christlich-Soziale Union
DC	Democrazia Cristiana
FDP	Freie Demokratische Partei
KDP	Kommunistische Partei Deutschlands
MRP	Mouvement Républicain Populaire
MSI	Movimento Sociale Italiano
PCF	Parti Communiste Français
PCI	Partito Comunista Italiano
PSI	Partito Socialista Italiano
PSIUP	Partito Socialista Italiano di Unità Proletaria
PS	Parti Socialiste
PSU	Parti Socialiste Unifié
RPF	Rassemblement du Peuple Français
SDS	Sozialistische Deutsche Studentenbund
SFIO	Section Française de l'Internationale Ouvrière
SPD	Sozialdemokratische Partei Deutschlands
SRP	Sozialistische Reichspartei

Acknowledgements

While working on this book, I often felt that writing was a rather solitary task. Now that the project is finished and I look back upon the past years, I must admit that the opposite is true. This project could never have been completed without the advice, assistance, and support of so many others. It is my pleasure to thank these people here.

This book started life as a PhD dissertation, which could never have been completed without Ido de Haan's ambition and his faith in the project, which often seemed too large. Ido has set a lightning example of what it means to be an academic. His sharp eye and criticism made the manuscript better than I could ever have imagined and have profoundly shaped me as a scholar.

I am deeply indebted to the Utrecht University History Department, which generously funded all my research travel and enabled me to present aspects of my work at conferences abroad. The department directors, Maarten Prak, Joris van Eijnatten, and Leen Dorsman, encouraged me in many ways; the way they value and foster the development of young scholars is praiseworthy. By also employing me as a lecturer, the department offered me the rewarding experience of teaching students. Teaching not only provided me with a valuable distance from library isolation, but the students' curiosity also inspired me throughout the project. My special thanks goes to some dear colleagues and friends at the department who have acted as sparring partners and mentors over the past few years and in particular to the colleagues at the political history section. Stefan Couperus, Liesbeth van de Grift, René Koekkoek and Christianne Smit deserve to be mentioned explicitly.

Moving beyond Utrecht, there are several institutes and people who have greatly contributed to this study. The Dutch-Flemish Research School of Political History enabled me to participate in a European network of PhD candidates. The Royal Netherlands Institute in Rome offered me indispensable support on the Italian side of the research. It was also an essential place for seclusion and late-hour library work, the importance of which cannot be overestimated. General assistance from the staff in Rome, and particularly Arthur Weststeijn's response to my manuscript, was extremely valuable.

I would also like to thank many others who, at conferences and elsewhere, commented on parts of the manuscript in draft form. Martin Conway, Jan-Werner Müller, Giovanni Orsina, and Henk te Velde deserve to be mentioned explicitly. So does Giulia Cartini, of the Italian Cultural Institute in Amsterdam, whose knowledge of Italian history prevented many potential inaccuracies in the manuscript. Many thanks to Mischa Hoyinck and Robert Chesal, who have quickly and professionally edited the manuscript. My gratitude also goes to the editorial teams at Routledge, and especially to Max Novick, for their support.

Special thanks go to friends and family who have always displayed a keen interest in my efforts to understand the more obscure aspects of democracy's postwar history. Nick and Simon deserve to be thanked for keeping their sense of humour when I feared to lose mine. My mother has been a continuous source of support in many ways.

As always, the most important people come last, as has probably too often been the case over the past few years. My gratitude for the love of Jo and Daniel at home is most heartfelt and has been the key to the project. Daniel has grown and developed at the same time as the manuscript and has made me so much prouder than this book could ever do. Jo, your understanding, sacrifices, and enthusiasm have always given me confidence in the book and in us. It is to you that this book is dedicated.

Amsterdam, March 2016

Introduction

Democracy in Europe appears to be in crisis. There are deep concerns about the relationship between democracy and free market capitalism in the wake of the recent economic recession. Political parties are facing declining membership, voter volatility, and changing modes of political participation, whereas politicians are finding it increasingly difficult to build coalitions in a fragmented and polarized political landscape. Most notably, the rise of new parties, often labelled as populist, is posing a challenge to governability and, more importantly, to the consensus among political elites on the principles of democracy.[1] All these developments are perceived as signs that the 'golden age' of democracy enjoyed in the decades following the Second World War is over and that this political model is now in steep decline.

The topic of democracy, especially in the post-1945 era, has gained increased attention from historians. Numerous national histories, many of outstanding quality, describe the development and crises of democratic systems and the debates they sparked. A recent strand of scholarship views the history of ideas in post-1945 Europe as a whole through the lens of democracy and aims to capture the spirit of democracy since 1945.[2] This book adds to this rapidly expanding body of scholarship by comparing various understandings of democracy among political elites in France, West Germany, and Italy and exploring how these ideas developed, influenced the contestation of political power, and ultimately led to a consensus on the principles of democracy. This study traces how the postwar democratic model was formed and disentangles the various democratic narratives it consists of.

Although it is tempting to see the contemporary history of democracy as a linear disintegration of a consensus model that existed immediately following the Second World War, this would ignore the fact that the principles of democracy were fiercely contested during the first postwar decades. The process through which political elites forged a broad consensus on the meaning of democracy was long and arduous. The elites clashed over democracy's form, over what it required in terms of social conditions and institutional design, and over who qualified as a democrat. Feeding into these disputes were concerns about the precarious democratization process after years of dictatorship, suspicions inherited from the fascist era, and domestic tensions that reflected the antagonisms of the Cold War. In 1945 and the immediate aftermath, there was no single universally endorsed model of democracy that political elites agreed on. Instead, competing democratic paradigms of rival parties and ideologies converged only gradually in an age when being seen as a true democrat was the key to political power.

To grasp the form of democracy that eventually emerged from this long conceptual struggle, we need to understand how politicians and others close to the centre of political power in the postwar period thought.[3] Political debates on the meaning of democracy in post-1945 Western Europe were not abstract, philosophical arguments. As democracy was the key to political legitimacy and eligibility, these debates directly affected the contestation of political power. This means that democracy, like many other political concepts, is an 'empty category' whose meaning has remained essentially contested[4] but also that it is arguably a key example of what the British philosopher Walter Bryce Gallie called an 'appraisive concept'.[5] In 1956, Gallie noted that democracy 'steadily established itself as the appraisive political concept *par excellence*', by which he meant that political actors all aimed to establish their conception of democracy as the only valid one.[6] He observed that there were 'dogfights' over the true meaning of democracy because virtually all political actors claimed to be democratic—and certainly more democratic than their political opponents. In other words, they aimed to delegitimize the claim other politicians laid to the meaning of democracy in favour of their own definition. Recently, historian Jan-Werner Müller convincingly put forward a similar argument, stating that any scrutiny of modern European politics should concern the analysis of political actors' 'attempts to create new conceptual meanings by recontextualizing ostensibly democratic values'.[7]

The image of 'dogfights' over the meaning of democracy contrasts with the dominant scholarly understanding of democracy in post-1945 Western Europe. Most studies take as their starting point the question of how Europe was able to avoid the political abyss of the interwar period. This has generated a broad historiographical agreement that the democracies of the post-1945 era were 'transformed democracies' with an institutional outline designed specifically to limit the chance of another democratic breakdown.[8] According to this view, political elites largely agreed on what democracy meant and on the socioeconomic conditions and political institutions essential for it to function well—in contradistinction to their counterparts in the interwar years.[9] Consequently, consensus among political elites on how democracy should be understood and practiced is thought to have played an important role in the surprisingly resilient renaissance of democracy after 1945. From this perspective, postwar politics seems to have been a matter of consensus based on a broad and structural consent on what constituted democracy.[10] Particularly the period between 1945 and the mid-1970s is seen as a 'golden age' characterized by a deep consensus among major political actors on the nature of democracy.[11]

The prevailing scholarly view held that this consensus among political elites resulted primarily from the limitation of popular influence on the decision-making process. Because mobilization of the masses brought democracy to the brink of collapse in the 1920s and 1930s, postwar political elites agreed that democracy should be 'restrained democracy'.[12] This type of system was characterized not only by restrictions on the people's influence on decision making, but also by institutional mechanisms to safeguard the status quo against a potential radicalization of the popular will, and by a confinement of liberty to individual rights. From this perspective, the protests of 1968 are often understood as a revolt against these limitations on political participation. However, the protests failed to change the restraining principles of postwar democracy. In other words, democracy was finally 'made safe for the world' after the volatile will of the people had jeopardized it in the interwar years.[13]

The second major ingredient of the postwar consensus, as understood in the prevailing historiographical view, was the principle of 'coordinated capitalism', which underpinned the economic boom of the 1950s and 1960s and contributed significantly to political stability.[14] Historiographical understandings of this second characteristic are not universally shared. Some historians emphasize the liberal traits of the social market economy, whereas others see the postwar renewal as the triumph of a model of social democracy that held bourgeois elites in check.[15] Historians do, however, share a perception that capitalism and democracy were accepted as compatible and that this idea was even embraced by the moderate European Left, which despite its revolutionary discourse was solidly on the way to reform. This acceptance of capitalism not only distinguished Western European democracies from the 'people's democracies' in the East, but it also fit in with the predilection for restricted freedom and protection of individual liberties. The Western European communist parties, which claimed to be both democratic and anti-capitalist, are often excluded from studies of democratic discourse in this period.[16]

Some of the smaller Western European countries such as Belgium, Austria, and the Netherlands might seem to have fit in neatly with this image of elite consensus, limited popular involvement, and coordinated capitalism. But the contrast between this generic model and national historiographies becomes sharper if one looks at the historiography of democracy in post-1945 France, Italy, and to a lesser extent, the Federal Republic of Germany. These were all countries where democracy most dramatically failed in the interwar period and where the Cold War had the biggest domestic impact. It is also these three countries which provide the most insight into the nature of democracy's postwar transformation, as France, West Germany, and Italy wrote new constitutions after 1945 and were determined to construct a postwar model of democracy distinct from their recent past. In contrast with the image of rapid success and consensus that predominates in the historiography on democracy in Western Europe as a whole, individual histories of these three countries emphasize the frequent and sometimes fierce conflicts between politicians throughout the postwar era on how democracy should function and who was deemed a democrat.

Prevailing historiography explains the problematic nature of European democracy's postwar transformation mainly as the result of specific national circumstances, leaving the question of how it related to broader pan-European developments largely unanswered. The uniquely problematic nature of democracy in the post-1945 era is most obvious in Italian historiography. The rise of Mussolini, the fascist regime, violent domestic conflicts in the final years of the war, and the role of the resistance in particular, all left indelible marks on Italian historiography, in which these topics occupied a major place.[17] Since the collapse of Italy's First Republic in the early 1990s, historiographical attention has shifted to the nature of Italy's democracy. Although some scholars caution their peers not to frame Italian democracy's problems mainly in terms of national peculiarities,[18] an expanding strand of scholarship emphasizes the unique features of Italian democracy.

Italian politician Aldo Moro, coining a phrase popularized in the decades since, once called Italy a particularly 'difficult democracy'.[19] The reasons for this difficulty have frequently been the subject of heated debate in the post-1945 era. Some point to the position of the Italian Communist Party, the largest communist party in Western Europe, which ruled out the possibility of government alternation and gave Italy's politics an 'imperfect two-party system'.[20] Others refer to the continuities between the fascist regime and the postwar state, referring either to state employees and socioeconomic interests[21] or to a specific Italian way of conducting politics in which elites were divorced from the average citizen.[22] Such debates have intensified since the early 1990s. The breakdown of the old party system ushered in a phase of protracted political transformation whose outcome, if any, is still unknown. It has confirmed, however, the widely perceived 'Italian exception', particularly with regard to the relationship between political parties, the state, and society in the postwar era.[23]

The historiography of the Federal Republic bears a closer resemblance to the general European trend towards a restrained democracy that went hand in hand with capitalism. Historians have generally developed a rather positive view of the Federal Republic's democratic achievements. Of course, this enthusiasm is not universally shared, and intellectual history in particular has pointed to the resistance that the Federal Republic encountered in its nascent phase.[24] Some argue that Germany's democracy was not always as consensual as it seemed,[25] in part because the Sozialdemokratische Partei Deutschlands (SPD) was relatively late to reform itself into a social democratic people's party.[26] Most historians, however, are more concerned with explaining democracy's resilience and vitality and conceive the postwar success of democracy as a break with the troubled relationship between the state, the nation, and (democratic) liberalism in German history.

In the latter view, it has been argued that Germany only gradually left its *Sonderweg* and unequivocally embarked on the 'long road West' over the course of the postwar era.[27] In explaining this success, scholars point not only to the influence of the Allies in sidelining political extremes in a crucial phase of political reconstruction[28] but also to the way in which the Federal Republic's founding figures developed institutional mechanisms to guarantee stability and arm democracy with useful means to defend itself, such as the constitutional court.[29] In this view, West Germany's institutional outline arguably epitomized the 'restrained' democracy of the post-1945 era, in which a broad party political consensus and an exclusion of popular influence ensured political stability. This order was challenged during the 1960s and 1970s, but its resilience was underlined by its ability to absorb the social movements that questioned the democratic legitimacy of the system and protect the state against political violence through democratic means.[30] This confirmed the leading perspective in which the Federal Republic became not only a mature but also a 'successful' democracy.[31]

In comparison with the largely negative evaluation of democracy in Italy, and the success story of the Federal Republic, the history of democracy in France has received mixed reviews. What it shares with Italy and West Germany's historiographies is that historians have mainly seen French postwar democracy, too, in terms of national exceptions. This has everything to do with the fact that France was the first country on the European continent to experience a democratic revolution. The legacy of the French Revolution haunted the French and in the nineteenth century deeply divided them on the reconciliation of popular sovereignty and state authority.[32] This resulted not only in five consecutive republics but also in experiences with dictatorship that rested on both authoritarian rule and a direct appeal to the will of the people.[33] Even before they were explicitly framed in democratic terms, these competing views of French politics pivoted either on parliamentary representation as a counterweight to strong executive power or on a strong leader who embodied the unity of all French citizens and acted on their behalf.

Initially, it seemed as if France's postwar history was to continue along these lines as the Fourth Republic bore many similarities to its predecessor. In addition, its sharp political polarization, with both the Gaullists and the communists in opposition, made an uneasy fit with the general pattern of Western European postwar consensus.[34] It is widely agreed upon that only the Fifth Republic has brought the country political stability, but whether it has resolved the problems of French democracy is still a moot point. Both the way in which De Gaulle returned to power and the reforms he put in place were deeply polarizing. To Gaullists, these facts demonstrated how, after every disaster in France's history, a strong leader emerges and takes the nation by the hand.[35] To others, they showed how politics repeatedly turned violent in mid-twentieth-century France[36] or constituted a continuation of nineteenth-century plebiscitary notions of politics.[37] Pierre Rosanvallon argued that these facts contributed to a broader acceptance of a 'modified Jacobinism', an equilibrium between the desire for popular influence and the necessity of executive power.[38] In his view, it is arguable that De Gaulle's return and reforms at least contributed to ending the 'French exception'.[39] But on this point, too, scholars are divided. Many have continued to emphasize the problems of French democracy and to analyze them in terms of typical French peculiarities.[40] It can be asserted that Gaullist democracy created the preconditions for the populism of the Front National[41] or that it failed to solve a crisis of public confidence in representative institutions partially caused by the strong centralist state.[42]

The national historiographies of Italy, France, and West Germany differ from more generic European studies in two ways. On the one hand, national historiographies correctly point out that many contemporary observers in these three nations did not perceive the first few postwar decades as an age of consent on the principles of democracy, let alone a 'democratic golden age', thus revealing the problematic and drawn-out transformation of postwar democracy often overlooked by more generic studies covering the entire continent. On the other hand, the national historiographies are more 'parochial' than transnational studies in that they analyze the problems and setbacks of postwar democracy and the debate this engendered, mostly in national terms.[43] In other words, historians often discuss the problems of postwar democracy in terms of national peculiarities, even though many of the most pressing problems of democracy that politicians sought to resolve were not unique. Every country in Europe had to address issues such as how democracy related to capitalism, whether parties were compatible with democratic government, how the separation of powers should be organized, how democracy should react to civic protests, and perhaps most importantly, which political actors were true democrats.

By comparing three national debates between politicians who exemplify the transformed democracies, and weaving the resulting comparisons together, this study unveils the problematic and prolonged process of establishing a consensus among political elites on the principles of democratic government after the Second World War. It shows that the history of democracy in postwar Western Europe is not a history of national exceptions. Instead, it is fair to speak of an entangled history because politicians in France, West Germany, and Italy had to contend with very similar issues and often responded to them in comparable ways. The debates in these countries also developed in broadly similar ways as they were based on the major ideologies' competing democratic paradigms.

These different democratic paradigms clashed frequently, especially for the first fifteen postwar years. This was not only the case in France and Italy, which had large communist parties that laid claim to the meaning of democracy every bit as much as the Christian Democrats did, but also in the more stable Federal Republic, which saw deep divisions between the social democrats and Christian Democrats on the question of who embodied West Germany's democratic values. Such tensions slowly eased from the 1960s onwards; the protests in 1968 and the economic crisis of 1973 strengthened the consensus among political elites on the principles of democracy. By the time the Berlin Wall fell, the prevailing democratic model that had taken so long to agree on also contained the first seeds of discontent with that consensus. Sections of the population felt an increasing dissatisfaction with the way in which political elites consensually defined the boundaries of the democracy—and delegitimized those who proposed political alternatives to how societies should be governed. The model that had emerged from the protracted debate among the major political actors of the postwar order was therefore not an unequivocal success. Rather, it constituted yet another example of a democratic paradigm that has come under attack.

The five chapters of this study disentangle the long and problematic formation of the postwar democratic order between the end of the Second World War and the 1980s. Chapter One discusses the political debate from the time of the liberation to the signing of the countries' new constitutions, roughly from 1943 to 1949. It argues that Western Europe witnessed a 'democratic moment' that coincided with national liberations and shows how the semantic confusion over the meaning of democracy was linked to the struggle for political power. Chapter One goes on to discuss how the explanations political actors gave for the failure of interwar democracies intersected with postwar power constellations. It also shows how different notions of democracy were reflected in the countries' postwar constitutions.

Chapter Two centres on the iciest phase of the Cold War in Western Europe. In terms of the debate on democracy, contemporaries did not consider the 1950s a decade of stability, reconstruction, and economic growth but one of (perceived) threats (of communism, neo-fascism, Gaullism, and authoritarianism) and of tensions related to the question of who deserved democratic legitimacy.

Chapter Three shows how, after the starkest divisions were overcome around 1960, the socialists, social democrats, and Christian Democrats in West Germany and Italy reached consensus on the rules of the democratic game. The chapter compares these developments with the fall of the Fourth Republic in France, which heralded a change in power relations in which the Gaullists gradually institutionalized their conception of democracy but continued to encounter challenges to their democratic legitimacy.

Chapter Four discusses the sense of crisis surrounding democratic government, as expressed by extra-parliamentary forces in the late 1960s in response to the growing consensus among political elites on the principles on democracy. It foregrounds the similarities between the conceptions of democracy propagated inside and outside parliament and takes a close look at how parliaments reacted to extra-parliamentary challenges to their political legitimacy.

Chapter Five discusses the major transformation in the debate on democracy in all three states from the mid-1970s onwards. It highlights the various challenges posed to the postwar consensus, such as social movements, activism, political violence, and the economic downturn and demonstrates how these resulted in a further convergence of the political elites' conceptions of democracy. These developments left France and West Germany with a broad consensus among political elites on the rules of the democratic game, but the same consensus between major political parties worsened Italian democracy's problems and contributed to the fall of the First Republic in the early 1990s.

The book concludes with an analysis of the major themes that characterized the postwar debate on democracy in Italy, France, and West Germany and connects these to the current debate on the state of democracy.

Notes

1. Y. Mény and Y. Surel eds., *Democracies and the Populist Challenge* (Basingstoke: Palgrave McMillan, 2002); C. Mudde and C.R. Kaltwasser eds., *Populism in Europe and the Americas. Threat or Corrective to Democracy?* (Cambridge: Cambridge University Press, 2013).
2. See, most notably: J.W. Müller, *Contesting Democracy. Political Thought in Twentieth Century Europe* (New Haven: Yale University Press, 2011).
3. J.W. Müller, 'European Intellectual History as Contemporary History', *Journal of Contemporary History*, vol. 46, no. 3 (2011), pp. 574–590.
4. W. Conze, H. Maier, C. Meier and H.L. Reimann, 'Demokratie', in: O. Brunner, W. Conze and R. Kosellek eds., *Geschichtliche Grundbegriffe* (7 vols., Stuttgart, 1972–1992), Volume I, pp. 821–899, on p. 898.
5. W.B. Gallie, 'Essentially Contested Concepts', *Proceedings of the Aristotelian Society*, vol. 56 (1955–1956), pp. 167–198, esp. pp. 183–187.
6. Gallie, 'Essentially Contested Concepts', p. 184.
7. Müller, 'European Intellectual History as Contemporary History', p. 589.
8. The term was coined by M. Mazower, *Dark Continent. Europe's Twentieth Century* (London: Lane/Penguin Press, 1998), p. 287.
9. T. Buchanan, 'Anti-fascism and Democracy in the 1930s', *European History Quarterly*, vol. 32, no. 1 (2002), pp. 39–57.
10. G. Eley, *Forging Democracy. A History of the Left in Europe 1850–2000* (Oxford: Oxford University Press, 2000), ch. 19; C.S. Maier, 'Democracy since the French Revolution', in: J. Dunn ed. *Democracy: The Unfinished Journey 508 BC–1993 AD* (Oxford: Oxford University Press, 1992), pp. 125–152, on p. 138; D. Sassoon, 'Politics', in: M. Fulbrook ed., *Europe since 1945* (Oxford: Oxford University Press, 2001), pp. 14–52.
11. M. Conway, 'The Rise and Fall of Europe's Democratic Age 1945–1973', *Contemporary European History*, vol. 13, no. 1 (2004), pp. 67–88; D. Stone, *Goodbye to All of That? A Story of Europe since 1945* (Oxford: Oxford University Press, 2014), ch. 1 and 3; K. Jahrausch, *Out of Ashes. A New History of Europe in the Twentieth Century* (New Jersey: Princeton University Press, 2015), ch. 15; G. Eley, 'Legacies of Antifascism: Constructing Democracy in Postwar Europe', *New German Critique*, vol. 67 (1996), pp. 73–100.
12. See most notably: Müller, *Contesting Democracy*, p. 128; T. Buchanan and M. Conway, 'The Politics of Democracy in Twentieth Century Europe: Introduction', *European History Quarterly*, vol. 32, no. 1 (2002), pp. 5–12; M. Conway, 'Democracy in Postwar Europe. The Triumph of a Political Model', *European History Quarterly*, vol. 32, no. 1 (2002), pp. 59–84.
13. Maier, 'Democracy after the French Revolution', p. 126.
14. J.B. Eichengreen, *The European Economy since 1945: Coordinated Capitalism* (New Jersey: Princeton University Press, 2007), ch. 2.
15. Eley, *Forging Democracy*, ch. 17 and 18.

16 M. Conway and V. Depkat, 'Towards a European History of the Discourse of Democracy: Discussing Democracy in Western Europe, 1945–60', in: M. Conway and K.K. Patel eds., *Europeanization in the Twentieth Century. Historical Approaches* (Basingstoke: Palgrave McMillan, 2010), pp. 132–156, on p. 149.

17 It was for this reason that some historians remarked that republican Italy did not receive sufficient attention from historians: N. Tranfaglia, *Il labirinto italiano. Il fascismo, l'antifascismo, gli storici* (Florence: La nuova editrice, 1989), p. 13.

18 P. Ginsborg, *Italy and its Discontents: Civil Society, Family, State, 1980–2001* (New York: Penguin, 2003); M. Lazar, 'Testing Italian Democracy', *Comparative European Politics*, vol. 11, no. 3 (2013), pp. 317–336;

19 Moro's speech dates from 1976; see also: F. Spotts and T. Wieser, *Italy: A Difficult Democracy. A Survey of Italian Politics* (Cambridge: Cambridge University Press, 1987); G. Bedeschi, *La prima repubblica (1946-1993). Storia di una democrazia difficile* (Soveria Mannelli: Rubbettino editore, 2013).

20 G. Galli, *Il bipartismo imperfetto: comunisti e democristiani in Italia* (Bologna: Il Mulino, 1966).

21 G. Crainz, *Storia del miracolo italiano* (Rome: Donzelli editore, 2004).

22 G. Orsina, *Storia del berlusconismo in Italia* (Venice: Marsillio editore, 2013).

23 S. Lupo, *Partito e antipartito. Una storia politica della prima repubblica (1946–1978)* (Rome: Donzelli editore, 2004); P. Scoppola, *La repubblica dei partiti. Evoluzione e crisi di un sistema politico* (Bologna: Il Mulino, 1997).

24 S.A. Forner, *German Intellectuals and the Challenge of Democratic Renewal. Culture and Politics after 1945* (Cambridge: Cambridge University Press, 2014).

25 A. Bauerkämper, 'The Twisted Road to Democracy as a Quest for Security: Germany in the Twentieth Century', *German History*, vol. 32, no. 3 (2014), pp. 431–455.

26 C.C. Hodge, 'The Long Fifties: The Politics of Socialist Programmatic Revision in Britain, France and Germany', *Contemporary European History*, vol. 2, no. 1 (1993), pp. 17–34.

27 H.A. Winkler, *Germany: The Long Road West* (2 vols., Oxford: Oxford University Press, 2006).

28 D.E. Rogers, 'Transforming the German Party System: The United States and the Origins of Political Moderation 1945–1949', *Journal of Modern History*, vol. 65, no. 3 (1993), pp. 512–541.

29 S. Ullrich, *Der Weimar-Komplex. Das Scheitern der ersten deutschen Demokratie und die politische Kultur in der frühen Bundesrepublik* (Göttingen: Wallstein Verlag, 2009); F.R. Alleman, *Bonn ist nicht Weimar* (Cologne: Kiepenheuer & Witsch, 1956); K. Sontheimer, *Die Adenauer Ära: Grundlegung der Bundesrepublik* (München: Deutscher Taschenbuch Verlag, 2003); M. Roseman, 'Restoration and Stability: The Creation of a Stable Democracy in the Federal Republic of Germany', in: J. Garrard, V. Tolz and R. White eds., *European Democratization since 1800* (Basingstoke: Palgrave Macmillan, 1999), pp. 141–160.

30 P. Hockenos, *Joschka Fischer and the Making of the Berlin Republic. An Alternative History of Post-war Germany* (Oxford: Oxford University Press, 2006); K. Hanshew, *Terror and Democracy in West Germany* (Cambridge: Cambridge University Press, 2012).

31 E. Wolfrum, *Die geglückte Demokratie: Geschichte der Bundesrepublik Deutschland von ihren Anfang bis zur Gegenwart* (Bonn: Bundeszentrale für Politische Bildung, 2007).

32 R. Gildea, *Children of the Revolution. The French 1799–1914* (Boston: Harvard University Press, 2010).

33 S. Hazareesingh, 'Bonapartism as the Progenitor of Democracy. The Paradoxical Case of the French Second Empire', in P. Baehr en M. Richter eds., *Dictatorship in History. Bonapartism, Caesarism, and Totalitarianism* (Cambridge: Cambridge University Press, 2004), pp. 129–152.

34 P. Facon, *La IVe République. De la libération au 13 Mai* (Paris: Pygmalion, 1997).
35 M. Agulhon, 'De Gaulle et l'histoire de France', *Vingtième Siècle. Revue d'histoire*, vol. 53, no. 1 (1997), pp. 3–12.
36 R. Vinen, *France 1934–1970* (Basingstoke: Palgrave McMillan, 1996).
37 S. Berstein, 'De la démocratie plébiscitaire au Gaullisme: naissance d'une nouvelle culture politique républicain', in: S. Berstein ed., *Les cultures politiques en France* (Paris: Éditions du Seuil, 1999), pp. 153–187.
38 P. Rosanvallon, *Le modèle politique français. La société civile contre le jacobinisme de 1789 à nos jours* (Paris: Seuil, 2006), p. 416.
39 J. Jennings, *Revolution and the Republic. A History of Political Thought in France since the Eighteenth Century* (Oxford: Oxford University Press, 2012), p. 568.
40 T. Chafer and E. Godin eds., *The End of the French Exception? Decline and Revival of the French Model* (Basingstoke: Palgrave McMillan, 2010).
41 C. Fieschi, *Fascism, Populism and the French Fifth Republic. In the Shadow of Democracy* (Manchester: Manchester University Press, 2004).
42 N. Hewlett, *Democracy in Modern France* (London: Bloomsbury Publishing, 2005).
43 In this way, it arguably reflects broader historiographical developments: S. Berger, 'A Return to the National Paradigm? National History Writing in Germany, Italy, France, and Britain from 1945 to the Present', *The Journal of Modern History*, vol. 77, no. 3 (2005), pp. 629–678.

1 Transforming Democracy After the Second World War

The end of World War Two signalled the beginning of a European era of constitution making that has been compared those at the end of the eighteenth century.¹ From the onset, the alliance of antifascist parties that undertook this task was fragile, and the political debate on the reform of democracy revealed deep divisions. These rifts ran roughly along the lines between the Left and conservatives that had marked the 1920s and 1930s and were exacerbated by rising Cold War tensions and different explanations of democracy's collapse in the interwar period. The divisions directly affected the way the political institutions of France, West Germany, and Italy were reformed after 1945. Thus, these countries' new constitutions did not just reflect a fear of a repetition of the events of the 1920s and 1930s, but they also mirrored the competing democratic narratives put forward in this age of political reconstruction.

At first glance, the postwar debates might not seem so divisive, thanks to the universal tribute politicians paid to the notion of democracy. As the future West German President Theodor Heuss noted in 1947, 'all the world is talking about democracy'.² However, whereas all forces claimed to be democratic, their visions on what this entailed were far apart. The communists enjoyed a unique moment of political legitimacy,³ thanks to which Maurice Thorez could claim that they embodied a 'renewed democracy' while also asserting that the Soviet Union was 'the most complete form of democracy'.⁴ The communists sat side by side in the provisional government with De Gaulle, who proclaimed before the consultative assembly that he would 'return democracy' to France.⁵ Likewise, the Italian National Liberation Committee (CLN) was composed of parties whose discourse was permeated with references to democracy. Italy's Christian Democratic Party still had within its ranks many of the same people who had belonged to its predecessor, the Popular Party, but it too explicitly expressed an aspiration to mark a new, democratic beginning for Catholic-inspired politics.⁶ The Italian Communist Party, like its French counterpart, claimed to stand for a new and 'progressive democracy',⁷ whereas the socialists called upon their supporters to go 'from the palace revolution of 25 July to the popular democratic revolution, struggle for a socialist republic of workers, affirming the postulates of liberty, of democracy and of social equality'.⁸ Even in

Germany, where in contrast to France and Italy, the Allies took complete control of political reconstruction, the liberation coincided with a surge in tributes to democracy. SPD leader Kurt Schumacher reacted with some scepticism to this sudden dedication to the democratic ideal. 'For the rest of the world it is both astonishing and bitter that in this country of hostility against democracy, suddenly all people want to be democrats', he remarked.[9]

The tendency to invoke democracy was universal; it came not only from the antifascist parties but also those who questioned the equation between antifascism and democracy. The CLN's attempts to democratize Italy, for instance, were contested by forces that were anti-antifascist but still claimed to be democratic. The Common Man's Front, founded in Naples in 1945, rejected the CLN as an elitist clique acting in authoritarian fashion and argued that the Front proposed a democratic solution for postwar Italy.[10] With their objective of 'inculcating genuine democratic values' in the average Italian,[11] the parties in the CLN were accused of having a steeply hierarchical and therefore anti-democratic conception of political leadership.[12] So universal was the appeal to democracy that even the Movimento Sociale Italiano (MSI), the main heir to the fascist party, claimed 'to represent the forces of law and order and thus of unity, and thus of democracy'.[13]

The imperative felt by every political party to assert its democratic credentials was arguably one of the major consequences of the Second World War. This turned 'democracy' into a contested term; in the immediate aftermath of the war, crucial political divisions emerged between the Left and conservatives on the transition to democracy. Their clashes centred on four main issues: the disputed lessons of interwar democracy; the reform of party democracy; the reform of representative institutions; and the relationship between capitalism and democracy. The different views on these issues were reflected in the postwar constitutions, mirroring the preoccupations of the postwar reformers. Therefore it can be said that the debates in this time of constitution signing had a lasting influence on the shape of postwar democracy.

The Disputed Lessons of Interwar Democracy

The different conclusions politicians drew from the failures of interwar democracy informed their debates about the kinds of institutions and socio-economic conditions needed to make the transition to democracy. These politicians displayed an instrumentalist conception of the past, using history to contest others' current democratic legitimacy and assert their own. Based on their past behaviour, Kurt Schumacher, for one, stated that 'all enemies of democracy are sitting in the dock'.[14] The communists 'should plead guilty', he argued, because 'without their obstruction the death of parliamentarianism in Germany would have been impossible'.[15] The same held for the 'bourgeois' parties, which as protectors of German capitalism were also responsible for Weimar's failure. Konrad Adenauer, leader of the nascent Christlich Demokratische Union (CDU), responded to Schumacher, arguing that Hitler was able to rise to power because the SPD prime minister of Prussia and the SPD interior minister had 'refused to do anything'.[16] Such direct accusations were obviously political rhetoric, but they show how politicians used the past to delegitimize their opponents' democratic credentials. At the same time, the recriminations revealed more fundamental disagreements about the conclusions to be drawn from the troubles of interwar democracy. The Left on the one hand, and Christian Democrats and Gaullists on the other, often adopted diametrically opposed positions on the lessons of the past and how these should be applied to the present.

For the major left-wing parties, the roots of democracy's troubles lay partially in the failed integration of the masses into the state. Especially in Germany and Italy, the Left argued that the average citizen lacked sufficient political development to enable such integration. The Italian resistance hero Ferrucio Parri stated that fascism had exacerbated the average Italian's lack of civic education.[17] Similarly, Schumacher wrote that Germans had remained subjects and not become citizens.[18] He believed that 'the longing for democracy' was 'alive in large parts of the population'[19] but that the 'problem for democracy currently is that the masses should first be taught the ability to judge'.[20] In the Left's view, the absence of a democratic spirit had offered elites the opportunity to mobilize against the people and thwart democratic government. This suggests that progressives were suspicious of the elites' intentions and reveals their latent confidence in the political abilities of the people—once they had been taught how to behave like democrats.

Obviously, the lessons drawn by the Left from interwar events were not the same everywhere, especially when it came to the relationship between communism and democracy. For the Italian Left, the *biennio rosso* and the rise of fascism were 'proof' that it would be impossible to secure democracy 'without the unity of the working class'.[21] This resulted in the formation of the Popular Front, an alliance that existed until the mid-1950s.[22] The communists quickly gained the upper hand in the Popular Front, leading to a rupture with those who mistrusted them. Giuseppe Saragat founded his own social democratic party.[23] In France, the strained collaboration between socialists and communists continued for several years. Their eventual break up occurred in 1947, and even though the gap between them was large, the rupture was less definitive than in Germany. There, the antagonism between the SPD and the communist KPD, inherited from the 1930s, proved impossible to resolve in the war's aftermath. Any attempt by the SPD and KPD to work together met with resistance from the Allies, Schumacher, and rank-and-file members, whereas the Communist Party in the Soviet occupation zone quickly established dominance over the KPD.[24]

Notwithstanding these differences, left-wing parties universally blamed the capitalist system for the problems of democracy in the interwar years. Togliatti expressed the concerns of many on the Left when he stated that 'the roots of fascism still exist. If we do not eradicate these roots, fascism can return'.[25] The KPD stated in its first major postwar declaration that the German 'catastrophe' had been caused by 'big capital such as Krupp and Siemens'.[26] The communists were not the only ones to reject capitalism; this position was broadly shared in progressive circles. Italian socialist leader Pietro Nenni claimed that the working class could have come to power after the Great War, '[b]ut then [fascism] turned to the bourgeoisie and started to gain support. Under the mask of nationalists and imperialists, fascism has always been a movement of the most corrupt and most reactionary guardians of capitalism'.[27] Schumacher, too, felt that 'big capital had been an enemy of democracy'.[28] Capitalism and democracy were incompatible, they argued, because to capitalists democracy had merely instrumental value. Ultimately, capitalism wanted 'democracy out of this world'.[29] Ideas like these also sowed doubt about the democratic credentials of their political rivals, the bourgeois parties. When Schumacher stated that the Catholic *Zentrum* party had displayed an 'authoritarian capitalism' that paved the way for Nazism,[30] he also launched an assault on the Christian Democrats because 'the leaders of the bourgeois parties still live in the pre-1932 world'.[31]

The progressives' major problem with free market capitalism was that it harmed social equality, a core notion of the left-wing understanding of democracy. Léon Blum, leader of the French socialists until 1946, argued that democracy was suffering from the absence of true equality. 'To recognize popular sovereignty, majority rule is the only rule acceptable, or even the only rule conceivable, and, for the composition of the majority, all citizens are necessarily considered equal', he argued.[32] Yet Blum saw mere political equality as 'false' equality. Because capitalism forced citizens to compete with each other, it was egoism rather than healthy individualism that ruled modern societies. Only if the state actively intervened to foster social as well as political equality would 'true equality take the place of false equality' and could the weaknesses of democracy be overcome.[33]

Even though hardly anyone disputed the necessity of far-reaching socio-economic reforms, both conservatives and liberals challenged the left-wing notion that democracy's failures had mainly resulted from the economic system. Instead, they argued that democracy had failed because representative institutions had been unable to meet the challenge of mass politics—referring to the rise of either fascism or left-wing militancy. Seen from this perspective, the democracies of interwar Europe had not been limited democracies constrained by civic immaturity, social inequalities, and elite sabotage but rather what French resistance groups close to De Gaulle called an 'excess of democracy' in which the masses, often by means of militant parties, had been able to harm political stability and individual freedoms.[34]

In the eyes of many conservatives, the institutional outlines of the Italian liberal state, the Weimar Republic, and the French Third Republic had failed to provide stability and secure individual liberties. The rise of movements that either successfully or unsuccessfully challenged interwar democratic regimes, and the access of the masses to politics through mass parties, had proven that democracy needed solid and rigid mechanisms to defend itself and the freedoms of its citizens. For obvious reasons, concerns about radicalization of the popular will were most profoundly felt in the western zones of Germany. When the delegates of the parliamentary council wrote the Basic Law in 1948, they did so on the explicit agreement that German democracy needed to be 'militant' to avoid the Weimar abyss. This militancy, based on Karl Loewenstein's notion of democratic self-defence[35] and supported by the SPD, comprised a commitment to the strictly representative nature of democracy, an overt intolerance of those opposing or manipulating democratic values, and institutional mechanisms to safeguard governmental stability.[36]

The situation in West Germany differed from that in France and Italy. In the latter two countries, the penchant for institutional reform aimed primarily at governmental stability was much more prevalent among conservatives than among Leftists. In one of its first programmes, written in March 1943, Italy's Christian Democratic Party (DC) proclaimed that the 'state should be constructed on the basis of liberty', with guarantees for the stability of government, a strong executive, and an independent judiciary.[37] Political liberties, often also explained in terms of religious liberties, had been insufficiently protected under the liberal regime and should in future be constitutionally secured, the party argued. As Christian Democratic leader Alcide de Gasperi claimed, '[W]e have to learn from the mistakes of the past, from 1919'.[38] Reformed institutions were needed to protect Italy from the threat that 'thanks to a *piazza* coup, a coup by the head of state, or both, we [could] lose our constitutional liberty, something that [should] never happen again'.[39] This explanation of the rise of fascism emphasized the lack of institutional mechanisms to prevent anti-democratic mass movements from abusing democratic freedoms.

De Gasperi's words showed that the conservatives' views of present-day political relations were clearly informed by their characterization of the past, which he clearly felt, also included the threat posed by socialists and communists to Italian democracy. He stated that 'the parties to which we refer here are totalitarian complexities. . . . Their party is a philosophical system, a creed, a teaching of a doctrine . . . a surrogate of religion and it assumes the doctrinal functions of a Church'.[40] At the party's first congress in 1946, the DC stated that the communist notion of a 'progressive democracy' was 'fake' and a cover to install the dictatorship of the proletariat.[41] Aided by the fact that it won a relative majority in the 1946 elections for the constituent assembly, the conviction that the DC was the only truly democratic Italian mass party gained ground. The party came to consider itself solely responsible for the development of Italian democracy.[42]

Whereas the failures of Italy's pre-war liberal regime influenced debates in Rome, the French past cast a shadow over debates about the Fourth Republic. In the eyes of the Left, history had shown that the danger to democracy lay in a leader who derived political authority from direct ties with the people and as such undermined representative democracy. Unsurprisingly, both De Gaulle's constitutional ideas and his popularity aroused such fears. The Left rejected direct election of the president by universal suffrage, at least in the current circumstances, because the 'passage from presidential power to personal power ... is a known danger and has proven to be a menace to democracy'.[43] The Gaullists, in turn, were deeply influenced by the instability of the Third Republic in the formulation of their ideas on democracy's transformation. To them, the historical problem of French democracy was that both parliament and the political parties were far too powerful. 'The embarrassment' of France in 1940 was 'indivisibly connected to the old parties, to the men who led them',[44] and 'the infection of the system by political parties is the first sign of decadence', they claimed.[45] In De Gaulle's view, the Third Republic had failed most visibly in preventing party strife and guaranteeing a strong and stable executive. The 1875 constitution resembled a 'dictatorship' of the assembly with too much power, and this caused difficulties 'above all in the difficult period in which we find ourselves. We have had several experiences with a unique and omnipotent assembly. These experiences almost always ended badly'.[46]

Echoes of the past were used not only to cast doubt on the democratic credentials of opponents but also as an aid to formulate the requirements for democracy's future success. The debates were sometimes characterized by pompous rhetoric. The German SPD, which it has been argued, was the 'only party' to intensively debate the issue of national socialism immediately after the war,[47] exemplified this. 'All the other parties needed the Anglo-Saxons to discover democracy', Schumacher claimed. 'We would have been democrats even if the Anglo-Saxons had been fascists'.[48] Yet below the surface of this rhetoric, the ideological differences between parties were very real, and sharply different notions of democracy steered the parties' contributions to the debate in the era of constitution writing. Based on their understanding of the rise of fascism, the Left aimed to render postwar democracy more inclusive by fostering integration between citizen and state; this required that institutions be representative but also directly responsive to popular sovereignty. The Left also explained democracy in terms of social equality, which required the extension of the state's influence over the economy. These components of a transformed democracy were fully endorsed by the Left in France and Italy but even found support in the more cautious SPD. This party claimed, in the words of Willy Brandt, that the difference between postwar and Weimar democracy 'does not lie in the foundation or non-foundation of parties and political parliaments, but [must lie] in the adaption of parliamentarianism to the requirements of a modern democracy. It should first of all be connected to a truly democratic redesign of relationships in society'.[49] By contrast, the Gaullists and the Christian Democrats in West Germany and Italy put top priority on the stability of the executive and a firm guarantee of individual freedom, which would protect democracy against potential radicalizations of the popular will.

Not all topics divided politicians in the aftermath of the war. The 1920s and 1930s had aggravated concerns about the average citizen's ability to make informed political decisions. This cast suspicion on more plebiscitary conceptions of democracy as well as other forms of direct popular influence. With the notable exception of the Gaullists, left-wing and conservative parties agreed that democracy ought to be parliamentary, which also implied the importance of political parties as vehicles of political emancipation.[50]

This was most obvious in Germany, where unlike Italy and France, politicians were in agreement on the institutional causes of interwar democracy's failure. They agreed that the lack of a successful democracy in German history was partly due to the relationship between citizen and state in post-unification Germany. The SPD felt the masses had 'accepted their fates silently' when Hitler came to power.[51] Heuss argued that democracy had never been 'nationalized' in Germany. As a consequence, he wrote, citizens had either retreated into political apathy or embraced a romantic notion of the state.[52] Like left-wing leaders, the conservative Adenauer agreed that Germans held an incorrect view of the role of the state and its relationship to the individual. Germans had 'put the state on the altar' and consequently 'undercut' individual liberties.[53] Due to their distrust of the people, politicians concurred that institutional reform was necessary. Reform, they felt, would stem the possible rise of anti-democratic forces and ensure stability. German politicians agreed that reform should take the shape of a 'militant' democracy with strong means to defend itself against anti-democratic forces and should include special guarantees to ensure political stability.

In Italy, different readings of the past created two political divides which ran through the history of the First Republic: one divide between the major parties and those who held anti-party sentiments and another among the parties themselves. The first of these divides pitted the biggest parties— the Partito Socialista Italiano (PSI), the Partito Comunista Italiano (PCI), and the DC—against the antagonists of the emerging party political system. All the major parties assumed a certain pedagogical stance with regard to the civic education of citizens and held that they, as parties, were exclusively responsible for integrating the masses into the state.[54] In liberal Italy, however, political parties had traditionally been parties of the state and had always stood at a remove from society.[55] Their dominance was therefore contested from the outset; before the war was even over, the first reference had been made to the parties as a homogeneous and elitist *partitocrazia*.[56] However, this division between party and anti-party was, temporarily at least, masked by the deepening rift among the parties, most notably between the DC and the Left. Like in Germany and France, these tensions had partly to do with economic policy but also with international alliances.[57]

The contours of the French debate on democracy in the postwar period became visible in the various analyses of the fate of the Third Republic. On the one side was the Left, which argued that the Third Republic should be replaced by a new system but which remained committed to the supremacy of parliament and parties. Even the communist Maurice Thorez claimed it was 'normal' that in a pluralist society, large parties existed which represented different interests. In his view, 'only reactionaries' argued that the role that political parties had played in the Third Republic had been 'excessive'.[58] On the other side were the Gaullists, who advocated large-scale institutional reform to diminish the role of parliament and parties and establish a strong executive led by a powerful head of state. Although the two sides came to a consensual arrangement on state interference in the economy, the institutional outline and the role of political parties in France continued to be divisive issues for decades.

Party Democracy, Its Reformists and Critics

The second fault line in the debate on the transformation of democracy was related to the reform of party democracy. Given the widespread discrediting of pre-war politics, it was obvious that the transformation of democracy could be successful only if it was accompanied by a new institutional outline. Only in France did the electorate decide, by means of a referendum, that the assembly it elected in the first postwar elections should be a constituent assembly. In Italy, the decision to hold elections for a constituent assembly was made by decree as part of the wartime agreements on the formation of the government of national unity. In West Germany, the decision to write a new constitution was made by the Allies, who moved decisively to construct the future West German state. They installed a parliamentary council comprised of prominent party politicians and instructed them that the constitution should be federalist and guarantee individual rights.[59] Party politicians dominated debates in these national constituent assemblies and councils, and this almost naturally implied that the transformation of democracy centred on the crucial position of political parties. But whereas parties emphasized their own importance in the democratic process, several other political actors disputed this claim and argued that parties thwarted democracy's transformation. This turned the question of how parties related to democracy into a polarizing issue in the debate.

To those who defended party democracy, parties were crucial forces that connected citizens to the state. Moreover, they aided the political emancipation of citizens, the expression of political views, and the stimulation of a public debate because, as the DC argued, 'ideas do not move by themselves, but need actual stimulation'.[60] Even Adenauer felt the success of West German democracy required that 'people should be involved in politics', but on one condition: 'all political activities should go through the parties'.[61] Even stronger advocates of party democracy were found on the Left. To them, the party was not only a vehicle for political emancipation but also the central platform for the expression of certain socioeconomic interests. In Léon Blum's view, there was 'no viable and stable democracy outside a parliamentary regime, and there is no viable and stable parliamentary regime without the organization of parties'.[62] Even Thorez argued that parties were essential because they voiced the interests of different classes. His acceptance of party political pluralism was still provisional because the French Communist Party (PCF) assumed that when class antagonisms eventually ebbed away, multiple parties would become obsolete. Nonetheless, Thorez's view demonstrates that parties were central to the French communists' conception of democracy.[63]

Whereas in France the supremacy of parties and parliaments was part of the republican tradition, the tribute to party democracy in the western zones of Germany and in Italy was due in part to their totalitarian pasts.[64] In Italy, the role of political parties was particularly important because it had been the parties that had led the armed resistance against fascism. If antifascism was 'the original and historical connotation of Italian democracy', then the parties, as embodiments of antifascism, were a crucial part of Italian democracy.[65] They facilitated popular participation, expressed the interests of different sections of society, and articulated popular sovereignty. Socialist Lelio Basso's view of the link between parties and democracy exemplified how the three Italian mass parties saw this issue.[66] He stated, 'The citizen who has to be politically involved nowadays, who genuinely wants to participate in the exercising of popular sovereignty, can do this every day. . . . [H]e is able to control day by day, to influence day by day, the political orientation of his party, and as such the political orientation of parliament and government'. Party democracy was therefore the 'highest form of democracy'.[67] To fulfil the promises of a vibrant and stable party democracy, politicians advocated breaking with the interwar style of party democracy in three ways. They felt it necessary, firstly, to overhaul intra-party relations; secondly, to restrict the political process to truly democratic parties; and thirdly, for parties to reform themselves as a means of reforming party democracy.

In terms of intra-party relations, there was widespread agreement in West Germany in particular that parties should avoid harmful political polarization.[68] Indeed, prominent SPD member Carlo Schmid argued that what defined a party as democratic was whether it gave priority to a sense of responsibility rather than to its particular ideology or the desire to challenge political opponents.[69]

By insisting only 'democratic' parties would be allowed to participate in the political process, politicians felt they were protecting democracy from what Willy Brandt called 'camouflaged anti-democratic parties'.[70] In West Germany, this led to the delegitimization and eventual banning of not only the extreme Right but also the Communist Party. To Schumacher, the communists used 'methods recognizable in any dictatorship. They speculate on the fear of violence among the masses. They are not even impressed by the knowledge that nothing damages democracy more than abusing the word democracy. To them, democracy is only an opportunity to attack democracy using democratic means'.[71] This immediate and broadly shared delegitimization of the communists as democrats set West Germany apart from France and Italy, where the compatibility between democracy and communist parties remained a contested issue.

For party democracy to work, politicians felt that parties that considered themselves democratic had to be able to reform themselves. This became most obvious in the formation of the Christian Democratic parties.[72] The formation of the CDU signified the birth of a Christian Democratic party that united Catholics and Protestants politically for the first time.[73] In France and Italy, the Christian Democrats divorced politics more clearly from clerical influence and established parties with a clear inter-class appeal.[74] This kind of renewal also took place on the Left. The SPD claimed that it was important to reach out to 'all classes that depend on labour' and thereby aimed to broaden its base beyond its traditional, working-class constituency.[75] In addition, the French and Italian communist parties aimed to reinvent themselves. Most illustrative of such reinvention was the PCI's transformation into a *partito nuovo*, symbolized by the return of their leader Palmiro Togliatti to Italian soil, in Salerno, in April 1944. The PCI made it a priority to defeat fascism in Italy and collaborated in a government of national unity. Togliatti argued that the PCI should become a more inclusive party which took responsibility. He stated that 'the working class should give up its politics of opposition. . . . The new party should also be a national Italian party, incorporating all the progressive traditions of the country'.[76] Yet even though its transformation was very real, the party remained marked by its 'dual loyalty' to the Italian constitution and the Soviet Union. The party was 'democratic and constitutional on the outside', while it had a rigid internal hierarchy and remained tied to Moscow.[77]

Whereas parties made an effort to improve the image of party democracy, other political actors argued against political parties, especially in France and Italy.[78] In France, the issue of party democracy became the main sticking point between the Gaullists and the 'republican' parties. While, to the Left, the party was the key to political emancipation and the instrument that most efficiently expressed diverse socioeconomic interests in a powerful parliament, to De Gaulle it was the source of political divisions and instability. Democracy centred not on particular interests but on the general interest, and parties were therefore a danger to democracy, he asserted.[79] In his last major speech as prime minister, on 31 December 1945, De Gaulle denounced the principles of party democracy in firm language and opposed it with a plea for a limited role for the assembly and in favour of the separation of powers. If parties failed to acknowledge that democracy was about the general interest, history could repeat itself, De Gaulle warned. 'If you act without learning lessons from our political history of the last shocking years, and in particular, of what happened in 1940, if you do not realize the absolute necessity of the authority, dignity and responsibility of government, you err in a situation where some day, I predict, you will bitterly regret having taken the road you have taken'.[80]

The parties rebuffed De Gaulle's challenge to party democracy, and he stepped down in January 1946. He re-entered the debate about the drafts of the constitution with speeches in Bayeux and Épinal that spring. The construction of the Fourth Republic as a *régime de partis* was again the main target of his criticism. De Gaulle argued that the Fourth Republic's constitutional draft ensured 'that these parties have at their discretion directly and without counterweight all the powers of the Republic'.[81] He predicted that this would lead to 'anarchy' and 'tyranny'.[82] It was therefore 'indispensable for the future of the country and democracy' that the new institutions guarded themselves against the threat that parties posed to democratic government.[83]

A similar contestation of party democracy occurred in Italy, although no opponent of party democracy could match De Gaulle's stature, and the legacy of fascism had cast a shadow over the democratic credentials of any anti-party position.[84] Rejection of the emerging *partitocrazia* was expressed most vociferously by the Common Man's Front, whose brief electoral surge was an early sign that the dominance of political parties in Italy was contested from the very beginning.[85] The Common Man's Front claimed that parties in general, and the CLN parties in particular, jeopardized democratic government. These antifascist forces, like the fascists, claimed that without the leadership of an aristocratic class of politicians, the country would make no political progress. Such views put their efforts to emancipate citizens in a completely different light. Like the fascists, the CLN parties were still in favour of an 'ethical state' that politicized civil society through mass parties.[86] The demise of the Front after 1947 meant the neo-fascist MSI was the only sizable political party left that denounced the emerging *partitocrazia*. The MSI lambasted the *partitocrazia* for governing through compromise and shady backroom deals and thereby worsening divisions in Italian society. Their political power also jeopardized the 'neutrality' of the state, the MSI claimed, stating that 'we cannot allow the parties to violate or betray popular sovereignty, to take over the public administration and reduce it to impotence, exhaustion, disorder, and anarchy'.[87]

Established political parties contested the democratic credentials of such anti-party sentiments. In their view, a system not based on mediation by political parties was either based on a direct bond between the executive and the people, which could only lead to a dictatorship, or it jeopardized political pluralism by adhering strictly to the principle of majority rule. The SDP's Carlo Schmid grasped these two objections. He understood that the prevalent *Zeitgeist* worked against parties, thanks to the failure of the Weimar Republic, but also because of 'the evil tyranny that for twelve years has been carried out in the name of the word "party" '.[88] However, he argued that parties were an indispensable part of democracy because 'groups that form around the same interests advocate these interests through political parties. If one criticizes the party, this means that one criticizes the possibility to politically voice concerns and interests. Even if one wished to, one could not bypass parties, because that would lead to career politicians, bureaucracy and dictatorship'.[89] The attack on parties was therefore seen as an assault on democracy as such. In France, Léon Blum claimed that De

Gaulle's speech in Bayeux 'scared every republican'.[90] De Gaulle's attack on the parties 'opposed the democratic system' and underscored 'the danger of a personal conception of power in a democracy'.[91] In Italy, the Common Man's Front was attacked as a remnant of fascism and was characterized by Aldo Moro as 'ready to accept any dictatorship'.[92]

Reforming Representative Institutions: Popular Sovereignty Versus Distrust of the People

The third division in the debate on the transformation of democracy had to do with the reform of representative institutions. The need for such reform went hand in hand with the imperative to write new constitutions. Although it was obvious that popular sovereignty was the only legitimate source of government, politicians also had to face the fact that the Nazi, Vichy, and fascist dictatorships had claimed to rule in the name of the people and had rested at least on some measure of popular consent. As already noted, this sowed a distrust of popular sovereignty, which underscored the importance of parliaments and parties. Distrust of the people's power was most obvious in West Germany, where Adenauer went so far as to suggest that the German people 'should be remade in their entire being'.[93] The SPD, the major party on the Left, also endorsed unelected intermediate institutions because they were a key component of the 'strong and militant democracy' the party desired.[94] The party characterized democracy as 'something that requires commitment', which meant it should be made clear to everyone that democracy was 'the only and last chance of life for the German people'.[95] These reservations resonated with the Allied occupiers of Germany, who were concerned that Germans were not 'ready' to become democrats.[96]

How exactly the representative institutions should be reformed was another bone of contention, particularly in France and Italy, where the Left and the conservatives held opposing views. Based on its analysis that interwar democracies had been limited democracies whose institutions were prone to elitist manipulation, the Left argued that the representatives of the new institutions should all be elected by universal suffrage. The conservatives, on the other hand, were far more cautious and envisioned a system of checks and balances which could limit the power of directly elected representatives.

The Left generally saw intermediate institutions as a threat to the integration of the masses in the state because they did not directly reflect the will of the people. At the centre of their ideas for institutional reform stood a powerful and preferably unicameral assembly in which the representatives of the people made laws directly. This meant that political powers would be united in a parliament, whose duties would not be confined to enacting legislation but would include the formation of a government with executive power, guaranteeing that the executive, too, mirrored popular sovereignty. In France, this preference was part of the republican tradition, which to Blum entailed that the unicameral assembly 'represents national sovereignty. Only [the assembly] votes on laws. Only [the assembly] nominates the government'.[97] Blum consequently rejected a constitutional court as undemocratic because it could only exist 'under a constitution which is systematically founded on the separation of powers, which is not and will not be the case for us'.[98] In Italy, the PCF and PCI expressed support for a similar, strong unicameral parliament at the centre of the postwar outline.[99] Togliatti, too, was initially opposed to constitutional guarantees for the judiciary because popular sovereignty 'should not be harnessed through the creation of organizations which would thwart the supreme decision of all, by creating a system which would have nothing to do with democracy'.[100] With the same goal of empowering a parliament elected by universal suffrage, the Left contested the installation of a second chamber based on the principles of representation of organized interests. Basso stated that 'men cannot be separated from these [socioeconomic] interests. When one votes, one votes for the entire aspect of politics'.[101]

The conservatives deeply distrusted the Left's support for representative institutions that directly reflected the will of the people. After all, they felt, the problems of the interwar period had resulted at least in part from the failure of representative institutions to safeguard democracy against the volatility of the popular will. To the conservatives, the successful transformation of democracy depended on an elaborate system devised to protect democratic government. This meant representative institutions should not be based solely on universal suffrage but should achieve a balance between elected and non-elected people. The Gaullists and Christian Democrats shared this view and in these respects jointly opposed the Left's preference for a powerful parliament. The Gaullists stood in a French plebiscitary tradition of democracy in which it was not representation that featured prominently but the direct expression of popular sovereignty by means of referendums or the ties between the president and the people. The Gaullist model of democracy was, in concurrence with the Left, presented as particularly 'republican' and democratic, but it advocated a limited role for parliament and direct ties between the head of state and the people.[102] By contrast, the Christian Democrats started from the assumption that the people's will was volatile, so they were traditionally more reluctant to accept plebiscitary elements.

In any case, the views of the Gaullists and the Christian Democrats clashed with the left-wing preference for a strong parliament as the cornerstone of a new institutional outline, prompting them to oppose this principle by formulating the following goals and concerns pertaining to institutional reform. Firstly, they advocated a firmly entrenched separation of powers to protect individual liberties and the democratic order against the volatile will of parliamentary representatives. Secondly, they proposed limitations on the powers of the directly elected chamber of parliament. And thirdly, they were against the direct expression of popular sovereignty in representative institutions as this would weaken the executive.

The proposed separation of powers showed an emphasis on institutional checks and balances that had already been present in the earliest documents published by the Christian Democrats. In its first major publication, in June 1945, the West German CDU stated that 'justice is the fundament of the state. The *Rechtstaat* will be reinstated. The judiciary is free and independent; its only guiding star is the law, before which all are equal'.[103] In Italy, the Christian Democrats also embraced this principle in their earliest political programmes.[104] Moro emphasized that 'after the fascist experience', the leading principle should be the 'sovereignty of the law' rather than the 'sovereignty of the people'.[105] The DC called for a 'Court of Guarantee' to defend the spirit and the letter of the constitution and for the head of state to play a role in guaranteeing and protecting the constitution. In this way, the DC aimed to reconcile popular sovereignty with stability because 'permanent democracy means anti-revolution'.[106] In France, De Gaulle also talked about a separation of powers, saying that 'all the principles and all the experiences which require government, legislative, executive, judicial, will be neatly separated' and would need to be accompanied by 'the establishment of a national arbitration', even though it was in principle the French president rather than the judiciary who assessed the constitutionality of laws.[107]

The Gaullists and Christian Democrats' second goal was to limit the power of the directly elected chamber of parliament. Therefore, they embraced the establishment of a second chamber representing organized interests or regional representation. This body's task would be to diminish the risk of quick fluctuations in popular opinion affecting stability. According to the DC, enacting laws was not only a matter of articulating the will of the people 'but also of reflection'.[108] The French Christian Democrats argued that organized interests should be represented in a second chamber because this would contribute to a 'more democratic republic'.[109] Similarly, De Gaulle advocated a second chamber housing representatives of families, intellectuals, and economic life, whose task it was to 'complement' parliament and debate legislation that the first chamber would 'neglect'.[110] In West Germany, the same tendency could be seen in the Christian Democrats' emphasis on the federalism of the state and their preference for the upper chamber to be composed of regional representatives rather than directly elected national representatives—as the SPD advocated.

The Christian Democrats and Gaullists' third concern was that the direct expression of popular sovereignty in representative institutions would result in a weak executive. Prominent DC politician Guido Gonella stated that parliament should 'not govern but legislate' and that a successful democracy required 'stability and homogeneity of government'.[111] As for De Gaulle, his entire political vision was dominated by the fear of what he called an 'omnipotent' assembly. More so than in the Christian Democrats' case, this had to do with the aim of establishing national grandeur.[112] But it had the same ultimate effect on his views on the transformation of democracy; like the DC, De Gaulle concluded that democracy required stability and a strong executive and that it could not be steered by the force of a parliament that was subordinate to the divisions and changing opinions of the people and its MPs.

There were many similarities in the politico-ideological positions on the reform of representative institutions in the three countries, but the extent to which these positions influenced the constitutional outline and power relations greatly depended on domestic circumstances. In France, institutional reform dominated the debate because this was what divided Gaullists and anti-Gaullists most deeply at the time. In Italy and West Germany, where the political arena was divided between the Left and the Christian Democrats, the economy was the most divisive issue. In these two countries, it proved much easier to reach compromises on institutional issues. In West Germany, this political agreement consisted of the imperative to stress the representative character of the postwar West German state and to shelter it from direct civic involvement.[113] The liberal party even stated that the objective of elections in a democracy was to put the 'most suitable' people into political office rather than to establish an accurate representation of the people.[114] In Italy, the Left eventually agreed to accept some essential features of the DC's outline of postwar Italian democracy. Even the PCI agreed that the Italian constitution should be a 'rigid' constitution not easily amended by fluctuating majorities, a stance which ultimately led the communists to accept a constitutional court as well.[115]

The Relationship Between Capitalism and Democracy

The fourth and final major fault line in the debate on the transformation of democracy was the socioeconomic dimension of democracy. On this issue, too, the actors were divided into two competing camps initially tied to their respective economic blueprints for the postwar age. Conservatives endorsed a form of social market economy in which the state intervened in the market economy to foster social justice. The Left went much further, envisioning extensive limitations on the free market economy, which some even felt should be abolished altogether. The communists were perhaps most explicit, with Thorez stating that 'we have a conception of democracy as defined by Condorcet, a democracy in which all social institutions aim for social, intellectual and physical betterment of the most numerous and poorest class'.[116] The socialists had their own interpretation of Marxism, which differed from that of the communists. They sought to unite political liberties with social equality or, following Schumacher, to render democracy 'socialist in its economy and democratic in its politics'.[117] Despite these distinctions, the socialists, too, felt that any transformation of democracy hinged on social equality; their notion of democracy was deeply class centred. The economic programmes of both conservatives and the Left were couched in explicitly democratic terms. Whereas conservatives argued that the market economy guaranteed individual liberties and hence democracy, socialists and communists claimed capitalism could never ensure the substantive degree of social equality they felt essential to democracy's realization.

All the major left-wing parties tried to reconcile their image as 'new' parties with a commitment to structural economic reform. Some combined this stance with revolutionary pretensions. In Germany, Schumacher claimed that Marxism was far from old-fashioned in its conception of history and said he accepted Marxist class struggle as a reality.[118] In France, the socialists and the PCF were split over the methods but not the ultimate aim of socioeconomic reform: a socialist society.[119] The socialists were quite militant, as illustrated by their decision to replace Blum and make Guy Mollet leader of the French Section of the Workers' International (SFIO) in 1946.[120] As Mollet wrote, '[T]he actual situation proves that [the class struggle] is more real than ever and it is a fact that we will endeavour to establish a society without classes. . . . It is for this reason that it is our party's task to take the initiative, in all areas, to strive for revolution'.[121]

All parties on the Left fiercely contested the link between democracy and capitalism. The 1946 SPD party programme proclaimed that socialism was revolutionary by definition and that 'while socialism without democracy is impossible, democracy is endangered by capitalism. Because of the special history and spiritual development of Germany, German democracy needs socialism. . . . German democracy must be socialist, otherwise the antirevolutionary forces will jeopardize it again'.[122] Schumacher presented social equality and state-led planning as ways to 'democratize' the economy[123] because he held that 'democracy should be socialist or it will not be'.[124] The Left considered sweeping socioeconomic reforms an intrinsic component of democracy's transformation because, without social equality, political equality would be meaningless. Schumacher stated that 'there are no constitutional guarantees for democracy, except for the change of social structure that renders it impossible to mobilize the average person against the ideas of democracy and socialism'.[125] Italian leftist political leader Pietro Nenni similarly claimed that 'if the republic does not have a social component, it will be dominated by the old reactionary interests' and said it was impossible to change Italy 'on the basis of current relationships in ownership and production'.[126]

Another nearly universal sentiment among the Left was their belief in an 'expansion' of democracy, meaning that democracy should transcend the traditional boundaries of 'liberal' or 'formal' democracy. Italian socialist Giuseppe Saragat expressed this left-wing differentiation between different kinds of democracy when he stated 'political democracy is limited, because it is bourgeois democracy. It is weak. Fascism proved this by speculating against bourgeois democracy'.[127] In line with this reasoning, the Left largely concurred that the postwar constitutions should be 'programmatic' constitutions that also declared socioeconomic rights and expressed the state's imperative to realize these rights in the future.[128] This aspiration was enshrined most clearly in the Italian constitution, which proclaims Italy a republic 'founded on work' and which has particular relevance in terms of the distinction between a 'political' and a 'true' democracy that includes all citizens. Basso worded it as follows:

> Labour is the fundamental base of the Italian Republic. . . . We believe that if democracy defends itself we should not diminish the powers of the state, we should not aim to impede or erect obstacles against the activities of the powers of the state, but, on the contrary, we should make all citizens participate in the life of the state. . . . We only truly realize a democracy if everyone effectively participates in collective political and economic life.[129]

The Left based their position on the premise that postwar democracy involved the 'protection of people by the state' and required the nationalization of banks, insurance companies, big industries, and the energy sector. By contrast, the Christian Democrats started from the premise that people should be protected against the state. Indeed, as Adenauer remarked, it was in personal 'freedom and independence [that] the state finds both its limits and its orientation'.[130] This did not necessarily mean that postwar conservatives were less committed to socioeconomic reform than their interwar predecessors.[131] Initially, Christian Democrats seemed to concur at least partly with the left wing's rejection of capitalism. In its role as a resistance party, the DC claimed that 'democracy without social justice would be illusory and misleading. Aside from the "formal" democracy, we should construct a "substantial" democracy, which means reforming the social structure'.[132] West Germany's Christian Democrats expressed similar reservations about capitalism in its *Ahlener Programm*, which posited that the 'capitalist economic system has not served the political or social interest of the German people'.[133] The Christian Democrats aspired to be cross-class parties,[134] yet they were always committed to the defence of private property. Therefore, they disagreed with the left-wing idea of 'expanding' democracy and were convinced that because democracy centred on individual liberty rather than social equality, only—reformed—capitalism could ensure individual freedom.

As individual liberty increasingly became the core of the DC's conception of democracy, the party's economic platform started to centre on deflationary policies, limited state intervention, and socioeconomic reforms.[135] In Germany, the CDU explicitly challenged the SPD's conception of democracy and its critique of capitalism so that by the end of the 1940s, two 'fundamentally different economic concepts confronted each other'.[136] The Christian Democrats emphasized the similarities between the SPD and communism and stated, 'Now every voter has to decide whether to belong to the Christian or the Marxist Front'.[137] Adenauer stated that 'to ensure political freedom, property rights should be guaranteed', and Ludwig Erhard saw the 'struggle for more democratic freedom' as inextricably linked with 'unalienable rights' such as consumer freedom. Statements like these made democracy contingent on the market economy.[138] So in terms of socioeconomic reforms, the Christian Democrats transformed their ideological mistrust of extensive state power into an emphasis on individual freedoms and strong guarantees against the possible threats to democracy associated with excessive state interference in the economy. In this vein, Adenauer remarked that 'personal liberty is the most important right of Man', and he warned of excessive state intervention.[139] Similarly, De Gasperi emphasized that because the socialists and communists were advocating a 'radical democracy', Italy needed a strong 'stabilization of the rights of Italians' akin to the late eighteenth-century declarations in France and the United States.[140] This shows that Christian Democrats in West Germany and Italy, where this debate was most divisive, made no distinction between a 'political' democracy in which these rights were guaranteed and a so-called 'true' democracy in which state interference in the economy was considered an intrinsic part of democracy.

The relationship between democracy and capitalism continued to divide Christian Democrats and the Left throughout the first few decades after the war, but to what extent these ideological divisions affected political power relations depended on national circumstances. This was least the case in France, where the debate was dominated by the clash between Gaullists and anti-Gaullists over the balance between executive and legislative power. The main political actors settled on the nationalization of the industrial and financial sectors and agreed on the principle of a planned economy in the framework of the free market.[141] Plans on the Left to establish a 'new republic' combining political liberalism with socialist economics won wide support, even from De Gaulle.[142] Blum captured the essence of this consensus when he noted that 'the word socialism has entered the vocabulary of all parties' because 'everyone sees the necessity of collectivization of production and the sharing of wealth',[143] whereas De Gaulle called it 'banal to say that economic and social renewal are the first prerequisite' for national renewal.[144] By contrast, the West German and Italian constitutional debates continued longer, became increasingly intertwined with the Cold War, and were characterized by a rift between a left-wing and a Christian Democratic camp. As a result, the economy became the most divisive issue in these countries' debates on democratic reform.

Conclusion: Competing Democratic Narratives After the War

In the postwar years of constitution writing, many politicians in Italy, West Germany, and France were keen to establish their own democratic credentials by contesting the credentials of others. Sometimes this descended into mere political bashing with the aim of delegitimizing opponents. Adenauer, for instance, said of Schumacher that 'the essence of democracy is not yet clear to him. He does not respect other parties and believes the socialist world view is the only right world view'. On the alleged similarities between Marxist and Nazi totalitarianism, Adenauer added, 'It is not the first time I hear this conviction'.[145] The SPD similarly questioned the democratic credentials of the CDU by claiming that the socialists constituted 'the only truly democratic force',[146] whereas the CDU was a 'hiding place for reactionaries and Nazis' that used Nazi-like 'methods and slogans', such as 'Christianity or Bolshevism', akin to 'Nazism or Bolshevism'.[147] In reference to Adenauer, Schumacher said, 'I believe that in Germany many have yet to learn what democracy means in spirit and practice'.[148]

Mud-slinging between politicians was mostly for effect but also reflected an undercurrent of competing narratives on what democracy was and how its principles should be established in the wake of past conflicts. At least four such narratives can be distinguished. Together these defined the debate on democracy's transformation. The first, and arguably most dominant, narrative was the Christian Democratic narrative of democracy. This centred on the distance between people and professional politicians, checks and balances on the power of parliament, individual freedom in the framework of reformed capitalism, and anti-Marxism.

On the Left, there were two narratives. The communists' conception of democracy favoured social equality over individual liberty. Particularly in Italy, the communists were clearly committed to the postwar constitution and the institutions of representative democracy. However, their commitment to social equality and their conception of democracy in terms of the working class's interests meant they had an ambiguous stance on individual freedoms and unconditional support for representative democracy as an aim in itself.

In the second leftist narrative, the socialists also battled with these questions to some extent because the SFIO, SPD, and PSI had not abandoned their Marxist roots and remained committed to a class-centred notion of democracy. Yet, especially the French and West German socialists aimed to reconcile the overthrow of capitalism with the protection of individual liberties and stressed their detachment from communism. As for the reform of representative institutions, the Left, with the exception of the SPD, was positive about more popular involvement within the framework of parliamentary party democracy; it aimed to limit the influence of intermediate institutions that could block the expression of the popular will in representative institutions. Of all ideologies, it was the Left that also cherished the principles of party democracy most strongly.

The fourth and final narrative, the Gaullist ideology, had key points in common with the Christian Democratic perspective, but it opposed party dominance and focused on the general interest instead, advocating a weaker, 'rationalized' parliament with a powerful head of state. Aside from these four predominant narratives, there were also less influential conceptions of democracy such as the one articulated by Italy's Common Man's Front, which centred on a rejection of party democracy and a depoliticization of civil society.

Obviously, the constitutions ratified between 1946 and 1949 reflected the different democratic narratives. Despite important national differences in the constitutions and the way they influenced debates on democracy in the following decades, a few transnational commonalities stand out in the way democracy was conceived after the war. The most notable of these was that constitutions united the guarantee of individual freedoms with a commitment to socioeconomic reform, thereby endorsing a positive conception of liberty in which democracy was defined both in socioeconomic and political terms. Germany's Basic Law declared Germany a 'social' state and paid explicit tribute to the SPD programme by declaring 'socialization' a 'purpose' in itself for which 'land, natural resources and the means of production' could be 'transferred into public ownership'. Italy's postwar democracy was established as a 'republic founded on work' with a 'duty to remove those obstacles of economic and social nature that in fact limit the freedom and equality of citizens'. Additionally, the constitutions either implicitly or explicitly paid tribute to political parties and parliaments as the cornerstones of democracy. This was a direct response to the instability of parliamentary democracy and the antagonism between parties and the state in the interwar years. As a result, parties received constitutional recognition in both Italy and West Germany. The Left succeeded in impeding the installation of a corporatist chamber of parliament.[149] Although all regimes became representative democracies, the new postwar constitutions were also infused with the promise of popular sovereignty, especially in France. This resulted in strong parliaments and weak executives and enabled popular referendums. The West German constitution showed the most explicit distrust of the people. The Basic Law created strong intermediate and unelected institutions, most notably the constitutional court. West Germany was the only state to create a strong and stable executive.[150] Italy took the middle ground with both constitutional references to referendums and a constitutional court. The progressive character of the Italian constitution was, however, undermined by a court ruling that distinguished between articles that were to take immediate effect and those that might be enforced in the future.[151]

The constitutions did not solely reflect the lessons politicians learned from the 1920s and 1930s; they also mirrored political differences among parties. In West Germany and Italy, the constitutions reflected the different notions of democracy held by the Christian Democrats and the Left. Contemporaries were aware that the constitutions had resulted from political compromises. Togliatti noted deep tensions between the constitution's progressive and conservative elements.[152] The fact that the constitutions were the result of cross-party collaboration in West Germany and Italy was highly significant. The documents struck a clever balance between social equality and individual rights and between parliamentary sovereignty and unelected institutions. In addition, the collaboration that underpinned the constitutions also contributed to their long-term stability and resilience because, in disputes, the parties always implicitly accepted the constitution and did not call it into question. This fostered a joint commitment to the Basic Law in West Germany but, more importantly, also bound the Italian communists to Italian democracy and drew them into the 'constitutional arch'.

By contrast, the major fault line in France ran between Gaullists and anti-Gaullists, and the French constitution was not a compromise between their conceptions of democracy. Rather, the 1946 constitution was a victory for the parties over the general, and the republic was therefore launched without the support of the major resistance force from which it should have drawn its legitimacy. The parties' traditional fear of a strong executive became entangled with a distrust of De Gaulle, who was portrayed as an anti-democrat.[153] De Gaulle had no formal powers to influence the constitution because he was not represented in the constitutional assembly, and he presented his own alternative to the constitutional drafts at a relatively late stage.[154] The 'republican' forces that formed the majority in the constituent assembly successfully parried the Gaullist challenge. Partially thanks to its anti-Gaullist inspiration, the Fourth Republic has been referred to as a 'negative constitution'.[155] Hence, the main divisions in the conceptualization of democracy were not reflected in the constitution, which put the French constitution itself at the centre of the debate on democracy. On his return to power in 1958, De Gaulle lamented with some justification that the Fourth Republic's constitution had been 'written against me'.[156]

The period between the end of the Second World War and the ratification of constitutions revealed the main rifts that shaped the debate on democracy for the next fifteen years. This period laid the groundwork for a form of democracy based on party political dominance, capitalism, parliamentarianism, and limited civic participation that eventually gained broad societal support. At the time, however, politicians argued about the trade-off between these principles and how to balance them with other issues such as social equality, the general interest, and civic commitment. In this debate, the parties often contested each other's understandings of democracy and accused each other of being anti-democratic. Such divisions only got worse when the Iron Curtain separated East and West and the Cold War froze domestic political divisions in the 1950s.

Notes

1 Eley, 'Legacies of Antifascism'.
2 T. Heuss, 'Das deutsche Schicksal und unsere Aufgabe' (1947), in: Heuss, *Politiker und Publizist. Aufsätze und Reden* (Tübingen: Wunderlich, 1984), pp. 337–346, on p. 340.
3 D. Sassoon, 'The Rise and Fall of West European Communism 1939–48', *Contemporary European History*, vol. 1, no. 2 (1992), pp. 139–169, on p. 149.

4 M. Thorez, 'Une politique française. Renaissance—démocratie—unité. Rapport au Xe congrès du Parti communiste français' (1945), in: Thorez, *Une politique du grandeur française* (Paris: Editions Sociales Paris, 1945), pp. 263–366, on p. 338.
5 C. de Gaulle, 'Discours prononcé à l'assemblée consultative provisoire' (9 novembre 1944) in: de Gaulle, *Discours et Messages. Pendant la guerre juin 1940-janvier 1946* (Paris: Plon, 1970), pp. 471–474, on p. 472.
6 P. Scoppola, *La democrazia cristiana in Italia dal 1943 al 1947* (Milan: Dott. A. Giuffrè editore, 1975), pp. 177–180.
7 A. Agosti, 'Partito Nuovo e democrazia progressiva nell'elaborazione dei comunisti', in: C. Franceschini, S. Guerrieri and G. Monina eds., *Le idee costituzionali della resistenza. Atti del Convegno di studi Roma 19, 20 e 21 ottobre 1995* (Rome: Presidenza del Consiglio dei ministri, 1995), pp. 235–248.
8 Quoted by: G. Scilanga, *Le Due Italie dalla Resistenza alla Repubblica* (Bari: Laterza, 2010), p. 112.
9 K. Schumacher, 'Konsequenzen deutscher Politik' (1945), in: K. Schumacher ed., *Turmwächter der Demokratie. Ein Lebensbild von Kurt Schumacher. II. Reden und Schriften* (Berlin: GMBH Verlags, 1953), pp. 25–50, on p. 32.
10 A.M. Imbriani, *Vento del Sud. Moderati, Reazionari, Qualunquisti 1943–1948* (Bologna: Il Mulino, 1996).
11 R.A. Ventresca, 'Mussolini's Ghost: Italy's *Duce* in History and Memory', *History and Memory*, vol. 18, no. 1 (2006), pp. 86–119, on p. 91.
12 See, for instance: G. Orsina, 'L'antipolitica dei moderati: dal qualunquismo al berlusconismo', *Ventunesimo secolo*, vol. 30, no. 1 (2013), pp. 91–111.
13 Movimento Sociale Italiano, *Situazione politica e blocchi* (1946), Fondazione Ugo Spirito e Renzo di Felice, Archivio del Movimento Sociale Italiano, Serie 2, busta 19, 56.
14 Schumacher, 'Konsequenzen deutscher Politik', p. 26.
15 *Ibid.*, p. 30.
16 K. Adenauer, 'Zeigt daβ Ihr auf dem Wege der politische Reife seid. Wahlkampfrede in Pulheim bei Köln' (1946), in: K. Adenauer ed., *Die Demokratie ist für uns eine Weltanschauung. Reden und Gespräche 1946–1967* (Bonn: Konrad Adenauer Stiftung, 1998), pp. 10–26, on p. 17.
17 F. Parri, 'Per la chiarezza democratica' (1946), in: F. Parri ed., *Scritti 1915–1975* (Milan: Feltrinelli, 1976), pp. 207–221, on p. 207.
18 K. Schumacher, 'Aufgaben und Ziele der deutsche Sozialdemokratie' (1946), in: Schumacher, *Turmwächter der Demokratie. II*, pp. 75–101, on p. 77.
19 Schumacher, 'Konsequenzen deutscher Politik', p. 30.
20 *Ibid.*, p. 45.
21 F. Onori, *Democrazia progressiva* (Rome: l'Unità, 1945), p. 17.
22 N. Tranfaglia, 'Socialisti e comunisti nell'Italia repubblicana: Un dialogo sempre difficile', *Studi Storici*, vol. 33, no. 2/3 (1992), pp. 499–511.
23 R. Di Scala, *Renewing Italian Socialism. Nenni to Craxi* (Oxford: Oxford University Press, 1988), p. 53.
24 P. Major, *The Death of the KPD. Communism and Anti-Communism in West Germany 1945–1956* (Oxford: Clarendon Press, 1997), ch. 2.
25 P. Togliatti, *Avanti verso la democrazia. Discorso pronunciato 21 settembre 1944 a Roma* (Rome: l'Unità, 1944), p. 5.
26 K.P.D., *Aufruf zum des Zentralkomitees der KPD vom. 11 Juni 1945 an das deutsche Volk zum Aufbau eines antifaschistisch-demokratischen Deutschland* (1945), in: M. Reimann ed., *Dokumente der Kommunistische Partei Deutschland 1945–1956* (Berlin: Dietz Verlag, 1965), pp. 1–8, on p. 1.
27 P. Nenni, *Che cosa vuole il Partito Socialista? Discorso pronunciato alla Sala Roma di Napoli il 3 Settembre 1944* (Roma: Consiglio Nazionale del PSI, 1944), p. 6.

28 K. Schumacher, 'Sozialismus—Eine Gegenwartsaufgabe' (1947), in: Schumacher, *Turmwächter der Demokratie. II*, pp. 102–108, on p. 106.
29 Schumacher, 'Von der Freiheit zur sozialen Gerechtigkeit', p. 137.
30 K. Schumacher, 'Von der Freiheit zur sozialen Gerechtigkeit' (1948), in: Schumacher, *Turmwächter der Demokratie. II*, pp. 111–138, *On* p. 137.
31 Schumacher, 'Aufgaben und Ziele der deutsche Sozialdemokratie', p. 77.
32 L. Blum, 'Notes d'Allemagne (1943–1945)', in: L. Blum ed., *L'Œuvre de Léon Blum V. 1940–1945 Mémoires de la prison et le procès: À l'échelle humaine* (Paris: Éditions Albin Michel, 1955), pp. 500–514, on p. 505.
33 *Ibid.*, p. 506.
34 Comité Général d'Étude, 'Le problème constitutionnel français' (1944), in: H. Michel and B. Mirkine-Geutzévitch eds., *Les Idées politiques et sociales de la Résistance* (Paris: Presses Universitaires de France, 1954), p. 288; S. Berstein, *Histoire du Gaullisme* (Paris, 2001), p. 61.
35 K. Loewenstein, 'Militant Democracy and Fundamental Rights I', *The American Political Science Review*, vol. 31, no. 3 (1937), pp. 417–432; K. Loewenstein, 'Militant Democracy and Fundamental Rights II', *The American Political Science Review*, vol. 31, no. 4 (1937), pp. 638–658.
36 Ullrich, *Der Weimar-Komplex*, pp. 272–302.
37 D.C., 'Linee di ricostruzione (redatto da De Gasperi, marzo 1943), in: F. Malgeri ed., *Storia della Democrazia Cristiana. Vol. I 1943–1948. Le origini: La DC dalla resistenza alla repubblica* (Rome: Edizione Cinque Lune, 1987), pp. 377–379, on p. 377.
38 A. de Gasperi, 'La democrazia cristiana e il momento politico (1944)', in: Malgeri, *Storia della Democrazia Cristiana. Vol. I*, pp. 453–462, on p. 460; C. Campanini, 'I programmi del partito democratico cristiana', in: Malgeri, *Storia della Democrazia Cristiana. Vol. I*, pp. 205–229.
39 De Gasperi, 'La democrazia cristiana e il momento politico (1944)', p. 460.
40 A. de Gasperi, 'Il programma della Democrazia Cristiana' (1944), in: A. de Gasperi ed., *Scritti politici di Alcide de Gasperi* (Milan: Feltrinelli, 1979), pp. 274–287, on p. 279.
41 D.C., '24–27 Aprile 1946. Roma. I Congresso Nazionale della DC. Il programma della DC per la nuova costituzione', in: A. Damiliano ed., *Atti e documenti della democrazia Cristiana 1943–1967. Vol I* (Rome: Edizione Cinque Lune, 1968), pp. 233–251, on p. 233.
42 G. Galli, *Storia della DC 1943–1993: mezzo secolo di Democrazia cristiana* (Rome: Kaos editore, 2007), pp. 73–74.
43 L. Blum, 'Les problèmes constitutionnels' (1946), in: Blum, *L'œuvre de Léon Blum VI*, pp. 217–224, on p. 218.
44 Résistance, 'Des partis, oui, mais d'autres' (1943), in: Michel and Mirkine-Geutzévitch, *Les Idées politiques et sociales de la Résistance*, pp. 115–116, on p. 115.
45 Comité Général d'Étude, 'Le problème constitutionnelle français', p. 295.
46 C. de Gaulle, 'Discours radiodiffusé (12th July 1945)', in: de Gaulle, *Pendant la Guerre*, pp. 581–585, on p. 583.
47 E. Wolgast, *Die Wahrnehmung des Dritten Reiches in der unmittelbaren Nachkriegszeit (1945–1946)* (Heidelberg: Universitätsverlag Winter, 2001), p. 112.
48 Schumacher, 'Aufgaben und Ziele der deutsche Sozialdemokratie', p. 80.
49 W. Brandt, 'Zur Nachkriegspolitik der deutschen Sozialisten' (1944), in: W. Brandt ed., *Berliner Ausgabe. Band 2. Zwei Vaterländer. Deutsch-Norweger im swedischen Exil—Rückkehr nach Deutschland 1940–1947* (Berlin: Willy Brandt Stiftung, 2000), pp. 154–205, on p. 196.
50 Conway, 'Democracy in Postwar Europe', pp. 64–68.

51 Schumacher, 'Konsequenzen deutscher Politik' (1945), p. 25.
52 T. Heuss, *Die deutsche Nationalidee im Wandel der Geschichte* (Stuttgart: Mittelbach Verlag, 1946), p. 28.
53 K. Adenauer, 'Die Demokratie ist für uns eine Weltanschauung. Grundsatzrede im Nordwestdeutschen Rundfunk über das Programm der CDU' (1946), in: K. Adenauer, *Die Demokratie ist für uns eine Weltanschauung*, pp. 1–9, on p. 2.
54 Orsina, *Il Berlusconismo nella storia d'Italia*, esp. ch. 2 and 3.
55 M.S. Piretti, 'Continuità e rottura alla nascita del sistema dei partiti', in: Franceschini, Guerrieri and Monina, *Le idee costituzionali della resistenza*, pp. 206–212, on p. 209.
56 E. Capozzi, 'La polemica antipartitocratica', in: G. Orsina ed., *Storia delle destra nell'Italia repubblicana* (Soveria Mannelli: Rubbettino editore, 2009), pp. 179–206, on p. 184.
57 R. Ventresca, *Fascism and Democracy. Culture and Politics in the Italian Election of 1948* (Toronto: Toronto University Press, 2004).
58 Thorez, 'Une politique française', p. 340.
59 M.F. Feldkamp, *Der parlamentarische Rat 1948–1949* (Göttingen: Vandenhoeck & Ruprecht, 1998), pp. 18–19.
60 Democrazia cristiana, 'Il programma della Democrazia Cristiana (Vicenza, 1944)', in: Malgeri, *Storia della Democrazia Cristiana. Vol. I*, pp. 419–428, on p. 419.
61 Adenauer, 'Die Demokratie ist für uns eine Weltanschauung', p. 1.
62 L. Blum, 'La démission du général De Gaulle et le gouvernement Félix Gouin' (1946), in: Blum, *L'œuvre de Léon Blum. VI*, pp. 158–173, on p. 166.
63 S. Courtois and M. Lazar, *Histoire du Parti communiste français* (Paris: Presses universitaires de France, 1995), p. 220.
64 V. Otto, *Das Staatsverständnis des Parlamentarischen Rates. Ein Beitrag zur Entstehungsgeschichte des Grundgesetzes für die Bundesrepublik Deutschland* (Düsseldorf: Rheinisch-Bergische Druckerei und Verlagsgesellschaft, 1971), pp. 150–151.
65 Scoppola, *La repubblica dei partiti*, p. 131.
66 M. Salvati, 'Il partito nell'elaborazioni dei socialisti', in: Franceschini, Guerrieri and Monina, *Le idee costituzionali della resistenza*, pp. 249–267.
67 L. Basso, 'Sul progetto di Costituzione della Repubblica' (1947), in: L. Basso ed., *In difesa della democrazia e della costituzione. Scritti scelti* (Milan: Edizioni punto rosso, 2009), pp. 19–24, on p. 24.
68 P. Brandt, 'Germany after 1945: Revolution by Defeat?' in: R. Rürup ed., *The Problem of Revolution in Germany 1789–1989* (Oxford: Berg, 2002), pp. 129–160, on p. 132.
69 C. Schmid, 'Weg und Ziel der Sozialdemokratie' (1945), in: C. Schmid ed., *Politik als geistige Aufgabe. Gesammelte Werkte I* (Munich: Scherz Verlag 1973), pp. 12–33, on p. 17.
70 Brandt, 'Zur Nachkriegspolitik der deutschen Sozialisten', p. 204.
71 Schumacher, 'Von der Freiheit zur sozialen Gerechtigkeit', p. 133.
72 A. Pelinka, 'Die Christdemokraten als europäische Parteifamilie', in: M. Gehler, W. Kaiser and W. Wohnout eds., *Christdemokraten in Europa in 20. Jahrhundert* (Vienna: Böhlau Verlag, 2001), pp. 537–555, on p. 544.
73 W. Becker, 'Der Einfluß der Unionsparteien auf der politische Ordnung der Bundesrepublik Deutschland', in: E. Lamberts ed., *Christian Democracy in the European Union 1945–1995. Proceedings of the Leuven Colloquium* (Leuven: Leuven University Press, 1997), pp. 224–241, on p. 225.
74 J-M. Mayeur, 'La Démocratie d'inspiration Chrétienne en France', in: Lamberts ed., *Christian Democracy in the European Union*, pp. 79–92; Scoppola, *La democrazia cristiana in Italia dal 1943 al 1947*.

75 K. Schumacher, 'Die Wandlungen um den Klassenkampf' (1946), in: Schumacher, *Turmwächter der Demokratie. II*, pp. 292–298, on p. 297.
76 Togliatti, *Avanti verso la democrazia*, p. 5. See also: A. Vittoria, *Storia del PCI 1921–1991* (Rome: Carocci editore, 2006), p. 64.
77 P. di Loreto, *Togliatti e la "Doppiezza". Il PCI tra democrazia e insurrezione. 1944–1949* (Bologna: Il Mulino, 1991), p. 350. The 'svolta' was orchestrated by Stalin: S. Pons, *L'impossibile egemonia. L'USSR, il PCI e le origine della guerra fredda (1943–1947)* (Rome: Carocci editore, 1999), p. 157.
78 In West Germany, such resistance to party democracy was largely limited to intellectuals: S.A. Forner, 'Das Sprachrohr keiner Besatzungsmacht oder Partei. Deutsche Publizisten, die Vereinigten Staaten und die demokratische Erneuerung in Westdeutschland 1945-1949', in: Bauerkämper, Jarausch and Payk, *Demokratiewunder*, pp. 159–189; Forner, *German Intellectuals and the Challenge of Democratic Renewal*, esp. pp. 86–103.
79 V. Alibert-Fabre, 'La pensée constitutionnelle du général de Gaulle à « l'épreuve des circonstances »', *Revue française de science politique*, vol. 40, no. 5 (1990), pp. 699–713.
80 C. de Gaulle, 'Déclaration à l'assemblée constituante' (1945) in: De Gaulle, *Pendant la guerre*, pp. 661–664, on p. 662.
81 C. de Gaulle, 'Discours prononcé à Épinal' (1946): C. de Gaulle, *Discours et Messages. Dans l'attente 1946–1958* (Paris: Plon, 1970), pp. 26–33, on p. 31.
82 *Ibid.*, p. 29.
83 C. de Gaulle, 'Discours prononcé à Bayeux' (1946), in: C. de Gaulle, *Discours et Messages. Dans l'attente 1946–1958* (Paris, 1970), pp. 5–11, on p. 7.
84 See, for instance: R. Chiarini, 'La fortuna del gollismo in Italia. L'attacco della destra alla "Repubblica dei partiti', *Storia Contemporanea*, vol. 23, no. 3 (1992), pp. 385–424.
85 C.M. Lomartire, *Il Qualunquista. Guglielmo Giannini e l'antipolitica* (Milan: Mondadori, 2008); M. Tarchi, *L'Italia populista. Da qualunquismo ai girotondi* (Bologna: Il Mulino, 2003); Orsina, *Il Berlusconismo nella storia dell'Italia*.
86 'Due milioni di voti per l'Uomo Qualunque', *Fronte dell'Uomo Qualunque*, 30 June 1946, p. 1. Fondo Fronte dell'Uomo Qualunque, Fondazione Ugo Spirito e Renzo di Felice, Archivi delle Destre, Rome.
87 Movimento Sociale Italiano, *Primo Congresso Nazionale* (1948), Fondazione Ugo Spirito, Archivi della Destra, Fondo Mario Cassiano, Busta 5, 57.
88 Schmid, 'Weg und Ziel der Sozialdemokratie', pp. 13–14.
89 *Ibid.*
90 L. Blum, 'La constitution de 1946' (1946), in: L. Blum, *L'Œuvre de Léon Blum. VI. Naissance de la Quatrième République. La vie du parti et la doctrine socialiste 1945–1947* (Paris: Éditions Albin Michel, 1958), pp. 295–332, on p. 305.
91 Blum, 'La constitution de 1946', p. 313.
92 A. Moro, 'La politica dell'uomo qualunque' (1945), in: Moro, *Scritti e discorsi*, pp. 254–255, on p. 255.
93 K. Adenauer, 'Rede in der Aula der Universität zu Köln' (1946), in: K. Adenauer, *Reden 1917–1967. Eine Auswahl* (Stuttgart: Deutsche Verlags-Anstalt, 1986), pp. 82–106, on p. 89.
94 SPD, *Politische Leitsätze* (1946). Found on: http://germanhistorydocs.ghi-dc.org/pdf/deu/Parties%20WZ%202%20GER.pdf, accessed on 28 May 2015.
95 Schumacher, 'Konsequenzen deutscher Politik', p. 46.
96 H-J. Rupieper, 'Peacemaking with Germany. Grundlinien amerikanischer Demokratisierungspolitik 1945–1954', in: A. Bauerkämper, K.H. Jarausch and M. Payk eds., *Demokratiewunder. Transatlantische Mittler und die kulturelle Öffnung Westdeutschlands 1945–1970* (Göttingen: Vandenhoeck & Ruprecht GmbH, 2005), pp. 41–56, on p. 46.

97 L. Blum, 'La constitution' (1945), in: Blum, *L'œuvre de Léon Blum*. *VI*, pp. 144–157, on p. 144. See for the republican tradition for instance: S. Berstein, 'La modèle républicaine: une modèle politique syncrétique', in: S. Berstein ed., *Les cultures politiques en France* (Paris: Éditions du Seuil, 1999), pp. 119–151.
98 Ibid., p. 223.
99 M. Guerrieri, 'Le idee costituzionali del Pcf e del Pci all'indomani della Liberazione', *Studi Storici*, vol. 36, no. 3 (1995), pp. 863–882.
100 P. Togliatti, *La nostra lotta per la democrazia e per il socialismo: discorso pronunciato alla Conferenza nazionale d'organizzazione, Firenze 10 gennaio* (Rome: UESISA, 1947), p. 29.
101 Basso, 'Sul progetto di Costituzione della Repubblica'. p. 22.
102 Berstein, 'De la démocratie plébiscitaire au Gaullisme'.
103 C.D.U., *Kölner Leitsätze. Vorläufiger Entwurf zu einem Programm der Christlicher Demokraten Deutschlands* (1945), found on http://www.kas.de/upload/bilder/cdu_goslar1950/koelner_leitsaetze.pdf, accessed on 8 June 2015.
104 S. Tramontin, 'La Democrazia cristiana dalla Resistenza alla Repubblica', in: Malgeri, *Storia della Democrazia Cristiana. Vol. I Le origine*, pp. 13–177, on p. 125.
105 A. Moro, 'Tre pilastri della democrazia' (1947), in: A. Moro ed., *Scritti e discorsi I. 1943–1947* (Rome: Edizione Cinque Lune, 1982), pp. 453–463, on p. 457.
106 A. de Gasperi, 'Le basi dello stato democratico e la battaglia di domani' (1945), in: Malgeri, *Storia della Democrazia Cristiana. Vol. I*, pp. 463–469, on p. 468.
107 De Gaulle, 'Discours prononcé à Bayeux', p. 8.
108 L. Gonella, 'La DC per la nuova costituzione' (1946) in: Malgeri, *Storia della Democrazia Cristiana. Vol. I*, pp. 485–519: 513.
109 Mouvement Républicain Populaire, *Le M.R.P. parti de la Quatrième République* (1946), pp. 7–10.
110 De Gaulle, 'Discours prononcé à Épinal', p. 30.
111 Gonella, 'La DC per la nuova costituzione', p. 514; Becker, 'Der Einfluß der Unionsparteien, p. 229.
112 Agulhon, 'De Gaulle et l'histoire de France', p. 8.
113 A. Bauerkämper, 'The Twisted Road to Democracy as a Quest for Security: Germany in the Twentieth Century', *German History*, vol. 32, no. 3 (2014), pp. 431–455, on p. 446.
114 F.D.P., *Bremerplatform* (1949). Retrieved from: http://ia700405.us.archive.org/10/items/BremerPlattform/1949_Bremer_Plattform.pdf, accessed on 24 April 2013.
115 Guerrieri, 'Le idee costituzionali del Pcf e del Pci', p. 878.
116 M. Thorez, 'Une politique française', p. 340.
117 Schumacher, 'Aufgaben und Ziele der deutsche Sozialdemokratie', p. 86.
118 D. Orlow, 'Delayed Reaction: Democracy, Nationalism and the SPD 1945–1966', *German Studies Review*, vol. 16, no. 1 (1997), pp. 77–102.
119 A. Bergenounioux, 'Socialisme Français et social-démocratie européenne', *Vingtième Siècle. Revue d'histoire*, vol. 65, no. 1 (2000), pp. 97–108, on p. 99; A. Bergounioux and G. Grunberg, *Le long remords du pouvoir. Le Parti socialiste français 1905–1992* (Paris: Fayard, 1992), p. 172.
120 F. Lafon, 'Structures idéologiques et nécessités pratiques au congrès de la S.F.I.O. en 1946', Revue d'histoire moderne et contemporaine, vol. 36, no. 4 (1989), pp. 672–694.
121 G. Mollet, 'Démocratie et révolution' (1946), in: G. Mollet ed., *Textes choisis. Le socialiste et le républicain 1945–1975* (Paris: Bruno Leprince éditeur, 1975), pp. 44–47, on pp. 45–46.
122 SPD, *Politische Leitsätze* (1946). Found on: http://germanhistorydocs.ghi-dc.org/pdf/deu/Parties%20WZ%202%20GER.pdf, accessed on 28 May 2015.

123 Schumacher, 'Von der Freiheit zur sozialen Gerechtigkeit', p. 127.
124 K. Schumacher, 'Kontinentale Demokratie' (1946), in: Schumacher, *Turmwächter der Demokratie. II*, pp. 410–423, on p. 422.
125 K. Schumacher, 'Demokratie und Sozialismus' (1948), in: Schumacher, *Turmwächter der Demokratie. II*, pp. 51–74, on p. 66.
126 Nenni, *Che cosa vuole il Partito Socialista?*, p. 15.
127 G. Saragat, 'Il discorso di Firenze' (1946), in: Saragat, *Quaranta anni di lotta per la democrazia. Scritti e discorsi 1925–1965* (Rome: U. Mursia, 1966), pp. 285–316, on p. 301.
128 With the notable exception of the PCF, see: Guerrieri, 'Le idee costituzionali del Pcf e del Pci', p. 867; p. 874.
129 Basso, 'Sul progetto di Costituzione della Repubblica', p. 20.
130 K. Adenauer, 'Grundsatzrede des 1. Vorsitzenden der Christlich-Demokratischen Union für die Britische Zone in der Aula der Kölner Universität' (1946), in: Adenauer, *Reden*, pp. 82–106, on p. 86.
131 M. Dumoulin, 'The socio-economic impact of Christian Democracy in Western Europe', in: Lamberts ed., *Christian Democracy in the European Union 1945–1995*, pp. 369–374; T. Judt, *Postwar. A History of Europe since 1945* (London: Heinemann, 2005), ch. 3.
132 DC, 'Linee di ricostruzione', p. 378.
133 CDU, *Ahlener Programm der CDU für die Britische Zone* (1947). Found on: http://www.kas.de/upload/themen/programmatik_der_cdu/programme/1947_Ahlener-Programm.pdf, accessed on 25 April 2013.
134 Or, to be more precise, the bourgeois-farmer alliance, see: M. Conway, 'The Age of Christian Democracy: The Frontiers of Success and Failure', in: T. Kselman and J.A. Buttigieg eds., *European Christian Democracy. Historical Legacies and Comparative Perspectives* (Notre Dame: University of Notre Dame Press, 2003), pp. 43–67.
135 Campanini, 'Le programmi della Democrazia Cristiana', p. 227.
136 G.L. Glossner, *The Making of the German Post-War Economy. Political Communication and Public Reception of the Social Market Economy after World War II* (London: I.B. Tauris Publishers, 2010), p. 79.
137 Adenauer, 'Zeigt daß Ihr auf dem Wege der politische Reife seid', p. 13.
138 L. Erhard, 'Marktwirtschaft im Streit der Meinungen' (1948), in: L. Erhard ed., *Gedanken aus fünf Jahrzehnten* (Düsseldorf: Ludwig Erhard Stiftung, 1988), pp. 134–152, on p. 133; K. Adenauer, 'Rede zum Programm der CDU' (1946), p. 2. Found on: http://www.kas.de/upload/ACDP/CDU/Reden/1946-03-06-Rede-Neheim-Huesten.pdf, accessed on 30 July 2014.
139 K. Adenauer, 'Eine Hoffnung für Europa. Eröffnungsrede zum 2. Parteitag der CDU der Britischen Zone in Recklinghausen' (1948), in: Adenauer, *Reden*, pp. 122–133, on p. 124.
140 De Gasperi, 'Le basi dello stato democratico', on p. 467.
141 P.V. Dutton, *Origins of the French Welfare State. The Struggle for Social Reform in France 1914–1947* (Cambridge: Cambridge University Press, 2002), pp. 202–219; R.F. Kuisel, *Capitalism and the State in Modern France. Renovation and Economic Management in the Twentieth Century* (Cambridge: Cambridge University Press, 1983); P. Nord, *France's New Deal. From the Thirties to the Postwar Era* (New Jersey: Princeton University Press, 2010), ch. 3.
142 J.P. Rioux, *The Fourth Republic 1944–1958* (Cambridge: Cambridge University Press, 1987), p. 48.
143 L. Blum, 'Les devoirs et les tâches du socialisme' (1945), in: Blum, *L'œuvre de Léon Blum*, pp. 5–11, on p. 8.
144 C. de Gaulle, 'Discours prononcé à l'assemblée consultative' (1945), in: de Gaulle, *Pendant la guerre*, pp. 521–532, on p. 531.
145 Adenauer, 'Rede in der Aula der Universität zu Köln', p. 101.

146 Schumacher, 'Aufgaben und Ziele der deutsche Sozialdemokratie', p. 80.
147 Schumacher, 'Konsequenzen deutscher Politik', p. 34.
148 Schumacher, 'Aufgaben und Ziele der deutsche Sozialdemokratie', p. 78.
149 On the 'supremacy of parliaments' as a constitutive element of postwar democracy, see also: Conway, 'Democracy in Postwar Europe', p. 64.
150 Ullrich, *Der Weimar-Komplex*, pp. 269–280.
151 Lupo, *Partito e antipartito*, p. 56.
152 P. Togliatti, *Tre minacce alla democrazia italiana. Rapporto al 6 Congresso del P.C.I.* (Rome: Centro diffusione stampa del PCI, 1948).
153 F. Broche, *Une histoire des antigaullismes des origines à nos jours* (Paris: Bartillat, 2007), p. 289.
154 J. Conwans, 'French Public Opinion and the Founding of the Fourth Republic', *French Historical Studies*, vol. 17, no. 1 (1991), pp. 62–95.
155 P. Coutier, *La Quatrième République* (Paris: Presses Universitaires de France, 1986), p. 12.
156 C. de Gaulle, 'Conférence de presse tenu au Palais d'Orsay' (1958), in: C. de Gaulle ed., *Discours et Messages. Avec le renouveau 1958–1962* (Paris: Plon, 1970), pp. 4–10, on p. 6.

2 Contesting Democratic Legitimacy During the Cold War

The period between the late 1940s and late 1950s was the decade when the balance of political power between government and opposition was most static and when divisions over democratic legitimacy ran deepest. In all three states, political actors distrusted each other's democratic credentials so much that power did not change hands in the decade following the first postwar parliamentary elections; government and opposition remained in their respective places. The Cold War played a major role in creating and consolidating these stark divides. It definitively broke up the antifascist coalitions in France and Italy in the spring of 1947 and played a major role in West Germany, too. There, the SPD criticized the Christian Democrats' commitment to firmly anchoring the country in the Western alliance, whereas Adenauer expressed anti-Marxism Cold War antagonisms among political parties over who deserved democratic legitimacy. At the time, people experienced the democratization of Western Europe as precarious and threatened by setbacks.

The first major elections signalled the beginning of the decade's debates. In West Germany and Italy, the Christian Democrats used anti-Marxism to blur distinctions between communists and socialists and highlight totalitarian elements of a planned economy. The left-wing opposition in turn pointed to similarities between postwar Christian Democrats and pre-war conservatives or even fascist regimes. In France, historical continuities also played an important role in the pre-election debate on democracy in the 1950s. De Gaulle highlighted similarities between the defects of party democracy in the Third and Fourth Republics, whereas the defendants of the 1946 constitution depicted De Gaulle as a dictator.

After the elections, in which the anti-Gaullists retained the upper hand in France, as did the Christian Democrats in West Germany and Italy, the political divisions and the democratic narratives that justified them stayed in place for a decade. No alternation of power between government and opposition occurred. The failure to build broader coalitions affected the degree of consensus among political elites on the principles of democracy. Issues such as the flaws of party democracy and the relationship between democracy and capitalism remained contested. This meant the question of who embodied democratic values and who constituted a threat to them also continued to be hotly disputed in this crucial decade of postwar reconstruction. Only at the end of the decade did these sharp divisions start to crumble, either suddenly, as in the collapse of the Fourth Republic, or more gradually, as was the case in West Germany and Italy.

The Contestation of Democratic Credentials and Struggle for Political Power in the Late 1940s

The first postwar polls in West Germany and Italy and the rise of the Gaullist movement *Rassemblement du Peuple Français* culminated in the division of postwar political elites into two camps. In France, the 'Third Force', comprised of anti-communists and anti-Gaullists, emerged victorious, whereas in Italy and West Germany coalitions led by Christian Democrats won the elections. The election campaigns had been dominated by anti-Marxist voices in the latter two countries and by anti-communist and anti-Gaullist rhetoric in France. At the same time, opposition forces were often able to turn the notion of democracy against the governing coalitions. The conceptions of democracy expressed during the campaign, and the political divisions they reflected, remained in place for at least a decade. As such, these election-time debates offer a perspective on how democratic concepts were disputed throughout that entire period.

In Italy and West Germany, the major fault line in this debate ran between the Christian Democrats and the Left. In West Germany, the election campaigns were so harsh and polarized that at times, it seemed as if the friend–enemy thinking that dominated the Third Reich had returned. Voters were told they faced a choice between a 'socialist' and a 'Christian' future.[1] The situation in Italy was even more extreme. The country was in 'a state of ideological war'.[2] The possibility of a Popular Front victory gave the elections enormous international significance, and outside powers did not idly stand by. Whereas the Marxist Left enjoyed the support of the Soviet Union, the U.S. supplied the 'bourgeois' parties with cash, threatened to withdraw Marshall funds in case of a left-wing victory, and organized covert support for the Christian Democrats and their allies through the Central Intelligence Agency (CIA).[3] The Vatican, too, intervened on the DC's side, with the Pope suggesting that those who voted for the Marxist parties would place themselves 'outside God's law'.[4]

During the election campaigns in Italy and West Germany, the Christian Democrats endorsed three key principles that challenged their opponents' democratic credentials. In the context of the international situation, the first was the Christian Democrats' allegiance to the West; they argued that no party could contest the Western alliance and yet claim to be democratic. Even though the West German SPD, unlike the Italian socialists, took an anti-communist position, their opponents in the CDU deliberately blurred the distinction with the communists to cast doubt on the SPD's democratic values. By this logic, because the SPD had not foresworn Marxist principles and was critical of the Federal Republic's integration into the West, the party's democratic legitimacy was questionable.[5] The Italian Christian Democrats upheld the U.S. as the prime example of democratic freedoms while asserting that the PSI and PCI were simply totalitarian forces controlled by Stalin.

The second principle endorsed by the Christian Democrats was a commitment to the market economy. They did not favour unbridled capitalism but advocated a social market economy that united capitalism with social policies and freedom with social justice. They saw the free market not merely as an economic principle but as a democratic one too because it guaranteed individual liberty. Based on this assumption, the CDU argued that there was no difference between socialism and communism and that the SPD's plans for far-reaching economic reforms harkened back to a totalitarian past.[6] Adenauer, in a Heidelberg speech in July 1949 that can be considered typical of his campaigning style, asserted that it was 'terrifying' to see how dogmatic the SPD was because the party had not formulated a new agenda after the war and still adhered to its 1925 programme. 'Socialism', Adenauer warned his audience, 'will lead to a total state. It is against human nature to have such a planned economic life. The main aim of the election campaign is to prevent it; we do not want to go *back* to a planned and oppressed community'.[7] The fact that both Marxism and Nazism had been 'materialist' ideologies was used as another basis for questioning the democratic credentials of the SPD.[8]

The third Christian Democratic proposition followed from their endorsement of the market economy; this was the emphasis on individual freedoms and the attendant claim that any form of Marxist-inspired politics would lead to totalitarianism. As early as 1947, Adenauer instructed his party members to emphasize that the SPD's alleged hunger for power was akin to that of the Nazis.[9] He also began saying that extensive planning was fatal for individual liberties. In an address to voters, Ludwig Erhard similarly linked the SPD to the end of a free and democratic order. 'Based on historical experience', Erhard stated, 'we reject any form of bureaucratic state and centralized plan economy. We consider job and consumer freedom inalienable rights of human freedom which should lead to a real democracy'.[10] In Italy, De Gasperi held that the DC was defending democratic freedoms against potential abuse by those who aimed to overthrow democracy and that the communists allegedly preferred 'the politics of action' above parliamentary procedures.[11] The DC's famous 'appeal to the people' for the elections expressed the distinction even more starkly. The party claimed that

> [o]n the 18th of April, you can save or destroy your freedom. . . . The choice is between an inhuman totalitarianism that concentrates and suffocates everything in the state, and a human concept of politics, in which citizens, associations, parties collaborate freely for the common good . . . between Bolshevist totalitarianism that hides between the mask of the Popular Front and the sincerely democratic parties.[12]

The Left countered these attacks on its democratic credentials by stating that the Christian Democrats were fundamentally no different from the pre-war conservatives who had lacked a real commitment to democracy. Schumacher did not consider the CDU a genuinely democratic party; he saw many similarities between the CDU and the conservatives of the Weimar Republic.[13] According to the SPD, the social market economy was yet another version of the free market capitalism that had sowed the seeds of Nazism. The party consequently tried to expose the 'lie of the free market economy'.[14] The SPD argued that the 'socialization' of key industries and financial institutions should be seen as democratization because it ensured that control of these organizations was given to the German people. 'Socialization is the best protection for democracy', the party claimed.[15]

The Marxist parties in Italy linked democracy to antifascism, social equality, and structural economic reforms—all within the context of the Italian constitution that, according to this interpretation, allowed for sweeping socioeconomic reform. From the Popular Front perspective, the 1948 elections were about revealing the true nature of the DC as a party that defended the same interests as fascism. By abandoning the antifascist unity, 'excluding' the working class, and pursuing the politics of economic 'privileges', the DC proved itself a major threat to Italian democracy in the eyes of the Front.[16] Indeed, Togliatti argued, the DC itself was like the fascists because with its slogan ' "For or against Christ", it has commenced a sharply anti-democratic and totalitarian kind of politics'.[17] The PCI claimed the DC 'does not want a true democracy. The DC does not want structural reforms that would deprive the groups to which the party is connected of their economic dominance'.[18] The conclusion could only be that 'the DC is a totalitarian party'[19] and that the communists and socialists had to be 'united in their duty to save Italian democracy'.[20]

Those who contested the Christian Democrats' democratic credentials also focused on their foreign policy preferences. Despite obvious and fundamental differences between the SPD and the Popular Front, they both took issue with the Christian Democrats' equation of the Western alliance with democracy. Unlike the Marxist Left in Italy, the SPD distanced itself from Moscow. However, it remained in line with the PSI and PCI in disputing the equation of Western capitalism with democracy. While the SPD contested two of the CDU's three basic democratic principles, the communists and socialists in Italy went much further. Above all, they were held together by their so-called internationalism in foreign policy, which effectively meant defending and legitimizing the Soviet Union.[21]

In France, the major fault lines between Gaullists and anti-Gaullists resurfaced some six months after the first parliamentary elections, in which the communists were voted out of government and De Gaulle's Rassemblement du Peuple Français (RPF) surged in local polls. As Raymond Aron put it, the communists and Gaullists jointly formed the 'double opposition' of the Fourth Republic.[22] This analysis overlooked the ambivalent position of the communists. Constitutional reform was an issue that every participant in the French debate on democracy had to take a position, on and this led to the PCF's 'ambiguous republicanism' in which the party supported the Fourth Republic's institutional outline but attacked its governments.

De Gaulle constituted the true structural opposition to the Fourth Republic. He was motivated most of all by his denouncement of party politics and his desire to reverse the outcome of the referendum he lost on the Fourth Republic's constitution.[23] De Gaulle toured the country to discredit the parties' democratic credentials, casting doubt on their claims to be defenders of the Republic's values. True democrats and republicans were in the RPF, he asserted, which 'reforms the republican state in order to put it in the service of the national interest'.[24] The party 'separatists', as De Gaulle called them, had left the country 'in disorder' and 'under threat'. Claim as they might to be the 'champions of democracy', they were in fact out to 'destroy' it, he argued.[25] The RPF emphasized that the constitution was democratically illegitimate because it was only supported by a 'faction of the people' and was 'a compromise between anarchy and dictatorship'.[26] Finally, the RPF denounced communism. At a rally in Rennes, De Gaulle famously described the Soviet threat to be no further away than 'two stages of the tour de France' and suggested that the divided parties could never protect French freedoms against Cold War threats.[27]

The 'double opposition' of communists and Gaullists prompted the creation of the 'Third Force', a coalition composed of Christian Democrats, socialists, and radicals whose aim was to defend the Fourth Republic.[28] Of these, the socialists identified most strongly with the republic's institutional outline.[29] At the SFIO's 1947 congress, Blum presented the French Section of the Workers' International as the natural defender of democracy in France. He denounced the PCF as an assembly of 'foreign agents who want to install a dictatorship',[30] and claimed that if De Gaulle's plans for constitutional revision were realized, 'there would be no more democracy in France, no longer the reality of a republic'.[31] De Gaulle's rejection of political parties entailed 'the end of the parliamentary regime', he wrote.[32] 'Everything' De Gaulle did 'contradicts the republican tradition'.[33] Even though he was 'no Louis Napoleon', De Gaulle's 'personality' illustrated the danger of a 'personal conception of power in a democracy' in Blum's view.[34]

In conclusion, the first postwar elections and their aftermath established a division of political power which persisted through the late 1940s and the 1950s. Opposition groups contested these divisions on democratic grounds, most notably by criticizing the lack of reform in postwar capitalism. The Left feared that capitalism in the postwar era would render democracy vulnerable to being dismantled in the same way as in the interwar years. In France, the Left also pointed to similarities between the pre-war and post-war *régime de partis*. However, those in government legitimized their stance by adopting the paradigms of anti-Marxism (in West Germany and Italy) and anti-communism and anti-Gaullism (in France).

As the dividing lines between those in government and opposition crystallized, the continued contestation of democratic credentials on all sides contributed to the general tendency of ruling parties to equate the strength of numbers in the parliamentary majority with democratic legitimacy. The best example of this tendency was the justification of the May 1947 expulsion of the Left from Italy's government. In support of the expulsion, De Gasperi stated that a government without the Marxist parties meant a return to 'regular parliamentary politics' and was a means of 'guaranteeing liberty'.[35] The Marxist parties, for their part, claimed that the Christian Democrats were jeopardizing Italy's transition from fascism to democracy. They argued that a normal vote of confidence in the constitutional assembly, which De Gasperi relied on to legitimize his decision to ditch the Left, was insufficient because the government did not derive its democratic legitimacy from its parliamentary support but from its struggle to eradicate fascism. By ditching the Left, the DC showed that Italy had 'not yet returned to the practices of a democratic regime', as Togliatti put it.[36] In response, De Gasperi stated, 'I do not accept Togliatti's argument with regard to the democratic method. The true essence of the democratic method is the responsibility of the [parliamentary] majority'.[37]

The Social Market Economy's Democratic Pros and Cons

The socioeconomic reforms of the postwar period are believed to have laid the groundwork for sustained economic growth and the expansion of the welfare state.[38] It is widely understood that these reforms centred on increased state intervention in the economy, particularly in terms of coordination and planning, and on fostering corporatist arrangements that were intended to counter class antagonisms. The vision underpinning these reforms is generally referred to as the Keynesian paradigm, which both social democracy and the Christian Democratic social market economy could identify with.[39] Although various parties' concrete socioeconomic measures and proposals were not always that far apart, essential differences persisted concerning the democratic function and objective of these reforms. The PSI and the PCI were still allied and in outright opposition to the Christian Democrats. The French socialists under Mollet combined a defence of the Fourth Republic with a revolutionary discourse to carve out electoral space against the communists. Even the SPD, arguably the most moderate major party on the Left, assumed that the contradictions of capitalism in the Federal Republic would result in economic collapse.[40] All left-wing parties argued that postwar capitalism made democracy vulnerable to threats similar to those in the 1920s and 1930s and that it failed to foster the social equality so essential to democracy. The Christian Democrats, on the other hand, linked democracy primarily to individual liberty and held that a capitalist market economy was the best guarantee of individual freedoms and therefore of democracy.

The Left's differences with the Christian Democrats over the economy surfaced most strongly in West Germany and Italy because of the ideological fault lines between government and opposition. Especially in the early 1950s, the Christian Democratic governments in these countries were reluctant to embark on massive socioeconomic reforms that depended on state interference in the economy and redistribution.[41] In the period of postwar reconstruction that preceded the economic miracle years, the most notable reform in Italy was arguably the establishment of the *Cassa per il Mezzogiorno*, through which Rome supplied large sums of money to develop the South. There were few large-scale nationalizations or welfare state provisions in either country's reforms in the early 1950s. On the occasions when these did occur, Christian Democrats hardly saw these reforms as an intrinsic component of the transformation of democracy. A pamphlet published by five-term Prime Minister Amintore Fanfani in 1954 illustrates this point. Fanfani, one of the more progressive Christian Democrats, listed the DC's achievements in defence of the party's socioeconomic track record but did not link these to the development of Italian democracy.[42] Socioeconomic reforms were mainly regarded in pragmatic terms and intended to enhance social justice and stability rather than democracy.

The social market economy was based in part on the free market principle of supply and demand and a rejection of central state planning. Negative effects of the market economy were to be countered by redistribution of the free market economy's surplus for all of society's benefit.[43] To the Christian Democrats, a free economy was a precondition for individual liberty, which was in turn a distinctive characteristic of democratic society.[44] As Erhard argued, '[T]he social market economy is the economic foundation of a democratic state, which has human freedom as its sacrosanct value. It is therefore self-evident that a free market economy is founded on the principle of freedom'.[45] In Erhard's view, income redistribution and state planning of the economy led to 'the disempowerment of individuals and growing dependence on either collective or on the state'. He opposed 'this dangerous road to the welfare state, with at its end the social subject and the patronizing guarantee of material security by an omnipotent state'.[46] This, he wrote, was why SPD plans failed to conform to the standards of democracy; the socialists' 'seemingly benevolent paternalism creates dependency, can only create subjects, and necessarily kills a free civic attitude'.[47]

Despite the obvious economic progress in the 1950s, the Left was reluctant to embrace this form of capitalism and held that without massive state intervention, nationalizations, and economic planning, both the economy and the development of democracy were in jeopardy. As a result of this rejection of capitalism, left-wing politicians came to share a conception of democracy with four main features that were consistent with their thinking on the same topic in the 1940s: democracy required social equality; the working class had to be integrated into the state; there was a need for agricultural and industrial reforms and massive economic planning; and the economic structure was inextricably linked to the institutions of political democracy.

Firstly, the Left was convinced that without social equality, there could be no democracy. Italian socialist Nenni claimed in 1954 that

> the troubles of our country today are not different from those we found ourselves in after the First World War. They are characterized by the inadequacy of the Italian political centre to confront and resolve the social question. . . . When eleven million Italians live in dire social circumstances, the process of developing national democratic life is being hindered and undermined every step of the way, and all the time.[48]

Similarly, Schumacher told the SPD party congress, '[T]he foundation of democracy as an economic principle [was] more strongly than ever before' necessary to 'strengthen West German democracy'.[49] The government's current 'social passivity motivated by class politics' was planting 'the seed of fascism and dictatorship', he said. The SPD's struggle to reform the social structure was foremost a part of the 'struggle for democracy in Germany'.[50]

Secondly, left-wing politicians insisted that democracy could only be secured by integrating the working class into the state; after all, it had been the absence of such integration that had rendered democracy fragile in the interwar years. Schumacher saw in the composition of the CDU-led government, comprised solely of 'bourgeois' parties, a 'great danger that this new state becomes an authoritarian, property-protecting state . . . which in turn raises the spectre of alienating working people from the state'.[51] Integration of the working class into the state was an issue of special significance in Italy, where collaboration between state and workers' organizations was weaker than in the Federal Republic and France. In the 1950s, Italy's labour unions were divided, and small firms made collective wage negotiations more difficult.[52] Interior Minister Mario Scelba, a Christian Democrat, initiated a policy of 'exceptional laws' to clamp down on disobedient workers and protesters.[53] Figures on state repression show that it was relatively high; from 1948 to 1952, Italian police killed sixty-five protesters, compared with three in France and six in West Germany.[54] The Left perceived this as an example of how the state apparatus was used to protect capitalist interests; they redoubled their commitment to the ideal of integrating the people into the state so that the state could no longer be seen as 'the enemy of the masses'.[55] Their priority was therefore 'the democratization of the state'.[56]

Thirdly, the Left stressed the importance of agricultural and industrial reforms and large-scale economic planning. Not ends in themselves, these were intended as a means to 'democratize' society and were therefore an integral part of the parties' conception of democracy. In France and West Germany, these reforms, like 'socialization' and the integration of workers into the state, were all about giving workers co-decision-making power in the economy, both at a microeconomic and a macroeconomic level.[57] In

Italy, the PCI adopted the economic plans of the communist trade union, which advocated nationalization of the electricity industry, agricultural reform, and substantial investments in housing, schools, and hospitals.[58] At its 1951 party congress, the PCI accordingly called for state investment in industry, land reform to benefit landless sharecroppers and peasants, nationalization of the mining and electrical industries, and support for small- and medium-sized businesses.[59] The PSI stressed that agrarian reform and state control of key industries was merely the fulfilment of democratic promises made in the Italian constitution.[60]

A fourth and final principle of democracy shared by left-wing politicians was that the economic structure could not be separated from the institutions of political democracy. In its programme for the 1951 parliamentary elections, the SFIO stated that 'there is no true liberty without social justice' and that the party aimed to construct a 'true economic democracy'.[61] Democracy should be seen as more than mere political rights, they argued. 'Democratic liberties' should be developed 'with an eye to the full equality of rights and duties among citizens, with an eye to a broad liberation in all economic domains'.[62] By the time of the 1956 elections, the party programme had become even more explicit about the link between mere 'political' and formal democracy and 'true' democracy, which comprised the 'democratization' of the economy: '[p]olitical democracy allows for the emancipation of the citizen; it does not allow for the emancipation of the worker, which will not be possible until political liberties—which ought to be protected and developed—are accompanied by the exercise of economic and social rights'.[63]

Although the Left's criticism of capitalism in all three countries shared these four features, the political conflicts this engendered played out very differently from country to country. In France, the successive governments were true coalitions in which Christian Democrats, radicals, and socialists cooperated, and the Christian Democratic Mouvement Républicain Populaire (MRP) supported large-scale state interference in the industrial and financial sectors.[64] The *économie concertée* principle was widely endorsed in Paris, although the substance of economic planning was often hotly debated, and the coalition continued to allow the free market principle to operate.[65] In West Germany and Italy, the sharply divided political constellation of a conservative government and a left-wing opposition gave rise to a more polarized debate. Even when government and opposition were able to reach an agreement on particular economic reforms, they still had different ideas of how these reforms would transform democracy.[66] The 1951 West German co-decision laws in the mining industry, a milestone in postwar West German economic history, were one such example of this rare, cross-party support that still meant something completely different to both parties.[67] To the socialists, securing workers' influence on the running of factories was part of the democratization of the economy. But Adenauer viewed the same achievement as an instrument to foster social peace and explicitly stated that the law did not advance the SPD's aim of 'socialization'.[68]

Party Democracy's Woes in the 1950s

Despite the deep-seated dissent over foreign policy issues and principles such as capitalism's compatibility with democracy, political elites in the 1950s did share some basic notions. The most obvious of these concerned the lessons learned from the troubled interwar period regarding the importance of party democracy and parliament. Political parties gained a lot of power in the 1950s, and the parties in government sometimes blurred the line between party and state.[69] Even in France's Fourth Republic, where the weaknesses of party democracy were most evident and soon surpassed those of the Third Republic, parties managed to defend their position.[70] This triggered a reaction from those who rejected the principles of representative party democracy and exposed great dissatisfaction with the postwar political settlement. Except in France, political elites successfully parried this critique by scrutinizing the democratic credentials of any political force that questioned the link between parties and democracy.

Dissatisfaction with party democracy heightened the mood of crisis that already plagued the three democracies. Outspoken criticism affected the dominant conception of democracy as a matter for professional party politicians but did so in sharply different ways. In West Germany and Italy, anti-party rhetoric was quickly viewed from the perspective of the totalitarian past. While this did not impede the expression of anti-party sentiments, it made delegitimization of anti-party critique easier than in France. Thanks to De Gaulle's credibility as a resistance leader, the Gaullist critics of political parties were able to establish themselves as the main rival of the Fourth Republic.

De Gaulle's own sometimes harsh public interventions overshadowed a more subtly articulated Gaullist concern with the problems of party democracy. Michel Debré, one of De Gaulle's closest allies, argued that parties distorted the process whereby people delegate power. He formulated three objections to party democracy. Debré argued, firstly, that because parties present a list of candidates at elections, there is no transfer of 'sovereignty' from one citizen to another, but from one citizen to the party. The party then acts in its own interest and in the interests of those it represents rather than for the common good. Parliamentarians are consequently unable to freely discuss the national interest because they have to follow the party line, whereas democracy 'means always governing in the general interest. Society, the state and politics are indivisible'.[71] Debré's second argument was that political parties thwart the neutrality of the state. Because the composition of democratic power is unstable by nature, the Gaullists felt a strong state was needed to provide political stability. This implies a clear division 'between the will that expresses power and the instrument used by power to arrive at its ends'.[72] In other words, state impartiality is necessary to be able to govern in the general interest, but parties always extend their control beyond parliament alone and influence affairs in many other state institutions. These institutions in turn begin to reflect the political preferences and privileges of the parties instead of neutral state interests. To Debré, no idea could be 'more wrong or crazy' than the division of public power among different groups.[73] However the weakest link between parties and democracy, in his view, was that parties absolve ordinary citizens of their sense of political and public responsibility and of the civic duty to be politically involved. As a result of this, 'power and nation follow diverging tracks, the electorate, among which scepticism grows with each election, does not harbour the profound attachment for democracy that secures the protection of the system'.[74]

In Italy and West Germany, too, several critics contended that the dominance of political parties thwarted the original function of parliament. This 'parliamentary party critique' acknowledged the importance of parliament but posited that parliament had lost its function as a meeting place for representatives who discussed the general interest. Instead, parliament had become an institution through which various parties competed for state power. In Italy, this critique was reflective of a more general concern about the apparent merger between the largest party and the state.[75] Luigi Sturzo, the former leader of the Popular Party and a senator for life in the early 1950s, was one of the people who expressed this concern most clearly.[76] He asserted that the dominance of political parties within the democratic system at large had affected the democratic character of the state and public confidence in institutions. Like Debré, Sturzo did not denounce parties in principle but stressed that they had become too powerful and thereby distorted the working of democracy, making the system 'unhealthy' and 'dysfunctional'.[77] The organization of parliament in party factions had, in Sturzo's opinion, 'exacerbated the errors' of the post-World War One era, when mass democracy was established in Italy, and had 'strengthened the stimuli of the *partitocrazia*'.[78] The parties' control of government effectively prevented government from acting in the general interest and entailed a significant strengthening of the power of the executive because parliament had lost its place as a centre for democratic control and free discussion of executive policy in which members of parliament (MPs) could vote according to their conscience. Sturzo argued that resistance to the *partitocrazia* was necessary, lest Italy 'degrade parliament and annul its function'.[79]

The legacy of fascism ensured that criticism of the party system only gained a small platform in Italy.[80] This was also the case, and arguably even more so, in West Germany, where it was mainly actors at some remove from direct political influence who criticized party democracy. Many intellectuals saw the Adenauer era as a restoration of something resembling the pre-1945 order.[81] Political parties were particularly suspect in this regard as they left little room for active citizenship and were susceptible to the influence of organized interests. In this critical assessment of political parties in the Federal Republic, parties were characterized as dominating the state and detached from the people. Critics decried parties' failure to bridge the gap between citizen and state, saying this impeded popular participation. Instead of fostering a democratic spirit and enabling popular involvement, the 'Fathers of the Basic Law have fallen into the opposite extreme and have overemphasized the representative character of our system of government', the intellectuals asserted.[82]

The proponents of party criticism still appreciated the central place of parliament in democracy, although some only in 'rationalized' form. One of the reasons politicians were able to delegitimize even this more moderate critique was that it existed side by side with an overt rejection of party democracy on the far right, for instance, from the Poujadist movement in France. Poujadism evolved from a tax revolt into a radical right movement over the course of the 1950s.[83] It was led by Pierre Poujade, who claimed that 'republican values [were] endangered' because, as he saw it, political parties had turned their backs on society and were only interested in the survival of the system.[84] He claimed the party system was oligarchic and elitist and bemoaned the gap between the parties' rhetoric about 'democracy' and the reality of ordinary French people's lives.[85] The Italian MSI, too, denounced the *partitocrazia*, envisioning corporatist representation of group interests as the basis of the political system, and was therefore in favour of a *democrazia qualificata*.[86] In West Germany, the main political expression of anti-party sentiment came from the Socialist Reichs Party. The party aimed for a personalization of politics such that people would vote for individuals rather than parties. Although the SRP claimed to respect the principle of the *Rechtstaat*, it also aimed to 'challenge' the West German party system and 'detoxify German political life' of the influence of the parties.[87] This discourse and its internal practices placed the party clearly outside of the realm of the politically acceptable in West Germany. Although it proved problematic to prosecute the party solely on the basis of its programme,[88] the Federal Constitutional Court outlawed the SRP because it was based on the *Führerprinzip* and a continuation of the NSDAP, making it incompatible with the Basic Law.

The Poujadists, MSI, and SRP were the heirs to a fundamentally hostile position not only towards political parties but the principle of parliamentary democracy too. To those in power, the far right's rejection of party democracy served to emphasize that only parties could guarantee democratic government. Political parties rejected criticism of party democracy as undemocratic, reinforced their emphasis on the role of political parties as a bridge between high politics and society, and stressed parties' crucial function in raising democratic awareness in the populace. This justification of the importance of political parties was typical of how French politicians like Mollet and Pierre Mendès France of the Radical Party challenged the 'personal power' of De Gaulle. Mendès France saw parties as indispensable for involving citizens in the political process and fostering political commitment, thus contributing to a 'fusion' of citizen and state. He considered parties part of the 'essence of a real democracy', a democracy in other words that valued this kind of popular participation.[89] Yet the government parties of the Fourth Republic were proving increasingly unable to form coherent governments, especially now that the Algerian War absorbed all their attention. This fuelled criticism of party democracy.

In Italy too, parties rallied to the defence of party democracy. The membership of the DC broadly accepted the conception of parties as a link between state and society. Within the party, the 'Democratic Initiative' arose in the early 1950s, motivated by a desire to instil in citizens a new sense of trust in democratic institutions. This movement emphasized the need to connect citizens to the state.[90] It saw parties as a crucial part of this process because only they could restore public faith in political institutions. They provided democratic inspiration and enthusiasm among the population and thus fostered, in the words of Christian Democrat Mariano Rumor, 'an alliance between government and the people'.[91] At the 1954 DC party congress, De Gasperi stressed that parties had a double function: they were an instrument to foster political commitment and a means 'to give a political direction to representatives and legislators'. To De Gasperi, this was an essential feature of the 'exercise of democracy, that is [to advocate] the decisions of [party] militants in the assembly'.[92]

In West Germany, the political elites were just as eager to defend party democracy. Schumacher felt parties provided the only viable alternative to dictatorship in an age of mass societies.[93] Erich Ollenhauer, who succeeded him as SPD leader in 1952, said in a major speech in parliament, '[W]e have to be very careful when criticizing political parties in a nascent democracy. We know they have their strengths and weaknesses, but there is no better . . . expression of the political will and formation of the political will than political parties'. Particularly because young adults in West Germany had little experience with party politics, prudence was required when critically assessing the relationship between parties and democracies. For Ollenhauer, 'every attack on the parties is essentially an attack on democracy', even if this criticism was launched 'with good intentions'.[94] However, criticism of the party state nonetheless pointed to a growing concern: how to engage the people. West Germany, according to philosopher Karl Jaspers, had to become a democracy 'of hearts and minds' rather than a democracy that was merely a form of government.[95]

Anti-Marxism and Its Detractors During the Rule of Adenauer and De Gasperi

In both Italy and West Germany, Christian Democrats in government felt responsible for safeguarding newly won democratic freedoms. The DC and the CDU saw the notion of 'protected democracy', which included the use of state institutions to battle political extremes, as a justification for taking measures that were sometimes considered controversial, for example, excluding the communists from government. At the level of ideas, the defence of democracy focused mainly on defeating Marxism; this affected the position of not only the communists but the socialists too. The Left challenged anti-Marxism, the dominant narrative of postwar democracy. They pointed to the problems of postwar democratization led by the Christian Democrats and expressed concerns about the party using its majority to push through controversial policies. This resulted in a fierce ideological battle between the Left and Christian Democrats on who embodied Europe's postwar democratic values.

The main difference between West Germany and Italy lay in their respective notions of a 'militant' or 'protected democracy' and how this idea was applied. 'Protected democracy', an idea first put forward by the Christian Democrats in Italy, was highly controversial because Italy had the largest communist party in all of Western Europe. Christian Democrat measures targeted the Left much more than the neo-fascists, which made the measures even more controversial.[96] In West Germany, however, the SPD and the Christian Democrats agreed that both neo-fascism and communism were enemies of democracy, uniting the two in their 'anti-totalitarianism'.[97] The SPD supported the notion of militant democracy as an important pillar of democratic self-defence. In his first parliamentary speech as chancellor, Adenauer promised to 'use every legal means available' to combat extremism and defend democracy.[98] This entailed that the Christian Democrats saw the state rather than the people as the ultimate line of democratic defence[99] and led to the banning of both the neo-Nazi Socialist Reichs Party and the Communist Party of Germany, even though the latter had won 5.7 per cent of the vote in 1949. The Federal Constitutional Court banned the Communist Party in 1956.

The debates in West Germany and Italy showed similarities. In both countries, the governing Christian Democrats sought to establish anti-Marxism as the dominant ideology during the 1950s and equated democracy with the parliamentary majority they enjoyed. In West Germany, this happened in the context of the debates about rearmament and the integration into the Western alliance. Adenauer linked foreign policy to the militant defence of democracy. He stated that 'the Federal Republic of Germany is part of this Western world. . . . [T]he German people, who love peace, will never give up the hope that peace can be maintained'. This required the Federal Republic to 'be prepared to make a reasonable contribution to the construction of this defensive front . . . to secure the freedom of its citizens'.[100] By linking democracy to the West, Adenauer instilled fears of the 'Marxist' SPD. He presented the CDU as a 'wall against Marxism',[101] claimed that 'all Marxist roads [led] to Moscow', and stated that the 1953 elections hinged on one issue: 'whether Germany falls for the materialist world view or remains Christian'.[102]

In Italy, the political tensions were greater and the polarization deeper, but the principles upheld by the Christian Democrats were the same. To a significant extent, democracy meant anti-Marxism and the force of the parliamentary majority was used to justify controversial decisions aimed at protecting democracy. This became visible for instance when a fanatic shot Togliatti and nearly killed him in front of parliament in the summer of 1948. This led to mass left-wing protests, occupation of the FIAT factories in Turin, roadblocks in Venice, and the occupation of the exchange controlling all telecommunications between the centre and north of the country. The PCI leadership aimed to diffuse the tensions; from the hospital Togliatti famously called upon the protesters 'not to lose their heads'. But many feared Togliatti had met the same fate as Giacomo Matteotti twenty-five years earlier.[103] In a speech to parliament in response to the unrest, De Gasperi stated that politics could only be conducted in parliament, so going on strike to bring down the government was an 'attempt to undermine the democratic order'. There were no grounds for any such demand because 'the government had won the confidence of parliament and the electorate'.[104]

The parliamentary majority was also used to defend Italian democracy against whatever influence Marxist parties could exert. The DC largely ignored the programmatic character of the Italian constitution and postponed the implementation of its most progressive articles for fear that the Marxist Left could use these to strengthen its power position.[105] De Gasperi postponed the establishment of a constitutional court, devolution of powers to the Italian regions, and the institutionalization of referendums—all instruments that could temper the influence of the parliamentary majority—because it was important to 'go *adagio* with the constitution'.[106]

De Gasperi took the view that the new republican state lacked 'methods to defend itself' and that 'what is necessary is a democracy that defends itself, otherwise there is no liberty'.[107] The assumption that recently established republican institutions had to be protected from the Marxist parties justified the DC's 'exceptional laws'. These laws resulted in the arrests of hundreds of people for selling the communist newspaper *l'Unità*, restricted the right to strike, justified crackdowns on land occupations,[108] and precipitated the sacking of socialist and communist civil servants, schoolteachers, and university professors.[109] In the collective memory, the DC's claim of defending the democratic order is associated first and foremost with the passage of an electoral reform law before the 1953 general election. The 'Scelba Law', as it is known, provided for the awarding of a majority premium of two thirds of the parliamentary seats to the party or coalition of parties that obtained 50 per cent plus one of the ballots cast. In the words of De Gasperi, the law was legitimate because it 'sublimes the existing principle that the majority rules'.[110]

The Scelba Law shows how the Italian Christian Democrats aimed to secure their power, stabilize government, and raise a wall against Marxism. Democratic legitimacy was increasingly equated with the parliamentary majority's support, which the party could use to justify controversial policies. In the hope of sustaining their majority and creating stability, the CDU, too, aimed for electoral reform to prevent the 'splintering' of parliament.[111]

This led to the introduction of the 5 per cent electoral threshold at national level for the 1953 elections and to (failed) attempts to introduce a majority voting system.[112] The co-decision laws discussed earlier can also be seen as an attempt to limit the scope for extra-parliamentary action as they gave politics influence over labour relations. 'It should be prevented', Adenauer argued, that 'in a democracy strikes have a power which laws do not'.[113] Many of the Christian Democrats' measures and declarations built upon the conviction that any change in government posed a threat to democracy, either because a new government might lack the commitment to militarily defend democracy against communism, or because the Marxist might make good on their aspirations to drastically expand the state, or in the case of the PCI and PSI, because democracy could be destroyed by international alliances and secretly harboured authoritarian tendencies.

The Left also perceived democracy to be in danger in the 1950s, but in their view the threat came from the Christian Democrats in government and the measures they took ostensibly to safeguard democratic freedoms. From the Left's perspective, the integration into the West was undemocratic. The Marxist Left in Italy used the notion of democracy to denounce the Christian Democrats' international orientation as belligerent. The same tendency was at play in the SPD's reading of the Cold War. Formally, the party was committed to the West, and both Schumacher and his successor, Erich Ollenhauer, realized that their ideal of social democracy was at odds with Soviet practices and ideology. Nonetheless, the SPD distinguished between being 'for' and 'with' the West and rejected virtually all the CDU's major foreign policy initiatives.[114] The socialists connected their resistance to rearmament with their contestation of the CDU's democratic credentials. The SPD argued that the remilitarization of West Germany flew in the face of the pacifist character of the Basic Law; they sued the government to prevent ratification of the European Defence Community treaty, but the constitutional court ruled in the government's favour.[115] Ollenhauer moreover stated that 'securing democracy socially must have priority over securing it militarily. Our first obligation is therefore to formulate an answer to the methods of the Cold War by means of politics which render democracy worthy of defence in the consciousness of the entire German people'.[116]

Concerns on the Left about the governments' practice of making far-reaching foreign policy decisions based solely on a parliamentary majority reflected a broader left-wing consternation about the quality of democracy under Adenauer and De Gasperi. The SPD feared that West Germany could de-democratize and argued that fundamental issues could not be decided on so weak a basis as a majority in parliament, particularly not when the quickly changing global situation confronted the German government with developments that were unimaginable at the time when they were elected. The SPD deeply distrusted the Christian Democrats and considered the 'autocracy of the chancellor' to violate the spirit of the constitution.[117] Christian Democratic MPs lacked 'any inner connection' to democracy, while the government had no respect for the parliamentary minority and displayed a 'tendency towards authoritarian and autocratic action against parliament'.[118]

Whereas the SPD expressed concerns that German Christian Democratic politicians felt only an instrumental and superficial affinity for democracy, the Left in Italy viewed the DC mainly from an antifascist perspective.[119] Recalling the infamous Acerbo laws through which Mussolini intended to perpetuate his rule, the Left saw the approval of the Scelba Law on electoral reform as a sign that the DC had fascist leanings. Togliatti claimed that the Scelba Law was 'an electoral swindle law, a copy of the analogous fascist law'.[120] Basso asserted that for De Gasperi and Scelba, 'democratic means that the majority can make laws', and 'the government is always right, because the government has a majority that has in this way abandoned its rights and obligations of parliamentary control'. Underlining the similarities with fascism, Basso argued that 'we find ourselves confronted with a government that is always right, just like another one that preceded it'.[121]

The Left tried to position itself as the true defenders of Italy's republic. Left-wingers viewed the DC's stance on the republican constitution from an antifascist perspective because 'at its origins are not fragile majorities that can also become minorities, but the sacrifices, the blood of the Resistance, that is to say, indestructible values that will never collapse again, whatever happens'.[122] Nenni pointed out that the one institution qualified to assess the constitutionality of the electoral reform; that is, a constitutional court, 'is exactly the institution not yet created' by the DC due to its refusal to enforce certain articles of the constitution.[123] In this sense, Nenni argued, 'a silent but therefore no less effective coup d'état has taken place' because 'abandoning the constitution or impeding its proper functioning' was 'the same thing'.[124]

These attacks between Christian Democrats and the Left demonstrate that grave concerns persisted about the state of postwar democracy in the 1950s. To those in government, anti-Marxism was not merely an electoral scare tactic but also a paradigm in which the democratic credentials of opponents were tested. This legitimized the sharp division of political power. The Left, by contrast, used the notion of democracy to contest this distribution of power. They felt democracy was threatened by the rule of the Christian Democrats, who acted in many ways like the pre-war conservatives.

Condemned From Birth: The Fourth Republic

In France, political forces disputed each other's democratic credentials in the 1950s, but the situation was different from West Germany and Italy in two important ways. Firstly, the political spectrum was divided between changing and unstable coalition governments supported by the MRP, radicals, and SFIO on the one hand, and the PCF and the Gaullists on the other, rather than a lasting, sharp division between Christian Democrats and the

Left. Secondly, a significant part of the opposition did not identify with the postwar constitution but wanted to replace it. The continuing instability of the Fourth Republic's successive governments, their inability to silence criticism of the malfunctioning party system, and the colonial wars all discredited the major parties of the Fourth Republic and the institutional outline they identified with.

In the face of growing criticism, the government parties tried to save what they saw as the only truly democratic and republican model. Mollet claimed that the socialists should be 'in government when democracy is menaced',[125] and he denounced the Gaullists as a 'neo-fascist' threat to democracy aimed at establishing a regime based on 'personal power'.[126] De Gaulle wanted 'to discredit and ruin [France's] parliamentary institutions' by 'installing a personal dictatorship', he asserted.[127] As in West Germany and Italy, the parties in government used their power to 'defend democracy' and change the rules of the game. In the 1951 elections, they changed the electoral system to their own advantage. Just like in West Germany and Italy, this move was defended as a move to guarantee political stability and protect democracy. The reform benefited parties who formed alliances, something that the parties in government could do but was of course unthinkable in the case of the PCF and RPF. So even though the PCF and the RPF got the most votes, the Third Force retained its parliamentary majority, which aided in the RPF's definitive electoral demise.[128]

In the opposition, the French communists were ambivalent in their contestation of democratic legitimacy in the 1950s.[129] Although the PCF was against many of the government's policies, it did not oppose the Fourth Republic as such.[130] On the one hand, the party challenged the democratic credentials of the governments based on class politics. The PCF distinguished itself by envisioning no 'democracy in general' but 'a new and popular democracy in which the working class plays a decisive role'.[131] On the other hand, the PCF sided with the government parties against Gaullism in defence of the Fourth Republic's institutions. Thorez defended the Fourth Republic's basic institutional outline and warned of the risks of a presidential system for France. In his view, the country risked falling into the hands of a regime of 'personal power' with 'fascist methods' precisely because it was so strongly centralized.[132] Particularly after Stalin's death, his party started taking a more collaborative stance towards the government, for example, during the 1953 presidential election and the parliamentary vote granting the Mollet government special powers during the Algerian war.[133]

The real, structural opposition in France came from the Gaullists. The RPF experienced its heyday in the early 1950s when De Gaulle successfully presented the RPF as the only viable alternative between 'two extremes: communism that wants to destroy everything, and the party regime that cannot change anything'.[134] The party stayed true to the principles of the Bayeux programme outlined by De Gaulle in 1946 and saw the Fourth Republic's party animosities as proof that only a comprehensive review of the country's institutions could save French democracy. The Gaullists rejected any party's attempts to hold onto their position of power in the name of defending democracy. De Gaulle claimed that the electoral reforms of 1951 were a violation of democracy by the parties. '[I]n order ' "to block", as they say, "the road to De Gaulle", they risk flouting democracy by pushing countless citizens into the separatist camp in case their scam succeeds'.[135]

The political parties managed to cope with the crises of the Fourth Republic for several years, but it has been said that the Fourth Republic was 'condemned from birth'.[136] The resistance of De Gaulle, the surge of the Poujadists, the feeble coalitions, but above all the colonial crises put immense pressures on the parties trying to keep the institutions in place. Instability increased when the Cold War broke up the three-party alliance among MRP, SFIO, and PCF soon after the constitution was ratified.[137] As a result, the question of who embodied democratic values in postwar France became an even bigger bone of contention than in West Germany and Italy. It was not just the interpretation of the constitution but the value of the constitution itself that was up for discussion in this ideological debate on the principles of democracy.

Conclusion: Ingrained Divisions on the Cusp of Change

In the 1950s, political debates on the nature of democracy were characterized by deep rifts.[138] The divisions reflected fundamental differences of opinion on the relationship between democracy and capitalism, the role of political parties, foreign policy, and the rights of the parliamentary majority. Even the ratification of the new constitutions did nothing to reconcile these divergent conceptions of democracy. At the end of the 1950s, the Gaullist, communist, socialist, and Christian Democratic narratives of democracy were still largely unchanged. Although all were in favour of limiting popular involvement, and with the exception of the Gaullists, the principles of party democracy and existing representative institutions, they continued to define democracy—and the form of government this required—on their own terms.

Discord over democracy's meaning and requirements was the deciding factor in the division of political power in this decade. This goes a long way to explaining the persistent, sharp division between government and opposition in the 1950s. In West Germany and Italy, the major political parties all supported their constitution but emphasized different parts of it. This difference in emphasis pertained not only to integration into the West but also to what Christian Democrats did about the social renewal implicitly promised in the constitutions of 1948 and 1949. The main political parties repeatedly questioned whether their opponents deserved to be called democratic at all. This mood of instability and fear for the safety of the democratic order was felt even more strongly in France, where even the constitution itself was openly questioned. Whereas the debates in Italy and France were more polarized than in the Federal Republic and, in the case of France, soon turned out to have wider implications, the political divisions in all three nations were of similar gravity. The Algerian War doubtlessly exacerbated the French crisis of democracy, but it was merely a sign and not the cause of the collapse of the Fourth Republic. Of the three, France was the only state with a real coalition government in which diverse political ideologies were represented. This made it very difficult to create a parliamentary majority, but it also prevented a Left-Christian Democratic rift like the divisions that took shape in the Federal Republic and Italy.

The distrust that permeated the debates on democracy in the 1950s culminated in alarmist claims about the state of democracy at the end of the decade, particularly in France. As the Algerian conflict continued to grow more violent, it increasingly disrupted French politics and was seen as more proof of the crisis of democratic values in the Fourth Republic.[139] The French government denied that the political class was dragging the country into a dishonourable war. Rather, the government 'made up of Resistance veterans committed to left-of-centre, progressive values, claimed to be upholding the very highest principles of the French republican tradition'.[140] Mendès France stated that there were several concurrent crises at work in France: social, economic, and colonial. 'But in the final analysis, dominating the other debates is the crisis of democracy, the crisis of our republican regime, to which we are attached, but which we feel is ill'.[141]

In West Germany and Italy, too, there was growing concern over the impact the division of power between government and opposition was having on democracy. Adenauer's conception of leadership, which left little room for active citizenship, gradually came to be perceived as an obstacle to the democratic development of the Federal Republic rather than a stabilizing factor. His landslide victory in the 1957 elections sparked further doubts about the democratization of West Germany, in which elections seemed a plebiscite on the office of chancellor.[142] In Italy, too, concerns about the state of democracy grew as the decade wore on. The Scelba Law was annulled, and the DC and its centrist allies lost their parliamentary majority, which increased governmental instability. In response, the Christian Democrats sought a rapprochement with the neo-fascists in a quest for parliamentary support. But this legitimization of the MSI raised concerns about the price that was being paid for the continued exclusion of the Left.

To sum up, the 1950s were a period of continuing concerns about the state of democracy. The static division of power between government and opposition belied the fact that this was also a time of rapid change that would eventually provide the opportunity for political elites to bridge some of their differences. The easing of Cold War tensions after Stalin's death and the Hungarian uprising gave communist parties more room for manoeuvre but most of all ended the Frontism of socialists and communists in Italy. Strong economic growth enabled Christian Democratic governments to legislate welfare facilities but also forced socialists to reconsider their fierce rejection of capitalism as undemocratic. These developments affected the major parties' conceptions of democracy and eventually led to swift political changes at the start of the 1960s.

Notes

1. Wolfrum, *Die geglückte Demokratie*, p. 46.
2. F. Barbagallo, *Dal '43 a '48. La formazione dell'Italia democratica* (Turin: Einaudi, 1996), p. 149.
3. Ventresca, *From Fascism to Democracy*, p. 88.
4. Bedeschi, *La prima repubblica*, p. 62.
5. H-O. Kleinmann, *Geschichte der CDU. 1945–1982* (Stuttgart: Deutsche Verlags-Anstalt, 1993), p. 150.
6. M.E. Spicka, *Selling the Economic Miracle. Economic Reconstruction and Politics in West Germany 1949–1957* (Oxford: Berghahn Books, 2007), p. 59.
7. K. Adenauer, 'Wahlrede bei einer CDU/CSU Kundgebung am Heidelberger Scloß' (1949), in: Adenauer, *Reden*, pp. 137–149, on p. 145. My emphasis.
8. M. Mitchell, 'Materialism and Secularism: CDU Politicians and National Socialism, 1945–1949', *The Journal of Modern History*, vol. 67, no. 2 (1995), pp. 278–308.
9. F. Bösch, *Die Adenauer-CDU. Gründung, Aufstieg und Krise eine Erfolgspartei 1945–1969* (Munich: Deutsche Verlags-Anstalt, 2001), p. 85.
10. L. Erhard, 'Wahlaufruf zum ersten Bundestag' (1949), in: Erhard, *Gedanken aus fünf Jahrzenten*, pp. 214–215, on p. 214.
11. A. de Gasperi, 'Non serviamo l'America, non osteggiamo la Russia, difendiamo l'Italia' (1948), in: F. Malgeri ed., *Storia della Democrazia Cristiana. Vol II. De Gasperi e l'età del centrismo, 1948–1954* (Rome: Edizione Cinque Lune, 1987), pp. 444–456, on p. 445.
12. DC, 'L'appello al Paese per le elezioni politiche' (1948), in: Malgeri, *Storia della Democrazia Cristiana. Vol II*, pp. 442–443, on p. 442.
13. Orlow, 'Delayed Reaction', p. 81.
14. SPD, *Wahlaufruf der Sozialdemokratischen Partei Deutschland. Für ein freies Deutschland in ein neues Europa* (1949), p. 6. Found on: http://library.fes.de/spdpd/1949/490801-sondervers.pdf, accessed on 18 August 2015.
15. SPD, *Wahlaufruf der Sozialdemokratischen Partei Deutschland. Für ein freies Deutschland in ein neues Europa* (1949), p. 3. Found on: http://library.fes.de/spdpd/1949/490801-sondervers.pdf, accessed on 18 August 2015.
16. P. Togliatti, *Tre minacce alla democrazia Italiana. Rapporto al 6 Congresso del PCI* (Rome: Centro diffusione stampa del PCI, 1948), p. 12.
17. *Ibid.*, p. 51.
18. PCI, *Chi sono i nemici della patria e dell'indipendenza nazionale, i nemici della libertà e della democrazia?* (PCI, supplemento al numero 6–7 di *Propaganda*, 1948), p. 21. Istituto Gramsci Rome, F.D. PCI Op. 2861 134170.
19. *Ibid.*, p. 23.
20. Togliatti, *Tre minacce alla democrazia Italiana*, p. 65.
21. F. Barbagallo, 'Classe, nazione, democrazia: La sinistra in Italia dal 1944 al 1956', *Studi Storici*, vol. 33, no. 2/3 (1992), pp. 479–498, on p. 492.
22. R. Aron, *Le grand schisme* (Paris: Gallimard, 1948), pp. 199–200.
23. See, for instance: C. d'Abzac-Épezy et al., *Charles de Gaulle et le Rassemblement du Peuple Français 1947–1955* (Paris: Colin, 1998), pp. 849–851.
24. C. de Gaulle, 'Déclaration' (1947), in: de Gaulle, *Dans l'attente*, pp. 109–110.
25. C. de Gaulle, 'Discours prononcé à Vincennes' (1947), in: de Gaulle, *Dans l'attente*, pp. 122–128, on p. 126.

26 Rassemblement du Peuple Français, *La Constitution* (N.P., 1947), p. 4. International Institute for Social History, Amsterdam. IISG Bro F 270/33.
27 C. de Gaulle, 'Discours prononcé à Rennes' (1947) in: de Gaulle, *Dans l'attente*, pp. 97–104, on p. 102.
28 J. Charlot, *Le gaullisme d'opposition 1946–1958. Histoire du gaullisme* (Paris: Fayard, 1983), p. 114 Broche, *Une histoire des antigaullismes*, p. 295.
29 Bergounioux and Grunberg, *Le long remords du pouvoir*, p. 162.
30 L. Blum, 'Communisme et Gaullisme' (1948), in: L. Blum, *L'œuvre de Léon Blum. VII (1947–1950) La fin des alliances, la troisième force, politique Européenne, pour la justice* (Paris, 1963), pp. 239–244.
31 L. Blum, 'Motion pour un congrès extraordinaire de la S.F.I.O.' (1947), in: Blum, *L'œuvre de Léon Blum VII*, pp. 109–113, on p. 111.
32 L. Blum, 'La formation de la double opposition' (1947), in: Blum, *L'œuvre de Léon Blum VII*, pp. 395–415, on p. 401.
33 L. Blum, 'L'intervention de De Gaulle et le referendum du 1946' (1946), in: Blum, *L'œuvre de Léon Blum. VI*, pp. 305–319, on p. 315.
34 *Ibid.*, p. 313.
35 A. De Gasperi, 'Le ragioni del "governo di emergenza"'(1947), in: De Gasperi, *Scritti politici*, pp. 316–339, on p. 338.
36 P. Togliatti, *Per l'unità di tutto il popolo contro il governo della discordia* (Rome: Superstampa, 1947), p. 4.
37 De Gasperi, 'Le ragione del governo "di emergenza"', p. 338. See also: A. Agosti, 'Il Partito comunista italiano e la svolta del 1947', *Studi Storici*, vol. 31, no. 1 (1990), pp. 53–88, on pp. 83–86.
38 Eichengreen, *The European Economy*, pp. 86–99; F. Nullmeier and F-X. Kaufmann, 'Post-war Welfare State Development', in: F. Castles et al. eds., *The Oxford Handbook of the Welfare State* (Oxford: Oxford University Press, 2010), pp. 81–101; I. de Haan, 'The Western European Welfare State beyond Christian and Social Democratic Ideology', in: D. Stone ed., *The Oxford Handbook of Postwar European History* (Oxford: Oxford University Press, 2012), pp. 299–318; M. Hanagan, 'Changing Margins in Post-war European Politics', in: R. Wakeman ed., *Themes in Modern European History since 1945* (London/ New York: Routledge, 2003), pp. 120–141.
39 Dumoulin, 'The Socio-economic Impact of Christian Democracy in Western Europe', p. 371; Eley, *Forging Democracy*, pp. 311–320.
40 Hodge, 'The Long Fifties', p. 21.
41 L. Avagliano, 'Democrazia cristiana e politiche economiche', in: Lamberts ed., *Christian Democracy in the European Union*, pp. 363–368, on p. 371; F.J. Stegmann, 'Sozio-ökonomische Vorstellungen der Unionsparteien CDU/CSU', in: Lamberts ed., *Christian Democracy in the European Union*, pp. 295–312, on pp. 299–301.
42 A. Fanfani, 'L'azione DC per le zone depresse' (1954), in: A. Fanfani, P. Campilli and E. Colombo, *La Democrazia cristiana per le zone depresse. Documenti* (Rome: Edizione Cinque Lune, 1954), pp. 9–21.
43 Stegmann, 'Sozio-ökonomische Vorstellungen der Unionsparteien CDU/CSU', on p. 299.
44 H.F. Wünsche, *Ludwig Erhards Konzept der Sozialen Marktwirtschaft. Erläuterungen und Interpretationen auf der Grundlage von wissenschaftlichen Schriften Erhards* (Freiburg, 1985), pp. 90–111.
45 L. Erhard, 'Die Ziele des Gesetz gegen Wettbewerbsbeschränkungen' (1955), in: Erhard, *Deutsche Wirtschaftspolitik*, pp. 267–275, on p. 267.
46 L. Erhard, *Wohlstand für Alle* (Düsseldorf: ECON Verlag, 1957), p. 264.
47 L. Erhard, 'Wohlstand für Alle' (1957), in: L. Erhard, *Wirken und Reden. 19 Reden aus die Jahre 1952–1965* (Ludwigsburg: Martin Hoch Druckerei, 1965), pp. 343–360, on p. 348.

48 P. Nenni, *Dialogo con la sinistra cattolica* (Milan: Avanti, 1954), p. 22; p. 24.
49 K. Schumacher, 'Der Parteitag der SPD vom 21 bis 25 Mai 1950 in Hamburg. Grundsatzreferat Schumachers: Die Sozialdemokratie im Kampf um Deutschland und Europa' (1950), in: Schumacher, *Reden—Schriften—Korrespondenzen*, pp. 746–780, on p. 746.
50 *Ibid.*, p. 770
51 K. Schumacher, 'Die Aufgabe der Opposition' (1949), in: Schumacher, *Turmwächter der Demokratie. II*, pp. 166–185, on p. 168.
52 Eichengreen, *The European Economy*, p. 96; p. 114; P. Ginsborg, *A History of Contemporary Italy. Society and Politics 1943–1980* (London: Penguin Press, 2003), p. 189.
53 L. Paggi, 'Violenza e democrazia nella storia delle Repubblica', *Studi storici.*, vol. 39, no. 4 (1998), pp. 935–952, on p. 943.
54 Vittoria, *Storia del PCI 1921–1991*, p. 68.
55 P. Nenni, 'Relazione di Pietro Nenni al 31 Congresso' (1955), in: P.S.I. *31 Congresso Nazionale del Partito socialista italiano. Nel decennale della Liberazione, unità del popolo per restaurare la democrazia nello Stato, nelle fabbriche, nelle campagne* (Milan: Avanti, 1955), pp. 37–89, on p. 51.
56 Nenni, *Dialogo con la sinistra cattolica*, p. 33.
57 SFIO, *Élections législatives de 2 janvier 1956. Programme d'Action du parti socialiste—S.F.I.O.* (1955), p. 10. International Institute for Social History, Amsterdam, Bro 58/23 fol.
58 Ginsborg, *A History of Contemporary Italy*, pp. 188–190.
59 PCI, *Risoluzioni e decisioni del VII Congresso nazionale del Partito comunista italiano. Roma 3–8 aprile 1951* (Rome: l'Unità, 1951), pp. 21–23.
60 PSI, *31 Congresso Nazionale del Partito socialista italiano. Nel decennale della Liberazione, unità del popolo per restaurare la democrazia nello Stato, nelle fabbriche, nelle campagne* (Milan: Avanti, 1955), p. 26.
61 SFIO, *Élections législatives du 17 juin 1951. Programme d'Action. Un seul espoir: le socialisme !* (1951), p. 5. Insternational Institute for Social History Amsterdam, F 1371/470 fol.
62 *Ibid.*, p. 4.
63 SFIO, *Élections législatives de 2 janvier 1956. Programme d'Action du parti socialiste—S.F.I.O.* (1955), p. 10. International Institute for Social History, Amsterdam, Bro 58/23 fol.
64 Callot, *Le Mouvement Républicaine Populaire*, p. 145.
65 Kuisel, *Capitalism and the State in Modern France*, pp. 248–260; Eichengreen, *The European Economy*, pp. 106–110.
66 Becker, 'Der Einfluß der Unionsparteien auf der politische Ordnung der Bundesrepublik Deutschland', p. 229.
67 H. Thum, *Mitbestimmung in der Montanindustrie. Der Mythos vom Sieg der Gewerkschaften* (Stuttgart: Deutsche Verlagsanstalt, 1982), esp. pp. 93–97.
68 Kleinmann, *Geschichte der CDU*, pp. 152–156; Thum, *Mitbestimmung in der Montanindustrie*, pp. 116–119.
69 R. Forlenza, 'A Party for the *Mezzogiorno*: The Christian Democratic Party, Agrarian Reform and the Government of Italy', *Contemporary European History*, vol. 19, no. 4 (2010), pp. 331–349, esp. on pp. 346–349; S. Padgett, 'The Chancellor and his Party', in: S. Padgett ed., *Adenauer to Kohl. The Development of the German Chancellorship* (London: Hurst, 1994), pp. 44–77, on p. 46.
70 D. Hanley, *Party, Society, Government. Republican Democracy in France* (Oxford: Berghahn Books, 2002), ch. 6.
71 M. Debré, *La République et son pouvoir* (Paris: Nagel, 1950), p. 41.
72 *Ibid.*, p. 50.
73 *Ibid.*, p. 60.

74 *Ibid.*, p. 105.
75 P. Allum, 'The Changing Face of Christian Democracy', in: C. Duggan and C. Wagstaff, *Italy and the Cold War: Politics, Culture, Society* (Oxford: Berg, 1995), pp. 117–130.
76 Lupo, *Partito e antipartito*, p. 8; p. 156.
77 L. Sturzo, 'Democrazia e partitocrazia' (1954), in: L. Sturzo, *Opera omnia di Luigi Sturzo. Seconda serie. Saggi—Discorsi—Articoli. Volume 13. Politica di questi anni. Consensi e critiche (1954–1956)* (Rome: Istituto Luigi Sturzo, 1966), pp. 30–35, on p. 31.
78 L. Sturzo, 'Partiti e partitocrazia' (1951), in: L. Sturzo, *Opera omnia di Luigi Sturzo. Seconda serie. Saggi—Discorsi—Articoli. Volume 12. Politica di questi anni. Consensi e critiche (1951–1953)* (Rome: Istituto Luigi Sturzo, 1966), pp. 39–43, on p. 43.
79 L. Sturzo, 'Partitocrazia e Parlamento' (1950), in: L. Sturzo, *Opera omnia di Luigi Sturzo. Seconda serie. Saggi—Discorsi—Articoli. Volume 11. Politica di questi anni. Consensi e critiche (1950–1951)* (Rome: Istituto Luigi Sturzo, 1966), pp. 254–258, on p. 256.
80 See, for instance: Chiarini, 'La fortuna del gollismo in Italia'.
81 J.W. Müller, *Another Country. German Intellectuals, Unification and National Identity* (New Haven: Yale University Press, 2000), pp. 33–40; K. Sontheimer, 'Intellectuals in the Political Life of the Federal Republic of Germany', in R. Pommerin ed., *Culture in the Federal Republic of Germany, 1945–1995* (Oxford: Berg, 1996), pp. 75–92.
82 E. Fraenkel, *Die repräsentative und die plebiszitäre Komponente im demokratischen Verfassungsstaat* (Tübingen: J.C.B. Mohr, 1958), p. 56.
83 R. Souillac, *Le mouvement Poujade. De la défense professionnelle au populisme nationale (1953–1962)* (Paris: Sciences-Po Presses, 2007), p. 394.
84 P. Poujade, *J'ai choisis le combat* (Saint Cère: Société Générale des Éditions et des publications, 1955), p. 208.
85 *Ibid.*, p. 113.
86 P. Ignazi, *Il polo escluso. Profilo storico del Movimento Sociale Italiano* (Bologna: Il Mulino, 1989), p. 47.
87 Sozialistische Reichspartei, 'Aktionsprogramm Sozialistische Reichspartei' (1951), in: O.K. Flechtheim ed., *Dokumente zur parteipolitische Entwicklung in Deutschland seit 1945. Vol. 2* (Berlin: Verlag Dr. Herbert Wendler & Co, 1963), pp. 489–493, on p. 489.
88 H. Hansen, *Die Sozialistische Reichspartei. Aufstieg und Scheitern einer rechtsextremen Partei* (Düsseldorf: Droste Verlag, 2007), p. 265.
89 P. Mendès France, 'La crise de la démocratie' (1955), in: P. Mendès France, *Œuvres complètes. Vol. IV. Pour une République moderne* (Paris: Gallimard, 1987), pp. 81–102, on pp. 82–89.
90 F. Malgeri, *L'Italia democristiana. Uomini e idee dal cattolicesimo democratico nell'Italia repubblicana (1943–1993)* (Rome: Gangemi editore, 2004), p. 80; A. Giovagnoli, *Il partito italiano. La Democrazia cristiana dal 1942 al 1994* (Bari: Laterza, 1996), p. 58.
91 M. Rumor, 'Una forza popolare' (1952), in: Malgeri, *Storia della Democrazia Cristiana. Vol II*, pp. 558–559.
92 A. de Gasperi, *Nella lotta per la democrazia* (Rome: Edizione Cinque Lune, 1954), p. 24.
93 K. Schumacher, 'Um die Lebensnotwendigkeit des Volkes' (1950), in: Schumacher, *Turmwächter der Demokratie. II*, pp. 186–220, on p. 190.
94 E. Ollenhauer, 'Voraussetzungen der Demokratie' (1949), in: Ollenhauer, *Reden und Aufsätze*, pp. 182–194, on p. 184.

95 K. Jaspers, 'Wahrheit, Freiheit und Friede' (1958), in: K. Jaspers ed., *Hoffnung und Sorge. Schriften zur deutsche Politik* (Munich: Piper, 1965), pp. 174–184, on p. 181.
96 F. Ferraresi, *Minacce alla democrazia. La destra radicale e la strategia di tensione in Italia nel dopoguerra* (Milan: Feltrinelli, 1995), p. 56.
97 Sontheimer, *Die Ära Adenauer*, p. 90.
98 K. Adenauer, 'Erste Regierungserklärung von Bundeskanzler Adenauer' (1949), in: Adenauer, *Reden*, pp. 153–169, on p. 163.
99 See: Hanshew, *Terror and Democracy*, ch. 1.
100 K. Adenauer, 'Regierungserklärung vor dem Deutschen Bundestag' (1950), in: Adenauer, *Reden*, pp. 193–200, on p. 200.
101 Bösch, *Die Adenauer-CDU*, p. 152.
102 Adenauer, 'Ansprache vor dem Bundesparteiausschuß der CDU' (1952), in: Adenauer, *Reden*, pp. 263–280, on p. 269.
103 Di Loreto, *Togliatti e la "Doppiezza"*, p. 291 ff.
104 A. de Gasperi, 'Dopo l'attentato a Togliatti' (1948), in: de Gasperi, *Scritti politici*, pp. 339–343, on pp. 339–340.
105 Lupo, *Partito e antipartito*, p. 56.
106 A. de Gasperi, 'Costituzione e riforma elettorale' (1952), in: de Gasperi, *Scritti politici*, pp. 383–386, on p. 383.
107 De Gasperi, 'Le ragioni di una politica anticomunista', p. 370.
108 G. Scarpari, *La Democrazia cristiana e le leggi eccezionali 1950–1953* (Milan: Feltrinelli, 1977).
109 Crainz, *Storia del miracolo italiano*, pp. 4–14.
110 A. de Gasperi, 'La legge maggioritaria. La DC e la dottrina sociale cattolica' (1953), in: de Gasperi, *Scritti Politici*, pp. 392–396, on p. 393.
111 C.D.U, *Hamburger Programm* (1953), p. 6. Found on: http://www.kas.de/upload/ACDP/CDU/Programme_Bundestag/1953_Hamburger-Programm.pdf, accessed on 30 July 2015.
112 M. Görtemacher, *Geschichte der Bundesrepublik. Von Gründung bis zum Gegenwart* (Munich, C.H. Beck Verlag, 1999), p. 75.
113 K. Adenauer, Mitbestimmung (1951), in: K. Adenauer, *Bundestagsreden* (Bonn: AZ Studio, 1972), pp. 79–83, on p. 80.
114 G.D. Drummond, *The German Social Democrats in Opposition 1949–1960. The Case against Rearmament* (Norman: University of Oklahoma Press, 1982), pp. 25–33.
115 *Ibid.*, pp. 69–74.
116 E. Ollenhauer, 'Es geht um mehr als Divisionen' (1952), in: E. Ollenhauer, *Reden und Aufsätze* (Hannover: Dietz Verlag, 1964), pp. 195–205, on p. 197.
117 K. Schumacher, 'Gesellschaftsumbau—Ein nationale Aufgabe' (1951), in: Schumacher, *Turmwächter der Demokratie. II*, pp. 249–281, on p. 252.
118 E. Ollenhauer, 'Bericht über die bisherige Tätigkeit der sozialdemokratische Bundestagfraktion', in: S.P.D., *Es gibt nur eine Wahrheit. Kurt Schumacher und Erich Ollenhauer auf dem Hamburger Parteitag der Sozialdemokratische Partei Deutschlands im Mai 1950* (Bonn: Vorstand der SPD, 1950), pp. 32–48, on pp. 34–35.
119 M. Degli'Innocenti, *Storia del PSI. Vol. III Dal dopoguerra a oggi* (Bari: Laterza, 1993), p. 111.
120 PCI, *Per un governo di pace e di riforme sociali. Per un'Italia democratica e indipendente. Rapporto al consiglio nazionale del P.C.I. di 15 aprile 1953* (1953), p. 7. Istituto Gramsci, Rome, Archivio del P.C.I., F. Col. Op. 91 000071303.
121 L. Basso, *Due totalitarismi. Fascismo e democrazia cristiana* (Rome, 1951), p. 152; p. 174.

122 P. Nenni, *Legge truffa e costituzione. Ragioni dell'ostruzionismo socialista* (Milan: Avanti, 1953), p. 21.
123 Nenni, *Legge truffa e costituzione*, p. 12.
124 Nenni, 'Relazione di Pietro Nenni al 31 Congresso', p. 57.
125 G. Mollet, 'Participation au gouvernement de Mendès France ?' (1954), in: G. Mollet, *Textes choisis. Le socialiste et le républicain 1945–1975* (Paris: Bruno Leprince Éditeur, 1995), pp. 83–94, on p. 87.
126 G. Mollet, *Nous travaillons pour une bonne cause* (Arras: Société d'éditions du Pas-de-Calais, 1949), p. 7.
127 L. Blum, 'A la recherche d'une majorité' (1949), in: Blum, *L'œuvre de Léon Blum. VII*, pp. 252–262, on p. 255.
128 Charlot, *Le gaullisme d'opposition*, pp. 226–240.
129 Courtois and Lazar, *Histoire du Parti communiste français*, p. 262; M. Lazar, 'Forte e fragile, immuable et changeante . . . La culture politique communiste', in: Berstein, *Les cultures politiques en France*, pp. 227–257, on p. 250.
130 Courtois and Lazar, *Histoire du Parti communiste français*, p. 301.
131 M. Thorez, 'Le combat pour l'unité' (1947), in: M. Thorez ed., *Ouvres Choisies en trois volumes. Tome 2 1938–1950* (Paris: Éditions sociales, 1965), pp. 476–491, on p. 487.
132 M. Thorez, 'Intervention au comité central d'Arcueil' (1956), in: M. Thorez ed., *Ouvres Choisies en trois volumes. Tome 3 1953–1964* (Paris: Éditions sociales, 1966), pp. 71–93, on p. 73.
133 Y. Santamaria, *Le parti de l'ennemi ? Le parti communiste française dans la lutte pour la paix (1947–1958)* (Paris: Armand Colin, 2006), p. 265.
134 C. de Gaulle, 'Allocution prononcée à la radiodiffusion française' (1951), in: de Gaulle, *Dans l'attente*, pp. 435–438, on p. 438.
135 *Ibid.*, pp. 437–438.
136 J.P. Rioux, *La France de la Quatrième République. 2. L'expansion et l'impuissance 1952–1958* (Paris, 1983), p. 344.
137 Hanley, *Party, Government, Society. Republican Democracy in France*, pp. 139–143.
138 P. Corduwener, 'Democracy as a Contested Concept in Postwar Western Europe: A Comparative Study of Political Debates in France, West Germany and Italy', *Historical Journal*, vol. 59, no. 1, pp. 197–220.
139 Rioux, *The Fourth Republic*, p. 256 ff.; R. Vinen, 'The Fifth Republic as Parenthesis? Politics since 1945', in: J. McMillan ed., *Modern France 1880–2002* (Oxford: Oxford University Press, 2003), pp. 74–10, on p. 84.
140 M. Evans, *Algeria: France's Undeclared War* (Oxford: Oxford University Press, 2012), p. 155.
141 Mendès France, 'La crise de la démocratie', p. 81.
142 Pulzer, *German Politics 1945–1995* (Oxford: Oxford University Press 1995), p. 66.

3 Converging Conceptions of Democracy at the Turn of the 1960s

The late 1950s rang in political changes that were inextricably linked to changing conceptions of democracy among the major political parties. The political constellation was overhauled with the establishment of the Fifth Republic in France, the formation of the first centre-left government between PSI and DC in Italy, and the SPD–CDU coalition talks which ultimately led to the Grand Coalition. That these new alliances were possible is often attributed to the socioeconomic changes that ushered in Western Europe's 'Age of Affluence'; to the era of 'peaceful coexistence' between East and West following Stalin's death; to the twentieth party congress of the Soviet communist party (CPSU); and, in France, to the Algerian War.[1] Whereas these events doubtlessly played a role, a key condition had to be fulfilled to make the formation of the new political alliances in France, the Federal Republic, and Italy possible. The political actors in these countries had to first accept each other as democrats who shared broadly similar notions of democracy.

From the turn of the decade, political elites increasingly looked at democracy in similar terms; the different conceptions of democracy that had pervaded debates during the first fifteen years after the war started to converge. This was most evident in West Germany and Italy, where Christian Democrats and socialists now accepted each other as democrats, due mainly to changing conceptions of democracy on the Left. The same happened in France, where De Gaulle's reforms in the late 1950s and early 1960s—although they were considered polarizing at the time—ultimately settled the disputes on French democracy over the course of the next few decades. Whereas these changes did usher in an age of increased consensus on the principles of postwar democracy, the new political constellations continued to be questioned on their democratic substance. In France, De Gaulle's reforms of 1958 and 1962 did not immediately settle differences on the principles of democracy. The debate on who was a true democrat picked up where the same debate under the Fourth Republic had left off—only now with reversed power relations. In West Germany, the broad political consensus among parliamentary actors over the principles of democracy met with growing resistance to the principles of party democracy and the lack of opportunity for civic involvement. In Italy, the formation of a centre-left coalition fuelled resistance against the 'republic of the parties' and discontent with the continued exclusion of the communists from power.[2]

Democracy as an End in Itself: A New Notion for the SPD and PSI

Although the PSI and SPD had made attempts to move closer to the political centre earlier in the 1950s, it was only at the end of the decade that the socialists and Christian Democrats bridged the main differences in their views of democracy. The fact that both socialist parties eventually accepted the market economy as democratic was due to some extent to the sustained economic growth under Christian Democratic leadership that went hand in hand with a weakening of traditional class allegiances and with enhanced social security and equality.[3] As Nenni put it, '[A] whole new world is on the move, and because of it, higher levels of democracy, liberty, social justice and equality are achievable'.[4] This led the PSI and SPD to adjust their ideas on the relationship between democracy and capitalism. Whereas they had previously denied that democracy could exist in a capitalist system and hence advocated large-scale nationalization, social equality, and popular control over the economy, the two parties now endorsed the market economy as democratic and expressed unconditional support for individual freedoms.

The SPD reformulated its principles in its 1959 *Godesberger Programm*, which explicitly aimed to strengthen the democratic credentials of the SPD by making the party 'ready for the market economy'.[5] Heinrich Deist, head of the economic affairs commission that prepared the Godesberger conference, argued that the totalitarian experiments of the century, both Nazi and communist, had demonstrated that freedom could not exist in a state-led economy. This entailed that a 'liberal socialist movement' should necessarily endorse a 'liberal economic order'.[6] 'Freedom in the economy, which is inconceivable without a minimum of independent thought and decision making, necessarily leads to the fostering of freedom in other areas of life as well. This is illustrated in particular by the major transformations Russia and its satellite states are currently undergoing', Deist asserted.[7]

In re-evaluating capitalism, the SPD had to include individual freedom as a core principle of the party's conception of democracy. 'Freedom' gained prevalence over 'equality' in SPD discourse about democracy and was explicitly linked to the denotations of 'democracy' because 'the form of state that corresponds best to freedom and human dignity is democracy'.[8] Willi Eichler, president of the Godesberger programme commission, stated that 'equality' in the SPD's terms meant 'equality of opportunity, because without personal freedom equality evolves into equalization'.[9] In Erich Ollenhauer's words, 'democracy means everyone enjoys the greatest possible freedom to develop their skills and talents, their political rights, their economic initiatives, and to sustain their spiritual, religious and cultural life'.[10]

This emphasis on freedom also clearly delineated the difference between the SPD and communism; the socialists abandoned their previous ambivalence towards Marxism. Marx was not mentioned once in the ultimate Godesberger programme; Ollenhauer argued that the programme 'closed the book on' the party's Marxist legacy.[11] He stated that 'the principle and unbridgeable contrast between democratic socialism and any kind of totalitarianism lies in the relationship to democracy' because communism entails 'the suppression of human freedom'.[12] The SPD's denunciation of Marxism meant it no longer distinguished between a 'bourgeois' democracy and a 'true' democracy, thereby uniting political freedoms with a socialist economy. The SPD also embraced parliamentary democracy as an end in itself, as explained by Eichler, because 'the socialist is not committed to [democracy] as a road to an objective, but as an order, without which the socialist society cannot exist'.[13]

The PSI did not officially abandon its Marxist roots, but it underwent a programmatic transformation similar to that of the SPD.[14] After the brutal crackdown on the Hungarian Uprising, the PSI distanced itself from communism and denounced it as undemocratic.[15] It also distanced itself from the Italian Communist Party because the PCI's response to 1956 and Khrushchev's de-Stalinization speech failed to ask 'how [someone who] is nowadays portrayed as a criminal was able to govern the Soviet Union for thirty years'.[16] Nenni criticized Stalin's personality cult and the USSR's conceptions of socialism, power, and the party as variations on a dictatorship.[17] The PSI condemned the communist conception of democracy, characterized it as fake, and stated that 'when the formula of "popular democracy" was launched in 1947–1948, it seemed to indicate a new political turn, the synthesis of two experiences, socialist and communist, [but] in the face of the Hungarian insurrection of 1956, popular democracy is nothing but a variety of the dictatorship of the proletariat, that is to say, communist party dictatorship'.[18]

But the changes in the PSI were more than a rupture with the communists alone. Like the SPD, the PSI also reformulated its understanding of the relationship between democracy and capitalism. Where the party had previously supported replacing capitalism and had denounced the Christian Democrats as defenders of the same interests as fascism, the Italian socialists now advocated 'in clear contrast to the anti-system philosophy' of the postwar years, a policy 'of public intervention . . . oriented towards economic development and the market'.[19] The PSI made its transformation explicit at its 1957 party congress in Venice, where Nenni, in a clear break with the socialist understanding of the DC in the early 1950s, asserted that 'reformism' had replaced 'clerical-fascism' as the dominant ideology of the country's economic and political elites.[20]

The PSI accepted the market economy as democratic, but more so than the SPD, the party argued in favour of state planning, which it felt Italy's specific situation required. Because parts of Italy lacked 'autonomous [economic] development', the economic gap between Italy's North and South required a level of state interference beyond the Keynesianism practiced in other Western European economies. Because the South had no functioning market economy, government intervention was needed to establish it, they argued.[21] Yet the PSI clearly distanced itself from the Soviet-style state planning aimed at organizing the entire economy in advance on the basis of fixed plans. The PSI acknowledged that 'we have to operate in a market economy . . . in which the state coordinates *post hoc* entrepreneurial decisions'.[22] On the subject of state planning, too, the socialists brought their conception of the relationship between democracy and capitalism more in line with that of the DC-led government. The government had an economic policy based on private initiative, but it had recently created a ministry for state intervention in the economy. 'Our conception of the operation and intervention of public enterprises is inspired on the conception of the economy in two sectors: a public and a private sector. This economy based on two sectors could already exist *de facto* in Italy: *Italy is a socialist country without knowing it*', the PSI stated in an attempt to encourage the government to step up their effort in this regard.[23]

To both the PSI and the SPD, democracy was now both a means and an end in itself: 'By saying democracy, we express our allegiance to universal suffrage, to parliament, to the multi-party system', Nenni said.[24] The PSI made 'a definitive choice for democracy and the democratic method' and stated that democracy has 'perennial values'.[25] This meant that the PSI no longer saw democracy as a stepping stone to a socialist society. It also stopped distinguishing between 'bourgeois' and 'true' democracy, as it had done since the Second World War, and now connected democracy explicitly to liberty. The latter figured less prominently in PSI programmes than in the SPD discourse, however. To Nenni, liberty meant 'emancipating men from misery' and 'the protection of constitutional liberties' and was no longer equated with the struggle to overthrow the capitalist system.[26]

In their quest for democratic legitimacy, the PSI and SPD had to do more than accept capitalism and unconditionally embrace individual liberties. They also needed to accept the West and pledge willingness to defend their democracies, even by military means, against communism. The PSI claimed to be officially neutralist in foreign policy but simultaneously stated that it did not 'question Italian membership in NATO and the obligations which come with it, because it does not, in the current situation, entail the risk . . . of seeing the country dragged into a third world war'.[27] Nenni explicitly denounced the party's allegiance to Moscow and its claim that accession to the North Atlantic Treaty Organization (NATO) was a threat to peace and democracy.[28] The SPD's foreign policy shift stressed the SPD and CDU's *Gemeinsamkeiten* in defence of the Western alliance and underscored the West German Socialist Party's commitment to defending democratic values militarily.[29] At the Godesberger conference, prominent party member Herbert Wehner had advocated that the SPD reconcile its conflicting messages;

how could the SPD claim to be the embodiment of democratic values in West Germany but refuse to make a military commitment to defending those values? 'The commitment to the defence of the democratic order and the commitment to national defence are inextricably linked', Wehner stated.[30] One year later, in a major foreign policy speech in parliament, he stressed the common foreign policy objectives shared by the Christian Democrats and the SPD, with the explicit aim of helping to establish a set of shared democratic principles in the Federal Republic. The SPD accepted NATO, a rearmed West Germany, and a common foreign policy and was committed 'in word and deed to the defence of the free and democratic order' so that, 'there is no democratic alternative to the present government in West Germany'.[31] This can be seen as a deliberate quest for consensus on the principles of West German democracy as Wehner claimed that 'domestic political contradictions revive democracy, but a hostile relationship ... ultimately kills democracy. West German democracy cannot bear an incurable mutual hostility between Christian Democrats and social democrats'.[32]

Christian Democrats and the 'Expansion' of Democracy

Once the SPD and PSI reconfigured their conceptions of democracy around 1960, the Christian Democrats were forced to reconsider their rejection of both parties' democratic legitimacy. Although reluctantly at first, the Christian Democrats eventually accepted the SPD and PSI as democrats. This paved the way for government collaboration between the two forces. In both West Germany and Italy, this resulted in a political framework where political parties, regardless of whether they were together in a government coalition or not, agreed on what democracy meant and which political actors were democrats. This consensus shaped the debate on the meaning of democracy and defined political power relationships for decades to come, although these new constellations would in turn come to be criticized as undemocratic.

In West Germany, the convergence between SPD and Christian Democrats and their acceptance of each other as democratic forces went rather smoothly. Initially, there had been a slight hitch when the Christian Democrats reacted with some hostility to the SPD's reforms, and Ludwig Erhard contended that the Godesberger programme was mere tactics and not a true reconfiguration of the SPD's conception of democracy.[33] The 1961 election campaign, in which the octogenarian Adenauer ran against Willy Brandt, echoed the campaigns of the 1950s; Adenauer proclaimed that the SPD would 'sell Germany out to the Russians' and that it would be 'an insult for democracy and all democratic parties to equate the SPD with democracy'.[34] However, the CDU was soon forced to come to terms with the SPD's newly established democratic credentials and its competition for the political centre. The 1961 polls, which resulted in a narrowed margin between SPD and the Christian Democrats, are considered 'crucial' in the political history of the Federal Republic because they mark the moment when the SPD and CDU accepted each other as democratic actors and hence as potential coalition partners.[35] The first negotiations between the two took place in the autumn of 1961, when the CDU decided to explore the possibilities of a Grand Coalition. The symbolism of acceptance was key, even though the Christian Democrats only sought the talks to put pressure on their preferred coalition partner, the Freie Demokratische Partei (FDP). The two parties continued to discuss a coalition in the years that followed, culminating in the Grand Coalition of 1966.[36] When Adenauer left office in 1963, even he conceded that his job had become easier over the years thanks to a 'milder' opposition.[37]

In Italy, the PSI and DC accepted each other as democrats too, but their reconciliation was much harder won than in West Germany. Resistance to socialist participation in government was still strong in the Catholic Church, the DC, and the upper-middle classes.[38] Guido Gonella, a former Christian Democratic Party leader, for instance, compared collaborating with the PSI to warming up to the PCI. 'Times change, but principles stay the same', he said. The DC had always been a centre party and had in so doing protected Italian democracy, Gonella argued. 'Saying no to the opening to the Left will . . . lend new zeal to our battle for the consolidation of democracy'.[39]

Events in July 1960 were crucial to the mutual acceptance between PSI and DC as democrats. They cast a shadow over the democratic credentials of the DC, leaving an alliance with the PSI as the only way to secure Italy's democracy. In the spring of that year, a new DC government led by Fernando Tambroni came to power by winning a confidence vote in parliament with support from the neo-fascist MSI. The neo-fascists soon provoked progressive Italy by staging its party congress in Genoa, a city that had played an important role in the antifascist resistance. Demonstrations in Genoa, protesting what was seen as government legitimization of neo-fascism, were harshly suppressed. This sparked mass protests and strikes in several cities and clashes between rival protesters. The government continued the crackdown; police killed several protesters and wounded dozens of others.[40]

In the eyes of the Left, a DC government supported by neo-fascists that cracked down on popular protests was the culmination of a decade of Christian Democratic assaults on democracy. Defending the protesters, Nenni said the government had acted 'in violent opposition to the entire democratic tradition in Italy and the values of the resistance on which the Republic is founded'.[41] Even Saragat, whose party had supported many DC governments in the 1950s, argued that there had been an 'erosion' of democracy under the DC's stewardship because the working class had lost its trust in the state. The government, he said, had 'underestimated the antifascism of the people'.[42] Tambroni, for his part, justified the suppression of the protests with arguments that echoed De Gasperi's defence of the suppression of rallies following the Togliatti shooting in 1948, claiming that 'the true threat' to Italian democracy was the PCI. Tambroni equated democratic legitimacy with his government's parliamentary majority and stated that 'the inclusion of the working class in the life of the state, which we sincerely aspire to, should be by means of and a victory of democracy, not something imposed by violence on the *piazza*.... If parliament is liberally and legally elected... if the masses can let their influence on the government of the state be heard by means of universal suffrage, Nenni's rhetoric can be nothing but a danger antithetical to democracy'.[43] Tambroni's words could even be interpreted as a reflection of the comments made by the MSI, which argued that it had to protect Italy against 'the Marxist aggression' and that an opening to the Left would necessarily entail an opening to communism because socialism and communism were two peas in a pod.[44]

The DC claimed to be both popular and antifascist but seemed to be neither in the summer of 1960. A decisive push in the direction of the socialists, who had broken away from the PCI, now seemed the only option to strengthen the party's democratic credentials and secure Italian democracy. The progressive wing of the DC, which had been advocating collaboration with the PSI since 1956, now gained the upper hand.[45] From a democratic viewpoint, there were two strong arguments for an alliance with the PSI. Firstly, it would lead to the exclusion of parties on the political fringes. Aldo Moro argued that the DC '[had] the greatest responsibility for the democratic development of Italy' and that, given the electoral gains of the MSI and the PCI, a 'parallel convergence' between PSI and DC was essential for the security of Italian democracy.[46] A centre-left government was considered the best way to isolate the communists. Moro felt that 'isolation of the communists [would be] a defensive measure' and that one of the instruments available 'in the struggle against communism [would be] the expansion of democracy'.[47] Secondly, inclusion of the PSI was portrayed as the inevitable outcome of socioeconomic developments; rather than excluding the working class in the spirit of the 'exceptional laws' of the 1950s, economic progress required inclusion and political consensus. Progressive Christian Democrat Amintore Fanfani argued that socioeconomic progress meant it was no longer strictly necessary to exclude the socialists. Collaboration with the PSI, he asserted, would help to 'democratize' the party, thereby furthering the cause of democratizing Italy.[48] Moro, too, saw inclusion of the PSI as a way to strengthen the relationship between citizens and the state. It could forge the 'reconciliation of the masses with the state, the overcoming of the opposition between the top and the base' and create 'a state not of some, but of all, and rather than the fortunes of the few, a social solidarity made possible by the maturation of democratic consciousness'.[49] Hence, the inclusion of the PSI can also be regarded as a deliberate attempt to overcome the harsh polemics in Italian democracy by forging a coalition that would facilitate the integration of the working class into the state.

The bloodshed of July 1960 tipped the balance in favour of a Christian Democratic alliance with the socialists. Facing a major controversy after the police crackdown, the DC eventually compromised. Tambroni stepped down, a centrist government was formed, and the MSI was discredited and excluded from government for decades to come.[50] This paved the way for collaboration with the PSI.[51] Nenni could now present a centre-left government as a guarantee of democracy in Italy and a way to prevent a new DC shift to the right.[52] The DC's collaboration with the PSI after the events of July 1960 clarified the DC's identity; it showed the people that the party was not just anti-communist but antifascist too.[53] Just as in Germany, a broad alliance was formed in Italy in which former antagonists now accepted each other as democrats and spoke about democracy in increasingly similar terms.

Converging Conceptions of Democracy, Deepening Discontent

Despite important similarities in both substance and chronology, the establishment of consensus on the principles of democracy in West Germany and Italy was marked by three crucial differences. The first of these differences was the balance of power and how this determined which party had to compromise its principles, whereas the second difference was the motives behind convergence. The third and final difference was how convergence influenced the political constellation in each country.

In West Germany, the convergence of conceptions of democracy entailed SPD acceptance of the two principles on which it had most vocally contested the democratic credentials of the CDU in the 1950s: the market economy and the alignment of a rearmed West Germany with the West. Thanks to a 1957 landslide election victory for the Christian Democrats, the only way the SPD could gain democratic legitimacy was by fully accepting the main principles of democracy laid out by the CDU. There was no room for compromise. In Italy, however, it was more a process of 'parallel convergence', as Moro put it. Whereas the PSI accepted NATO accession and the market economy, the DC committed to the implementation of the as-yet-unenforced articles of the Italian constitution. Fanfani, the first prime minister with PSI support in 1962, declared that the government would proceed with the institutionalization of the Italian regions, an ideal long cherished by the socialists. This also involved the 'democratization' of the education system, a relaxation of censorship laws, and the nationalization of the electrical energy sector. Nationalization of key sectors of the economy had always been a PSI goal, as part of the overall aim of economic democratization, but the DC had so far always dismissed this. Fanfani now embraced the move because, in his words,

> electrical energy is so inextricably linked to the civil and economic development of the nation, in all aspects, that it is the duty of the state to make it available to citizens under the best conditions and with the best guarantees. In other words, the decision made by the government to transfer the electrical industry into public hands has its foundation in the nature of the public service of the industry itself.[54]

A second difference between convergences of the Christian Democrats and socialists in West Germany and Italy was the motives behind the move. External events eventually motivated both the PSI and SPD to fundamentally revise their programmes. In Italy, these were the events of 1956 in the Soviet Union and Hungary.[55] A 'parallel convergence' was also necessary because the DC could no longer count on a stable parliamentary majority—as its experiment with the MSI underscored. The coalition with the PSI solved this problem by providing the DC with broader parliamentary support. In West Germany, the CDU did not need the SPD's help; it won an absolute majority in 1957 and ruled in a coalition with the FDP from 1961, which explains why it was mostly the SPD that redesigned its ideas on democracy.[56] The SPD's motive was to establish a shared democratic framework and to attain democratic legitimacy in the eyes of centrist voters, moves that historians have characterized as 'tactical'.[57] The West German and Italian motives behind the convergence differed in a more fundamental way, too, however. In Italy, politicians feared that differences in the country ran so deep that the democratic order as such was at risk. During the Tambroni government's rule, the country witnessed the eruption of a decade of tensions between the Left and the DC. Saragat remarked that 'the country was not [yet] on the brink of civil war, but it was getting close'.[58] So the Italian socialists' quest for democratic legitimacy also originated in their belief that Italian democracy was in jeopardy. This fear may have been justified to some extent. After all, the DC seemed to prefer collaboration with the neo-fascists over the socialists, whereas the state also held onto more legacies from the era of fascism than in West Germany.[59] For example, both the penal code and the education system stemmed directly from the fascist era, whereas the security services still had the same attitude towards the Left and even employed people who were in their ranks during the fascist regime.[60] Thinking of the end of the *Biennio Rosso*, when the Left's confrontation with the state ended in the establishment of the fascist regime, the PSI argued the only way to safeguard democracy was to take a parliamentary path and to include the socialists in government, in other words, to integrate the Left into the state.[61] The socialists' fear that democracy was in jeopardy was underscored in 1964, for instance, when a *Carabinieri* commander planned a coup d'etat. The plot, which was never attempted, called for the arrest of hundreds of left-wing politicians, an armed takeover of strategic positions in Rome, and the blocking of socialist inclusion in the government.[62]

The third difference between the West German and Italian convergences pertains to their impact on the political constellation. In both countries, broader agreement on the principles of democracy fuelled the growth of resistance to the dominant democratic paradigm, which was based on Keynesianism, parliamentarianism, and a party democracy that tolerated less and less opposition. In West Germany, the three parties represented in parliament had now all accepted each other as 'democratic'; the SPD had succeeded in its conscious effort to establish a broad front of forces that acknowledged each other's democratic credentials. In Italy, the convergence between PSI and DC had less harmonious overtones; it was also a means to isolate the PCI,[63] which left the country with a large and powerful opposition party that had yet to define its stance on the new political constellation.

With the mutual acceptance of credentials by the SPD, FDP, and Christian Democrats, West Germany became the first of the three states discussed in the book to achieve such a broad political agreement on the core principles of democracy. However, this process of convergence was neither complete nor completely uncontested, in particular on two issues. The first issue was how to engage the people in West German democracy and to what extent civic commitment should be encouraged. The CDU continued to be wary of any civic participation that eluded the control of political elites and the parties. The party was searching for a new identity suited to an increasingly secular, affluent society, but in its programme, the CDU did not adjust its conception of democracy and stuck with the ideas it had expressed since the 1950s.[64] Erhard, Adenauer's successor, regarded democracy as a form of government that should secure the general interest and counter pluralism in a modernizing West German society.[65] Therefore, the CDU remained committed to a formal conception of democracy that equated this form of rule with a set of representative institutions determined by parliamentary majority and to the principle that democracy was protected by the state rather than citizen involvement.

In contrast with the Christian Democrats, the SPD increasingly emphasized the importance of civil society.[66] Brandt argued that the CDU was more concerned with governmental efficacy than democratic freedoms and that Adenauer 'jeopardized the democratic order' by blurring the difference between party and state.[67] Controversies such as the *Der Spiegel* Affair, which forced CSU hardliner Franz-Joseph Strauss to resign, revealed the power of public opinion in the 'new West Germany', where democracy resided not only in state institutions but in civil society too.[68] Brandt approved of this development and argued that it was time to overcome distrust in the people, a remnant from the German past. To make West German democracy healthy, the nation had to 'be a mature [*mündiges*] people' with an active notion of citizenship.[69] This required a lively public debate and greater tolerance for different opinions, Brandt felt. As a consequence, he opposed the Christian Democrat model based on the general interest and limited civic involvement. Instead, Brandt supported citizenship and pluralism because 'we need more free spirits and tolerance in the life of the state'.[70] In this vein, the SPD also pushed for more opportunities for co-decision in the workplace, an effort aimed at ensuring 'autonomy' in a free economy and making relationships less hierarchical.[71]

Despite his attempts to push back against Christian Democratic notions of democracy, Brandt took care to preserve the common ground he had sought with the CDU for several years. He stressed that society must be spared 'any dogmatic world view and ideological rigidity' and that ideological conflict between the major parties had to be avoided.[72] This points to the second issue that dominated political debates in West Germany, an issue that became more important as the differences between SPD and CDU diminished, namely that West German democracy suffered increasingly from a lack of parliamentary opposition. In this light, the apparent lack of popular involvement became even more pressing and concerns about the influence of political parties more urgent.[73] Intellectuals had started expressing such worries as early as 1960, but from the mid-1960s onwards these ideas gained real traction. In 1960, philosopher Karl Jaspers had theorized that West German citizens showed little affection for political freedom and refrained from participating in political decision making because that freedom had been imposed on the Federal Republic rather than won by it. Jaspers even claimed that no 'true democratic consciousness' had taken root under the long period of Adenauer's rule.[74] Conservative intellectual Karl Dietrich Bracher warned of the lack of civic commitment in relation to the power of political parties. The wealth, consensus and stability in the Federal Republic could be

> harmful to the development of civic consciousness. . . . [T]he increasing power of the executive, the advance of the bureaucratic administrative state, the retreat of Parliament, which is further reinforced by the plebiscitary escalation of the elections, but also state funding of parties, all hinder the political participation of citizens and harbour the danger of a crisis in which citizens are alienated from those in power.[75]

The convergence of conceptions of democracy only served to fuel these concerns about the state of parliamentary democracy. Whereas the SPD channelled some of those concerns into advocacy for a more active civil society, the party remained beholden to preserve the basic consensus with the CDU on the principles of democracy. This meant that the criticism aimed at the power of parties, the lack of parliamentary opposition, and the low level of civic participation went unaddressed but kept gaining ground throughout the 1960s, both inside and outside parliament.

In Italy, the centre-left government initially seemed to be turning over a new leaf. It aspired to resolve the old antagonism between the DC and the Left and the gap between the working classes and the state by forging an alliance in touch with the rapid changes taking place in society. In his government declaration, Moro stated that the parties had joined forces with one objective: to create 'a wider base of consensus and therefore a more solid democratic state . . . in these times of great transformation of Italian society'.[76] Nenni called the collaboration with the DC 'not just an alliance, but a way to create a modern state', which resulted in 'a democratic security that this county has never known'.[77] But the Italian coalition also encountered fierce criticism from two sides. At first, the communists argued that the alliance did not contribute to the democratization of Italy. Later, when the centre-left coalition shifted the perimeters of political alliances and gradually integrated the PCI into the party system, those who questioned the dominance of political parties as such became more sharply critical of the political system as a whole. It was the latter criticism that most profoundly influenced the debate on democracy.

The PCI initially argued that the centre-left coalition did not solve the structural problems of Italian democracy, most notably social inequality and the lack of working-class integration into the state. However, the suppression of the Hungarian Uprising in 1956 once again threw doubt on the PCI's own democratic credentials, as Togliatti by and large defended the Soviet Union and denounced the Hungarian Uprising as an 'anti-communist, anti-socialist and anti-democratic campaign'.[78] Although the PCI did go slightly further than the French communists in criticizing Moscow, historians have branded this a 'missed opportunity' because the party refrained from firmly denouncing the Soviet model as undemocratic.[79] The PCI did not alter its position on democratic centralism, and it remained firmly entrenched in international socialism.[80]

The PCI's proclamation of an 'Italian road to socialism' within the context of the Italian constitution underscored its ambivalence towards the formation of the centre-Left coalition and the Italian party system as a whole. The PCI argued on the one hand that Italian governments, with or without the PSI, were undemocratic because, in the capitalist system, 'democratic liberties are always limited and at risk of being destroyed'.[81] As Togliatti put it, 'Every capitalist state is a dictatorship of the bourgeoisie'.[82] To the communists, 'democracy only ha[d] value if it touche[d] upon economic life, if it contribute[d] to social relationships'.[83] They felt democratic liberty should be imbued with 'new substance' because liberty was not valuable as an end but only as a means 'to well-being and economic progress' and because 'holding elections once in a while is not enough to establish a democratic regime'.[84] On the other hand, Togliatti stressed that the socio-economic aspects of democracy could be attained within the context of the Italian constitution because the constitution expressed 'the intention to extend democratic principles to encompass the economic sphere'.[85] This goes to show that the communists slowly toned down their resistance to government economic programmes in the 1960s,[86] then started to admit that capitalist states 'exist in different degrees', and finally acknowledged that in Italy, despite all its problems, 'a democratic order' existed.[87] In this way, the PCI gradually relinquished its vehement opposition to the DC and became part of the mainstream party political constellation.[88]

As the PCI made its way into the Italian party system in the 1960s, the system itself became the target of increasingly fierce criticism.[89] The formation of the centre-Left coalition and the PCI's integration into the political framework reinforced antifascist sentiments, a political ideology that had been eclipsed by anti-communism in the iciest phase of the Cold War. The re-emergence of antifascism not only reinforced the consensus among the major parties; it also underlined the importance of the political parties as heirs of the antifascist resistance and enabled them to establish themselves as the 'central and commanding institutions of Italian politics'.[90] Especially under Fanfani's leadership, the DC made an effort to bridge the gap between high politics and society.[91] In the same antifascist vein, however, Nenni reaffirmed his commitment to party democracy and spoke in favour of state financing of political parties, citing their crucial function in democracy.[92] So although the centre-Left coalition was intended to increase citizen involvement in the state, the parties negated their own effort by continuing to see themselves as indispensable for managing the relationship between citizen and state.

Politicians' defence of the intimate relationship between parties and democracy in the centre-Left era only fostered resistance to the *partitocrazia*.[93] Criticism was aimed firstly all at how the DC blurred the lines between the party and the state, a problem that the PSI–DC coalition did nothing to address.[94] Some in the PSI, including prominent member Lelio Basso, left the party to found the Italian Socialist Party of Proletarian Unity (PSIUP).[95] Basso explained the move, saying the coalition only existed for 'the DC [to] retain its monopoly on power'.[96] However, now even the PSI had been drawn into the clientelistic system of distribution of state benefits which the DC had built up over the course of the 1950s.[97] The shifts in the party system fed criticism of party democracy as it functioned in Italy. Naturally, the criticism came from the MSI, the fascist movement that exuded distrust of Italians in the political class and decried the growing gap between the world of politics, or *paese legale*, and the real world, or *paese reale*.[98] However, there was also criticism from within the party system itself. Prominent DC politician Guido Gonella, for one, partly shared the MSI's dim views of the way party democracy functioned and denounced it. Because Italian democracy had been born in 1945 as 'a party state' that had conserved some of the negative elements of fascism, Gonella felt parliament had 'a purely instrumental function. The general will is not determined by the free convergence of single representatives of the people but by the deals between leaders of groups. These groups are in control, not the individuals. . . . In the party regime, free suffrage leads to the legitimization of oligarchies'.[99] So rather than bridging the gap between society and politics, parties were increasingly taking control of society. The parties, Gonella said, shared an

> ability to dispose of positions and money, to have leaderships shrewdly supported by majorities, to cleverly create plans with which the top can control the base (thus reversing the terms of democratic logic), to expertly nurture the courtliness of patronage, to intimidate by blackmail, and to distort reality by advertising. This is the pathology of all parties and therefore of the system, the anti-democracy of democracy.[100]

To counter such fundamental criticism of Italian democracy, the centre-Left needed to enact reforms. As historians have pointed out, however, the centre-Left's reformist zeal petered out rather quickly. Following the first major reforms in education and the energy sector, the long-awaited regional reforms did not happen until 1970.[101] Some historians even argued that 'the centre-Left as a project' for renewal in Italian democracy was over by 1964, even though the coalition remained in place for a long time thereafter.[102] As a result, class relations and the power of political parties continued to dominate the debate on democracy in 1960s Italy.

The growing consensus among West Germany and Italy's political elites on the meaning of democracy led to coalitions with greater political power. This was a thorn in the side of those who held different views of democracy and pointed to the new coalitions' failure to deliver on democratic promises. In Italy, the new power relations meant that the old division between the Marxist Left and the DC was replaced by an equally deep divide between the centre-Left and the PCI, although over time the latter was subsumed into the party system. The new centre-Left coalitions sparked new disagreements. One of these was the dispute between the communists and the government parties regarding social equality and the communists' democratic credentials as the communists remained allies of Moscow. The other dispute pitted the increasingly homogeneous political elite who used political parties to strengthen their grip on the country against those who resisted this consolidation of power. Unlike in Italy, the West German government and parliamentary opposition fully accepted each other as democrats. The West German parties succeeded in establishing a truly broad and secure framework of shared democratic principles. However, this broad consensus also led to an increasing similarity between the West German political parties, a development that drew criticism, just like the sparse room the West German parties created for active citizenship.

The Fifth Republic: A Quest for Democratic Consensus

Whereas in West Germany and Italy, political alliances broadened, and formerly opposing conceptions of democracy converged, France moved in a decidedly different direction in the late 1950s and early 1960s. The establishment of the Fifth Republic was postwar Western Europe's most profound political change up until that point, but it did not immediately lead to a convergence of conceptions of democracy. Even though the Algerian War forced political antagonists to work together, De Gaulle's reforms remained contested, and the fiercest backers of a 'republican' democratic model assailed them as anti-democratic. Their dispute with De Gaulle was bolstered by his constitutional reform of 1962. Aside from a short period of cooperation at the height of the Algerian War, the debate on French democracy continued along the lines established just after the Second World War. Gaullists and anti-Gaullists held different conceptions of democracy and denied each other's democratic credentials. The only difference was that the power constellation was the opposite of what it had been in the Fourth Republic.

The democratic legitimacy of De Gaulle's return to power in 1958 is still a divisive issue in French historiography.[103] From the mid-1950s onwards, the war in Algeria spiralled out of the Fourth Republic government's control. While they adhered to the principle that Algeria should remain under French rule, they failed to reassure the *pieds-noirs* of the future of a French Algeria. As a result, they faced violent opposition from two sides: from the Algerians fighting for decolonization and from those who wanted to keep Algeria French.[104] The tensions came to a head in the spring of 1958, when on 13 May, the army established a Committee of Public Safety in Algiers and publically called for the return of De Gaulle. De Gaulle declared he was ready 'to assume the powers of the republic' but aimed to do so in a way that was at least formally legal.[105] Hence, at the height of the crisis, there were three centres (and types) of power: the government with legal power in Paris, the military with the force of arms in Algiers, and De Gaulle exerting moral influence from his home in Colombré.[106]

In the following weeks, while tensions mounted in Algeria and the army took control of Corsica, De Gaulle carefully 'played politicians and the army off' against each other.[107] The political parties that supported the Fourth Republic initially closed ranks in a 'republican front' to protect French democracy from De Gaulle, while anti-Gaullists, including François Mitterrand and Pierre Mendès France, organized a mass protest rally in Paris. At the same time, however, many radicals and socialists believed the Gaullists could protect the republic from the threat of a military coup. It was at this juncture that President René Coty intervened and asked 'the most illustrious of all the French' to form a government, thus sealing the fate of the Fourth Republic. In short, 'it was no coup d'état, but the threat of a coup d'état that convinced the leaders of the republic to step down'.[108] De Gaulle formed a coalition that resembled a government of national unity, including his former antagonist Mollet, for one.[109] The majority of the parties of the Fourth Republic subsequently approved six-month emergency powers for the general and entrusted him with the power to write a new constitution. They did insist on five conditions; among these, the government had to be answerable to parliament, and universal suffrage was to be the source of all power.[110]

A commission appointed by De Gaulle set to work and produced a constitution that was both inspired by the Bayeux programme and at the same time a compromise between De Gaulle and his former antagonists' conceptions of democracy. This was how the two major democratic paradigms in France, 'republican' and Gaullist, converged under the pressures generated by the Algerian War.[111] De Gaulle announced their achievements at the Place de la République, a venue chosen to send the message that he was not threatening but saving the republic.[112] The constitution was subsequently approved by more than 80 per cent of the electorate in a referendum.

The new French constitution built upon three key principles. Firstly, it was to safeguard governmental stability and state authority by protecting institutions from party influence. Michel Debré, who played a major role in writing the constitution, argued that democracies in general, and French democracy in particular, were badly equipped to defend themselves. They required stability to overcome political divisions.[113] So stability was provided by a two-tier electoral system intended to prevent the fragmentation of parliament; a constitutional council; and a powerful president with the authority to appoint the prime minister, dissolve parliament, and invoke far-reaching emergency powers should the need arise. Most importantly, the president was to be elected by a broad electoral college rather than by the parties in parliament. This meant the president now stood above party divisions. The presidency incarnated the sovereignty of the French people and the general interest rather than that of parties. In Debré's words, now 'more than ever, the president of the republic will also be the president of France'.[114] This is why De Gaulle's descriptions of himself should be considered applicable to any president who succeeds him. In his capacity as president, De Gaulle embodied democratic legitimacy 'because I am a man alone, I do not subscribe to any party, any organization. . . . I am a man who belongs to no-one and who belongs to everyone'.[115]

The second principle underpinning the new constitution clearly shows the hand of the Gaullists: referendums. Faithful Gaullist René Capitant called democracy 'the popular participation of citizens in public affairs' and said 'the more active this participation is, the more democratic a nation is'.[116] To the Gaullists, referendums were precisely the type of active political participation that the Fourth Republic had prevented. Capitant viewed them as 'the most perfect expression of democracy' because people directly voted on laws.[117] This element of the constitution signalled a shift from the Fourth Republic's ideal that the popular will was to be represented and expressed exclusively by the national assembly to a situation in which the president embodied sovereignty and could call upon the support of the entire electorate. By successfully reaching over the heads of professional politicians directly to the people, De Gaulle contested the parties' claim that they embodied democratic legitimacy.

The third principle in the new constitution had to do with the revised role of the national assembly, which still enjoyed considerable powers, most notably the right to force governments appointed by the president to resign. This meant that the Fifth Republic was still a parliamentary regime, albeit in 'rationalized' form so as to prevent the instability associated with the Third and Fourth Republics. Debré argued that French democracy was 'unthinkable' without a major role for parliament. Parliament's 'new task', he stressed, 'reasonable and at the same time revolutionary, is to renovate, to rejuvenate the parliamentary regime, or, rather, dare we say it, to finally form a parliamentary regime'.[118] The 'regime of the assembly' was replaced by a 'parliamentary regime, that is, a regime in which power is assured by the collaboration of independent bodies', Debré explained, pointing to the separation of powers so cherished by the Gaullists.[119] Whereas parties had first been able to control government, the Fifth Republic aimed to limit their role to parliament and hoped to render parliament a place where these parties discussed issues of general interest—just as Debré had argued in the early 1950s. The separation of powers was made complete by the establishment of a constitutional council, which slowly gained in importance.[120]

The Fifth Republic was not based solely upon the Bayeux programme but also upon a fine balance between the presidency and parliament.[121] During the campaign for approval of the constitution by referendum, its supporters stressed that it was not just a truly democratic and republican constitution but that it would also, finally, ensure a system of real parliamentary democracy in France. This two-pronged approach underscored the flexibility of the republican tradition in France and enabled De Gaulle to place himself in this tradition to strengthen his democratic credentials.[122] This view was reluctantly accepted by many, both Left and centre, who saw De Gaulle as the only one who could save democracy during the Algerian War.[123] Even Mollet, who had previously not hesitated to link Gaullism to fascism, used this argument to justify his collaboration in the constitutional project. It was a clever balancing act between a right-wing coup and a communist insurrection.[124]

Unrelenting Resistance to Gaullist Democracy

Just as in Italy and West Germany, once a dominant democratic paradigm in France had been established, it encountered resistance. Opposition to the constitutional reforms came from some prominent Fourth Republic politicians, most notably François Mitterrand and Pierre Mendès France, as well as from the French communists. The opposition parties were united, firstly, in their view that De Gaulle had come to power by way of a coup d'état.[125] Mitterrand argued that his presidency was illegal from a democratic perspective: 'I cannot forget that General De Gaulle, president of the council . . . was called upon first and foremost by an undisciplined army. Legally, General De Gaulle has been given his power by the national assembly, but actually, he has held on to it since his *coup de force*'.[126] Mendès France also refused to support a motion of confidence in De Gaulle's government, adding, '[A]bove all, I cannot consent to casting a vote constrained by the insurrection and the threat of a military coup. Because the decision that the Assembly makes—as everyone knows—is not a free decision; the consent that will be given is flawed'.[127]

The critics also took aim at the content of the Fifth Republic's constitution. Mendès France considered the document an assault on democracy and decried what he considered an imbalance between presidential and parliamentary powers. He admitted that the Fourth Republic had been plagued by demagogic methods, lobby groups with too much power, and politicians lacking in courage. But despite all this, he argued, the 1958 constitution was not necessarily an improvement. The constitution clashed with Mendès France's 'republican' ideal because it provided for checks and balances on the power of parliament. The Fifth Republic would rob the people of influence and harm democracy, he claimed, because 'the essential bodies of the new Constitution, we know, the president of the republic, elected by inverse proportional suffrage, the prime minister, the constitutional council, the Senate . . . can, in every way possible, paralyze the Assembly, the only direct representation of universal suffrage'.[128] Referendums, too, were the target of criticism from adherents of a pure parliamentary democracy. Such critics compared them to the nineteenth-century Bonapartist plebiscites, which were not genuine attempts to involve citizens in political decision making but an instrument to assure popular affirmation of presidential politics. Moreover, the critics asserted, the questions De Gaulle posed in the referendums were always 'ambiguous' and intended to mislead, rather than involve, the people.[129]

The chief reason critics gave for rejecting the constitution was that it was undemocratic because it gave the president too much power. Mendès France called the president a 'non-hereditary monarch' who owing to his emergency powers could 'go as far as legally declaring a dictatorship'.[130] There was no true separation of powers because the president also had legislative powers. In addition, the president was elected by an electoral college in which rural regions, often politically conservative, were overrepresented. And this constitution, Mendès France argued, was tailor-made for one man only. Even if De Gaulle did not abuse the extensive powers given to him, no one could guarantee that his successor would show the same restraint. For these reasons, Mendès France called the Fifth Republic the 'De Gaulle's dictatorship'[131] and when the constitution was ratified announced that 'without a doubt, in 1959 the French no longer live in a democracy'.[132]

Whereas the non-communist Left was divided over the democratic credentials of the Fifth Republic, the communists were unified in their rejection. The PCF found itself in a tight spot after the Hungarian Uprising and the speech in which Khrushchev denounced Stalin's personality cult. In the crucial year of 1956, the PCF took a position 'diametrically opposed' to the Italian Communist Party,[133] which on its 'Italian road to socialism', cherished 'parliamentary illusions'.[134] In France, Thorez defended Stalin and pleaded for a policy of international communist unity. He acknowledged that the French people were 'attached to parliamentary institutions' and that the struggle for social change would 'probably' take place through these institutions. Yet he added that 'history has taught us that the forms of the struggle cannot always be peaceful'.[135] This statement cost the party dearly; the PCF faced protests, had managed to alienate the party faithful, and lost members as a result.[136] Despite Thorez's firm language, the party's ambiguous stance towards parliamentary democracy resurfaced when De Gaulle came to power. The PCF rallied to the defence of the Republic and denounced the events of May 1958 as a fascist coup.[137] Thorez had already dismissed the presidential system as dangerous in a country as strongly centralized as France,[138] but now he also decried De Gaulle's novel majoritarian voting system. He called the system undemocratic, claiming that only a system of proportional representation justly reflected the popular will.[139] Finally, Thorez claimed that the constitution posed 'a threat to the working classes' because it did not envision large-scale socioeconomic changes and nationalizations.[140] This led him to seek collaboration with the socialists in the early 1960s in the hope of 'assuring the victory of workers and democracy' in France.[141]

The conflict between the 'parties' and De Gaulle resurfaced in 1962, once the Algerian War had been settled with the Evian Accords. An attempt on De Gaulle's life by terrorists opposed to this treaty prompted a plan that divided the political spectrum into Gaullists and anti-Gaullists once again: direct election of the French president by universal suffrage.[142] Instead of taking the parliamentary road to amending the constitution, De Gaulle submitted the plan in a referendum to the French electorate. The Gaullists provided a range of arguments as to why a universally elected president was perfect for the democratic and republican tradition. Firstly, a universally elected president would enhance state authority and protect the presidency from party politics. De Gaulle held that only a president elected by the people would have enough authority to act in the general interest. In a televised speech, De Gaulle argued that the president had to be universally elected 'to maintain and strengthen the future of our institutions vis-à-vis the factious assemblies of any kind, or manoeuvres of those who, in good or in bad faith, would bring [back] the disastrous old system'.[143] Capitant portrayed the parties' resistance to the plan as a sign they wanted to preserve their privileges. It was '[an act of] attempted revenge by the political oligarchy dispossessed in 1958, which is fiercely determined to stop France from embarking on the journey to direct democracy'.[144]

Apart from protecting the presidency, the reform also enriched democracy, the Gaullists argued. In De Gaulle's words, '[N]othing is more republican, nothing is more democratic', than a universally elected president.[145] The Gaullists made their case by frequently appealing to the 'will of the people' and the 'people's sovereignty' and juxtaposing this with parliamentary authority. Capitant referred to left-wing opponents in parliament as part of the old oligarchy who treated the people 'like a big child' and who unjustly felt citizens were unqualified to decide on matters such as the constitution.[146] The Gaullists, on the other hand, 'believe the people are the sole legitimate sovereign. . . . We no longer support those who are elected as the guardians of a people of minors, but we want to be the agents of citizens in full possession and use of their rights. That is why we consider it democratic progress that the president will now be elected by universal suffrage'.[147]

Despite the Gaullists' efforts, all political parties except De Gaulle's own movement turned against the reform. Its opponents considered it unconstitutional and a threat to the balance between parliamentarianism and presidentialism established in 1958.[148] Mendès France stated that the president would have almost unlimited powers for 'seven years during which he governs without any control and without any accountability'.[149]

The PCF argued that France was moving in the direction of 'a de facto dictatorship' and saw the Gaullists as exponents of the capitalist system preparing a fascist takeover.[150] The communists continued to put forward a plan for 'democratic renewal' that centred on social equality, large-scale nationalizations, and a central role for parliament. The governmental instability of the Fourth Republic was 'not at all the consequence of an excess of democracy; on the contrary, [it was] the result of a systematic violation of the principles of democracy: Democracy should always be in the interest of the—qualitatively and quantitatively—most important section of the people: the working class'.[151] The PCF advocated the establishment of a new constitutional assembly that would write 'a democratic constitution' and bring 'an end to the regime of personal power'.[152]

Even those who had supported the establishment of the Fifth Republic now turned against De Gaulle. Paul Reynaud, who had helped draft the 1958 constitution, stated in a parliamentary speech that De Gaulle's plan was an attack on parliament. 'In all civilized countries, parliament is considered the representative of the nation, with its qualities and defects, with its diversities and even its contradictions.... For us France is *here* ... [and the MPs] are the nation and there is no higher expression of the will of the people' than parliament.[153] Guy Mollet argued that a 'unity of all democratic forces' should rise up against De Gaulle's plans. He accused De Gaulle of having authoritarian intentions because referendums and presidential elections by universal suffrage were an assault on the rights of the minority. 'The essential rule of democracy', Mollet argued, is that 'the majority forms a community which governs in the interest of all, but in so doing, it has no right to infringe upon certain fundamental rights that every one has'.[154] Moreover, Mollet felt the reform jeopardized the balance between presidency and parliament. 'Democracy cannot rest upon a person' but should instead be based upon 'the nation itself, in the measured decisions of its representatives and the harmonious functioning of its institutions'.[155] Mollet also bemoaned De Gaulle's reforms aimed at diminishing the role of political parties, arguing that parties were 'the only means of staying in permanent touch with the people'.[156]

De Gaulle ultimately won the referendum, which made the year 1962 synonymous with the 'second foundation' of the Fifth Republic.[157] This had somewhat paradoxical consequences. In the short run, it ensured that De Gaulle's democratic credentials and the presidential character of the Fifth Republic would continue to be contested throughout the 1960s. At the level of political ideas, the Fifth Republic therefore failed to forge an agreement between Gaullists and anti-Gaullists on the principles of democracy. Despite the momentous political changes between 1958 and 1962, the political debate on democracy in France in a sense resumed the debate under the Fourth Republic: Gaullists and anti-Gaullists still held different conceptions of democracy and questioned each other's democratic credentials.

In the long run, 1962 fostered the formation of two distinct political sides of the spectrum, left-wing and Gaullist, and led to a further stabilization of the political system.[158] Amidst the tensions generated by the Algerian War, former political enemies such as Mollet supported the General by default; this was made more palatable by the fact that the Fifth Republic was presented as a 'parliamentary' regime. The new system also provided the Left with better odds of gaining political power, which was an incentive for them to accept the system. The unifying power of the Fifth Republic became fully evident only after De Gaulle, the towering and polarizing figure with whom the institutions were identified, had stepped down; it was then that the Fifth Republic's true capacity to unify diverse visions on French democracy became clear.

Conclusion: Notions of Democracy, Their Convergence, and Limits in the Early 1960s

At the turn of the 1960s, a new political constellation took shape in West Germany and Italy, where the PSI, the SPD, and the Christian Democrats acknowledged each other's democratic credentials and endorsed a broadly similar conception of democracy. These parties equated parliamentary democracy with democracy as such. Even the PSI, which was still nominally Marxist, now accepted parliamentary democracy as an end in itself rather than as a stepping stone to socialism. The parties to the new consensus also shared a commitment to individual liberties and used this, amidst increasingly visible assaults on individual liberties in communist-ruled Eastern Europe, to strengthen their democratic credentials. The latter played a particularly important role in Italy. Here, Aldo Moro claimed in 1962 that 'communism changes the hierarchy of values, mortifies man, essentially dissolves men into a collective machine which does not regard equality as equal dignity, but requires that the autonomous value of each individual be renounced'.[159] This embrace of individual liberty was already part of the Christian Democratic vocabulary but now became a prominent part of the PSI and SPD's discourse as well, a move motivated by the left-wing parties' acceptance of the market economy as part of democracy. Prominent SPD politician Carlo Schmid illustrated this shift on the Left by formulating the new objectives of his party, as follows: 'It is no longer necessary for the entire economic structure to be restructured . . . but it is necessary to divide the social product more justly, to prevent the abuse of economic power and to grant the working people co-decision rights in the economic process'.[160] To pave the way for this left-wing acceptance of the market economy, the Christian Democrats embarked on a more explicit economic policy of public intervention and redistribution than in the 1950s.[161] Yet another expression of convergence had to do with party democracy. Political changes at the turn of the decade arguably strengthened the principles of party democracy. The Christian Democratic parties in both West Germany and Italy sought new ways of connecting to society, whereas the PSI and the SPD, which enjoyed a large membership base, continued to stress the importance of parties in the democratic process; Nenni denounced criticism of the *partitocrazia* as 'right-wing polemics' opposed to democracy.[162]

In retrospect, France, like West Germany and Italy, slowly grew towards consensus on a few key principles, although this was not so obvious to contemporaries because it was obscured by far-reaching institutional changes, De Gaulle's polarizing personality, and controversies over the constitutionality of De Gaulle's 1962 reform. At first glance it seemed that discord, and not consensus, ruled the day. The establishment of the Fifth Republic failed to bring about an immediate, broad agreement on the principles underpinning French democracy. To make matters worse, the reform of 1962 confirmed many former Fourth Republic politicians' fears that De Gaulle was no democrat and convinced them that another constitutional revision was needed to protect parliamentary democracy and save French democracy per se. So the role of parliament and political parties remained a debatable question between Gaullists and anti-Gaullists, whereas the French socialists and communists still claimed to uphold the revolutionary aim that capitalism should be overcome to establish a true democracy.[163] Yet, by emphasizing the republican tradition and the Fifth Republic's parliamentary characteristics, the Gaullists had managed to secure the endorsement of the 1958 constitution by their future political adversaries. Later on, the new constitution unexpectedly turned out to give political parties room to adjust to the new institutional outline and retain significant political influence.[164]

The changes around the turn of the 1960s occurred against the backdrop of different power constellations in Italy, West Germany, and France. As a result, the debates in the three countries showed differing levels of consensus on the principles of democracy. West Germany was the first country where all the main political parties acknowledged each other as fully democratic. This consensus came about largely through the reforms symbolized in the SPD's Godesberger programme and the CDU's readiness to accept the SPD as a democratic partner. Even if it took several more years for a Grand Coalition to be formed, the parties had evidently moved beyond the fundamental contestation of each other's democratic legitimacy based on competing economic and foreign policy orientations. However, this consensus could not conceal two issues of growing importance in West German democracy: the differences between the SPD and Christian Democrats' concepts of civic participation and concerns over the lack of fundamental opposition in a system dominated by political parties.

Unlike in West Germany, the large parliamentary opposition in Italy continued to cling to its conception of democracy, which differed fundamentally from the government's democratic notions. Over the course of the 1960s, however, the PCI gradually toned down its opposition. Faced with further delegitimization of 'real existing socialism' and the new domestic political constellation, the party had to reconsider its outright dismissal of capitalism, its allegiance to the Soviet Union, and its depiction of the DC as an heir to fascism.[165] This process was informed partly by the events of 1956 in Moscow and Hungary and partly by the formation of the centre-Left coalition. The inclusion of a formally Marxist party in government, the government's commitment to enforcing as yet dormant articles of the constitution, and the successes of Italy's economic miracle created a new political climate in which the PCI's traditional distinction between the 'democratic' masses and an 'authoritarian' state sounded increasingly obsolete. Despite the continued communist exclusion from government, the main political parties seemed to coalesce towards a common set of ideas on democracy. As these developments unfolded over the course of the 1960s, the power of political parties, the gap between politics and society (*paese legale* and *paese reale*), and the limited alternative space for political participation became increasingly pressing issues. These issues would soon prove to be particularly explosive when they coincided with uneasiness about social inequality.

In France, many of De Gaulle's rivals ruled out a return to a regime like the Fourth Republic but were equally opposed to the Gaullist interpretation of democracy. Continued discord on this issue had an impact on the political landscape. Among the French socialists it impeded the kind of reform that its West German and Italian cousins, the SPD and PSI, managed to achieve. Of course, the French socialists made concessions towards the acceptance of the market economy in the early 1960s, yet they did not truly reform their notion of democracy because the party remained preoccupied with defending democracy from Gaullism.[166] Government-initiated reforms stimulated the formation of new political alliances, and the party system slowly polarized into two antagonistic camps with the Gaullists and the Left challenging each other.[167]

The turn of the 1960s was a crucial time in the debate on democracy. The great rifts that had characterized the first fifteen years after the war were partially replaced by a broader consensus among political elites on the meaning of democracy. This consensus, however, fuelled a growing resentment against political elites, who seemed increasingly alike in their conception of democracy and left little room for alternative thinking outside their notions of limited participation, parliamentarianism, state-coordinated capitalism, and especially in West Germany and Italy, the party system. These issues dominated the debate on democracy from the early 1960s onward and created a fertile breeding ground for the growth of the extra-parliamentary Left and the parliamentary opposition that remained outside the consensus.

Notes

1 Eichengreen, *The European Economy since 1945*, ch. 7; Judt, *Postwar*, ch. 10; Crainz, *Storia del miracolo italiano*, ch. 6; J. Horne, 'The Transformation of Society', in J. McMillan ed., *Modern France 1880–2002* (Oxford: Oxford University Press, 2003), pp. 127–149, on p. 149; Orlow, 'Delayed Reaction', p. 90; J.P. Rioux, *La France de la Quatrième République*, p. 44.

2 G. Orsina, 'The Republic after Berlusconi: Some Reflections on Historiography, Politics and the Political Use of History in Post-1994 Italy', *Modern Italy*, vol. 15, no. 1 (2010), pp. 77–92, esp. pp. 78–80.

3 Crainz, *Storia del miracolo italiano*, ch. 4; Degli'Innocenti, *Storia del PSI*, p. 270; Drummond, *The German Social Democrats in Opposition*, p. 261; C. Nonn, 'Das Godesberger Programm und die Krise des Ruhrbergbaus. Zum Wandel der deutschen Sozialdemokratie von Ollenhauer zu Brandt', *Vierteljahrshefte für Zeitgeschichte*, vol. 50, no. 1 (2002), pp. 71–97.

4 P. Nenni, 'La relazione di Pietro Nenni' (1963), in: P.S.I., *Il 35 Congresso Nazionale, Rome 25–29 Ottobre 1963. Resoconto integrale con una Appendice di documenti precongressuali* (Milan: Avanti, 1964), pp. 27–74, at pp. 32–33.
5 Lösche and Walter, *Die SPD*, p. 114.
6 H. Deist, *Wirtschaft von Morgen. Beiträge zur Wirtschaftspolitik der SPD* (Berlin: Dietz Verlag, 1959), p. 53.
7 *Ibid.*, p. 15.
8 W. Eichler, *Grundwerte und Grundforderungen im Godesberger Grundsatzprogramm der SPD* (Bonn: Vorstand der SPD, 1962), p. 20.
9 *Ibid.*, p. 11.
10 E. Ollenhauer, 'Das Grundsatzprogramm der SPD. Der Vorsitze der SPD Erich Ollenhauer auf dem Außenorderntliche Parteitrag in Bad Godesberg. 13.-15. November 1959', in: Miller ed., *Die SPD vor und nach Godesberg*, pp. 110–116, on p. 111.
11 E. Ollenhauer, 'Zum Godesberger Grundsatzprogramm' (1959), in: E. Ollenhauer ed., *Reden und Aufsätze* (Hannover: Dietz Verlag, 1964), pp. 275–306, on p. 283.
12 Ollenhauer, 'Zum Godesberger Grundsatzprogramm', p. 288.
13 Eichler, *Grundwerte und Grundforderungen*, p. 20.
14 Nonetheless, the PSI denounced the course of the SPD as a surrender to social democracy. See, for instance: F. Traldi, 'Il Psi di fronte ad Bad Godesberg', *Ventunesimo secolo*, vol. 8, no. 18 (2009), pp. 137–161.
15 Tranfaglia, 'Socialisti e comunisti', p. 501; Barbagallo, 'Classe, nazione, democrazia', pp. 496–497.
16 P. Nenni, 'Al 35 Congresso. Il primo governo Moro' (1963) in: P. Nenni ed., *Il socialismo nella democrazia. Realtà e presente* (Florence: Valecchi Editore, 1966), pp. 243–276, on p. 274.
17 P. Nenni, 'Al 32 Congresso' (1957), in: Nenni, *Il socialismo nella democrazia*, pp. 5–44, on p. 31; P. Nenni, 'I "vergognosi fatti" del rapporto segreto di Krusciov' (1956), in: P. Nenni ed., *Le prospettive del socialismo dopo la destalinizzazione* (Turin: Einaudi, 1962), pp. 33–51.
18 Nenni, 'Al 35 Congresso', pp. 275–276.
19 Degli'Innocenti, *Storia del PSI*, p. 220.
20 Nenni, 'Al 32 Congresso', p. 7.
21 PSI, *Convegno sulle Partecipazioni Statali. Atti e documenti, Roma, 3–4 maggio 1959* (Milan: Avanti, 1960), p. 212.
22 *Ibid.*, p. 21.
23 *Ibid.*, p. 25. Italics in original.
24 P. Nenni, 'Al 32 Congresso', p. 29.
25 P. Nenni, 'Al 33 Congresso' (1959), in: Nenni, *Il socialismo nella democrazia*, pp. 49–82, on p. 52.
26 P. Nenni, 'Al 32 Congresso', p. 30. See also: Degli'Innocenti, *Storia del PSI*, p. 224.
27 Nenni, 'La relazione di Pietro Nenni', pp. 54–55.
28 T. Nencioni, 'Tra neutralismo e atlantismo. La politica internazionale del Partito socialista italiano 1956–1966', *Italia Contemporanea*, vol. 260 (2010), pp. 438–470.
29 Drummond, *The German Social Democrats in Opposition*, pp. 263–270; B.W. Bouvier, *Zwischen Godesberg und Großer Koalition. Der Weg der SPD in die Regierungsverantwortung. Außen, Sicherheits- und Deutschlandpolitische Umorientierung und gesellschaftliche Öffnung der SPD 1960–1966* (Bonn: Diez Verlag, 1990), p. 60.
30 H. Wehner, 'Demokratie und Landesverteidigung. Diskussionsbeitrag vor dem Godesberger Parteitag der SPD' (1959), in: H. Wehner ed., *Wandel und*

Bewährung. Ausgewählte Reden und Schriften 1930–1975 (Frankfurt am Main: Ullstein Verlag, 1976), pp. 217–218, on p. 218.
31 H. Wehner, 'Außenpolitische Lage. Aussprache über die Regierungserklärung zur außenpolitische Lage' (1960), in: H. Wehner ed., *Bundestagsreden* (Bonn: AZ Studio, 1970), pp. 197–215, on p. 214.
32 *Ibid.*, p. 215.
33 L. Erhard, 'Soziale Ordnung schafft Wohlstand und Sicherheit' (1961), in: Erhard, *Deutsche Wirtschaftspolitik*, pp. 567–587, on p. 567.
34 K. Adenauer, 'Wahlrede auf einer Großkundgebung in Regensburg' (1961), in: Adenauer, *Reden*, pp. 413–423, on p. 418.
35 Bouvier, *Zwischen Godesberg und Großer Koalition*, p. 105.
36 R.J. Granieri, 'Politics in C Minor. The CDU/CSU between Germany and Europe since the Secular Sixties', *Central European History*, vol. 42, no. 1 (2009), pp. 1–32, on pp. 23–24.
37 K. Adenauer, 'Abschiedsansprache auf der Sondersitzung des Deutschen Bundestages' (1963), in: Adenauer, *Bundestagsreden*, pp. 453–456, on p. 455.
38 L. Radi, *Tambroni trent'anni dopo. La nascita del centro-sinistra* (Bologna: Il Mulino, 1990), p. 104. The Kennedy administration toned down its resistance to a government including the socialists; see: Crainz, *Storia del miracolo italiano*, p.164.
39 G. Gonnella, *L'apertura incondizionata* ([1962] Rome: Società nuova, 1963), p. 25.
40 P. Cooke, *Luglio 1960: Tambroni e la repressione fallita* (Milan: Teti editore, 2000).
41 P. Nenni, 'L'avventura di destra dell'estate '60 stroncata dalla sollevazione della coscienza antifascista della nazione' (1960), in: P. Nenni ed., *La battaglia socialista per la svolta a sinistra nelle terza legislatura 1958–1963* (Milan: Avanti, 1963), pp. 45–80, on p. 49.
42 G. Saragat, 'La restaurazione dei valori democratici' (1960), in: Saragat, *Quaranta anni di lotta per la democrazia*, pp. 536–543, on p. 537; p. 539.
43 F. Tambroni, *Un governo amministrativo. Discorsi pronunciato dal 4 aprile al 14 luglio 1960* (Rome: Editrice les problèmes de l'Europe, 1960), pp. 160–161.
44 Movimento Sociale Italiano, 'VI Congresso Nazionale Genova 2–4 Luglio 1960. Mozione unitaria', Fondazione Ugo Spirito. Rome, Fondo Movimento Sociale Italiano. Busta 1. Materiale di propaganda elettorale 1948–1983.
45 Giovagnoli, *Il partito italiano*, pp. 102–119.
46 A. Moro, 'Le ragioni delle convergenze parallele' (1960), in: A. Moro ed., *Scritti e discorsi Vol. II 1951–1963* (Rome: Edizioni Cinque Lune, 1982), pp. 794–813, on p. 797.
47 A. Moro, 'La relazione di Moro' (1962), in: Democrazia Cristiana, *Consiglio Nazionale D.C. 10-11-12 Novembre 1962* (Rome: Documenti SES Cenrale, 1962), pp. 49–50.
48 A. Fanfani, 'La D.C. di fronte al problema socialista. Relazione al Consiglio Nazionale della Democrazia Cristiana Vallombrosa' (1957), in: A. Fanfani ed., *Da Napoli a Firenze 1954–1959. Proposte per una politica di sviluppo democratico* (Rome: Garanzia editore, 1959), pp. 177–207, on p. 188.
49 A. Moro, 'Il congresso di Firenze' (1959), in: Moro, *Scritti e discorsi. Vol II*, pp. 637–718, on p. 685.
50 Cooke, *Luglio 1960*, p. 14.
51 Radi, *Tambroni trent'anni dopo*, pp. 127–128.
52 Di Scala, *Renewing Italian Socialism*, p. 133.
53 Lupo, *Partito e antipartito*, p. 164.
54 A. Fanfani, *Centro-Sinistra '62* (Rome: Garzanti, 1962), p. 116.
55 Degli'Innocenti, *Storia del PSI*, p. 185; Barbagallo, 'Classe, nazione, democrazia', p. 495.

56 Hodge, 'The Long Fifties', p. 22; Spicka, *Selling the Economic Miracle*, ch 6.
57 K. Schönhoven, *Wendejahre. Die Sozialdemokratie in der Zeit der Große Koalition, 1966–1969* (Bonn: Dietz Verlag, 2004), p. 37.
58 Saragat, 'La restaurazione dei valori', p. 542.
59 D. Della Porta, *Social Movements, Political Violence and the State. A Comparative Analysis of Italy and Germany* (Cambridge: Cambridge University Press, 1995), p. 194.
60 Crainz, *Storia del miracolo italiano*, ch. 1.
61 Nenni, 'La relazione di Pietro Nenni', p. 67.
62 The so-called Piano Solo Coup of 1964, see: Paggi, 'Violenza e democrazia nella storia delle Repubblica', p. 945; Crainz, *Storia del miracolo italiano*, p. 180.
63 Degli'Innocenti, *Storia del PSI*, p. 270.
64 Granieri, 'Politics in C Minor', p. 17; Bösch, *Die Adenauer-CDU*, p. 339.
65 Kleinmann, *Geschichte der CDU*, p. 241.
66 Hanshew, *Terror and Democracy in West Germany*, ch. 1.
67 W. Brandt, 'Das Regierungsprogramm der SPD. Rede Willy Brandt SPD Kongress Bonn' (1961), in: W. Brandt ed., *Berliner Ausgabe. Auf dem Weg nach vorn. Willy Brandt und die SPD 1947–1972* (Bonn: Verlag J.H.W. Dietz Nachfolger GmbH, 2000), pp. 230–257, on p. 233; p. 246.
68 Nichols, *The Bonn Republic*, p. 177.
69 Brandt, 'Das Regierungsprogramm der SPD', p. 233; p. 235.
70 *Ibid.*, p. 233; p. 246.
71 Deist, *Wirtschaft von Morgen*, pp. 107–113.
72 W. Brandt, 'Entscheidung für Deutschland' (1961), in: Brandt, *Berliner Ausgabe. Band 4*, pp. 257–264, on p. 263.
73 Hockenos, *Joschka Fischer and the Making of the Berlin Republic*, p. 47; Müller, *Another Country*, p. 45.
74 K. Jaspers, *Freiheit und Wiedervereinigung: über Aufgabe deutscher Politik* (Munich: Piper, 1960), p. 274.
75 K.D. Bracher, 'Die zweite Demokratie in Deutschland—Strukturen und Probleme' (1962), in: R. Löwenthal ed., *Die Demokratie im Wandel der Geschichte* (Berlin: Colloquium Verlag, 1963), pp. 113–135, on p. 135.
76 A. Moro, 'Il patto di Centro-Sinistra' (1963), in: A. Moro, *Scritti e discorsi. Volume II*, pp. 1351–1374, on p. 1351.
77 P. Nenni, 'La relazione di Pietro Nenni', p. 48.
78 P. Togliatto, 'Il rapporto al VIII Congresso' (1956), in: P.C.I., *Il PCI e la svolta di '56* (Rome: Rinascità, 1986), pp. 49–100, on p. 50.
79 Barbagallo, 'Classe, nazione, democrazia', p. 498.
80 Vittoria, *Storia del PCI*, pp. 88–93.
81 P. Togliatti, 'Elementi per una dichiarazione programmatica del P.C.I.' (1956), in: P.C.I., *Il PCI e la svolta*, pp. 113–141, on p. 116.
82 P. Togliatti, 'Linea democratica e prospettiva rivoluzionaria' (1961), in: P. Togliatti ed., *Democrazia e socialismo. Da l'Unità e la Rinascita. Febbraio—Aprile 1961* (Rome: Partito Comunista Italiano, 1961), pp. 15–20, on p. 15.
83 P. Togliatti, 'A proposito di socialismo e democrazia' (1961), in: Togliatti, *Democrazia e socialismo*, pp. 21–50, on p. 31.
84 *Ibid.*, p. 35.
85 *Ibid.*, p. 32.
86 Tranfaglia, 'Socialisti e comunisti', p. 507.
87 Togliatti, 'Linea democratica e prospettiva rivoluzionaria', p. 15.
88 Tranfaglia, 'Socialisti e comunisti', p. 507; Lupo, *Partito e antipartito*, p. 197.
89 G. Crainz, *Il paese mancato. Dal miracolo economico agli anni ottanta* (Rome: Donzelli editore, 2003), pp. 155–170.

90 Orsina, 'The Republic after Berlusconi', p. 78.
91 Giovagnoli, *Il partito italiano*, p. 120.
92 Nenni, 'La relazione di Pietro Nenni', p. 48.
93 Chiarini, 'La fortuna del gollismo in Italia'; Capozzi, 'La polemica antipartitocratica'.
94 McCarthy, *The Crisis of the Italian State*, ch. 2; Ginsborg, *A History of Contemporary Italy*, ch. 5.
95 Degli'Innocenti, *Storia del PSI*, p. 330.
96 L. Basso, 'Sulla comunicazione del governo' (1963), in: Basso, *In difesa della democrazia*, pp. 98–107, on p. 100.
97 Crainz, *Storia del miracolo italiano*, p. 227.
98 Movimento Sociale Italiano, *VI Congresso Nazionale Genova 2–4 Luglio 1960. Mozione unitaria*, Fondazione Ugo Spirito. Rome, Fondo Movimento Sociale Italiano. Busta 1. Materiale di propaganda elettorale 1948–1983.
99 G. Gonella, *Fedeltà e coerenza* (Rome: Società nuova, 1963), p. 25.
100 *Ibid.*, pp. 25–26.
101 R. Lumley, *States of Emergency. Cultures of Revolt in Italy 1968–1978* (London: Verso, 1990), p. 14; Tranfaglia, 'Socialisti e comunisti', p. 502.
102 Crainz, *Storia del miracolo italiano*, p. 240.
103 S. Berstein, 'De Gaulle and Gaullism in the Fifth Republic', in: Hough and Horne, *De Gaulle and Twentieth Century France*, pp. 109–123, on pp. 110–111.
104 Evans, *Algeria: France's Undeclared War*.
105 Berstein, *Histoire du Gaullisme*, pp. 207–211.
106 Facon, *La IVe République*, p. 390.
107 Vinen, *France 1934–1970*, p. 109.
108 Berstein, *Histoire du Gaullisme*, p. 216.
109 A. Knapp, *Parties and the Party System in France: A Disconnected Democracy?* (Basingstoke: Palgrave Macmillan, 2004), p. 34.
110 Berstein, *Histoire du Gaullisme*, p. 218.
111 S. Berstein, *The Republic of De Gaulle* (Cambridge: Cambridge University Press, 1993), p. 3.
112 Broche, *Une histoire des antigaullismes*, p. 389.
113 M. Debré, 'Construire enfin un régime parlementaire' (1958), in: M. Debré ed., *Refaire une démocratie un état un pouvoir* (Paris: Plon, 1958), pp. 15–35, on p. 18.
114 *Ibid.*, p. 17.
115 De Gaulle, 'Conférence de presse tenu à Palais d'Orsay', p. 5.
116 R. Capitant, 'La force du Gaullisme' (1961), in: R. Capitant ed., *Écrits politiques 1960–1970* (Paris: Flammarion, 1971), pp. 9–11, on p. 10.
117 R. Capitant, 'Nécessité et légitimité du referendum' (1960), in: Capitant, *Écrits politiques*, pp. 65–67, on p. 65.
118 Debré, 'Construire enfin un régime parlementaire', p. 22.
119 M. Debré, 'Pourquoi oui ?' (1958), in: Debré, *Refaire une démocratie*, pp. 73–79, on pp. 74–75.
120 S. Brouard, 'The Politics of Constitutional Veto in France: Constitutional Council, Legislative Majority and Electoral Competition', *West European Politics*, vol. 32, no. 2 (2009), pp. 384–403.
121 Berstein, 'De la démocratie plébiscitaire au Gaullisme', p. 176.
122 S. Hazareesingh, 'L'imaginaire républicain en France, de la Révolution française à Charles de Gaulle', *Revue historique,*, no. 659 (2011), pp. 637–654, on p. 647.
123 J. Jackson, 'General De Gaulle and his Enemies: Anti-Gaullism in France since 1940', *Transactions of the Royal Historical Society*, vol. 9 (1999), pp. 43–65, on p. 54.

124 G. Mollet, *13 mai 1958–13 mai 1962* (Paris: Plon, 1962), p. 3.
125 E. Duhamel, *L'UDSR ou la genèse de François Mitterrand* (Paris: CNRS Éditions, 2007), p. 305; Santamaria, *Le parti de l'ennemi ?*, p. 340; Broche, *Une histoire des antigaullismes*, p. 381.
126 F. Mitterrand, 'Réponse au discours d'investiture du général de Gaulle (1958), found on: http://www2.assemblee-nationale.fr/decouvrir-l-assemblee/histoire/grands-moments-d-eloquence/francois-mitterrand-1958-reponse-au-discours-d-investiture-du-general-de-gaulle-1er-juin-1958, accessed on 5 March 2015.
127 P. Mendès France, 'L'investiture du Général de Gaulle' (1958), in: Mendès France, *Œuvres complètes Vol. IV*, pp. 418–425, on p. 421.
128 P. Mendès France, 'Le rejet de la constitution de la Ve République', in: Mendès France, *Œuvres complètes Vol. IV*, pp. 435–452, on p. 438.
129 P. Mendès France, 'Gaullisme, Mendèsisme et la Ve République' (1961), in: Mendès France, *Œuvres complètes Vol. IV*, pp. 656–660, on p. 658.
130 Mendès France, 'Le rejet de la constitution', p. 439.
131 Mendès France, 'Gaullisme, Mendèsisme et la Ve République', p. 660.
132 P. Mendès France, 'Aucun démocratie est possible dans le mensonge', in: Mendès France, *Œuvres complètes Vol. IV*, pp. 525–527, on p. 527.
133 M. Dreyfus, *Le PCF. Crises et dissidences* (Brussels: Éditions complexes, 1990), p. 117.
134 Courtois and Lazar, *Histoire du Parti communiste français*, p. 296.
135 M. Thorez, 'Quelques questions capitales posées au XXe Congrès du Parti Communiste de l'Union Soviétique' (1956), in: M. Thorez ed., *Œuvres choisis en trois volumes. III 1953–1964* (Paris: Editons sociales, 1965), pp. 45–70, on p. 53.
136 Dreyfus, *Le PCF. Crises et dissidences*, p. 118.
137 Courtois and Lazar, *Histoire du Parti communiste français*, p. 306.
138 Thorez, 'Intervention au Comité Central d'Arcueil', p. 73.
139 M. Thorez, 'Intervention au Comité Central de Bezons' (1962), in: Thorez, *Œuvres choisis en trois volumes. III 1953–1964*, pp. 243–256, on p. 254.
140 M. Thorez, 'Discours Clôture au Comité Central d'Ivry (1958), in: Thorez, *Œuvres choisis en trois volumes. III 1953–1964*, pp. 94–119, on p. 97.
141 Thorez, 'Intervention au Comité Central de Bezons', p. 249.
142 Berstein, *The Republic of De Gaulle*, p. 71.
143 C. de Gaulle, 'Allocution radiodiffusée et télévisé au palais d'Élysée' (1962), in: C. de Gaulle ed., *Discours et Messages. Pour l'effort. Aout 1962—Décembre 1965* (Paris: Plon, 1970), pp. 20–24, on p. 23.
144 R. Capitant, 'Réfutation du « non »' (1962), in: Capitant, *Écrits politiques*, pp. 151–160, on p. 156.
145 C. de Gaulle, 'Allocution radiodiffusée et télévisé au palais d'Élysée 4 Octobre' (1962), in: de Gaulle, *Discours et Messages. Pour l'effort*, pp. 30–33, on p. 32
146 R. Capitant, 'Réfutation du « non »', p. 152.
147 *Ibid.*, p. 153.
148 N. Atkin, *The Fifth French Republic* (Basingstoke: Palgrave McMillan, 2005), p. 57; Jackson, 'General De Gaulle and his Enemies', p. 58; Broche, *Une histoire des antigaullismes*, p. 486.
149 P. Mendès France, 'La crise de Cuba et le Référendum sur l'élection du président de la République au suffrage universel' (1962), in: Mendès France, *Œuvres complètes Vol. IV*, pp. 894–902, on p. 896.
150 Thorez, 'Intervention au Comité Central de Bezons', p. 249. See also: Courtois and Lazar, *Histoire du Parti communiste français*, p. 306.
151 J. Duclos, *L'avenir de la démocratie* (Paris: Éditions sociales, 1962), p. 248.
152 *Ibid.*, p. 235.

153 P. Reynaud, 'Débat de censure' (1962). My emphasis. http://www2.assemblee-nationale.fr/decouvrir-l-assemblee/histoire/grands-moments-d-eloquence/paul-reynaud-georges-pompidou-1962-debat-de-censure-4-octobre-1962, accessed on 10 June 2015.
154 Mollet, *13 Mai 1958–13 Mai 1962*, p. 227.
155 *Ibid.*, p. 153.
156 *Ibid.*, p. 208.
157 Atkin, *The Fifth French Republic*, p. 58.
158 Berstein, *Histoire du Gaullisme*, p. 235; Berstein, *The Republic of De Gaulle*, p. 98; Fieschi, *Fascism, Populism and the French Fifth Republic*, p. 84; Courtois and Lazar, *Histoire du Parti communiste français*, p. 309; Atkin, *The Fifth French Republic*, p. 58.
159 A. Moro, 'Il partito e le scelte di fondo della politica nazionale' (1962), in: F. Malgeri ed., *Storia della Democrazia Cristiana Vol. III. Gli anni di transizione 1954–1962. Da Fanfani a Moro* (Rome: Edizione Cinque Lune, 1988), pp. 473–559, on p. 528.
160 C. Schmid, 'Der ideologische Standort der deutschen Sozialismus in der Gegenwart' (1958), in: C. Schmid, *Politik und Geist* (Stuttgart: Ernst Klett Verlag, 1961), pp. 245–278, on p. 260.
161 Spicka, *Selling the Economic Miracle*, pp. 214–215; Avagliano, 'Democrazia cristiana e politiche economiche', pp. 371–372.
162 Nenni, 'La relazione di Pietro Nenni', p. 48.
163 Bergounioux and Grunberg, *Le long remords du pouvoir*, p. 206.
164 Hanley, *Parties, Society, Government. Republican Democracy in France*, pp. 166–167.
165 Galli, *Storia del PCI*, pp. 194–198; Tranfaglia, 'Socialisti e comunisti nell'Italia repubblicana, p. 507.
166 Bergounioux and Grunberg, *Le long remords du pouvoir*, pp. 206–208; Hodge, 'The Long Fifties, p. 31.
167 Hanley, *Party, Society, Government. Republican Democracy in France*, ch. 7.

4 Political Elites and the Challenge to the Parliamentary Model

The 1960s saw the rise of the extra-parliamentary Left, whose actions infused Western Europe's debate on democracy with a new intensity. In some respects, the extra-parliamentary Left's conception of democracy was diametrically opposed to the conception political elites were increasingly concurring on. A prime example of this was the Left's rejection of parliamentarianism and political parties. As mass protests and suppression followed each other up in a cycle of escalating tension, political actors on all sides disputed each other's democratic credentials. Whereas conservatives denounced the extra-parliamentary Left as 'left-wing terrorists', communist politicians belittled the protesters as 'bourgeois', and protest leaders denounced the political establishment as an authoritarian or even fascistoid clique.

The extra-parliamentary intervention in the debate about the state of democracy did not occur in isolation. Within parliament too, minor forces of opposition started to question the functioning of parliamentary democracy following the shifts that marked the turn of the 1960s. They feared that the growing consensus on democracy was diminishing parliament's function as a place to air ideological differences and that the executive, the technocrats, and the political parties were taking over and undemocratically imposing their views. They wanted to put a stop to what they saw as the decline of representative democracy.

At first, political elites could not agree on how to respond to the challenge from critics inside and outside parliament, as the parliamentary Left was much more open to civic involvement than the conservatives. However, when the model of parliamentary democracy faced a challenge at the turn of the 1970s, the parliamentary Left and the conservatives closed ranks in defence of capitalism, existing representative institutions, and limited popular participation. As a result, their conceptions of democracy in the early 1970s were more uniform than at any point since the Second World War.

Parliamentary Opposition to the Decline of Parliamentary Democracy

As the major parties coalesced over the principles of democracy during the 1960s, smaller forces in the parliamentary opposition came to see this development as a decline or even crisis of democracy. They aimed their criticism primarily at the diminishing role of parliament, which, thanks to far-reaching agreements between parties, was no longer the arena where key political differences were debated. As parliament lost influence, power became concentrated in the executive, among technocrats, and in the political party establishments that were beyond parliamentary control. In terms of their ideas, the major political parties became harder to tell apart; they all claimed to govern in the general interest, sometimes even based on 'scientific' solutions to political problems.[1] A clear example of this was the broad embrace of Keynesian economic policy, but it was also reflected in the ambivalence many politicians apparently felt towards civic participation. In any case, such participation was hardly encouraged.

One of Italy's small opposition parties, the PSIUP, argued that the centre-Left government's intention to foster the integration of citizens into the state had descended into an authoritarian form of imposed consensus that negated the role of parliament. At the first PSIUP party congress in 1965, Party secretary Tullio Vecchietti argued that the centre-Left

> tends towards the organization of consensus, with a complex mediation between groups and capitalist sectors, between public and private sectors, between opposing classes. This complex mediation, which is taking place ever more outside the traditional instruments of democracy, most notably parliament, is the main reason why every government and every majority tend to transform into a regime and the centre-left is becoming their beacon to follow.[2]

In West Germany, the FDP was the only remaining parliamentary opposition after 1966. Party leader Walter Scheel argued that the SPD and CDU aimed to impede parliamentary checks on the executive and reduce natural ideological differences.[3] He stated that 'authoritarian thinking is gaining ground, and the "authorities", like governments a hundred years ago . . . want to run their affairs behind closed doors. . . . That democracy happens publically . . . seems to be more and more forgotten'.[4] The Grand Coalition equated democracy with stability and social harmony rather than with an open and potentially polarized debate between opposing interests, and thereby harmed democracy, Scheel argued. 'The development of democracy has been halted by a flawed understanding of democracy . . . fearful of conflicts', he stated.[5]

In France, the political debate in the 1960s continued to pivot on the issue of De Gaulle's democratic credentials. However, in terms of substance the discontent was similar to the criticism in West Germany and Italy. Mitterrand, Mendès France, the communists and the socialists were all concerned about the decline of parliamentary power in the Fifth Republic.[6] The communists intended to write an entirely new constitution that restored the national assembly to the heart of French democracy. Jacques Duclos compared De Gaulle to Louis Bonaparte and stated that 'we find many points of comparison between the behaviour of the Gaullists and that of the men of all the strands of the Second Empire'.[7] Mendès France proposed a new institutional outline in his pamphlet titled *La République moderne*, proposing the restoration of many of parliament's lost powers while stressing the importance of more popular participation in socioeconomic affairs and the development of a new 'civic spirit'.[8] Unlike the communists and Mendès France, Mitterrand envisioned merely constitutional revisions to restrict presidential powers rather than a new constitution.[9] He nonetheless contended that France was a dictatorship, 'even if it is a dictatorship that does not shed any blood and does not exercise terror'.[10] In his 1964 political pamphlet titled *Le coup d'état permanent*, Mitterrand argued that the 1958 coup d'état set De Gaulle apart from the republicans. De Gaulle's coup was permanent, he wrote, and consisted of 'the progressive crumbling of institutions, disappearance of parliamentary control, return of the force of legal exceptions, arbitrary police power, [and] totalitarian propaganda', for which 'General De Gaulle is fully responsible'.[11]

Concerns about the decline of postwar democracy surfaced most clearly in debates on socioeconomic reform. Here too, the major parties seemed increasingly indistinguishable in their views on economic planning and state intervention in the framework of the free market.[12] In West Germany, the SPD did not really challenge the status quo in the 1960s and was itself a major advocate of economic planning and 'scientific' solutions to political problems.[13] Similarly, an apparent consensus among the major parties existed in France and Italy, even though the communist parties had yet to formally accept the link between capitalism and democracy. De Gaulle was portrayed as the protector of capitalist interests, and Thorez, in one of the last speeches he gave before he died, still maintained that the 1958 constitution was 'against the working class and democracy'.[14] The Italian communists challenged the democratic credentials of the centre-Left coalition on the same grounds. The PCI stated that 'the regime in which we live is a regime characterized by a development in the interest of a single social group; those in possession of the most powerful means of production are in a position to dominate society and exploit the workers'.[15] However, because the communists also championed state interference and economic planning, they increasingly concurred with the Gaullists' and centre-Left's economic policies, even if these were not nearly as far-reaching as they had envisioned.[16] This put the communist parties in a quandary; formally they still advocated the abolishment of capitalism, but they had softened their stance considerably by reducing their ambitions for social equality to a pay raise for the workers and the nationalization of key industries.[17]

As shown by historian Gerd-Rainer Horn, newcomers on the Left in the French and Italian parliaments contested the growing consensus among the main political parties on what they called 'state capitalism' and proposed alternatives to the current relationship between democracy and capitalism.[18] The Unified Socialist Party (PSU) explained that it was less opposed to De Gaulle's 'personal power than [to] the institutional economic and social order that De Gaulle has become the embodiment of. We cannot judge the institutions of the Fifth Republic while neglecting its neo-capitalist arrangement'.[19] The PSU argued that the capitalist system needed efficiency and stability to survive and therefore led to a 'degeneration of the parliamentary system'.[20] This was also the reason for the PSIUP to criticize the centre-Left's economic 'reformism' based on economic planning. Integrating the working class into the state by enhancing the role of the state in the economy was no cure for the inherently undemocratic nature of capitalism nor for revaluating labour as a process of personal emancipation. The PSIUP claimed to lead the struggle 'against the reformism of the masses, which should be direct and reinforce class consciousness in the only possible way . . . [by] proposing solutions that inspire an alternative conception to the choices of modern capitalism'.[21] Lelio Basso conceived overcoming capitalism as a way to 'stop the negation of democracy, which is the negation of man, in the condition in which he is condemned to live in modern capitalist society; the alienated man, deprived of his conscious participation in collective life'.[22]

Concerns over the reduced role of parliament and the perceived authoritarianism in the technocratic approach to political problems coalesced with cries for more active civic participation in political affairs. The debate about the balance between civic participation and representative institutions was most urgent in West Germany. There, the debate took place in the shadow of Nazism and the distrust of the popular will that political actors had felt ever since the Federal Republic was founded. In the 1960s, a growing number of politicians amended their notion of democracy to make room for popular participation, which they felt should reflect current societal changes. This shift was epitomized by the FDP's more progressive attitude at the end of the decade.[23] The liberals' claim to be pro-civic involvement was made explicit in the debate on the 'emergency laws' that allowed the government, in certain circumstances, to suspend constitutional liberties.[24] Scheel criticized the Grand Coalition for having 'a conception of democracy that rejects a process of democratization'.[25] The liberals voted against the emergency laws because even 'in exceptional situations, in a democracy power belongs with its citizens'.[26]

The question of civic participation also continued to divide the SPD and Christian Democrats. The Christian Democrats under Ludwig Erhard described democracy as an 'organized society' (*formierte Gesellschaft*), which denoted that democracy was the expression of the general interest. Organized society was a political translation of Erhard's vision on the social market economy in which the state acted as a supreme arbiter of many societal interests and thereby actively encouraged the promotion of the 'common good' in society.[27] Erhard explained at the 1965 CDU party congress that

> [w]e have to be clear that our political order is also undergoing a natural development. The organized society therefore also requires new impulses from our political parties and from parliamentarianism

itself. Parliamentary democracy can no longer be controlled by organized interest; but instead requires . . . greater autonomy in our parliament. . . . Maybe we need a new type of specialists, namely specialists for the general interest.[28]

The SPD, for its part, increasingly stressed that pluralism and the participation of citizens were preconditions for democracy.[29] Brandt named 'democratization' one of the party's top priorities, with a particular eye to fostering political commitment among citizens and engaging a nation accustomed to regarding democracy as a thing that professional politicians did. In Brandt's view, the SPD's entry into government in 1966 began a second phase in the history of the Federal Republic that faced 'the task of democratization'. Brandt conceived of democracy as a continuous process and believed that without committed citizens, West German democracy could not be secure because 'the realization of democracy is very much dependent on individual citizens'. He warned that 'if the leaders . . . do not trust the citizens, it is going to be difficult to create a viable interest in political decision making'.[30] Hence, the SPD aimed to encourage the establishment of an active civil society in addition to parliament as a cornerstone of democracy.

In France and Italy, the issue of civic involvement also gained traction. The new left-wing parties PSU and PSIUP thought of democracy as something that happened outside traditional parliamentary representation too.[31] The PSU felt that 'the Left cannot be content to battle for a bourgeois parliamentary democracy'. It was essential, they argued, to overcome the issue that had dominated the French debate on democracy ever since 1875: 'balancing the executive and legislative' powers. Rather than just talking about gaining power through elections, the PSU should also focus on establishing 'new centres of political power and decision making'.[32] Leading PSIUP member Lelio Basso, one of the founding fathers of the Italian republic,[33] now argued that 'we should not limit ourselves to a purely parliamentary and electoral vision, we must not delude ourselves that parliament is the most perfect form of democracy. . . . [D]emocracy is the spirit which permeates the masses, its capacity for initiative, and its effective participation in the control of society'.[34]

Criticism of the parliamentary and party system was most severe in Italy because closing the gap between state and citizens had initially been one of the centre-Left coalition's main aspirations. As the coalition failed to enact the socioeconomic and political reforms that could align Italy's institutions with the quick modernization of society, its ambition to integrate citizens, and particularly the working class, into the state quickly proved an illusion.[35] According to the PCI this was 'the true problem . . . today for the entire working class and democratic movement in Italy'.[36] Concerns about the malfunctioning of the parliamentary party system were felt so acutely in Italy that they were expressed not only by opposition forces, as in France and West Germany, but also by the ruling Christian Democrats.[37]

At the 1967 party congress, DC leader Mariano Rumor claimed that the 'central problem of Italian democracy today is the lack of faith in politics and the party political system'.[38] He stated that the *boom economico* had created 'the conditions in which the essence of the constitutional design could be realized'. Thus, the phase in which democracy was mainly about guaranteeing political rights had been replaced by a new phase, in which 'a community of state, local entities, [and] civil society' would lead to further democratization.[39] Despite their awareness, the Christian Democrats had a rather patronizing way of stimulating this democratic development; they backed the very institutions that were being criticized for impeding the integration of citizens into the state. Indeed, Rumor claimed it was the political parties that were to be entrusted with fostering civic development, elevating public morality, and modernizing the state. Along the same lines, Aldo Moro, prime minister of successive centre-Left governments in the mid-1960s, called parliament 'the only authentic expression of the popular will'[40] because in a democracy 'above all there is parliament, custodian of national sovereignty and guarantee of the democratic life of the country'.[41]

All told, the parliamentary actors in West Germany, France and Italy held a vibrant and polarized debate in the 1960s, frequently expressing concerns about the state of democracy. The most vehement criticism came from those not included in the new coalitions that emerged after the turn of the decade: the PSU, the PSIUP and to a lesser extent the FDP after 1966. These parties decried the growing consensus among coalition parties and their tendency to reduce the meaning of democracy to their own principles. To counter this trend, the opposition posited that parliament should be reinforced as the core of democracy and protected from too much executive or party political influence, while civic participation should be encouraged.

Authoritarianism, the Rallying Cry of the Extra-Parliamentary Left

The extra-parliamentary Left entered the debate on democracy from the mid-1960s onwards. Initially it was students who dominated the protests; they were at the heart of the social movements and articulated their political ideas.[42] Particularly in Italy, however, the social movements succeeded in establishing ties between students and workers. Their collaboration lasted into the mid-1970s and reached levels unique in Europe.[43] Just like some of the parliamentary opposition voices already discussed, the leaders of social movements criticized the coalescence of political parties and accused them of being increasingly authoritarian in imposing their views. Likewise, they rejected the power of technocracy in 'state capitalism', stressing the importance of civic participation. However, the social movement leaders drew markedly different conclusions from opposition politicians. The problem of postwar democracy, they felt, did not lay in the decline of the parliamentary model but in the nature of parliamentary democracy itself. Instead of arguing for changes within the framework of existing representative institutions, they advocated delegation and direct democracy. Only these forms of participation could overcome what they saw as the authoritarian nature of representation and create the conditions for truly democratic self-government.

In their analysis of parliamentary democracy, the leaders of social movements reasoned from an anti-authoritarian perspective.[44] The shortcomings they identified can be summarized in three main conclusions: the homogeneity of the political system silenced opposition; the coalescence on a socio-economic policy and its execution by technocrats 'in the general interest' thwarted democracy; and finally, the model as a whole provided no room and no encouragement for personal autonomy and civic participation.

In decrying the homogeneity of the political system, social movement leaders concluded that the parliamentary opposition proposed no genuine alternative to the policies of those in government. In France, these accusations centred on the perceived similarities between the political parties and De Gaulle because 'even when voting for it, we feel that the parliamentary opposition of the Left, and a change of government, will not mean grand changes'.[45] Leftist student leader Daniel Cohn-Bendit remarked that even if the Left had won the parliamentary elections, 'we know perfectly well that different men would have promoted the same policies'.[46] Students warned of a 'thoughtless anti-Gaullism', the illusion that all of democracy's problems would be resolved with De Gaulle's departure.[47] French democracy was authoritarian, they argued, because the political parties collaborated with De Gaulle in the establishment of 'a bourgeois dictatorship'. These parties offered no real opposition, because the 'supporters of the Bonapartism of the Fifth Republic could be found among the old parties, allied with lobbies and pressure groups'.[48]

In West Germany, the social movements argued that liberation from the authoritarian system required a true democratization because the Bonn Republic had so far failed to distinguish itself clearly enough from the Nazi state.[49] The emergency laws served at as a catalyst for this view, as these laws could only be passed in the constellation of the Grand Coalition, revealing that there was no real difference between SPD and CDU. Student leaders drew comparisons between the emergency legislation and Hitler's rise to power in 1933.[50] The final declaration at a conference against the laws stated that 'serious dangers threaten the second German democracy' because the government 'wants to prepare a dictatorship by legal means. . . . To oppose the emergency plans of the federal government we declare the emergency of democracy'.[51] As if to confirm this 'state of emergency of democracy', police fatally shot protester Benno Ohnesorg in West Berlin on 2 June 1967. Student leader Rudi Dutschke responded, saying, '[I]t is clear what emergency laws mean to the police. We cannot trust a system where people reject police attacks against harmless demonstrators out of democratic convictions, but are part of a bureaucracy of professional politicians'.

Dutschke also said he saw a 'contradiction between those who rule us and those who want a radical democratization of all elements of society'.[52]

In Italy, resistance against protracted DC rule and concerns over the lack of real opposition by the PCI proved an explosive combination. The extra-parliamentary Left denounced the authoritarian nature of the 'DC state', calling the DC the 'party of the bourgeoisie monopoly in Italy', 'the oppressor of the masses' and 'against the majority of the working people.... Only a long and conscious struggle can defeat the DC's reactionary shift that is oppressing the masses'.[53] The *Movimento Studentesco* argued that '[t]he arrogance of the DC reaches intolerable heights. Every day it blatantly tramples the most elementary democratic liberties'.[54] The communists, too, became the object of extra-parliamentary criticism because of their ties to Moscow, their democratic centralism, and their complicity in the party system. This deprived Italian democracy of a true opposition party that could foster the integration of the working class into the Italian state.[55] The PCI's 'trust in bourgeois institutions and parliament, and [their] offer to collaborate with bourgeois parties' led to 'control of parliament by the forces of the bourgeoisie'. In this sense, the student movement argued, Italy's economy was run on a scheme similar to the orthodox planning schemes of 'real existing socialism', and the PCI presented no alternative because it was not against capitalism, 'but in favour of state-regulated capitalism'.[56] Guido Viale, a leader of Lotta Continua, one of the most prominent revolutionary social movements, therefore stated that 'we should not aim . . . to bring a working class to power under the leadership of the PCI'.[57]

The second major conclusion the extra-parliamentary Left drew about parliamentary democracy was similar to the PSU and PSIUP's analyses, which held that imposing a socioeconomic consensus in the name of the general interest and having this executed by experts had thwarted democracy. It had led to authoritarian forms of decision making in which technocrats and specialists ruled. By treating political problems as technocratic problems, political parties had patched over conflict and made all dissident voices out to be enemies of order as such. The French movement *Nous sommes en marche* stated that '[we] should not confuse the technical division of labour with the hierarchy of authority and power. We do not want to be passively governed anymore by "scientific laws", by the laws of the economy or by technical "imperatives"'.[58] Rudi Dutschke concluded that the attempt to co-opt all dissenting voices 'made it clear to us that the established rules of this unreasonable democracy are not our rules, and that the politicization of the student movement must start with consciously breaking those rules'.[59]

As the parliamentary Left had done earlier, extra-parliamentary actors disputed the relationship between democracy and capitalism because capitalism, they claimed, contributed to a 'verticalization' of power relations that negated political equality and impeded the realization of a true democracy.[60] This criticism was directed specifically at 'state capitalism' as it had evolved in postwar Western Europe. Whereas the parliamentary

Left advocated the democratization of the means of production, the extra-parliamentary Left advocated the democratization of the relations of production, that is, the social relationships on the work floor. The extra-parliamentary movements embraced personal autonomy and workers' self-determination and rejected bureaucracy and hierarchical relationships.[61] The struggle against the capitalist system was first and foremost a 'cultural' struggle whose prime objective was to emancipate the masses from their position of inferiority by establishing anti-hierarchical modes of decision making.[62] As Guido Viale claimed, '[O]ur first battle is an internal one: getting rid of our fear of our masters'.[63] This entailed that to build 'true' democracies, citizens should shift their priorities from economic prosperity to active participation in politics and society.

The third problem of parliamentary democracy, the social movements concluded, was that it offered neither room nor stimulus for personal autonomy and active civic participation. The extra-parliamentary Left saw democracy as an active political process. Democratization took place at the level of society rather than the state. It was the average citizen's apathy and lack of democratic commitment that enabled the state and the capitalist system to become authoritarian. As Daniel Cohn-Bendit put it, a police force and political apathy was all it took 'to sustain power in a modern society'.[64] Dutschke claimed that the 'fascist mindset has not been eradicated since 1945',[65] and called the masses 'dumb and passive'.[66] The economic miracle could not conceal that West Germans still had no true commitment to democracy: 'we are increasing our wealth, more and more, faster and faster, better and better, and that is our only motto'.[67] The Grand Coalition and its perceived authoritarian ambitions risked 'degrading democracy [and turning it into] a welfare state's luxury constitution'.[68]

Citizen participation in politics was a prerequisite for real democracy. In the words of a French Action committee, the extra-parliamentary movements ensured that politics 'ceased to be a disgusting thing ... of corrupt and careerist politicians and [instead] became everyone's right to play a role in society'.[69] The students not only considered the student protests at universities part of a broader quest for democratization, but they also contended that the protests were actually the core of what democracy was all about. Democracy, Cohn-Bendit reasoned, could be everywhere, in every political practice, because the practice itself was what constituted democracy. He illustrated this by saying that the organization of action committees in Paris had led to the involvement of local people in political decisions, after which 'democracy sprang from discussion of our immediate needs and the exigencies of the situation which required action'.[70]

The extra-parliamentary Left therefore argued that democracy should also be practiced in spheres previously considered apolitical. Initially, and most evidently, this quest to democratize society by means of active participation took place at the university. The social movements saw the university as a prime example of the authoritarian model society was organized by.

By addressing the lack of democracy at the university, this could be made more tangible. As Dutschke stated, the 'democratization of the universities' could then no longer be divorced from 'the democratization of society'.[71] In Trento, one of the hotbeds of Italy's student revolt, the movements claimed that 'only a global vision of the university problems . . . [could] achieve a democratic functioning of the university'.[72]

But the notion that democracy was about participation and the establishment of anti-hierarchical relationships rapidly spread beyond university walls and affected relations in the workplace. The extra-parliamentary Left's ideas on this theme went beyond co-decision and increased social equality. German students even denounced the SPD conception of co-decision as a 'hypocritical campaign' by the 'technocratic side of the authoritarian state'.[73] In France and Italy, 'democracy' was most visible on the factory floors, although French workers were, in Cohn-Bendit's words, bribed into 'obedience' by the government's pay raise and never reestablished the militancy and solidarity of May 1968.[74] In Italy, however, the workers' quest to establish anti-hierarchical social relationships, actively participate, and transcend established institutions merged in the thinking and actions of several revolutionary movements such as Lotta Continua. This movement was founded during the massive wildcat strikes in Turin in the autumn of 1969, which caused the trade unions to fear they would lose all control of the working class.[75] These strikes were devised mainly as 'political action[s]' and as part of the quest for democratization; the idea was to create a new model of democracy on the work floor beyond the purview of trade unions and political parties. In a description of the strikes in the eponymous newspaper *Lotta Continua* of 6 December, the organization wrote: 'spontaneously, thousands of metal workers form a *corteo* inside the factory. . . . . During the improvised assembly, a few workers explain the reasons for the struggle'. This spontaneous action ended, however, when union representatives entered and formulated clear economic demands. As a result, 'no political discussion was held, everything was immediately closed down'.[76] The trade unions had mistaken a political struggle for a merely economic argument for higher wages and benefits. As a consequence, the action had 'lost all significance thanks to the separation of economic from political struggle'.[77]

Alternatives to Parliamentary Democracy and Their Limitations

From their analysis of the three major problems of parliamentary democracy, it was but a small step for the extra-parliamentary Left to reject the institutions of representative democracy altogether. Representation, they reasoned, was a matter of politicians assuming authoritarian power, whereby they ruled the people and impeded their active involvement in politics. The extra-parliamentary Left envisioned forms of political decision making and participation that were not merely meant to supplement parliament, parties and trade unions but instead to replace them. The social movement leaders questioned the democratic legitimacy of contemporary democratic institutions, because, as Cohn-Bendit remarked, 'if the bourgeoisie is allowed to choose the arena, it will always cut the workers down to size'.[78]

Aside from parliament, political parties were the bodies most directly affected by the notion that representation was undemocratic. Unlike other postwar anti-party traditions, the extra-parliamentary Left did not reject party democracy because parties had disproportionate power or because they expressed the general interest in a distorted way. Instead, they considered political parties undemocratic simply because they were representative. The extra-parliamentary Left rejected not only the principle of representation but of authority too. All notions of authority should be banned from democratic practices, they asserted, because, as Cohn-Bendit put it, 'democracy is not corrupted by bad leadership, but by the very existence of leadership'.[79] Cohn-Bendit was perhaps the most outspoken proponent of the rejection of parties with his argument that 'democracy cannot even exist within the Party, because the Party itself is not a democratic organization'.[80] Similarly, Dutschke argued that political parties were undemocratic because they featured hierarchical power relations and were manipulated from above instead of being 'organized from below'.[81] Because parties should 'no longer be allowed to determine what was to be understood by democracy',[82] extra-parliamentary movements in West Germany and Italy also called themselves 'anti-parliamentary' rather than merely 'extra-parliamentary'. Dutschke claimed to be in favour of the 'cancellation of the parliamentary system as it currently exists'.[83] Mario Capanna stated that parliament is 'the instrument of bourgeois power that manipulates the masses by giving them the illusion of being involved in politics. . . . For this reason, the change by the *Movimento studentesco* from its initial position of extra-parliamentary position to an anti-parliamentary position is a basic strategic choice'.[84]

The extra-parliamentary Left subsequently aimed to 'demystify electoralism' by exposing its hidden authoritarian tendencies.[85] Instead of 'representation' by means of parliament and parties, it advocated and practiced a system of delegation and direct democracy. Delegates were different from representatives because they were elected from among the electoral body itself rather than chosen from a list composed by political elites. They could also be recalled immediately and did not have the liberty to vote as they pleased for a designated period of time. The continuous debate between delegates and their constituency opened the door to 'the *autogestion* of workers and students'—referring to the term used for workers' self-management—which had as its goal 'to fully achieve free participation in production and consumption, elimination of hierarchies, setting up workers' councils elected by themselves'.[86] In France, protesters advocated the formation of a workers' government, 'based on the proposals of rank-and-file committees'.[87] French workers experimented with new forms of collective decision making, in which rank-and-file committees practiced workers' self-management decided on the organization of tasks, promotions wages and hours; and elected their own delegates to negotiate with the firm. These delegates served only for short periods of time; half of them were replaced every three months, and they could always be recalled in case workers felt they did not live up to their promises.[88] Similarly, the *Movimento studentesco* was locally administered by means of a system of assembly democracy in which all decisions were made by the *assemblea* at a particular university. In Florence, for instance, students claimed that 'the power in the department is exercised by the general assembly. Those who are part of the general assembly publically recognize the principle of power, which comprises everyone's critical commitment to actively participate in the evolution of the department'.[89] These committees were to become the backbone of a truly democratized society because only they embodied the bottom-up, grass-roots approach to politics that qualified as truly democratic. Viale approvingly cited workers at a FIAT factory in Turin who collectively refuted the demand of representation with the cry: 'We are all delegates'.[90] Along the same lines, Dutschke advocated replacing parliamentary politics with 'council republics'. These council republics were meant to organize the decision-making process as close to the people as possible and to give everyone the opportunity to be politically involved; Dutschke considered them essential to the 'radical democratization' of West Germany.[91]

Lotta Continua wanted to bridge the gap between the working class's representation and action by sidelining the Communist Party and making grass-roots initiatives the new frame of reference for working class democracy. The movement stated that there was always 'a risk' that a vanguard would divide the working class by leading it politically. 'From now on we must avert this risk: we must act in a way that the most conscious working comrades . . . are not only the most resolute in conducting strikes . . . but also form the effective and real political direction, as they are the ones that know what the struggle on the workfloor means'.[92] In Italy, the assembly system was adopted by factory workers during and after the Hot Autumn of 1969.[93] By 1972, the country had more than sixty thousand elected delegates who represented more than six thousand factory councils.[94]

To fulfil the promise of participation and absolute political equality, the extra-parliamentary Left felt that only delegation and direct democracy were truly democratic. Their contestation of 'representation' was the extra-parliamentary Left's main contribution to the debate on democracy in the 1960s. However, it was also the position that definitively failed to change the way democracy was practiced. This takes nothing away from the impact of 1968 in terms of stimulating egalitarian political relationships and a culture of active citizenship. Yet the institutions of representative democracy, the major target of the extra-parliamentary critique, withstood the barbs of the 1968 generation unscathed. This was mainly due to the fact that any conception of democracy that did not feature existing representative structures was firmly rejected by virtually all parliamentary actors. But another important factor, the extra-parliamentary Left soon discovered, was that it was extremely difficult to sustain their activities based on ideals of absolute equality, full participation, and delegation, without a formal and centralized organization that could unite the various initiatives and determine a common political strategy. This dilemma was described by Dutschke as 'the problem of organization as the problem of revolutionary existence'.[95] In France and West Germany, the movements with a comprehensive political programme largely dispersed into the new social movements of the 1970s or into the parliamentary Left.[96] The German Socialist Student Union (SDS) epitomized the failure to provide a convincing answer to the organizational dilemma. Its final meeting concluded that 'no informal organization can continue democracy, plebiscitary decision-making structures, and individual emancipation in society as a whole . . . if the liberation of society is not immediately possible, the SDS should at least guarantee democracy and emancipation for itself'.[97] In other words, because it failed to stay true to its ideals of autonomy and direct democracy, it abolished itself rather than sacrifice those ideals in pursuit of political power. In France, the PSU played a crucial role in bridging the gap between the student movement and the world of high politics. PSU leader Michel Rocard emphasized the importance of decentralization; alternative decision-making bodies in schools, universities and factories; and new centres of economic power: he also articulated many of the issues of the 1968 revolt in parliament.[98]

In Italy, the 'problem of organization' was different than in France and West Germany, partly thanks to well-established ties between the student and working-class movements. The Italian social movements had a more openly revolutionary character and claimed to speak on behalf of a working class that was far less integrated into the system.[99] In terms of organization, this meant that the extra-parliamentary Left's claim to speak on behalf of the working class started to gain prevalence over its desire to establish new decision-making models and practices. On this subject, Viale said that Lotta Continua's main issue was 'not only that of organization . . . but also that of growing workers' autonomy in the face of all kinds of despotism and capitalist control, the gradual transformation of the proletariat from a separate class to a class that stands up for itself'.[100] More than in West Germany and France, the Italian extra-parliamentary Left responded to the problem of organization by giving priority to the 'working-class struggle' over the ideals of direct democracy and personal autonomy.

The Conservatives Dig in Their Heels

The massive protests across European cities from the mid-1960s onwards foregrounded existing concerns about parliamentary democracy. Once again, the questions of who deserved democratic legitimacy and who could put their conception of democracy forward most convincingly were in the spotlight. Whereas the extra-parliamentary Left claimed that professional politicians threatened the survival of democracy, conservative politicians in particular turned the concept of democracy against extra-parliamentary critics. CDU leader Franz-Josef Strauss argued that 'the democracies in Europe are in a critical situation . . . [T]he hesitance and feebleness of the democratic authorities' defence against the aggressive collective actions of the New Left reveals that democracy is no longer certain of its role as sole proprietor of all legitimizing values'.[101] The extra-parliamentary Left was antithetical to democracy, Strauss claimed. He spoke of 'Left-wing terror', describing it as 'cold, rational hatred against the law, civilization and order; the envy of the anti-socials; the destructiveness of negative elements who disguise their criminal stance towards society with political motives'.[102] De Gaulle, too, compared his followers' democratic values to what he saw as the extra-parliamentary Left's violent and anti-democratic nature. France was being 'threatened by dictatorship' as a result of 'intimidation, intoxication and tyranny expressed by organized groups', he said.[103]

Amidst the push for more active participation, Christian Democrats and Gaullists reaffirmed their conception of democracy as represented by institutions that safeguarded the general interest. Rainer Barzel, the leader of the CDU, argued that conflicts in a democracy were desirable 'as long as they do not infringe on the core values of others'.[104] The extra-parliamentary Left, by contrast, aimed 'to make the sociological fact of pluralist society into a qualitative, absolute standard'.[105] Helmut Kohl claimed that both the system of council republics and democratic socialism would mean a step backwards for democracy. He pointed to the general interest, arguing that democratization should be 'compatible' with the climate in which it was introduced and that 'society as a whole' rather than workers or students should decide what that climate should be.[106] Franz-Josef Strauss mocked the aim to democratize society as 'romanticized democracy'. By this he meant any conception of democracy that encompassed more than a form of government and that included domains that, in Strauss's view, should be left unpoliticized. He declared the economy 'impossible to democratize', for instance.[107] Similarly, Aldo Moro claimed that 'security comes first' and that 'the democratic state can and will not consent to any initiative of violence and disorder aimed at making the university the platform of a political game'.[108]

The French 'link' between president and people, over the heads of other political representatives, was epitomized by the Gaullist counter-rally on 30 May 1968, where André Malraux asserted that De Gaulle enjoyed 'historic power' supported by the will of the people.[109] But this glorification of the link between the president and the people went hand in hand with a tribute to parliamentary democracy. De Gaulle, claiming he was protecting democratic government from the supposed threats and disorder society was facing, took 'the only acceptable road, that of democracy', by calling snap parliamentary elections, which the Gaullists won by a landslide.[110] Even at moments when the Gaullists seemed most vulnerable to the 1968 critique of a highly centralized and authoritarian Fifth Republic, they resorted to the basics of their notion of democracy. This was most evident in 1969, when De Gaulle called a referendum on regional and senate reforms. One of the reforms proposed was that the senate would be indirectly elected and composed of socioeconomic interest groups. However, this was presented as a way to ensure more 'direct interaction and participation of the French in the affairs of the state'.[111] De Gaulle asserted that what French democracy needed was 'the Participation, a reform that is certainly both long-term and far-reaching'.[112] In reality, though, the proposal would have turned the senate into an unelected and advisory body. As such this proposition offered nothing new; the idea came straight out of the Bayeux plan of 1946.[113] So instead of adapting his conception of democracy to the cries for participation, De Gaulle resorted to the central premise of the Gaullist political programme from twenty years ago. He lost the referendum, resigned, and was succeeded by Georges Pompidou.

In Italy, the DC regarded the revolt of 1968 and 1969 as a sign that Italy's political class had failed to close the gap between state and society, one of the very motives for the formation of the centre-Left. Mariano Rumor had already cautioned his party about this at the 1967 congress. At the party congress two years later, DC leader Flaminio Piccoli spoke of a 'crisis of political parties' and a 'growing crisis in the political class'.[114] Rumor had similarly claimed that the main challenge for Italian democracy lay in confronting defiance of the party system. He pointed to the necessity of political change, saying 'in particular in regard to the young this need for participation seems ever more pressing in order to avoid a gap between the country and the political class. . . . [T]he theme of participation is essential for the survival and the democratic development of our country'.[115] These remarks did not indicate that the DC, any more than the CDU or the Gaullists, endeavoured to adopt positions backed by the extra-parliamentary Left but rather that a sense of crisis was now also permeating the discourse of Italy's leading party. The DC was neither able to initiate the political change Italy needed nor contribute to the integration of citizens into the state, issues that had both been on the agenda for decades. The party reaffirmed the central role of representative institutions, most notably the parties and parliament, and argued for the need to 'defend' the party system.[116]

So instead of showing openness to demands for more civic participation, the DC asserted that the solutions to the perceived democratic crisis lay within the party system. In his speech at the DC party congress in 1973, Moro observed that whereas society was changing quickly, the 'political system has never managed to find a way to keep pace'.[117] Political change was necessary, however, because Italy's democracy faced a dangerous polarization and 'risks moving into the frontal contraposition of two blocs'.[118] According to Moro, what was essentially wrong with this polarization was that it rendered government alternation impossible. He therefore called for a dialogue with the PCI, urging the communists to do more to alter their conception of democracy to 'enter the game'.[119] His cautious rapprochement with the communists implicitly confirmed the primacy of political parties in guiding the country's development and asserted the centrality of the DC in Italian democracy. Perhaps aware of this implication, Moro paradoxically called upon his party to 'become an alternative to itself' to contribute to the renewal of Italian democracy.[120] So, in search of a resolution to heightening social and political tensions, the biggest Italian party resorted to the principles of party democracy and elite collaboration.

Overtaken on the Left: The Parliamentary Left's Response to 1968

The Christian Democrats' outright rejection of the extra-parliamentary Left agenda was not unanimously shared. Left-wing parties in parliament, especially in West Germany and France, were much more susceptible to the cry for participation and self-government because their side of the political spectrum had always addressed questions of participation and democracy's relationship to capitalism more openly. Amidst the extra-parliamentary challenge, many of the themes of 1968, ranging from *autogestion* to co-decision at factories, permeated parliamentary left-wing discourse. The events of 1968, both in Western Europe and across the Iron Curtain in Prague, caused a breach between the PCI and PCF on the one hand and Moscow on the other, which in the PCI's case would never be healed. Despite these far-reaching effects, the parliamentary Left never fundamentally questioned the principles of representation or the existing institutions. In this respect, they formed a front with the Christian Democrats and Gaullists. And so the challenge to parliamentary democracy posed by the protests of 1968 and their long aftermath failed to upset the consensus among political elites on the principles of democracy. However, this challenge did have a noticeable influence on some progressive parliamentary forces.

The extra-parliamentary Left's influence on progressive parliamentary forces was most obvious in West Germany, where it reinforced the desire for civic participation and democratization expressed by progressive politicians earlier on in the 1960s. The SPD–FDP coalition formed by Willy Brandt in 1969, which has been characterized as the 'second foundation' of the Federal Republic,[121] co-opted key themes from the extra-parliamentary Left. Brandt claimed that

> we want to dare more democracy. We will . . . work towards this goal not solely by hearings in parliament, but also by constantly being in touch with representative groups of our people, by a full disclosure of government's policy, by giving every citizen the opportunity to participate in the reform of state and society. . . . Co-decision in the various spheres of our society will be a dynamic force in the coming years. We cannot create the perfect democracy. We want a society that offers more freedom and more shared responsibility.[122]

Democracy should not solely be conceived in terms of the state, Brandt argued, but 'must also be freely practiced in society'.[123]

Changes within the liberal FDP show that extra-parliamentary and parliamentary ideas on democracy were in fact influencing each other around the turn of the 1970s. The SPD's coalition partner transformed into a progressive party that advocated citizen participation in political affairs.[124] The FDP endorsed a range of reforms, including direct election of the federal president, referendums on major issues, increased parliamentary transparency, lowering the voting age, and greater influence for citizens on the organization of political parties.[125] The party's *Freiburger Thesen* were an explicit response to the extra-parliamentary Left, designed to formulate a 'political practice for this new spirit of democratization of society'. The party believed the youth protests denoted 'deep changes in consciousness', which akin to the French Revolution, were founded on the notions of freedom, equality and fraternity.[126]

In France and Italy, parliamentary expression of the extra-parliamentary Left's agenda was mainly confined to the PSIUP and the PSU. In Italy, the PSIUP, which experienced its electoral peak in 1968 when it captured 4 per cent of the vote, stood closest to the student and workers' movements.[127] It increasingly paid tribute to participation, workers' autonomy, and alternatives to state-led capitalism. At its party congress in 1969, the PSIUP moved beyond pure parliamentarianism, stating that 'in this revolt, it is becoming clear that we need to create new forms of democratic life, of control, and self-government in political life'.[128] The party proclaimed that

> [we] do not intend to take a legal and parliamentarian road that has no chance of success. . . . [We] intend to construct a revolutionary strategy of the working class and its organizations, based on developing a new and more modern relationship between party and class, [one that is] able to gather and unleash the full potential of class struggle, by developing new means of self-management in social struggles and new centres of democratic power in opposition to those of the capitalist state.[129]

The PSU, the most obvious link in France between the extra-parliamentary and parliamentary Left, launched an attack on both Gaullism and the left-wing opposition.[130] At the party's 1969 congress, the PSU argued that what really counted was not defeating ruling power but winning 'real power', which meant that the battle 'should primarily take place in the workplace'.[131] There should be 'a mobilization of the masses at all levels', the PSU stated, deliberately advocating politics beyond parliaments and parties because 'the revolutionary movement of the masses is the most authentic expression of democracy'. Where there is a 'crisis of the regime, illegal means such as strikes, manifestations, occupations of public spaces and buildings, and formation of counter-power units are all democratic actions of the masses', the party asserted.[132] The PSU was giving its stamp of democratic legitimacy to extra-parliamentary politics.

In addition to the extra-parliamentary movements' influence on left-wing parties, May 1968 had great impact on the relationship between the French Left and democracy in three key respects: the Left increased its backing for civic and worker participation; the socialists and communists agreed to jointly back social and economic democracy in a collaboration that would have long-lasting impact on the French political landscape; and finally, the Left gradually came to accept the institutional outline of the Fifth Republic.

The Left's crushing defeat at the 1968 parliamentary polls was a decisive catalyst for the formation of the *Parti Socialiste*, in which the French non-communist Left united under the leadership of Mitterrand.[133] At the Épinay congress in 1971, the party simultaneously paid tribute to two key concepts: the traditional left-wing critique of the Fifth Republic's centralized and presidential character and the participatory claims of the 1968 movements.[134] This was the congress where it was famously proclaimed there could be 'no real democracy in a capitalist society', and that the Parti Socialiste itself was revolutionary in nature.[135] Socialism entailed not only the nationalization of the means of production but worker participation too. Mitterrand endorsed workers' self-management, claiming that 'change is coming to France . . . replacing the relationship between an omnipotent state and its excessive administration with citizens, local authorities and local communities. Change in the very concept of democracy, which should become a daily experience for fully responsible citizens'.[136] In the spirit of 1968, Mitterrand had called the alternative to De Gaulle a 'liberal socialism'.[137]

The second key change in the Left's relationship to democracy also began at the Épinay congress, where Mitterrand made an overture to the PCF. He denounced 'ideological dialogue' and proposed an 'alliance in elections'.[138] His initiative met with a positive response from the PCF, which after the protests of 1968 in Paris and the brutal repression of the Prague Spring, had sought integration into the Fifth Republic's party system. In fact, the Soviet intervention in Prague triggered the PCF to reject Soviet policy, ringing in a decade of relative autonomy from Moscow.[139] The PS and the PCF agreed on a Common Programme in 1972, a document that exemplifies how the values of 1968 had become part of left-wing parlance. Some argue that the programme was only a pragmatic move that both parties made primarily for electoral reasons,[140] but all the same it reveals how the French Left's notions of democracy developed in the 1970s. In the document, the Left confirmed that a political democracy could not be separated from an economic democracy. In the words of PCF leader Georges Marchais, democracy had to be conceived of as more than a set of political institutions; it had to include social equality to be 'an advanced democracy. That is to say, a type of democracy that our country has never known and that would manifest itself in political and economic reforms with an unprecedented social significance. . . . In short, an advanced social and economic democracy made possible by the success of this programme . . . that would constitute a transition towards socialism'.[141]

The Common Programme also showed how the PCF had reconfigured its conception of democracy to make room for increased acceptance of civil liberties, individual freedoms, and political pluralism.[142] No longer did the party primarily view these liberties from the perspective of working class rights but rather as 'every individual's democracy and liberty.... We should guarantee individual liberties, liberty of thought, freedom and expression'.[143] Marchais asserted that the PCF had a 'rich conception of democracy' in which there was a place for universal suffrage, political party pluralism, local autonomy and free cultural associations.[144] He refuted critics who said a socialist society would necessarily be bureaucratic and restrictive of personal freedom. Instead, 'we are a long way from Étatism, from bureaucratic centralization', Marchais claimed, adding that 'the communist ideal is a society in which members govern themselves'.[145]

The third and final way the May 1968 movement influenced the French Left's relationship to democracy is that the Left gradually started to accept the institutional outline of the Fifth Republic after the departure of De Gaulle. This does not mean the Left stopped criticizing the Fifth Republic, but the discourse certainly became less polemical than during the De Gaulle presidency. In his 1973 pamphlet *Le rose au poing*, Mitterrand outlined constitutional reforms intended to diminish the power of the presidency, strengthen parliament and decentralize the state.[146] However, the PCF and PS's Common Programme no longer advocated an entirely new constitution. Mitterrand's argument that the constitution should be revised rather than replaced gained traction and encouraged an increased acceptance of the Fifth Republic on the Left. The prime objective, particularly for the PS, was to gain power. Mitterrand saw that the Fifth Republic's outline offered many opportunities in this regard.[147]

Compared to the PS and the SPD, the main left-wing party in Italy was less responsive to the extra-parliamentary Left's conceptions of democracy. The PCI responded 'by closing itself off, expelling those party members who came closest to expressing activist agendas at the centre of public attention in the *biennio rosso* of 1968–1969'.[148] One of the critical voices of the PCI belonged to Rossana Rossanda, a young PCI intellectual who had criticized the communists' contempt for the 1968 movement. Rossanda called the PCI's stance a 'grave error'.[149] The PCI, she claimed, had refused to recognize that the student movement was a 'political actor'. As such, the movement had an entirely different model of political organization than the Old Left, and 'this originality in its formation generates a strong distrust primarily of the way parties are organized: the students [are] egalitarian, the parties rigidly centralized and hierarchical'.[150]

The PCI's dismissal of the extra-parliamentary movement does not mean the party's conception of democracy was unaffected by 1968. Historian Silvio Pons argues that the PCI did change and that this change was due to the Cold War post-1968 détente and the concurrently rising social tensions, which in Italy reached heights unparalleled in Western Europe.[151] The country not only faced the continued dichotomy between Christian Democrats and communists, but it also went through a period of working-class militancy in the early 1970s. Just after the Hot Autumn of 1969, a terrorist bombing of a bank at the Piazza Fontana in Milan launched the beginning of what was termed the 'Strategy of Tension'. Although the bombing was initially blamed on anarchists, it was soon clear that neo-fascists with links to the security services had been responsible. The true nature and extent of the 'Strategy of Tension' is still a disputed issue, but in essence it was a coordinated effort by neo-fascists and elements in the security services to prevent the inclusion of communists in government. Their strategy was to commit terrorist acts that would scare the public and turn political opinion in favour of a right-wing, possibly even authoritarian, solution.[152] The effort included numerous neo-fascist terrorist bombings as well as a failed military coup in 1970.[153]

International events continued to play a role, particularly the deposal of Chile's democratically elected socialist leader Salvador Allende in Augusto Pinochet's right-wing coup. This confirmed new PCI leader Enrico Berlinguer's fears that even a hypothetical left-wing government in Italy would not be able to secure the future of democracy in the country.[154] Berlinguer aimed to overcome the domestic polarization that, he feared, threatened Italian democracy.[155] He felt this threat could only be overcome by establishing a broad consensus on Italy's antifascist and constitutional values. In his words, he envisioned a 'system of political relationships that favours a convergence and collaboration between all democratic and popular forces . . . a historic compromise between the forces that comprise and represent the grand majority of the Italian people'.[156]

Berlinguer knew the PCI would inevitably have to shift its conception of democracy to gain badly needed political legitimacy. He proposed a 'democratic turn' to 'block a reactionary attack on our democracy'.[157] His proposal was aimed at gaining democratic legitimacy in the eyes of the DC but also at reconciling the country's opposing subcultures and expressing greater independence from Moscow.[158] It signified a shift towards the DC's conception of democracy in two ways. Firstly, the PCI recognized the Christian Democrats as a democratic force and did so much more unequivocally than under Togliatti. 'We always recognized the link between the DC and the dominant groups of the bourgeoisie', Berlinguer said, but the DC also 'unite[s] other forces and social and economic interests'.[159] Secondly, Berlinguer emphasized the common ground between his party and the DC, as forces that had established parliamentary democracy in Italy. The PCI made this line of reasoning more explicit in the late 1970s, but it was already visible in their 1972 embrace of parliamentary democracy as an end in itself rather than as a means to a socialist end. Crucially, Berlinguer warned the communists not to

> resort to foolish anti-parliamentarianism. . . . We consider parliament an essential institution of Italian political life, and not just today, but also during our transformation to socialism and during its establishment. . . .

Parliament should therefore not, as in Lenin's time or as in other countries, be conceived as a mere platform for denouncing the evils of capitalism and bourgeois governments in order to propagate socialism.[160]

This statement also had repercussions for the PCI's earlier denouncement of the 'DC regime'. Whereas the PCI used to regard the state and the republic as two different entities, the party now said that the state needed defending to safeguard the republic.[161]

Berlinguer's attempt to reach out to the Christian Democratic Party coincided with Moro's plea for a prudent and gradual inclusion of the PCI in Italian democracy.[162] It underscored one of the major problems of Italian democracy in the 1970s: political polarization, partly caused by a lack of government alternation and the awareness that political parties were increasingly detached from society, was so extreme that it actually drew Christian Democrats and communists closer together. As a result, an alternative to the long rule of the Christian Democrats was still nowhere in sight. Hence, the move to make the PCI fit for government reaffirmed the primacy of political parties and parliamentary politics in Italian democracy: the very two institutions that were so often accused of malfunctioning.

Conclusion: After 1968, the Political Elites Close Ranks

The parliamentary Left, especially in France and West Germany, readily adapted to issues raised by extra-parliamentary actors, mainly because these issues were not entirely new; in fact, the social movements had merely seized upon themes that were already part of the political debate in the early 1960s. Criticism of authoritarian governments, capitalism, and the lack of civil liberties, and the desire for a more active type of citizenship, had all been part of the political debate throughout the 1960s, most notably in the discourse of parties like the PSU and the PSIUP but also among left-wing actors in general. On the conservative side, the Gaullists and Christian Democrats were less inclined to debate democracy from these perspectives. In the 1970s, they continued to emphasize state authority, stability, and the general interest.

It is tempting to conclude that the gap between the Left and the conservatives in parliament widened when the extra-parliamentary Left reignited themes already fiercely debated by the Left, the Christian Democrats and the Gaullists in the 1940s and 1950s. And while the parliamentary Left and Right certainly disagreed over these issues at the turn of the 1970s, and left-wing parliamentary actors in particular included concepts such as *autogestion* and participation in their notion of democracy, this apparent polarization did not make a dent in the parliamentary Left and Right's united front. They stood shoulder to shoulder in their rejection of the most far-reaching and innovative argument in the extra-parliamentary critique: the idea that representation per se is undemocratic. Virtually all parties rallied to the defence of representative institutions. As a consequence, they reached a deeper consensus on their conceptions of democracy in the 1970s than at any time since the Second World War. So ultimately, the protests of 1968 only strengthened the 1960s trend towards convergence among political elites.

Convergence even took place in France, where the nature of representative institutions had consistently divided Gaullists and anti-Gaullists. By the 1970s, the political spectrum had reached an uncharacteristic level of consensus when it came to the democratic legitimacy of the Fifth Republic. Compared with a decade earlier, the two sides disagreed less vociferously on the question of parliamentary versus presidential democracy. The formation of the PS and its Common Programme with the communists paved the way for a left-wing group that opposed the right wing, which was growing ever more divided after De Gaulle left office.[163] The PCF now agreed with Mitterrand that constitutional changes should take place within the framework of the Fifth Republic rather than outside of it. Guy Mollet concluded in 1973 that the constitution was no longer a topic of debate or popular protest, not even among the Left. He remarked that the Gaullists' political adversaries were 'not very concerned' with how the constitution functioned and that 'the protests of the French Left against the malfunctioning of our institutions are rare and timid'.[164]

The major parties' broader and deeper consensus on the principles of existing representative institutions was also visible in West Germany. This is not to say that the SPD and the Christian Democrats agreed in their assessment of the extra-parliamentary Left. The Christian Democrats rejected the push to democratize every sector of society and even accused the SPD of having adopted the extra-parliamentary Left's ideology.[165] However, the CDU and CSU's emphasis on parliament and political parties preserved their common ground with the SPD as these were exactly the institutions on whose importance the SPD was unwilling to compromise with the extra-parliamentary Left. Willy Brandt felt that 'as democratic parties, the Christian Democrats, Free Democrats and the Social Democrats shared a set of political *Gemeinsamkeiten* that they should all uphold'.[166] Like the Christian Democrats, Brandt warned of the consequences of unlimited 'democratization' by pointing out that it was actually 'a step backwards to apply the principles of democracy to every sphere of society'.[167] Brandt defended the controversial emergency laws, claiming that criticism of them was caused by an 'unjustified mistrust of the parties' democratic intent'.[168] Another issue on which the SPD, CDU and CSU concurred was the economy. The SPD continued to embrace the market economy as a system that 'performs its social and societal tasks better than other systems'.[169] Helmut Schmidt asserted that the 'basic principle' for the SPD remained 'our attachment to parliamentary representative democracy, trust in evolutionary change, and a rejection of revolution or the dictatorship of the proletariat'.[170]

In Italy, consensus grew in a different way. The PCI and the DC did not recognize each other as democratic equals. Nonetheless, the long period of tensions generated by the 1968 revolt brought the two parties closer together. They not only shared a concern over threats to state institutions and the division of the country into two subcultures, but they gradually met minds on parliamentary party democracy as the key principle of Italian politics, partly because of the PCI's 'democratic turn'. Therein lay a great paradox for the communists. If they wanted to remain connected to the broad societal resistance against DC rule, they had to wage fierce opposition against the Christian Democrats, but at the same time the extreme tension in Italy caused by terrorism and mass strikes required a reconciliation with them. The PCI was condemned to remain in opposition, which some saw as proof that the Italian political class had failed to keep in step with a society that was moving decisively to the Left. In this sense, the agreement between PCI and DC only exacerbated the notion that Italy had a homogenous political class detached from civil society.[171]

Italy faced unique problems at the turn of the 1970s. The political elites there were least affected by the discourse of the extra-parliamentary Left. Their increased collaboration seemed inspired more by unparalleled social and political polarization than anything else, but this meant that the solutions they sought still did not venture outside of the very system that was already under fierce criticism. Although in Italy too, the main parties agreed on their conception of democracy, the debate in this country started diverging more and more from that in France and West Germany. In the latter two countries, the consensus on democracy reflected a shared agreement on the underlying issues that had divided political actors since the 1940s. In Italy, the agreement between the PCI and DC was more a matter of necessity galvanized by dire challenges to the Italian state, and it actually appeared to worsen, rather than ease, the underlying dissatisfaction with the state of Italian democracy.

Notes

1 K. Schönhoven, 'Aufbruch in die sozialliberale Ära. Zur Bedeutung der 60er Jahre in der Geschichte der Bundesrepublik', *Geschichte und Gesellschaft*, vol. 25, no. 1 (1999), pp. 123–145, on p. 140; G. Metzler, 'Am Ende aller Krisen? Politisches Denken und Handeln in der Bundesrepublik in der sechziger Jahre', *Historisches Zeitschrift*, vol. 275 (2002), pp. 57–103; D. Gosewinkel, 'Zwischen Dikton ur und Demokratie. Wirtschaftliches Planungsdenken in Deutschland und Frankreich: Vom Ersten Weltkrieg bis zur Mitte der 1970er Jahre', *Geschichte und Gesellschaft*, vol. 34, no. 3, (2008), pp. 327–359.
2 Partito Socialista di Unità Proletaria, *1 Congresso Nazionale. Per la pace e la libertà contro l'imperialismo, per il socialismo contro lo sfruttamento e il potere del capitalismo, rafforziamo nelle lotta l'unità dei lavoratori* (Rome, 1965), pp. 33–34.
3 Becker, 'Der Einfluß der Unionsparteien auf der politische Ordnung der Bundesrepublik Deutschland', p. 231; Granieri, 'Politics in C Minor', pp. 23–24; Schönhoven, 'Aufbruch in die sozialliberale Ära', p. 132.
4 W. Scheel, 'Opposition: Kritik und Kontrolle', *Liberal*, vol. 11 (1967), pp. 806–809, on p. 806.

5 W. Scheel, 'Zum geistigen Standort der Liberalen in dieser Zeit', in: W. Scheel et al., *Formeln deutscher Politik. Sechs Praktiker und Theoretiker stellen sich* (Munich: Bechtle Verlag, 1965), pp. 15–50, on p. 18.
6 Broche, *Une histoire des antigaullismes*, pp. 501–507.
7 J. Duclos, *De Napoléon III à De Gaulle* (Paris: Éditions Sociales, 1964), p. 14.
8 P. Mendès France, 'La République moderne. Propositions' (1961), in: Mendès France, *Œuvres complètes Vol. IV*, pp. 737–888, on p.795; 878. Broche concludes that the proposal did not convince anyone, see: Broche, *Une histoire des antigaullismes*, p. 501.
9 See, for instance: A. Bergounioux and G. Grunberg, *L'ambition et le remords. Les socialistes français et le pouvoir (1905–2005)* (Paris: Fayard, 2005), p. 245. See also: Duhamel, *L'UDSR*, pp. 307–318.
10 F. Mitterrand, *Le Coup d'État permanent* (Paris: Julliard, 1984 [1964]), p. 270.
11 *Ibid.*, p. 269.
12 J-P. Dormois, *The French Economy in the Twentieth Century* (Cambridge: Cambridge University Press, 2004), pp. 57–62; Berstein, 'De Gaulle and Gaullism in the Fifth Republic', pp. 115–116; Gosewinkel, 'Zwischen Diktatur und Demokratie', pp. 343–347, and pp. 358–359.
13 Lösche and Walter, *Die SPD*, p. 116.
14 M. Thorez, 'Unité pour la démocratie, pour le socialisme' (1964), in: Thorez, *Œuvres choisis en trois volumes. III*, pp. 316–331, on p. 317.
15 P. Togliatti, 'Rilancio della DC', (1964), in: Togliatti, *Opere VI 1956–1964* (Rome: Editori Riuniti, 1984), pp. 759–761, on p. 760.
16 Tranfaglia, 'Socialisti e comunisti', p. 507; Degli'Innocenti, *Storia del PSI*, p. 285.
17 Galli, *Storia del PCI*, p. 194.
18 G.R. Horn, *The Spirit of '68. Rebellion in Europe and North America 1956–1976* (Oxford: Oxford University Press, 2007), pp. 148–151.
19 PSU, *Tribune Socialiste*, no. 371 (1968), p. 5. Found on: http://edocs.lib.sfu.ca/cgi-bin/Mai68?Display=3385, accessed on 30 June 2015.
20 *Ibid.*, p. 5.
21 PSIUP, *1 Congresso Nazionale*, p. 54.
22 *Ibid.*, p. 372.
23 J. Dittberner, 'FDP—Partei der Zweiten Wahl. Ein Beitrag zur Geschichte der liberalen Partei und ihrer Funktionen im Pateiensystem der Bundesrepublik' (Opladen: Westdeuscher Verlag, 1987), pp. 14–39 on pp. 17–18; E.J. Kirchner and D. Broughton, 'The FDP in the Federal Republic of Germany: The Requirements of Survival and Success', in: E.J. Kirchner ed., *Liberal Parties in Western Europe* (Cambridge: Cambridge University Press, 1988), pp. 62–92, on p. 83.
24 Wolfrum, *Die geglückte Demokratie*, p. 236.
25 Scheel, 'Zum geistigen Standort der Liberalen in dieser Zeit', p. 18.
26 W. Scheel, 'Zu den Notstandgesetze' (1968), found on: http://chronik.fnst.de/files/77/Scheel-Notstandgesetze_1.pdf, accessed on 30 July 2015.
27 H. Schot, *Die Formierte Gesellschaft und das deutsche Gemeinschaftswerk. Zwei gesellschaftspolitische Konzepte Ludwig Erhards* (Doct. Dissertation, Bonn, 1981), p. 27.
28 L. Erhard, 'Formierte Gesellschaft. Rede vor dem 13. Bundesparteitag der CDU' (1965), in: Erhard, *Gedanken aus fünf Jahrzehnten*, pp. 915–931, on p. 917.
29 Bouvier, *Zwischen Godesberg und Großer Koalition*, pp. 243–254.
30 W. Brandt, 'Artikel des Regierenden Bürgermeisters von Berlin und Vorsitzenden der SPD, Brandt, für Die Neue Gesellschaft' (1966), in: Brandt, *Berliner Ausgabe 7. Mehr Demokratie wagen. Innen- und Gesellschaftspolitik 1966–1974* (Bonn: Verlag J.H.W. Dietz Nachf, 2001), pp. 94–106, on pp. 102–103.
31 This is not to suggest that both parties had essentially similar ideologies, which was not the case, as has been shown. The PSIUP was much closer to communism

than the PSU, see: D.A. Gordon, 'A "Mediterranean New Left"? Comparing and Contrasting the French PSU and the Italian PSIUP', *Contemporary European History*, vol. 19, no. 4 (2010), pp. 309–330. Cf: G.R. Horn, *The Spirit of '68. Rebellion in Europe and North America 1956–1976* (Oxford: Oxford University Press, 2007), p. 151.
32 PSU, *Tribune Socialiste*, no. 371, p. 5.
33 Salvati, 'Il partito nell'elaborazioni dei socialisti', p. 263.
34 PSIUP, *1 Congresso Nazionale*, p. 378.
35 Ginsborg, *A History of Contemporary Italy*, pp. 276–283; N. Tranfaglia, 'Parlamento, partiti e società civile nella crisi repubblicana', *Studi storici*, vol. 42, no. 4 (2001), pp. 827–835.
36 P. Togliatti, 'Le strade del partito socialista' (1963), in: Togliatti, *Opere VI*, pp. 740–743, p. 742.
37 P. Castellani, 'La Democrazia cristiana dal Centro-sinistra al delitto Moro (1962–1978), in: F. Malgeri ed., *Storia della Democrazia cristiana. IV. Dal Centrosinistra agli "anni di piombo" (1962–1978)* (Rome: Edizione Cinque Lune, 1989), pp. 3–118, on p. 42; Malgeri, *L'Italia democristiana*, p. 101.
38 M. Rumor, 'Iniziativa dei democratici Cristiani per il rinnovamento dello Stato per lo sviluppo della democrazia per la libertà e per la pace' (1967), in: Malgeri, *Storia della Democrazia Cristiana. Vol IV*, pp. 423–466, on p. 424.
39 *Ibid.*, p. 439.
40 A. Moro, 'Il terzo governo Moro' (1966), in: A. Moro ed., *Scritti e discorsi. Volume IV 1966–1968* (Rome: Edizione Cinque Lune, 1987), pp. 2006–2045, on p. 2010.
41 A. Moro, 'Il X Congresso Nazionale della DC' (1967), in: Moro, *Scritti e discorsi. Volume IV*, pp. 2437–2465, on p. 2457.
42 M. Klimke, 'West Germany', in: M. Klimke and J. Scharloth eds., *1968 in Europe. A History of Protest and Activism, 1957–1977* (Basingstoke: Palgrave MacMillan, 2008), pp. 97–110; I. Gilcher-Holety, 'France', in: Klimke and Scharloth eds., *1968 in Europe*, pp. 111–123.
43 J. Kurz and M. Tolomelli, 'Italy', in: Klimke and Scharloth eds., *1968 in Europe*, pp. 83–96; D. Giachetti, *L'autunno caldo* (Rome: Ediessi, 2013).
44 P. Gassert, 'Narratives of Democratisation: 1968 in Postwar Europe', in: Klimke and Scharloth eds., *1968 in Europe*, pp. 307–324, on p. 315.
45 P. Claris and La Ruche Ouvrière, 'L'autogestion, l'état et la révolution'. *Supplément noir et rouge*, no. 41 (1968), found on: http://edocs.lib.sfu.ca/cgi-bin/Mai68?Display=3485, accessed on 5–11-2013.
46 D. Cohn-Bendit and G. Cohn-Bendit, *Obsolete Communism. The Left-wing Alternative* (translated from German, London: Penguin Books, 1969 [1968]), p. 139.
47 Various authors, 'The Revolutionary Action Committee of the Sorbonne' (1968), in: Feenberg and Freedman, *When Poetry Ruled the Streets*, pp. 152–168, on p. 164.
48 Militants des comités d'action Sorbonne, Vincennes, Nanterre, *Apres mai 1968 les plans de la bourgeoisie et le mouvement révolutionnaire* (1969), p. 4 p. 15, found on http://edocs.lib.sfu.ca/cgi-bin/Mai68?Display=1268, accessed on 4-11-2013.
49 M.A. Schmidtke, 'Reform, Revolte oder Revolution? Der Sozialistische Deutsche Studentenbund (SDS) und die Students for a Democratic Society (SDS), 1960–1970, *Geschichte und Gesellschaft*, vol. 17 (1998), pp. 188–206, on p. 192.
50 U. Bergmann, R. Dutschke, W Lefèvre and B. Rabehl, *Rebellion der Studenten oder die neue Opposition* (Berlin: Rowolt, 1968), p. 159. See also: N. Thomas, *Protest Movements in the 1960s in West Germany. A Social History of Dissent and Democracy* (Oxford: Berg, 2003), p. 123.

51 H. Schauer ed., 'Schlußerklärung des Kuratoriums "Notstand der Demokratie" zum Kongreß', in: H. Schauer ed., *Notstand der Demokratie. Referate, Diskussionsbeiträge und Materialien von Kongreß am 30. Oktober 1966* (Frankfurt am Main, 1966), pp. 209–211, on pp. 209–210.
52 R. Dutschke, 'Keiner Partei dürfen wir vertrauen' (1967), in: R. Dutschke ed., *Geschichte ist machbar. Texte über das herrschende Falsche und die Radikalität des Friedens* (Berlin: Klaus Wagenbach, 1980), pp. 86–88, on p. 86.
53 Movimento Studentesco, 'La DC, partito della borghesia' (1972), in: L. Cortese ed., *Il Movimento Studentesco. Storia e documenti 1968–1973* (Milan: Valentino Bompani, 1973), pp. 39–42, on p. 42.
54 Movimento Studentesco, 'La fascistizzazione dello Stato' (1974), in: Cortese ed., *Il Movimento Studentesco*, pp. 121–123, on p. 122.
55 Horn, *The Spirit of '68*, p. 144; M. Tolomelli, *Terrorismo e società. Il pubblico dibattito in Italia e Germania negli anni Settanta* (Bologna: Il Mulino, 2006), pp. 271–285.
56 Movimento Studentesco, *La situazione attuale e i compiti politici del Movimento Studentesco* (Milan: Sapere Edizioni, 1969), p. 14.
57 G. Viale, 'Cinquanta giorni di lotta alla FIAT' (1969), in: G. Viale ed., *S'avanza uno strano soldato* (Rome: Edizioni di Lotta Continua, 1973), pp. 49–58, on p. 56.
58 Nous Sommes en Marche, 'The Amnesty of the Blinded Eyes' (1968), in: A. Feenberg and J. Freedman eds., *When Poetry Ruled the Streets. The French May Events of 1968. Part 2. Documents of the May Movement* (Albany: State of University of New York Press, 2001), pp. 81–86, on pp. 84–85.
59 R. Dutschke, 'Professor Habermas, Ihr begriffsloser Objektivismus erschlägt das zu emanzipierende Subjekt!' (1967), in: Dutschke, *Geschichte ist machbar*, pp. 76–84, on p. 78.
60 M. Capanna, *Movimento Studentesco. Crescita politica e azione rivoluzionaria* (Milan: Sapere, 1968), p. 7.
61 Gassert, 'Narratives of Democratisation', p. 313.
62 Capanna, *Movimento Studentesco*, p. 34.
63 G. Viale, 'La Rivoluzione culturale nelle fabbriche italiane' (1969), in: Viale, *S'avanza uno strano soldato*, pp. 59–67, on p. 59.
64 Cohn-Bendit and Cohn-Bendit, *Obsolete Communism*, p. 128.
65 Bergmann, Dutschke, Lefèvre and Rabehl, *Rebellion der Studenten*, p. 58.
66 Dutschke, 'Keiner Partei dürfen wir vertrauen', p. 86.
67 E. Kogon, 'Die Verhängnisvolle Vorsorge' (1968), in: E. Kogon et al. ed., *Der totale Notstandstaat* (Frankfurt am Main: Stimme Verlag, 1968), pp. 3–9, on p. 4.
68 Schauer ed., 'Schlußerklärung des Kuratoriums "Notstand der Demokratie" zum Kongreß'.
69 Various authors, 'The Revolutionary Action Committee of the Sorbonne', p. 163.
70 Cohn-Bendit and Cohn-Bendit, *Obsolete Communism*, p. 80.
71 R. Dutschke, 'Demokratie, Universität und Gesellschaft' (1967), in: Dutschke, *Geschichte ist machbar*, pp. 61–75, on p. 61.
72 'La nuova fase politica del movimento studentesco trentino' (1968), in: Movimento Studentesco ed., *Documenti della rivolta universitaria* (Bari: Laterza, 1968), pp. 41–43, on p. 42.
73 SDS, 'Erklärung des SDS Vorstsandes zur Bundestagswahl 1969', Neue Linke, Studentenbewegung, Außerparlamentarische Opposition in Deutschland Collection, inventory number 127, International Institute of Social History, Amsterdam.
74 Cohn-Bendit and Cohn-Bendit, *Obsolete Communism*, p. 139.
75 M. Tolomelli, '1968: Formen der Interaktion zwischen Studenten und Arbeiterbewegung in Italien und der Bundesrepublik', *Geschichte und Gesellschaft*, vol. 17 (1998), pp. 82–100, on p. 98.

76 'Cresce organizzazione interno alla fabbrica', *Lotta Continua*, 6 December 1969, p. 3.
77 'Tra servi e padroni. La funzione del sindacato nella società capitalistica', *Lotta Continua*, 17 January 1970, p. 6.
78 Cohn-Bendit and Cohn-Bendit, *Obsolete Communism*, p. 139.
79 *Ibid.*, p. 250.
80 *Ibid.*
81 R. Dutschke, 'Unser Prozeß der Revolution wird ein sehr langer Marsch sein. Träume, Wünsche, Hoffnungen', in: R. Dutschke ed., *Mein langer Marsch. Reden, Schriften und Tagebücher aus zwanzig Jahren* (Reinbek bei Hamburg: Rowolt Verlag, 1980), pp. 11–29, on p. 13.
82 Bergmann, Dutschke, Lefèvre and Rabehl, *Rebellion der Studenten*, p. 161.
83 'Außerparlamentarische oder antiparlamentarische Oppisition? Auszug aus einem SPIEGEL-interview mit Rudi Dutschke vom 1967', in: K.A. Otto ed., *Außerparlamentarische Opposition in Quellen und Dokumenten (1960–1970)* (Cologne: Paul Rugenstein Verlag, 1989), pp. 170–171, on p. 171.
84 Capanna, *Movimento studentesco*, p. 27.
85 La Voie, *Elections bourgeoises ou action révolutionnaire* (1968), found on: http://edocs.lib.sfu.ca/projects/mai68/pdfs/POST_May_Perspectives.pdf, accessed on 4–11–2013.
86 Various authors, 'The Revolutionary Action Committee of the Sorbonne', p. 164.
87 *Ibid.*, p. 163.
88 *A New Form of Organisation in the Factories*: http://edocs.lib.sfu.ca/projects/mai68/pdfs/A_New_Form_of_Organisation_in_the_Factories.pdf, visited 4–11–2013.
89 'Mozione di 26 Febbraio. Firenze', in: Movimento Studentesco, *Documenti della rivolta*, pp. 362–363, on p. 362.
90 Viale, 'La Rivoluzione culturale', p. 66.
91 Dutschke, 'Demokratie, Universität und Gesellschaft', p. 64.
92 'Quale teoria e quanta? Il problema dello studio nell'organizzazione rivoluzionaria', *Lotta Continua*, 17 January 1970, p. 3.
93 Lumley, *States of Emergency*, p. 231.
94 Figures from: Giachetti, *L'autunno caldo*, p. 121.
95 R. Dutschke, Das Sich-Verweigern erfordert Guerilla-Mentalität (1967), found on: http://glasnost.de/hist/apo/67dutschke.html, accessed on 5 November 2013.
96 G. Koenen, *Das rote Jahrzehnt. Unsere kleine deutsche Kulturrevolution 1967–1977* (Cologne: Kiepenheuer & Witsch, 2001), p. 198; Tolomelli, *Terrorismo e società*, pp. 281–282; Hanshew, *Terror and Democracy*, p. 107.
97 SDS, 'SDS-BS Öffentliche BV Sitzung. Aus dieser BV-Sitzung muss über die Auflösung des SDS-BV entschieden werden', Neue Linke, Studentenbewegung, Außerparlamentarische Opposition in Deutschland Collection, inventory number 127, International Institute of Social History, Amsterdam.
98 PSU, *Tribune socialiste* (1971), found on: http://edocs.lib.sfu.ca/cgi-bin/Mai68?Display=3385, accessed on 15–6–2015.
99 Della Porta, *Social Movements, Political Violence and the State*, p. 28.
100 Viale, 'Cinquanta giorni di lotta alla FIAT', p. 57.
101 F.J. Strauß, 'Über die APO' (1968), in: F.J. Strauß ed., *Das Konzept der deutsche Rechten. Aus Reden und Schriften des F.J. Strauß* (Cologne: Pahl Rugenstein Verlag, 1971), pp. 43–48, on pp. 44–45.
102 Strauß, 'Über die APO', p. 46.
103 C. de Gaulle, 'Allocution radiodiffusée et télévisée prononcée au palais de l'Élysée (30 May 1968), in: C. de Gaulle ed., *Discours et Messages. Vers le terme 1966–1969* (Paris: Plon, 1970), pp. 291–293, on p. 293.

104 Barzel, *Gesichtspunkte eines Deutschen*, p. 273.
105 *Ibid.*, p. 94.
106 H. Kohl, *Zwischen Ideologie und Pragmatismus. Aspekte und Ansichten zu Grundfragen der Politik* (Stuttgart: Verlag Bonn Aktuell, 1973), p. 75.
107 F.J. Strauß, 'Strauß erklärt Wirtschaftsleben für nicht demokratisierbar' (1968), in: Strauß, *Das Konzept der deutsche Rechten*, pp. 39–40.
108 A. Moro, 'Invita alla partecipazione' (1968), in: Moro, *Scritti e discorsi. Volume IV*, pp. 2498–2507.
109 A. Malraux, 'Discours prononcé au parc des expositions' (1968), in: A. Malraux ed., *Essais. Œuvres Complètes VI* (Paris: Gallimard, 2010), pp. 512–517.
110 De Gaulle, 'Allocution radiodiffusée et télévisée prononcée au palais de l'Élysée' (30 May 1968), on p. 292.
111 C. de Gaulle, 'Allocution radiodiffusée et télévisée prononcée au palais de l'Élysée (11 March 1969), in: de Gaulle, *Vers le terme*, pp. 384–389.
112 *Ibid.*, p. 386.
113 Broche, *Une histoire des antigaullismes*, p. 541.
114 F. Piccoli, 'Idee, struttura e iniziative della Democrazia cristiana per il rinnovamento delle istituzioni nell'attuazione della Costituzione e nello sviluppo della società nazionale' (1969), in: Malgeri, *Storia della Democrazia cristiana IV*, pp. 457–506, on p. 470.
115 M. Rumor, 'La Democrazia cristiana raccoglie le sfide del futuro', (1968), in: M. Rumor ed., *Discorsi sulla Democrazia cristiana* (Milan: Franco Angelli, 2010), pp. 372–381, on p. 375.
116 Rumor, 'La Democrazia cristiana raccoglie le sfide del futuro', p. 377.
117 A. Moro, *Per una iniziativa politica della Democrazia cristiana* (Rome: Agenzia Progetto, 1973), p. 95.
118 *Ibid.*, p. 110.
119 *Ibid.*, pp. 126–127.
120 *Ibid.*, p. 128. See also: G. Cotturi, 'Moro e la transizione interrotta', *Studi Storici*, vol. 37, no. 2 (1996), pp. 489–511, on pp. 495–497.
121 K. Sontheimer, *So war Deutschland nie. Anmerkungen zur politischen Kultur der Bundesrepublik* (Munich: C.H. Beck, 1990), p. 90.
122 W. Brandt, 'Aus der Regierungserklärung des Bundeskanzlers Brandt vor dem Deutschen Bundestag' (1969), in: Brandt, *Berliner Ausgabe. Band 7*, pp. 218–224, on p. 219, p. 220.
123 W. Brandt, 'Perspektiven der neuen Mitten. Aus der Rede des Bundeskanzlers, Brandt, anlässlich der Verleihung des Theodor-Heuss-Preises in München' (1974), in: Brandt, *Berliner Ausgabe. Band 7*, pp. 480–490, on p. 486.
124 See also: Dittberner, *FDP—Partei der Zweiten Wahl*, pp. 17–18.
125 FDP, 'Praktische Politik für Deutschland', pp. 200–201.
126 FDP, *Freiburger Thesen zur Gesellschaftspolitik der Freien Demokratischen Partei* (1971), found on: http://www.freiheit.org/files/288/1971_Freiburger_Thesen.pdf, accessed on 7 November 2013.
127 Giachetti, *L'autunno caldo*, p. 141.
128 PSIUP, 'Tesi approvati del 2 Congresso', in: PSIUP, *2 Congresso Nazionale del PSIUP. Unità della sinistra per una alternative al centrosinistra e per un nuovo internazionalismo proletario. Napoli 18-21 dicembre 1969* (Rome, 1969), pp. 7–39, on p. 23
129 *Ibid.*, p. 21.
130 M. Rocard, *Le P.S.U. et l'avenir socialiste de la France* (Paris : Éditions du Seuil, 1969), p. 72.
131 PSU, 'Les 17 thèses du P.S.U. Adoptées au Congrès du Dijon mars 1969' (1969), in: M. Rocard ed., *Le P.S.U. et l'avenir de la France* (Paris: Éditions du Seuil, 1969), pp. 123–183, on p. 143.

132 Ibid., p. 164.
133 J. Moreau, 'Le congrès d'Épinay-sur-Seine du parti socialiste', *Vingtième siècle. Revue d'histoire*, vol. 65, no. 1 (2000), pp. 81–96.
134 Winock, 'Le parti socialiste dans le système politique français', p. 16.
135 Bergounioux and Grunberg, *Le long remords du pouvoir*, p. 257.
136 F. Mitterrand, '1974: les élections présidentielles et ses conséquences', in: Mitterrand, *Politique*, pp. 555–571, on p. 568.
137 F. Mitterrand, 'Mai 68 et ses conséquences' (1968), in: Mitterrand, *Politique*, pp. 478–507, p. 489. See also: J.-F. Sirinelli, *Mai 68. L'événement Janus* (Paris: Fayard, 2008), p. 280.
138 F. Mitterrand, 'Discours au Congrès de l'unité des socialistes. Épinay, 13 Juin 1971', in: M. Ouraoui, *Les Grands Discours socialistes français du XXe siècle* (Paris: Bibliothèque Complexe, 2007), pp. 142–161, on p. 159.
139 M. Lazar, *Le communisme, une passion française* (Paris: Perrin, 2002), p. 39.
140 Courtois and Lazar, *Histoire du Parti communiste français*, p. 352.
141 G. Marchais, *Préface. Programme Commun du gouvernement du Parti communiste français et du Parti socialiste (27 juin 1972)* (Paris: Éditions Sociales, 1972), pp. 38–39.
142 Courtois and Lazar, *Histoire du Parti communiste français*, p. 354.
143 Parti Socialiste and Parti Communiste Français, *Programme Commun du gouvernement du Parti communiste français et du Parti socialiste (27 juin 1972)* (Paris: Éditions Sociales, 1972), p. 143.
144 G. Marchais, *Le Défi Démocratique* (Paris: Éditions Grasset & Fasquelle, 1973), p. 122.
145 Ibid., p. 101.
146 F. Mitterrand, *La Rose au poing* (Paris: Flammarion, 1973).
147 Bergounioux, 'Socialisme français et social-démocratie européenne', p. 101; Moreau, 'Le congrès d'Épinay-sur-Seine du parti socialiste', pp. 81–96; Bergounioux and Grunberg, *L'ambition et le remords*, p. 241.
148 Horn, *The Spirit of '68*, p. 194; On the PCI's negative response to '68, see also: Crainz, *Il paese mancato*, p. 312; Ginsborg, *A History of Contemporary Italy*, p. 307. Cf: A. Höbel, 'Il Pci di Longo e il '68 studentesco', *Studi Storici*, vol. 45, no. 2 (2004), pp. 419–459.
149 R. Rossanda, *L'anno degli studenti* (Bari: De Donato editore, 1968), p. 135.
150 Ibid., p. 111.
151 S. Pons, *Berlinguer e la fine del comunismo* (Turin: Einaudi editore, 2006).
152 Ferraresi, *Minacce alla democrazia*, pp. 167–173.
153 Paggi, 'Violenza e democrazia nella storia della Repubblica', pp. 949–951.
154 F. Barbagallo, 'Enrico Berlinguer, il compromesso storico e l'alternativa democratica', *Studi Storici*, vol. 45, no. 4 (2004), pp. 939–949, esp. on p. 940.
155 Pons, *Berlinguer e la fine del comunismo*, p. 18.
156 E. Berlinguer, 'Riflessione sull'Italia dopo i fatti di Cile' (1973), in: E. Berlinguer ed., *La crisi italiana* (Editrice l'Unità, 1985), pp. 45–75, on p. 69, p. 75.
157 E. Berlinguer, *Per un governo di svolta democratica. Il testo integrale del rapporto tenuto al XIII Congresso nazionale del Partito comunista italiano* (Rome: Editori Riuniti, 1972), p. 80.
158 Vittoria, *Storia del PCI*, p. 115.
159 Ibid., p. 72.
160 Berlinguer, 'Riflessione sull'Italia dopo i fatti di Cile', p. 60.
161 Paggi, 'Violenza e democrazia nella storia della Repubblica', p. 951.
162 A. Giovagnoli, *Il caso Moro. Una tragedia repubblicana* (Bologna: Il Mulino, 2005), pp. 14–16; Barbagallo, 'Enrico Berlinguer, il compromesso storico e l'alternativa democratica'; Cotturi, 'Moro e la transizione interrotta'.

163 Moreau, 'Le congrès d'Épinay-sur-Seine du parti socialiste', p. 92.
164 G. Mollet, *Quinze ans après 1958–1973* (Paris: Éditions Albin Michel, 1973), p. 145.
165 R. Barzel, 'Regierungsprogramm CDU 1972. Wir bauen der Fortschritt auf Stabilität' (1972), found on: http://www.kas.de/upload/ACDP/CDU/Programme_Bundestag/1972_Regierungsprogramm_Wir-bauen-den-Fortschritt-auf-Stabilitaet.pdf, accessed on 13 November 2014.
166 Orlow, 'Delayed Reaction', p. 91.
167 W. Brandt, 'Politik in Deutschland—Wertvorstellungen unter Ideologieverdacht. Aus der Rede des Bundeskanzlers, Brandt, in der Evangelischen Akademie in Bad Segeberg' (1973), in: Brandt, *Berliner Ausgabe. Band 7*, pp. 444–456, on p. 452.
168 W. Brandt, 'Aus der Rede der Bundesminister des Auswärtigen. Brandt, vor dem Deutschen Bundestag' (1968), in: Brandt, *Berliner Ausgabe. Band 7*, pp. 148–156.
169 H. Schmidt, 'Für eine Politik der Vernunft' (1973), in: H. Schmidt ed., *Auf dem Fundament des Godesberger Programms* (Bonn: Verlag Neue Gesellschaft, 1973), pp. 9–34, on p.20.
170 Schmidt, 'Für eine Politik der Vernunft', p. 24.
171 Pons, *Berlinguer e la fine del comunismo*, pp. 14–15; R. Guarltieri, *L'Italia dal 1943 al 1992. DC e PCI nella storia della Repubblica* (Rome: Carocci editore, 2006), p. 200; Lumley, *States of Emergency*, p. 44.

5 Democracy Between Crisis and Consensus After the 1973 Oil Crisis

The second half of the 1970s was a decisive period in the debate on democracy in Western Europe. The 1973 Oil Crisis had interrupted almost thirty years of uninterrupted economic growth, and Europe saw the end of an era characterized by full employment and expanding social security arrangements. The Keynesian paradigm that a variety of ideological forces had embraced now collapsed. The downturn in the economy led to mass strikes, especially in France and Italy. As the decade wore on, politics turned increasingly violent in West Germany and Italy in particular as both states battled with domestic terrorism.[1] This explains why, by the time of the oil crisis, the 1970s was already being perceived as a decade of democratic crisis.[2] Western democracies had no answer to the social movements' demands for participation, especially not at a time of such economic hardship. The collapse of the postwar settlement is why the 1970s is seen as a watershed in the history of postwar democracy.[3] The democratic model appeared unable to meet the challenges it faced, while the material certainties underpinning it eroded under the pressures of economic decline. The crisis of democracy particularly affected the Western European Left, which faced the demise of the ideological hegemony of Keynesianism.[4] It was most deeply felt in France and Italy. Of the four major left-wing parties of France and Italy, only the Parti Socialiste survived into the early 1990s.[5]

Although the period from 1975 onwards was a time of crisis, coalescence on the principles of democracy continued. This is evident in the way political elites responded to challenges. To begin with, the Left showed a tendency towards agreement by quickly adopting the more liberal economic ideas of their conservative rivals. As a result, governments could quickly replace the collapsed Keynesian paradigm of social democracy with a narrative in which democracy would come to be equated with a smaller government and individual liberties. A second sign of consensus was the formation of new political parties that evolved from the movements of 1968. No longer rejecting parliaments and the party system as undemocratic, these parties endorsed the principle of representative democracy. A third and final sign was how the left-wing parties of France and Italy fully reconciled themselves with the Gaullist and Christian Democratic state. In France, this process culminated in the election of Mitterrand as president in 1981. In Italy, it led to the inclusion of the communists in the parliamentary majority as a semi-legitimized democratic partner following the 'crisis of the republic' at the end of the 1970s.

Following in the footsteps of West Germany, the political elites in Italy and France now conceptualized democracy in similar terms and largely came to accept each other's democratic credentials. This process of convergence had different consequences for the three states. In West Germany and France, the establishment of a broad consensus on the rules and principles of the democratic game was perceived as an answer to the most troubling issues of previous decades. Despite some remaining dissatisfaction with the political system's functioning, the major actors concurred on the current model, and for them, this settled the disputes that had dominated the postwar debate on democracy. Italy, however, was another matter. There, a similar process of convergence had revealed that the leading actors had in fact been unable to resolve the most pressing issues of postwar Italian democracy. As a result, the mood of democratic crisis had deepened, and all political actors, big and small, increasingly questioned the dominant democratic model.

Even though the Italian elites were not ready to accept the existing model of democracy in their country, at least, by the turn of the 1980s, all the leading political actors in Western Europe more or less agreed on what *ought to be* the core features of democracy. They saw eye to eye on the principles of party democracy, representation, the free market and an appreciation of civic participation—as long as this was confined to civil society rather than direct inclusion in political decision making. This consensus does not mean that their conceptions of democracy completely overlapped or that political actors stopped criticizing the functioning of their democracies and their political opponents. Nor does it mean that this model should be considered a success by either contemporary or present standards. Nevertheless, it was a model in which all major political actors generally considered each other democratic and shared similar views of democracy.

Economic Decline and the Shifting Postwar Consensus on Democracy and Capitalism

The 1971 breakdown of the pegged exchange rates agreed to at the Bretton Woods Conference, and the 1973 Oil Crisis, marked the beginning of a drastic change in the economic climate. The effects of this downturn, which lasted through the second half of the 1970s and early 1980s, were visible in all three states, but their gravity, the chronology of the crisis and the resulting impact on the debate on democracy differed considerably. In France, the economic crisis hit particularly hard in the early 1980s, when the interventionist economic policies of the Mitterrand government backfired and Paris devaluated the *franc* three times in two years.[6] In West Germany, the effects of the economic slowdown were severe but thanks to corporatist negotiations and an extensive welfare state, did not immediately lead to political instability.[7] Italy was strongly affected by the downturn. The nation battled with high levels of inflation and appealed to the International Monetary Fund (IMF) for financial support. In the worst year of the crisis, 1975, the economy shrunk by almost 4 per cent, while inflation rates topped 17 per cent.[8] As one *Financial Times* correspondent worded it in 1976, '[T]he country is not now on the verge of bankruptcy, it is theoretically bankrupt'.[9]

The economic crisis curtailed the 'social democratic moment' and ushered in a protracted period of welfare state reform. It forced politicians to rethink the economic dimension of democracy, which was increasingly debated in terms of congruence between democracy and the free market. This re-evaluation of the state's responsibilities was most evident among the Christian Democrats, who revived and built upon their 1940s tradition of valuing individual liberty and the market economy. The Left went along with the conservative response by adopting 'neoliberal economic policies'.[10] So even though the economic downturn eroded the social democratic paradigm, it did not bring about the demise of consensus per se. Instead, the consensus on Keynesian principles was replaced by a new consensus between the Left and the Christian Democrats on the relationship among the free market, individual liberty and democracy. The new consensus did not put a stop to political actors voicing their different opinions on the role of the state and social equality, but it did mean they generally agreed that the free market and democracy were compatible. As a result, the debate on the economy was decoupled from the debate on democracy; political actors now discussed democracy in terms of individual liberty rather than social equality.

This ideological shift towards the free market and individual liberty was most obvious in the Italian and West German Christian Democratic parties. As early as 1972, the Italian DC hosted a highly influential conference on state intervention in the economy.[11] The conference's concluding statement asserted that 'there is a large consensus here on the role of [free] enterprise and the function of the market' that contrasted with the 'limited success of past experiences with planning'.[12] Prominent party member Arnaldo Forlani added that the DC had opted to 'prefer a market economy. To us, the market economy means . . . recognition of companies' need for autonomy, and a place to organize man's creative and innovative capacities, and also that consumers enjoy freedom of choice. [This] secures the general interest . . . for all of society'.[13]

The DC's re-evaluation of the market economy implied a rejection of economic planning in party discourse and a revaluation of individual liberty. These two objectives were expressed as a single goal at the DC's 1981 annual meeting, when the DC declared that 'in comparison with the past, the conception of the role of "public intervention" [has changed]'. Economic planning was no longer 'intended as a vertical instrument [guiding] the productive structures, but as a horizontal instrument in the service of productive structures'. The party opted for 'the free economic initiative and the market to safeguard free individual initiative and an efficient use of resources'.[14] Statements like these aside, it became clear right away that the Christian Democrats did not practice what they preached because public debt continued to rise and state bureaucracy continued to expand over the course of the 1980s.[15] Nonetheless, the DC made a renewed ideological commitment to the relationship between individual liberty, capitalism and democracy, which the party felt would best be able to restore dynamism to the Italian economy.

The West German Christian Democrats were clearer still in their embrace of the triad of individual liberty, capitalism and democracy. A groundswell of opinion felt the SPD, which had led the government since 1969, had moved the Federal Republic dangerously far to the left. The growing resistance to the SPD, which reared its head in the second half of the 1970s, has been described as a *Tendenzwende* in the West German debate, voiced not only by intellectuals but also by the fierce Christian Democratic opposition to the Schmidt government.[16] The SPD's left-wing policies were increasingly perceived as a threat to individual freedom and therefore to democracy. In Franz-Josef Strauss's view, the West German *Rechtstaat* was a state of free individuals living under the rule of law and a constitution that protected against what he called 'an equalizing exercise of power'.[17] Strauss claimed that 'an equality which levels everything, as socialism wants, will render human freedom meaningless'.[18] He held that the social democrats 'proclaim the reform of capitalist society and their aim . . . is to terminate free order'.[19]

The Christian Democrats presented themselves as a liberal alternative to the social democrats who 'have overburdened the finances and the economy. They have overtaxed the system of social security'.[20] After the political *Wende* of 1982, in which the Christian Democrats and the liberals formed a government coalition, the Christian Democrats continued to blame many of the country's problems on the SPD's economic policies. The alternative proposed by the Christian Democrats was to link civic participation with individual responsibility and the free market.[21] This became the CDU's ideological point of reference as it steadily evolved into a typical centre-Right party that advocated budget cuts and lower taxes to strengthen individual liberties and decrease state intervention.[22] The party presented its renewed trust in the free market within the framework of the social market economy.[23] On the nintieth anniversary of Ludwig Erhard's birth in 1987, Chancellor Kohl stated that the social market economy was still essentially about fostering freedom, personal responsibility and solidarity. In line with these principles, it was the CDU's task

> to always make clear that freedom of choice, decentralization of decision making, protection of minorities and thrifty control of limited resources are part of the politically distinctive elements of the social market economy. There is no decision-making process which is more

democratic and more powerful than the 'invisible hand' of price and competition in our economic order, which brings together millions of different interests without force every day.[24]

In France, the Right also expressed a renewed appreciation for the market economy around the turn of the 1980s, a move that reflected developments in West Germany and Italy. Mitterrand's election victory pushed the Right in a liberal direction; they criticized Mitterrand's U-turn on the economy as insufficient to counter the country's problems.[25] Raymond Barre, prime minister under Valéry Giscard d'Estaing, remarked, '[N]ever have a country and a people paid such a high price for the blindness and irresponsibility of a political team', which then had been forced to go back on its promises and introduce 'such a radical change'.[26] Barre did not advocate that France adopt Reaganomics—nor incidentally did Christian Democrats elsewhere in Europe—but he did declare Keynesian economics obsolete.[27] The changing economic climate required a redefinition of the role of the state, which 'should do as little as possible. . . . This is my liberalism'.[28] Barre, too, framed the relinquishment of the state's responsibilities in terms of individual liberties. In 1984, he claimed that 'the state has penetrated too far into the most diverse private domains and that; we should restore as wide an array of activities as possible to individual initiative and responsibility'.[29]

The neo-Gaullists led by Jacques Chirac re-evaluated the role of the state too, waging tough opposition 'without concessions to the socialist power' and denouncing it 'in all respects'.[30] Chirac switched from left to right on many issues in the last quarter of the twentieth century. Even the manifesto of the neo-Gaullist *Rassemblement pour la République* was often ambiguous on where the party stood.[31] It was evident, however, that Chirac advocated a different notion of liberalism with a smaller role for government and a shift towards the free market.[32] He linked a free market economy to individual liberty, individual responsibility and opportunities for participation in an active civil society. Chirac stated that 'we advocate a course of freedom for business. . . . Our society should indeed become responsible again, we will never more accept that people are nothing but pawns, without initiative, programmed from birth to death'.[33]

In short, conservatives responded to the economic recession of the 1970s with a renewed emphasis on the link between the free market and democracy hinging on the notion of individual liberty, which had been snowed under by the emphasis on state intervention and economic planning in the postwar era. Christian Democrats in particular returned to their founding ideas from the 1940s, when they had rejected state control over the economy for this very reason. In the late 1950s and 1960s, the conservatives had toned down their criticism of state intervention, but after 1973, they dusted it off again when they started stressing the link between democracy and individual liberty and characterizing the state as an obstacle to democratic development.

The Left also had to come to terms with the effects of the new economic climate. Left-leaning governments were in power for a significant part of the 1970s and 1980s. The SPD ruled in West Germany until 1982, the PSI supplied Italy's prime minister, Bettino Craxi, from 1983 to 1987, and the French socialists won the presidential and parliamentary elections in 1981 and again in 1988. Yet even from a position of power, they often resorted to liberal solutions to the economic crisis as the 'neo-liberal idea that markets should be liberalised as much as possible' gained ground on the Left too.[34] This reflected a change at the level of ideas. Many left-wing parties had long since accepted the link between democracy and capitalism as a pragmatic measure, but now they ideologically embraced the connection between democracy and the free market, individual liberties, and a reduced role of the state. As political opponents discredited the economic cornerstones of democracy in left-wing thought—the welfare state, nationalization and economic planning—the Left failed to come up with any other concepts on the link between democracy and capitalism, aside from what their adversaries already endorsed: individual liberty and the market.[35] The Italian socialists embodied this development like none other.

In practice, the Italian Socialist Party had already embraced the market economy at the turn of the 1960s, although only in combination with state interference in the economy—a proviso the party dropped under Bettino Craxi's leadership, along with its ideological legacy and all references to Marxism.[36] PSI leader Craxi stated that 'the utopia of abolishing capitalism as the socialist transformation's endpoint ha[d] led to an underestimation of the problems that are crucial to . . . the construction of a new society'.[37] The party revamped its understanding of democracy, removing the link to social equality and the interests of the working class. The PSI posited the market as a key to overcoming Italy's economic problems and adapted itself to diminishing class loyalties in the 1980s, developing a conception of democracy disconnected from Marxist notions of class. In Craxi's view, social relations could no longer be seen in terms of 'the separation of classes and neatly divided categories: today the world of labour is a world of citizens who try to lead the same sort of life, tend to share customs and aspirations. Strong economic differences persist, but the social differences have diminished in the broad framework of common duties and rights'.[38]

In the new PSI analysis, the Marxist commitment to massive state intervention in the economy was irreconcilable with democracy because 'the monopoly on material resources leads to the fusion between economic and political power, that is, to total power. Far from liberating the worker, the "state-ization" of the economy forms the material foundation for the one-party dictatorship'.[39] Having rejected state intervention, the logical conclusion was to champion the free market. At the end of his premiership, Craxi asserted that Italy could never have overcome its economic crisis 'without the contribution of Italian entrepreneurship, without the dynamism and commitment of big and small enterprises'.[40] Craxi envisioned a 'reformist socialism, democratic and secular' that countered 'the crisis of the welfare state, the social state'.[41]

In an international perspective, the PSI's transformation was relatively radical, but it broadly represented the shift taken by French socialists too. Mitterrand had been elected on a platform of massive economic reform, including the nationalization of key industries, decentralization of decision making and increasing workers' autonomy.[42] Even before the polls, however, the socialist party had adopted a more moderate discourse that tempered some of the promises of the Épinay programme.[43] After Mitterrand's victory, many socioeconomic reform proposals were watered down. The Auroux laws, for instance, which were intended to strengthen workers' self-management instruments, were 'in effect primarily the work of technocrats, far more moderate than the Socialist Party's left wing had conceived when it drafted the electoral programmes in the 1970s'.[44] At the time it was written, the socialist economic programme had been based on the assumption that France would spearhead an economic revival. Instead, the French economy sank deeper into crisis in the early 1980s, forcing the administration to abandon many of its proposals and make a 'U-turn' in economic policy.[45] In practical terms, this meant the end of the socialist programme of nationalizations and state interference. Ideologically, it exposed the fact that socialist thought was 'in crisis', as Rocard had already noted in 1979, because the socialists had no real alternatives to a more liberal approach to the economy.[46] The PS's turnaround was personified by Mitterrand's prime ministers Laurent Fabius and, later, Rocard.[47] Both figureheads, from the progressive wing of the PS, tried to reconcile the economic policy changes with a new socialist discourse focused on 'modernization'.[48] No longer interested in a 'rupture with capitalism', Fabius asserted that 'it is vital that France revamp the role of the state' and that 'modernization mainly is the responsibility of businesses'.[49] In 1985, Rocard stated at the PS party congress that 'we have changed, because we have learned. . . . It has become evident that, whether nationalized [the full] 100% or [just] 51%, a public enterprise remains an enterprise. In any case, we have concluded that a mixed economy is in all circumstances preferable to a managed economy' because there should be 'harmony' between 'plan and market'.[50]

The PS's 1980s change of heart about the market economy was visible both in practice and its ideology.[51] Even the conservative Barre noted that 'a liberal discourse ha[d] emerged'[52] among the PS politicians who increasingly saw themselves as social democrats rather than socialists.[53] The PS made fewer direct references to 'democracy' in its discourse on the economy. Even Fabius, in his 1983 evaluation of the French government's nationalization policies, did not explicitly link these to democracy.[54] By inference, the PS had abandoned its vision of the economy as a tool for creating a democratic society based on social equality and aligned itself with the general appreciation of the market economy. The party set new objectives, like monetary stabilization, increased international competitiveness and budget deficit reduction, a clear sign that it acknowledged that 'there [could] not be a distinctive socialist economic policy'.[55] This exposed an existential problem among the French leftists. They had watered down their support for social equality and the working class, originally two core components of their notion of democracy. Yet the Left had nothing to fill this gap with, other than what Rocard called the 'rediscovery of the individual as the ultimate objective of life and social organization'.[56]

Unlike its cousins in France and Italy, West Germany's main left-wing opposition party had not disputed the concord between democracy and the market economy since the early 1960s. Moreover, West Germany withstood the initial shocks of the Oil Crisis with relative ease, which meant the SPD did not feel the need to reappraise its rather pragmatic approach to the economy. While at the helm of government, the SPD had followed the principles of the social market economy, although its economic agenda could be characterized as interventionist given the measures it took to transform the country's ageing industry and to facilitate worker co-decision.[57] In the mid-1970s, Schmidt seized upon the country's relative economic success by claiming credit for the German Model, which had brought unparalleled economic and political stability and social tranquility.[58] Brandt claimed that 'the Federal Republic is economically, socially, and politically more stable than almost any other state in the world'.[59]

The SPD programme did not mention increased commitment to the market economy until the 1980s, when the West German economy went through a deep recession, which caused a sharp rise in unemployment and a widening budget deficit. This exposed increasing differences between the FDP and the SPD over the issue of state intervention in the economy and brought down the coalition in 1982. Just like the Italian and French socialists, the SPD suddenly started referring to the concept of 'modernization' to disguise its crisis of thought and identity.[60] The SPD committed to the market economy in the 1980s and did not raise any fundamental objections to the economic principles of the Christian Democrats.[61] This was not a major leap; in practice, the SPD had already accepted the market economy in its 1959 Godesberger programme. Now all the party did was make its commitment more explicit. Hans-Jochen Vogel, SPD leader in the 1980s, still claimed that the central objective of social democratic economic policy was the development of every individual's 'personality in freedom', which required a 'mixed [economic] order, in which both autonomous market mechanisms and state influence ha[d] their place'.[62] This continuity was reflected in the party's first main political programme since the Godesberger programme. The SPD's 1989 Berliner programme stated that 'within the framework of democratic laws, market and competition are indispensable. The market coordinates the vast quantity of economic decisions. . . . Economic democracy requires entrepreneurial initiative and achievement, we recognize and foster these'. The SPD supported 'competition as much as possible, planning as much as necessary'.[63]

As the mainstream Western European Left failed to embed the relationship between democracy and capitalism in a new ideology, the PCF receded into orthodox obscurity, leaving the Italian Communist Party as the only left-wing party that attempted to provide a genuine alternative. This required the PCI to accept private economic initiatives and even the DC's deflationary politics. The PCI stated that 'the market should perform an important task as the stimulator of efficiency and entrepreneurship'.[64] However, the party gave a particular spin to its support for austerity measures at the end of the 1970s. Berlinguer characterized these reforms as a way to weed out the immoral aspects of capitalism and to tackle growing state corruption and its influence on society.[65] From this perspective, he argued, austerity should be seen as 'an instrument' to overcome 'a system immersed in a deep and structural crisis' as austerity meant 'rigour, efficiency, seriousness, and justice'.[66] Although his words conveyed a genuine critique of capitalism, they were nothing like the PCI's views on capitalism in the first decades after Second World War. Berlinguer envisioned a 'third way' between a capitalist model in crisis and the delegitimized 'real existing socialism' of the East to 'supersede the stage of capitalism we, in the industrialized and developed West, have reached . . . by constructing a socialism which manifests itself by safeguarding the protection of established democratic liberties'.[67] He argued that capitalism should be overcome through direct worker participation in factories, women's emancipation, peace and disarmament, and liberation from exploitation.

To summarize, political elites quickly found a new ground for consensus over the economic dimension of democracy after 1973. In the immediate aftermath of the Second World War, tensions between social equality and individual liberty had dominated the economic dimension of the debate on democracy. The underlying question was whether state interference nurtured or harmed democracy. Around the turn of the 1960s, politicians found middle ground between these two principles. The economic downturn of the early 1970s challenged this ideological equilibrium and undermined its material foundations. In response, virtually all political forces re-evaluated the relationship between free market capitalism and democracy, most obviously on the liberal and conservative side and in more veiled terms on the Left.

The new consensus over the link between democracy and capitalism had two major consequences. Firstly, the political debate on the qualities and principles of democracy ceased to hinge on democracy's relationship to economy. The economy was still debated, and extensively so, but the discourse remained confined to topics such as the sustainability of state finances, unemployment policies, prospects for entrepreneurs, and the individual freedom of citizens in the face of bureaucracy. Whereas all these themes are ultimately related to democracy, direct references to 'democracy' occurred ever less frequently. Secondly, individual freedom, rather than social equality, became the dominant notion informing democracy. This became evident around the turn of the 1980s. Until then, the balance between individual freedom and social equality had been the source of heated debate. State intervention, which the Left used to see as the main instrument to foster the democratic content of society, was now viewed with growing suspicion.

The Extra-Parliamentary Left's Acceptance of Parliamentary Democracy

The democratic narrative of the social movements of 1968 distinguished itself most clearly from established modes of conceptualizing democracy in its rejection of representation. This narrative regarded bodies such as parliament, which were distant from their constituencies, and parties, which were more centralized and hierarchical, as undemocratic. Social movements were initially unwilling to compromise on these ideals, as illustrated by the dissolution of the West German Socialist Student Union. However, as the 1970s proceeded and it became clear that the principles of democracy could not be changed from the outside only, some leaders and movements began the 'long march through the institutions'. 'Socialist policies cannot be built on naive dreams', Dutschke claimed in 1977.[68] As a result, some of the most prominent leaders of the 1968 movements adopted a new stance on representation. However, on the road to accepting parliamentary democracy as 'democratic', they took very different paths. The SPD and the PS not only co-opted the agenda of 1968, but they also enlisted many former social activists as members. France and West Germany also saw the formation of green parties. These parties raised awareness of new political issues but also aimed to reinvigorate party democracy by introducing some of the direct democracy practices from the social movements. In Italy, the social movements formed political parties based on strong internal hierarchies and Marxist orthodoxy. Despite the different roads to parliament that the social movements travelled in the 1970s, all showed that they accepted the principles of parliamentary and party democracy.

The transition from extra-parliamentary protests to parliamentary party was most successful in West Germany. The political organization of social movements became a particularly relevant issue at the end of the 1970s. It was partly for pragmatic reasons that the movements felt they needed to define their relationship to parliamentary democracy, but many also felt it imperative to distance themselves from the left-wing terrorism of the Rote Armee Fraktion (RAF).[69] Dutschke had earlier been ambivalent on the use of violence but now unequivocally embraced non-violence to contest political power. He stated that 'as a socialist I fight the representatives of the ruling political class by extra-parliamentary and parliamentary means in equal measure—not by the methods of individual terror that turns its back on the people'.[70]

The most obvious example of the shifting stance on representation was the establishment of the West German Green Party. Although the membership and leadership of the national party founded in 1980 and the movements of 1968 did not overlap entirely, the Green Party has been called a 'paradigmatic example' of the institutionalization of the extra-parliamentary Left.[71] Aside from campaigning for peace and the environment, the Green Party also advocated democratic renewal and presented itself as a 'social movement party'.[72] It held heated internal debates over how to reconcile the ideals and practices of a social movement with parliamentary politics.[73] In their initial phase, the Green Party was a 'branch' of the social movements, and founding member Petra Kelly regarded the party as both parliamentary and extra-parliamentary.[74] The Green Party called itself an 'anti-party party' and claimed that 'our internal organization and relationship with the people who support us and vote for us, is the exact opposite of the established parties in Bonn'.[75] The party distinguished itself from others through its notion of grass-roots democracy.[76] This was a form of democracy in which 'the control of all representatives, office holders and institutions [takes place] at the grass roots [level]'.[77] This would guarantee a maximum of transparency, accountability and direct democracy. The party proposed open and transparent meetings, limitations on re-election, and rotation of representative functions. For the country at large, it proposed the elimination of the 5 per cent threshold and 'unrestrained' freedoms of association, demonstration and speech, as well as referendums and other means of direct democracy.[78]

Despite these attempts to distinguish itself from the Federal Republic's 'established parties', the main heir to 1968 no longer denounced parties and parliaments in principle but merely the way party democracy functioned. The Green Party proposed measures to rejuvenate West German democracy and tried to introduce the social movements' agenda and practices into parliamentary politics. All of these endeavours were complementary to existing representative practices and institutions. The Green Party endorsed representative democracy as a legitimate means of conducting politics, stating that even 'grassroots democracy requires comprehensive organization and coordination'—which captures the changing way in which representation was conceived of since the SDS dissolution a decade earlier.[79] When the Green Party entered the federal parliament in 1983, Kelly stated that 'an autonomous, exclusively extra-parliamentary movement does not have as many opportunities to enforce proposals, for instance for a new security policy, as when the proposals are also made, imaginatively and peacefully, in parliament'. She concluded that 'facing the power relations in society, there is no other option than to relate to the political system as it is'.[80] This shift also meant the acceptance of parliament as the place 'where decisions are made about political issues'.[81] In other words, the Green Party no longer rejected parliament as an authoritarian institution and now accepted parties as a justified and legitimate instrument through which to conduct politics.

Just as in West Germany, France's social movements grew to accept the institutions of representative democracy. The social movement *La Voie* claimed that 'as long as it was clear what to do, spontaneity proved to be a good system'.[82] But after 1968, the objectives that social movements could spontaneously rally for became less evident. Even Cohn-Bendit, known for his emphasis on spontaneity, reconsidered his rejection of organizations. He ultimately joined the German Green Party in 1984. The formation of the French Green party, *Les Verts,* is another example of a social movement that moved from extra-parliamentarianism to parliamentarianism after 1968. Once it discovered the limitations of protest, in the early 1980s, the ecologist movement overcame its resistance to creating a structural party organization.[83]

This change was also visible in the French Unified Socialist Party (PSU). In 1968, the PSU was an important bridge between high politics and the social movements. Indeed, '[w]hatever aspect of "the 68 years" one looks at, from immigration to the environment, from workers' self management to student unionism, one so often seems to find the PSU centrally placed in the background somewhere'.[84] By the early 1970s, however, the PSU was facing an internal crisis and sought to establish ties with the established parties of the Left. Michel Rocard, who had been one of the prominent figures of May 1968 in Paris, left for the Parti Socialiste in 1974. Looking back on those years, Michel Rocard remembered how 'absolute priority was given to the political sphere and to elections, which replaced the disdain for the political sphere and the exclusivity given to social struggle which had characterized the previous period'.[85] Accepting representative institutions and competition for political power within those institutions as democratic had become the norm for those who had most fervently supported the ideals of 1968.

In Italy, too, some of the heirs of 1968 sought to enter the parliamentary system. Lotta Continua was a prime example of this shift from a decentralized and anti-hierarchical social movement to a centralized organization taking part in elections. However, the extra-parliamentary Left's inclusion in the party political system in Italy had very different consequences from that of their cousins in France and West Germany. This was the result of the very class-based disputes of the 1960s and 1970s. Lotta Continua was initially federalist in structure and ambivalent when it came to the use of violence to achieve its objectives. In the early 1970s, it lauded the killing of police officer Luigi Calabresi—for which Lotta Continua leader Adriano Sofri would be convicted in 1988—and sometimes only tactically condemned the violence of the Red Brigade.[86] But as Red Brigade attacks grew more lethal and frequent over the course of the 1970s, Lotta Continua faced a choice between 'an often violent *spontaneismo* and the search for institutional legitimacy'.[87] Just as it did for the social movements in West Germany, the escalation of political violence forced Lotta Continua to take a position on ideological and organizational issues as well as the principle of parliamentary democracy. The movement slowly shed its Marxist-Leninist orientation and settled on more 'generic left-wing positions on the social questions of the day'.[88] Concerning its organization, however, the question of how to reconcile its spontaneous, decentralized and participatory character with a more fruitful struggle for political power divided the movement.

Ultimately, Lotta Continua turned itself, a decentralized and loosely organized movement, into a national party organization with a strong and central command.[89] In 1975, the movement held its first national congress and was transformed into a political party. The new party emphasized that this was a pragmatic move and did not signify it had cut ties with its grass-roots supporters.[90] In other words, like the German Green Party, Lotta Continua endeavoured to remain firmly rooted in society and retain its social movement character while at the same time creating a party that 'constitutes a common base of political action much more efficient in its organization'.[91] Their process of accepting parliamentary politics as democratic became more evident when the PCI moved closer to the DC. In Lotta Continua's view, the major political parties were becoming indistinguishable because 'the major parties of the Left, PCI and PSI, in fact, do not make any left-wing demands in these elections, but propose a government of "national unity"'.[92] To offer the voters a more left-wing alternative, Lotta Continua decided to compete in the 1976 parliamentary elections, presenting a common electoral list with other far-left parties under the name of *Democrazia Proletaria*.[93] At its congress, the Democrazia Proletaria proclaimed that 'the choice between party and movement is a false choice, without a party capable of capturing the immediacy of the movements. . . . [T]he movements risk excluding themselves'.[94] So former social movements now sought democratic legitimacy by adhering to the rules of the democratic game as formulated by political parties, a premise they had previously rejected. They now accepted that political power was contested primarily, albeit not exclusively, by the ballot box and not just on the streets. Indeed, Lotta Continua now stated that '[v]oting [in parliamentary elections] has to be an instrument to reinforce the class movement'.[95]

Like the West German Green Party, Lotta Continua thereby gave prevalence to actually contesting power over contesting the system that distributed this power. Lotta Continua transformed from a decentralized movement based on working class-student collaboration into a party with strong top-down command structures and from a social movement that questioned the principle of representative democracy and its institutions to a political party that competed in parliamentary elections. But many grass-roots members felt the changes were too radical because they deprived the movement of its original identity. The far-Left common electoral list did poorly at the 1976 polls, and this threw Lotta Continua into existential turmoil, which soon led to the party's dissolution. To illustrate that acceptance of party and parliamentary democracy had become a goal in itself for the leadership, Adriano Sofri said at the party's final meeting that '[t]he clash that has occurred at this congress is exactly analogous to the 1968–1969 clash between the revisionists and the students and workers. We are repeating that clash today, only instead of Longo, Berlinguer and Amendola, it is Sofri, Viale and their companions who suffer the same fate'.[96] In other words, Lotta Continua had come to resemble the PCI in the worst respect.

Clearly, not all social movements experienced an equally successful or smooth entry into parliamentary politics, even though movements in all three countries this book deals with came to accept the principles of parliamentary democracy. In West Germany and, to a somewhat lesser extent, France, the formation of political parties based on the agenda of 1968 was successful. This was due partly to the fact that the extra-parliamentary Left was less closely connected to the working-class movement than in Italy and partly to the fact that in West Germany and France, the parliamentary Left was more open to the 1968 movements' conceptions democracy.[97] In fact, the movement La Voie had already noted in 1968 that the protest movement 'never succeeded in separating itself completely from parliamentary Left'.[98] From Brandt's 'daring more democracy' agenda to Mitterrand's nod to workers' self-management and the discourse of Michel Rocard, all of these resonated with themes advocated by the extra-parliamentary Left. The establishment of green parties in both countries and the integration of the extra-parliamentary Left in the SPD and PS also contributed to a changing conception of democracy within the political establishment, which became more open to alternatives to the tradition of parties and parliaments and adopted a more active conception of citizenship.

In Italy, the accession of extra-parliamentary movements to the parliamentary system was less successful. Guido Viale noted that the 'disintegration of the Christian Democratic regime' required 'centralization' and that as an almost natural consequence '*Lotta Continua* [became] a party'.[99] But the movements never structurally made it into parliament. Because of their strong class consciousness, Italian extra-parliamentary groups made more radical claims than their counterparts in other countries. Several were also radical in their methods and considered it justifiable to use 'offensive violence' against the police during strikes and demonstrations because their 'objectives were greater dignity and democracy'.[100] This supplied political elites with the arguments they needed to blur the distinction between violent radicals and peaceful protesters; it also seemed to confirm the idea that it would be better to entrust political parties and representative institutions with the democratic development of the country. The radicalism of the social movements' demands was a reaction to the closed nature of the Italian political class in an era of a historic compromise and part of a wider societal resistance to the consensus between the parliamentary Left and Christian Democrats that rendered political opposition indistinguishable. Understandable though the radicalism of the extra-parliamentary Left may have been, it was simultaneously the reason why these movements failed to enter the system.[101]

From Épinay to the Elyssée: The French Left Endorses the Fifth Republic

The French Left had vehemently contested the democratic legitimacy of its Gaullist opponents over several Gaullist measures: the establishment of the Fifth Republic, the 1962 reforms, and the Gaullist response to the extra-parliamentary challenge. In the 1970s, however, the Left's animosity gave way to an acknowledgement of the Gaullists and their ideas as democratic when it eventually realized that the Fifth Republic's institutional outline offered great opportunities for the contestation of political power. Meanwhile, the presidency of Valéry Giscard d'Estaing contributed to a more congenial atmosphere that eased the tension between Gaullists and anti-Gaullists. The Left, having contested the democratic legitimacy of De Gaulle and his conception of democracy ever since 1945, finally embraced the Fifth Republic as fully democratic.

This change of heart initially took place within the framework of the Common Programme of PS and PCF. The transition was made easier for the PCF by the Cold War détente and, more specifically, the party's relative independence from Moscow. The French communists recognized the plurality of political parties, embraced the acceptance of election results and government alternation, and guaranteed individual liberties such as freedom of thought and expression.[102] They insisted that 'liberty and socialism are inseparable' and declared that it would 'in all circumstances' accept the outcome of elections 'because it [the PCF] categorically rules out resorting to oppression, personal power, totalitarianism'.[103] In 1976, the party officially struck the notion of the 'dictatorship of the proletariat' from its programme.[104] However, the PCF's transition was not categorical; the ideological distance between the socialists and communists increased after the Common Programme was abandoned in September 1977. The PCF returned to its more orthodox ideas and sought to restore closer ties with the Soviet Union.[105]

Breaking with the PCF was a blessing in disguise for Mitterrand, not only because the PCF was electorally marginalized over the course of the 1980s but also because the rupture made it much harder for his main opponent, Jacques Chirac, to portray the PS as part of the Soviet camp.[106] It allowed the PS to establish itself more firmly in the electoral centre, not only by embracing the Fifth Republic but also by stressing its separation from the communists. The PS stated, for instance, that the 'socialist party, while according great importance to the theories of Marx, is not a Marxist party'.[107] With these moves, all of the main French parties now endorsed the constitutional settlement of 1958 nearly unconditionally. The underlying reasons for this consensus were threefold: the most radical leaders had left politics or died, leaving more consensus-minded politicians in their place; the socialists accepted the Fifth Republic as democratic; and they realized that the Fifth Republic offered them an opportunity to come to power.

The Fifth Republic lost its two most partisan leaders who embodied the ideological and divisive character of the constitution when De Gaulle left office in 1969 and his successor Pompidou died in 1974.[108] As a result, the Fifth Republic became less of a divisive issue and more of a political model endorsed by all political parties. The presidency of Valéry Giscard d'Estaing, who was by no accounts a Gaullist, contributed to this development. His election rung in 'a new era' for the Fifth Republic's institutions because, for the first time, the president could not count on a parliamentary majority.[109] This meant Giscard depended on fluctuating parliamentary majorities, including that of dissident socialist MPs. More than his predecessors, he invested in dialogue with the parliamentary opposition and valued the role of an active civil society,[110] and he is considered more of a 'citizens' president' who aimed to heal the wounds of 1968 by striking a conciliatory tone.[111] Giscard sought compromise and thereby brought an end to the polarization between left-wing and Gaullist politicians that had hampered a full reconciliation between the Left and the Fifth Republic's institutions. As Mitterrand put it, Pompidou had been the 'last projection' of Gaullism, and the ideology was now dead.[112]

Another factor that brought about full acceptance of the 1958 constitution was the fact that the French socialists finally accepted the Fifth Republic as democratic. They now perceived the Gaullist republic as a parliamentary system that concurred with their own traditional republican views. Mitterrand downplayed the differences between the Gaullist and 'republican' views of democracy by stating that in both presidential and parliamentary systems, popular sovereignty was the key feature. In contrast to his denouncement of the Fifth Republic as a 'permanent coup d'état', Mitterrand now stated that the socialist would 'not forget that the Constitution of 1958 is a parliamentary constitution'.[113] To him, this meant that 'if we were going reform certain aspects of our institutions, this would be within the framework of the same existing institutions'.[114] And as if to accentuate that a convergence of conceptions of democracy had taken place, Mitterrand stated that as president, 'I will be the most faithful interpreter of the institutions of the Republic'.[115] The '110 propositions' of the 1981 presidential campaign included limiting the presidential term to five years, restricting the president's right to appoint the members of the constitutional council, and introducing proportional representation for elections.[116] But of all these plans for institutional reform, only proportional representation for parliamentary elections was enacted—and annulled after it resulted in major losses for the socialists.[117]

The third reason for the consensus was that the socialists accepted the Fifth Republic's constitution partly out of strategic considerations. Although Mitterrand initially dismissed the direct election of the president by universal suffrage in 1962, he immediately realized the potential advantages of this reform.[118] In 1965, when he was just the leader of a minor left-wing party, direct election provided him with a national platform and visibility. After the Épinay congress, where he was elected leader of the PS, the struggle for power became the socialists' main motivation.[119] The constitution of the Fifth Republic provided great opportunities in this regard, easing the party's acceptance of it. The socialists knew that by endorsing the Fifth Republic, they gained political legitimacy within the existing political framework, which provided them with an inroad to political power.

When Mitterrand was elected in 1981, he said the socialist ascent to power and the inclusion of four communist ministers in his government should be placed in the tradition of the Popular Front of the 1930s and the institutionalization of the values of 1968.[120] However, the most remarkable consequence of his election was the definitive reconciliation between two opposing visions on French democracy that had marked the postwar era: the Gaullist and the 'republican' conceptions of democracy.[121] By emphasizing the socialist commitment to the institutional outline, Mitterrand not only confirmed the oft-praised 'flexibility' of the Fifth Republic's constitution and the 'republican tradition' as a whole,[122] but he also demonstrated that accepting these institutions as 'democratic' had become a requirement for any political actor to have a shot at reaching political office. Mitterrand had transformed from one of the staunchest opponents of the Fifth Republic into a president in the 'Gaullist' tradition.[123] In a sense, his election was the crown jewel of the 1970s process towards consensus on France's institutional outline that had been a long time coming since 1945.

Protecting the Republic: Italy's Emergency Government and Its Legacy

In Italy, the convergence of left-wing and conservative conceptions of democracy was a far more difficult process than in France. It was instigated by the nation's deep political and economic crisis in the 1970s, to which only the collaboration of the two major parties seemed to offer a solution. The PCI's conception of democracy underwent a genuine transformation. The party now endorsed civil liberties, political pluralism, and parliamentary democracy as ends in themselves. However, the Christian Democratic system the communists were endorsing was already past its prime, so the communists' consensus-oriented move had the net result of depriving the country of a genuine opposition. Whereas in France the rallying around the institutions of the Fifth Republic created a broad consensus on the rules of the democratic game, in Italy the convergence between PCI and DC was perceived as a sign of the *partitocrazia*'s inability to solve the problems of Italian democracy. This means the Italian Left's adaptation of its conceptions of democracy differed both in terms of causes and consequences from the left-wing transformation in France. Whereas in Paris, the convergence resulted from the diminishing polarization between Gaullists and anti-Gaullists during the more consensual Giscard presidency, the 'democratic turn' taken by the PCI took place at 'the most difficult moment for Italian democracy', in which the country faced social polarization and an economic crisis with double-digit inflation.[124] Most importantly, Italy was struggling with a wave of more than four thousand terrorist incidents that left 362 people dead.[125] Amidst these crises, the communists tried to put an end to the Cold War logic that had condemned them to permanent opposition and could, in the eyes of Berlinguer, jeopardize the democratic order.[126] Collaboration with the DC was vital to achieve this goal. Berlinguer therefore talked about providing 'democratic legality' and offering the communist party's 'solid and broad' support to help stem the crisis.[127]

By reconfiguring their stance on democracy, the communists continued the 'democratic turn' initiated by Berlinguer in 1972, which was based on the premise that the threats posed to democracy, required an effort akin to the antifascist collaboration that had spawned the Italian constitution. What shifted in the PCI was that it accepted the principles of liberal democracy, at least when it came to civil liberties, parliamentarianism, individual freedom and government alternation.[128] At a meeting of Western European communist parties in Brussels in 1974, Berlinguer explained that 'democracy' now had a different meaning and should no longer primarily be interpreted in terms of social relations. Consequently, the communists now regarded values they used to decry as mere 'bourgeois' democracy as valid goals to strive for. Berlinguer saw the 'affirmation of socialism as the coherent and full actualization of democracy'. This included

> the recognition and the guarantee of the value of personal liberties, the principles of a secular state, plurality of political parties, autonomy of labour unions, religious liberties, freedom of research, culture and science. This also includes for us a socialist solution to the economic problems . . . including coexistence and complementarity of various forms of initiative and management, both public and private.[129]

To emphasize the PCI's transformation and its eligibility for government, Berlinguer famously declared he felt 'safer being on this side' of the Iron Curtain.[130]

A second factor that aided the communists' shift was the DC's changing stance towards Berlinguer's PCI.[131] Aldo Moro aspired to construct an entirely new political system, the so-called 'Third Phase' of both the DC and Italian postwar democracy. It was not his intention to bring the PCI directly into government, so he continued to emphasize that only the DC could offer 'an authentic social and political pluralism',[132] but he also claimed that 'there is room for a responsible contribution by the communist party, which the extreme emergency in which we find ourselves requires'.[133] Mariano Rumor aptly described this semi-legitimization of the PCI when he said the communists' entry into the parliamentary majority was both an achievement and a problem. It was an achievement 'because it testifies to the evolution of the party in recent years' but problematic 'because despite its evolution the party has not superseded the contradictions of its programme: endorsing liberty while condoning the Soviet Union'.[134]

The ideological rapprochement between DC and PCI became more evident when the PCI moved closer to the centre. First the PCI abstained from a confidence vote on the DC-led government, and then it entered the parliamentary majority and signed a joint programme with the DC.[135] The PCI's transformation was most explicit during the Moro hostage crisis, when the communists defended the very same state institutions they had condemned in the 1950s. Moro was kidnapped in broad daylight on his way to parliament, where he was about to debate the formation of the first government with communist support since 1947.[136] This 'historic compromise' was originally intended to be a slow process of reconciliation but was catapulted into a crisis situation, where the discourse was conducted in terms of 'national solidarity' and 'emergency' government.[137] During the hostage crisis, the government opted for a policy of *fermezza*, a refusal to negotiate with the terrorists. It claimed that *raison d'état* had to prevail over saving individual lives because it would harm democracy if the government gave in to the terrorists' demand for a prisoner's swap. The communists supported the *fermezza*, albeit after prolonged debates that caused great tension. The PCI rebuked the DC for its decades-long exclusion of the communists and for wrongly 'identifying the enemy of democracy, of Italian democracy ... in the PCI', a move the party claimed had alienated part of the population from the state and sowed the seeds of violence.[138] But in the end the communists were 'above all preoccupied with defending the democratic institutions from the spread of terrorism, and securing their recently acquired participation in the government's majority'.[139] In short, the crisis was conducive to the PCI's acceptance of the Italian state and the Christian Democrats' main democratic conceptions.[140]

The 'historic compromise' ended in 1979 when the communists, dissatisfied with the lack of fundamental change, left the parliamentary majority. Their disappointment did not prompt them to revert to their earlier conception of democracy, however.[141] The PCI's changes, unlike the PCF's, were structural.[142] The Italian communists stayed true to the essentials of their reformed conception of democracy, including individual liberties and political pluralism. More and more, they also distanced themselves from the Soviet Union. When the Polish authorities imposed martial law to clamp down on the solidarity trade union in 1981, for instance, the PCI declared itself 'autonomous' from the Soviet Union and issued a statement to the effect that democracy and socialism could 'only be asserted in full respect of every people to decide over its own fortunes'.[143] Just two weeks after the fall of the Berlin Wall in 1989, the last PCI leader Achille Occhetto symbolized the party's transition by stating that 'democracy is the road to socialism. This means not only that there is no Chinese Wall separating democracy and socialism, but that socialism itself can only be conceived as an open-ended process, and indefinitely so, within the democratic system'.[144] This phase ultimately culminated in the dissolution of the PCI and its transformation into the Democratic Party of the Left (PDS) in 1991.[145]

Both the Italian communists and the French Left eventually fully accepted the rules of democracy that their political adversaries had outlined in previous decades. Despite the ostensible similarities, these processes were parallel rather than intertwined. Although the Cold War détente led to a convergence of democratic notions and there was a brief period of Eurocommunism in which French and Italian communists' ideas for reform overlapped, the net result of the convergence processes was dictated largely by national characteristics. As a consequence, the outcomes differed greatly.

In France, the convergence process had a positive impact on the stability of the democratic order and fostered agreement among the major forces on a set of rules and institutions universally considered 'democratic' and 'republican'. The Left adapted its conception of democracy to the new reality of the Fifth Republic. It did so on its own initiative and from a position of opposition in an atmosphere of lessening social and political tensions.

In Italy, the convergence did not bring about a structural solution to Italy's political problems, although it did help protect Italian democracy from serious and immediate threats.[146] Unlike its cousins in France, the Left did not revamp its understanding of democracy in a climate of relative social stability but at a time of national emergency when the democracy itself was in jeopardy. The 'democratic turn' that had been intended as a slow, bottom-up merger of the subcultures ended up an expedited decision by the top politicians. This exacerbated the image of Italian democracy as a closed circuit of dominant political parties detached from civil society.[147] Berlinguer's 'historic compromise' began at the PCI leader's own initiative, but it was executed in coordination with the Christian Democrats, above all with Moro.[148] Due to this compromise, the PCI lost many of the traits that distinguished the party from its rivals; it even shared in the spoils of corruption enjoyed by DC–PSI coalition partners that was revealed in scandals a decade later.[149] So in one sense, the merger of the PCI and DC's conceptions of democracy was too complete to settle the issues that dominated the Italian debate on democracy; many felt it deprived the country of a genuine opposition party and aggravated the worst features of the *partitocrazia*. However, in another sense the merger was not complete enough; the PCI never received full recognition from the other parties as a democratic partner, and this prevented government alternation and a break from DC rule.

Democracy Between Crisis and Consensus in the 1980s

The years 1975 to 1989 were a crucial period in the development of the debate on democracy in which political elites faced grave economic problems and challenges to their authority. In response, they closed ranks on how democracy should be defined and practiced. Mutual acceptance of democratic credentials and overlapping conceptions of democracy, which had been typical of West German politics since the 1960s, also took hold in France and Italy. Reaching a consensus on the principles of democratic rule was what enabled these countries to weather stormy times. However, this consensus should not be equated with the success of the model as a whole. The events in Italy in particular show that the increased consensus among political elites merely reinforced the perception that there was a lack of alternatives and increased the resistance to political elites, a development that became widely visible in the 1980s.

In West Germany, the main political actors generally considered the country's democracy a success. They credited its institutions with integrating the protest movements of the 1960s and 1970s.[150] There was, however, an undercurrent of discontent with the state of affairs in West Germany, which surfaced in various ways in the 1980s, for example, in the *Historikerstreit*, in growing criticism of the power of political parties and in the peace movement's mass protests.[151] Yet this dissatisfaction neither affected the main political actors' views on democracy nor jeopardized the common ground these actors had found. Even the Green Party, the most radical mainstream party in West German politics at the time, did not change parliamentarianism; rather, the practices of parliamentary democracy changed the party.[152]

West Germany's major political parties had become so monolithic that both of them endorsed the same three core concepts in their political programmes—freedom, justice and solidarity—and explained these terms in largely similar ways.[153] The CDU and the SPD praised each other for having played an indispensable role in forging the democratic order since 1949, saying that the 'solidarity of democrats stood at the cradle of the constitution'.[154] The SPD declared its conservative counterparts co-responsible for the perceived success of the German Model, an image of West Germany as a haven of political stability and economic prosperity in 1970s and 1980s Europe. Willy Brandt stated that '[o]ur constitutional order ... has developed in such a way that we can call it the freest order we have ever had in Germany. Every democratic force has contributed to our country's solid foundation: social democrats, Christian socialist, liberals and conservatives'.[155] So when the Berlin Wall fell, there was little doubt among politicians that the West German concept of democracy would become the model for a reunited Germany.

French democracy was less warmly and universally embraced in the 1980s. Intellectuals, for one, criticized the state of French democracy.[156] Another sign of dissatisfaction was the electoral breakthrough of the Front National in 1984, which seized on the people's growing dissatisfaction with political elites.[157] Despite these developments, however, the discourse on democracy in France sounded increasingly uniform.[158] Even the *Front National* did not contest the principles of the Fifth Republic but rather capitalized on the opportunities it offered.[159]

The dissatisfaction in France pertained to the increased consensus on the way democracy should be practiced. This consensus was evident, for instance, in the legitimization of the socialists' total turnaround on the economy after 1983, the Gaullists' new interpretation of participation under the leadership of Chirac, and the surprising resilience of party democracy despite persistent suspicions among Chirac's Gaullists of how the Left organized and practiced party politics.[160] But the consensus was most obvious in the settlement of the dispute regarding the balance of power between the executive and the legislature that had divided Gaullists and anti-Gaullists since 1945. The dispute was resolved through habituation and a wide acceptance of the Fifth Republic, further validated after Mitterrand's election in 1981.[161] Even Mitterrand's opponent Raymond Barre stated that 'regarding the institutions, the least we can say is that the exercise of constitutional power since 1981 has not been inspired by the anathemas of *Le coup d'état permanent*.[162] Mitterrand and his adversary Chirac even collaborated during the Fifth Republic's first period of *cohabitation*, demonstrating how previously antagonistic political families could join forces and work together within the framework of the Fifth Republic's institutions.[163] Throughout his presidency, Mitterrand defended the Gaullist principles of the Fifth Republic, even when the primacy of the president seemed to be threatened by Chirac during *cohabitation*.[164]

In Italy, the main political actors had also come together on some key principles of postwar democracy around the turn of the 1980s. The PCI's 'democratic turn' ensured that the party's ideas on democracy started to resemble those of the Christian Democrats and the socialists. This led to a broad agreement among these actors on the principles of party democracy, representation and, increasingly, the free market. The major political parties were wary of too much civic involvement and wanted political parties to manage participation. Despite this broad consensus, the major Italian political actors continued to debate solutions to what they saw as a crisis of democracy. There are five dimensions to this Italian debate that set it apart from discussions in Bonn and Paris.

The first idiosyncracy in the Italian debate on democracy was that Italy's main political parties in the 1980s still did not accept each other as full-fledged democratic partners. The DC combined its two previous main coalitions, the centrist and the centre-Left, in what was called the *pentapartito*, a five-party alliance that banished the PCI to perpetual opposition. Their attempts to delegitimize the PCI became increasingly difficult as the communists transformed themselves under Berlinguer's leadership. Even DC party leader Flaminio Piccoli acknowledged that 'the communist party has lost its ideological point of reference: the October Revolution and the socialist society of the East are no longer accepted models'.[165] All the same, the DC continued to justify the exclusion of the communists from government by pointing to their party's lack of democratic credentials. Around election time, the DC claimed that they and the communists were mutually exclusive alternatives and that the DC was Italy's bastion against 'authoritarian government' and an 'ambiguous international neutralism'.[166] The socialist party under Craxi's leadership took the same tack, launching a vicious attack on the democratic credentials of the PCI.[167] Simultaneously, the PCI cast doubt on the democratic credentials of the *pentapartito* and its leading party in particular. The communists held the DC accountable for Italy's political woes, and Berlinguer claimed that 'the country can no longer bear this leaden cloak of power and Christian Democratic arrogance, this is exactly what limits the liberal functioning of democratic institutions and threatens to suffocate them'.[168] The PCI portrayed itself as the 'democratic alternative' to the Christian Democrats, and Berlinguer advocated a 'complete overhaul of the deformation and distortions that have rendered Italian democracy "difficult" and "lame"'.[169] He was referring in part to corruption and links between politics and organized crime, which in his words, 'has by now become an internal challenge to the political system and the state'.[170]

Despite the dogfights over democratic legitimacy, there was a general consensus on democratic principles in Italy but one that met with much harsher and wider political resistance than similar agreements in France and West Germany; this is the second condition that made the debate in Italy so distinctive. The PCI did oppose the DC, but all the same the tensions between the parties gradually eased, a process that culminated in the 'historic compromise', which clearly demonstrated that the crisis of Italy's party system could only be resolved through the collaboration of the two previous arch-enemies.[171] However, as the PCI and DC lost support over the 1980s, the 'historic compromise' and the cooperation it spawned came to be associated with the hated *partitocrazia*, which was said to have caused all of Italian democracy's problems in which dominant political parties were completely detached from civil society.[172] Former communist Rossana Rossanda stated that the PCI's identification with the DC deprived the country of any opposition. Left-wing terrorism was part of what she called the PCI's 'family album'. The PCI, under Togliatti, had claimed that the DC was looking to install an authoritarian and clerical regime, so for the communists to suddenly contend that the DC was an antifascist and popular force left them, in Rossanda's view, open to criticism.[173] The MSI, Italy's fourth-largest party in the 1980s, claimed that the PCI's pledge of support for the government had created 'an elephant-size majority' in parliament and left the country without opposition. 'Choosing PCI nowadays equals choosing DC, and vice versa', the MSI's 1979 campaign manifesto argued.[174] Similar claims came from the progressive side of the political spectrum. The Radical Party, for one, decried the lack of opposition now that the PCI supported the DC in 'a unanimous parliament'.[175] As party leader Marco Pannella put it, '[T]he country and the people are tired, they do not understand anymore. The parties are retreating ever more into themselves'.[176] The 'most corrosive threat of all' was arguably the rise of the *Lega Nord* in the late 1980s, which not only challenged Italian unity but defied the party system as a whole.[177]

The widespread resistance to Italy's *partitocrazia* had partly to do with the political elite's particular views on the role of civil society, the third factor differentiating the debate in Italy from those in West Germany and France. In the latter two countries, the parliamentary Left had been susceptible to the agenda of the 1968 movements when it came to civic participation. Even the conservatives in both states started talking about civic involvement. In France, the presidency of Giscard d'Estaing played a major role in this regard.[178] Giscard went so far as to state that modern democracy was about giving 'power to the citizen'.[179] Gaullists, too, started incorporating the appreciation of an active civil society in their views on democracy. To the Gaullist Jacques Chirac, the institutions of the republic as such should not be questioned, but citizens should participate in them more than before.[180] 'One of the essential missions of the *Rassemblement*', Chirac said in 1978, 'will be to facilitate this participation: we will organize it so that there will be a place for reflection, for consultation, for suggestions and, if necessary, for critique'.[181] In 1976, he had already concluded that 'people want democracy on a day-to-day basis' and had claimed that participation, even in enterprises, was therefore of crucial importance.[182] Chirac assured that '[w]e want to commit resolutely to the path of participation in order to give our citizens a clearer notion of their rights, their duties, [and] their responsibilities'.[183]

The West German Christian Democrats had also altered their appreciation of civic participation during the 1970s, which had enhanced the party's identity as a 'modern' people's party open to an active civil society.[184] The new party leader Helmut Kohl was decisive in this shift.[185] In 1973, Kohl said about the CDU that it was 'committed in [its] party programme to a dynamic democracy, meaning further developing this democracy. Especially in this understanding of democracy, which is influenced by the demand for democratic organization and decision making in every sphere of society and the state, we need to ensure continued development'.[186] This new line was confirmed in the party's new political programme in 1978, in which the CDU explained its stance on democracy as follows: the party 'understands democracy to be a dynamic and developing political order that guarantees the cooperation of citizens and assures their freedom by separation and control of power. This order must be transparent for the individual and can only become reality if citizens feel responsible for its organization and are actively ... involved in it'.[187]

In Italy, the 1980s are referred to as the 'decade of civil society'.[188] However, this description belies the fact that civic involvement was not actively endorsed by the nation's ruling political class, which still thought mainly in party political terms. At the very moment it became evident that Italy's political parties were incapable of countering the growing sense of democratic crisis, the leading national party responded by embracing the institutions of party democracy rather than those of civic participation.[189] Even though the DC claimed to be 'an open party for an open society',[190] it did not embrace civic participation as explicitly as the conservatives in France and West Germany did in their views on democracy.

The fourth factor that differentiated the Italian debate from those in West Germany and France was that the discontent with democracy was not confined to fringe parties and intellectuals; the large Italian political parties were dissatisfied too.[191] Whereas the leading French politicians rallied around the flexible issue of republicanism as embodied by the Fifth Republic, and the West German leaders from the whole political spectrum embraced the German Model with its constitutional patriotism, Italian politics saw only a democracy in crisis. In truth, the postwar transformation of Italian democracy had been plagued by setbacks and problems. The Italian communists were included in the parliamentary majority, but their inclusion took place in response to what Moro called 'the most difficult moment' in postwar history. This moment was not just an economic and social crisis but also 'a crisis of the democratic order, a latent crisis, on some points acute', as Moro put it.[192] But the historic collaboration arguably only worsened Italy's political problems.[193]

Forces on the Left, inside and outside parliament, blamed Italy's democratic crisis on the fact that the DC remained in power. Mario Capanna, an influential figure in the extra-parliamentary Left, claimed that 'the DC system of power has permeated the structures of the state to the point of becoming identical to it. In this sense, it is justified to speak of a Christian Democratic *regime*'.[194] Berlinguer said there was 'a profound degeneration of the institutional mechanisms and the state, caused by the Christian Democratic system of power, which consists of a mutual infiltration between DC and the State. . . . The particular gravity and extension of the corruption of public life has its origin here'.[195] Communist politician Giorgio Napolitano remarked that various corruption scandals 'were a devastating, emblematic summary of the 30-year long identification of the dominant party with the state apparatus, of the arbitrary use of power by the Christian Democrats and, in varying degrees in various circumstances, by its government allies'.[196] The Christian Democrats turned this argument around, claiming that it aspired to a system with government alternation but was impeded by the lack of democratic alternatives on the opposition side. Moro had noted as early as 1973 that the problem of Italian democracy was the lack of alternatives to a DC government.[197] His words proved true, despite the 'historic compromise'. DC Party Secretary Ciriaco De Mita noted a decade later that 'the lack of this possibility [government alternation] generated the crisis, which, in the absence of adequately functioning politics, got worse'.[198]

As if it were a natural conclusion of Italy's crises, the theme of constitutional revision became part of the debate on democracy.[199] This fifth and final difference set the debate on democracy apart from those in Italy and West Germany. By the 1980s, the latter two countries had reached broad consensus on their constitutions, and so the constitution per se had disappeared from the debate on democracy. In Italy, by contrast, a new debate on the value of the constitution and institutional principles of democracy reared its head around the turn of the 1980s.[200] The socialists played a key role in this debate on constitutional reform.[201] Craxi stated that 'the system has had no answer to the two correlated demands for more efficiency and more democracy. . . . Democracy is therefore in need of renovation and this is the most urgent objective'.[202] In Craxi's view, the problems of Italian democracy were totally at odds with the renewed economic dynamism of the 1980s, which only made the country's democratic crisis more conspicuous. 'The question of institutional reform [had] become unavoidable', Craxi felt, because 'we lack an initiative that, based on the values of our

1947 constitution, tries to renovate our institutions in light of the necessary changes and past experiences'.[203] The socialists put forward a list of reforms, some of them sweeping, such as the replacement of the bicameral system with a unicameral system, more local autonomy, a shakeup of the country's bureaucracy and direct presidential elections.[204] On the Christian Democratic side, politician Ciriaco De Mita called for institutional reform, too, but was much more concerned than Craxi with preserving parliament's pivotal role.[205] De Mita denounced proposals to reform the bicameral system, for instance. 'The utility of unicameralism in respect to bicameralism seems indisputable, [but] in reality the question implies delicate problems of the political order and of democratic guarantees', he argued.[206] The PCI, by contrast, claimed that the most urgently needed measures were changes in the structure of the state, saying it proposed 'not solely adjustments, but profound acts of reform' of the bureaucracy.[207] None of these institutional reform projects materialized because of 'the impossibility of an agreement between the parties on a comprehensive renovation of the institutions'.[208] This resulted in a self-perpetuating catch-22 that historian Pietro Scoppola has called the 'paradox of institutional reform' in which the parties that stood to lose most from such reforms blocked any attempts to push them through, which in turn made the need for reforms even greater—and party resistance to it even stronger.[209]

In short, political actors in Italy saw the crisis plaguing their democracy deepen, while no real alternative seemed available from within the system. This was quite a different path than the developments in West Germany and France. Italy's failure to follow these other states' examples was at least partially caused by the fact that the parties refused to address their own position in the Italian democracy. In the views of those outside parliamentary circles, this lack of introspection was perhaps the biggest problem the country's political system faced. Although the parties continuously declared the urgency of institutional reform and voiced worries about the deep rift between politics and society, they also frequently reiterated their commitment to the party democratic system as it stood at the time. The pinnacle of this paradoxical discourse was the communists' claim they were committed to 'expanding the democratic involvement of citizens and thus to expanding political participation' on condition that 'the principle bodies of participation will remain the political parties, [as] they are and must continue to be the backbone of Italian democracy'.[210]

This failure to reform prompted Craxi in the 1980s to speak of Italy as a 'sick' country and to remark that in Europe, there was no other 'institutional system as incapable of adapting and innovating itself in the face of social change'.[211] The socialists felt that the parties had failed in their most fundamental task. According to them, 'the basic problem the republic's political forces were facing had been and still was the duty that both the liberal system and the fascist regime had failed to fulfil: to admit, or better yet, to integrate the masses into the state. . . . [E]ither the political system addresses this fundamental issue or, otherwise, this unresolved question will start to dominate the scene'.[212] The DC concurred with the socialists' analysis. Its prominent member Arnaldo Forlani noted that 'a serious fissure has opened between the people and the political institutions and parties. What we need is a serious commitment, befitting the extent and gravity of this situation'.[213] The 1980s then were a time when Italy descended into 'a state of mind that championed a kind of summary trial as well as a guilty verdict on the country's entire ruling class, with no possibility of appeal '. This was the fall of the so-called First Republic in the early 1990s.[214]

Conclusion: Democracy in the 1980s

The course of Italian politics since the 1980s shows that an agreement by political elites on the principles of democracy is no guarantee of democratic success. In simple terms, the broadening consensus on the meaning of democracy neither reflected an improvement in democratic substance nor led to more popular satisfaction with democracy. In fact, in all three states discussed in this book, many events in the 1980s pointed to the opposite, for example, the frequent mass political protests on issues ranging from the environment to nuclear disarmament and peace. The decade was rife with discontent and visible challenges to the status quo, both inside parliament and beyond. In addition to the protests, the decade also saw the electoral breakthrough of the Green Party in Germany and the Front National in France and the formation of the various Northern Leagues in Italy, all of which were signs that the electoral hegemony of the dominant postwar parties could no longer be taken for granted.

With the benefit of hindsight, it is easy to see these political challenges as an early sign of the high levels of dissatisfaction with politics that mark our current decade. At the time, however, this was far less obvious. On the contrary, the most visible and significant development was the growing consensus among political elites on how democracy should function and their mutual acceptance as allies and democratic partners. In this light, the fact that the 1980s social movements' activities were quite different in nature from previous decades is very significant because it reveals how these movements were adapting to the rules of representative democracy rather than contesting the legitimacy of those rules.[215] At the same time, however, these signs of discontent were also a response to the increased consensus among political elites and the way the elites guarded the boundaries of what they considered democratic. In this way, the growth of consensus opened up space for competing democratic narratives that fulminated against the status quo for failing to uphold important democratic values. Hence, the increased consensus among political elites from the 1970s onwards is inversely proportional to the signs of dissatisfaction at the time—and in subsequent decades.

Notes

1. For a discussion whether the 1970s was a time of delusion or promises, see: H. Kaelbe, *The 1970s in Europe: A Period of Disillusionment or Promise?* (London: German Historical Institute, 2009).
2. M. Crozier, S.P. Huntington, and J. Watanuki, *The Crisis of Democracy. What's Troubling the Trilateral Countries?* (New York: New York University Press, 1975).
3. Hanagan, 'Changing Margins in European Politics', p. 131; Judt, *Postwar*, ch. 17. Mazower, *Dark Continent*, p. 328; Stone, *Goodbye to All That?*, ch. 7.
4. Eley, *Forging Democracy*, ch. 24; Sassoon, *One Hundred Years of Socialism*, ch. 16.
5. M. Lazar, 'La gauche e la défi des changements dans les années 1970–80. Les cas français et italien, *Journal of Modern European History*, vol. 9, no. 2 (2011), pp. 241–262.
6. E. Cohen, 'A Dirigiste End to Dirigisme?' in: M. MacLean, *The Mitterrand Years.*, pp. 36–45.
7. Eichengreen, *The European Economy*, p. 268.
8. Crainz, *Il paese mancato*, pp. 424–427.
9. Quoted by: Ginsborg, *A History of Contemporary Italy*, p. 354.
10. Eley concludes that 'Left parties lost control over the crisis, adopting neoliberal economic policies even in power', see: Eley, *Forging Democracy*, p. 396.
11. See, most notably: P. Roggi, 'L'impegno della Dc nell'economia durante gli ultimi quarant'anni', in: Malgeri, *Storia della Democrazia Cristiana. Vol. IV*, pp. 197–246, on pp. 235–236.
12. DC, *I problemi dell'economia Italiana superamento della crisi e nuove prospettive di sviluppo sociale. Convegno nazionale di studi DC. Perugia, 9–12 Dicembre 1972. Vol 3. L'assemblea generale* (Rome: Edizione Cinque Lune, 1973), pp. 323–325.
13. *Ibid.*, p. 343.
14. DC, *Per la società nuova. Un grande partito di popolo. Assemblea nazionale DC. Roma 25–30 Novembre 1981* (N.P. 1981), pp. 23–24.
15. McCarthy, *The Crisis of the Italian State*, ch. 5; Ginsborg, *Italy and Its Discontents*, ch. 7.
16. On the *Tendenzwende*, see: Müller, *Another Country*, p. 53.
17. F.J. Strauß, 'Freiheit oder Abhängigkeit?' (1974), in: F.J. Strauß ed., *Signale. Beiträge zur deutschen Politik 1969–1978* (Munich: Verlag Bayernkurier, 1978), pp. 147–150, on p. 148.
18. Strauß, 'Freiheit oder Abhängigkeit?', p. 148.
19. F.J. Strauß, *Deutschland deine Zukunft* (Stuttgart: Seewald Verlag, 1975), p. 13.
20. H. Kohl, 'Handeln als Christliche Demokraten. Rede auf dem 31. Bundesparteitag der CDU in Köln' (1983), in: H. Kohl ed., *Der Kurs der CDU* (Stuttgart: Deutsche Verlags-Anstalt, 1993), pp. 205–227, on p. 208.
21. A. Cole, 'Political Leadership in Western Europe: Helmut Kohl in Comparative Perspective', in: C. Clemens and W.A. Paterson eds., *The Kohl Chancellorship* (London: Port Class, 1998), pp. 120–142, on p. 123; Wolfrum, *Die geglückte Demokratie*, p. 361.
22. Granieri, 'Politics in C Minor', p. 31.
23. P. Hoeres, 'Von der "Tendenzwende" zur "geistig-moralischen Wende". Konstruktion und Kritik konservativer Signaturen in den 1970er und 1980er Jahren', *Vierteljahrshefte für Zeitgeschichte*, vol. 61, no. 1 (2013), pp. 93–119, esp. 101–104.
24. H. Kohl, 'Das Erbe Ludwig Erhards—Herausforderung an die Wirtschaftspolitik' (1987), in: H. Kohl ed., *Reden zu Fragen der Sozialen Marktwirtschaft*

(Bonn: Presse und Informationsamt der Bundesregierung, 1990), pp. 7–26, on p. 17.
25 J. Hayward, 'Moins d'État or Mieux d'État: The French Response to the Neoliberal Challenge', in: M. MacLean ed., *The Mitterrand Years. Legacy and Evaluation* (Basingstoke: Palgrave McMillan, 1998), pp. 23–35, on p. 26.
26 R. Barre, *Réflexions pour demain* (Paris: Hachette, 1984), p. 25.
27 R. Barre, *La crise des politiques économiques et sociales et l'avenir des démocraties industrielles* (Rome: Banco di Roma, 1983), p. 41.
28 R. Barre, *Une politique pour l'avenir* (Paris: Plon, 1981), p. 105.
29 Barre, *Réflexions pour demain*, p. 36.
30 Berstein, *Histoire du Gaullisme*, p. 438.
31 *Ibid.*, pp. 421–423 Knapp, *Parties and the Parties in France*, p. 239.
32 Bell, *Parties and Democracy in France*, p. 66.
33 J. Chirac, *La Bataille de France. Discours prononcée au Rassemblement du 11 Février 1978* (Paris: Création Publicité Impression, 1978) p. 16.
34 Sassoon, *One Hundred Years of Socialism*, p. 457.
35 Berger, 'Democracy and Social Democracy', p. 29; S. Berger, 'Communism, Social Democracy and the Democracy Gap', *Socialist History*, vol. 27 (2005), pp. 1–20, on p. 13; Sassoon, *One Hundred Years of Socialism*, p. 457.
36 M. Gervasoni, *Storia d'Italia degli anni ottanta. Quando eravamo moderni* (Venice: Marsilio editore, 2010), p. 10; Di Scala, *Renewing Italian Socialism*, p. 200; Degli'Innocenti, *Storia del PSI*, p. 420; S. Gundle, 'The Rise and Fall of Craxi's Socialist Party', in: Gundle and Parker, *The New Italian Republic*, pp. 85–98;
37 B. Craxi, *L'alternativa dei socialisti. Il progetto del PSI presentato da Bettino Craxi* (Milan: Edizione Avanti, 1978), p. 31.
38 Craxi, *Una responsabilità democratica*, p. 25.
39 B. Craxi, *Marxismo, Socialismo e Libertà. Discorso pronunciato a Trevieri il 4 Maggio 1977* (Roma: Biblioteca Rossa, 1977), p. 13.
40 B. Craxi, *Una responsabilità democratica. Una prospettiva riformista per l'Italia che cambia. Relazione introduttiva al 44 Congresso, Rimini 31 marzo-5 aprile 1987* (1987), p. 16.
41 PSI, *Governare il cambiamento. Intervento alla conferenza di Rimini 4 aprile 1982* (Rome: Sezione propaganda e sezione del P.S.I., 1982), p. 6; p. 16.
42 S. Berstein, 'The Crisis of the Left and the Renaissance of the Republican Model 1981–1995', in: Maclean, *The Mitterrand Years*, pp. 46–65, on p. 53.
43 Moreau, 'Le congrès d'Épinay-sur-Seine du parti socialiste', p. 96.
44 M. Tracol, *Changer le travail pour changer la vie? Genèse des lois Auroux, 1981–1982* (Paris: L'Harmattan, 2009), p. 207.
45 Winock, *La Gauche en France*, pp. 424–425; Moreau, 'Le congrès d'Épinay-sur-Seine du parti socialiste', p. 96; Bergounioux, 'Socialisme français et social-démocratie européenne', p. 102. For an economic perspective, see: Eichengreen, *The European Economy*, pp. 287–290.
46 M. Rocard, 'La pensée socialiste est en crise' (1979), in: M. Rocard ed., *A l'épreuve des faits. Textes politiques 1979–1985* (Paris: Seuil, 1986), pp. 21–31, on p. 27.
47 Berstein, 'The Crisis of the Left', p. 60.
48 Bergounioux and Grunberg, *Le long remords du pouvoir*, p. 433.
49 L. Fabius, 'Moderniser et rassembler. Discours d'investiture' (1984), in: L. Fabius ed., *Le Cœur du Futur* (Paris: Almann-Levy, 1985), pp. 49–62, on pp. 54–55.
50 M. Rocard, 'Nous avons changé, osons le dire' (1985), in: Rocard, *A l'épreuve des faits*, pp. 37–49, on p. 43.
51 See also: Winock, *La Gauche en France*, p. 426.
52 Barre, *Réflexions pour demain*, p. 46.

53 Bergounioux, 'Socialisme français et social-démocratie européenne', p. 102.
54 L. Fabius, 'L'impact des nationalisations' (1984), in: Fabius, *Le cœur du Futur*, pp. 209–211.
55 Sassoon, *One Hundred Years of Socialism*, p. 461.
56 M. Rocard, 'La redécouverte de l'individu' (1985), in: Rocard, *A l'épreuve des faits*, pp. 203–205, on p. 203.
57 Sassoon, *One Hundred Years of Socialism*, pp. 510–513.
58 W. Brandt and H. Schmidt, *Theorie und Grundwerte. Weiterarbeiten am Modell Deutschland. Reden von Willy Brandt und Helmut Schmidt* (SPD, 1976), p. 24.
59 W. Brandt, 'Aus der Erklärung von Parteivorstand, Parteirat und Kontrollkommission der SPD zur Bundeskonferenz in Recklinghausen 17 Februar 1975' (1975), in: W. Brandt ed., *Berliner Ausgabe. Band 5. Die Partei der Freiheit. Willy Brandt und die SPD 1972–1992* (Bonn: Dietz Verlag, 2002), pp. 151–157, on p. 151.
60 Lösche and Walter, *Die SPD*, pp. 119–128.
61 G. Brauntahl, 'Opposition in the Kohl Era: The SPD and the Left', in: Clemens and Paterson, *The Kohl Chancellorship*, pp. 143–162, on p. 146.
62 H-J. Vogel, 'Politischer Ausblick' (1984), in: A Möller ed., *Wirtschaftspolitik in den 80er Jahren* (Bonn: Verlag Neue Gesellschaft, 1984), pp. 210–215, on pp. 212–213.
63 SPD, *Grundsatzprogramm der Sozialdemokratische Partei Deutschlands* (Berlin, 1989), p. 43. Found on: http://library.fes.de/pdf-files/bibliothek/retro-scans/fa90-00398.pdf, accessed on 10 June 2015.
64 PCI, 'La proposta di alternative per il cambiamento. Documento politico con gli emendamenti approvati dal XVI Congresso' (1983), in: E. Berlinguer ed., *Economia, stato, pace: l'iniziativa e le proposte del PCI. Rapporto, conclusioni e documento politico del XVI Congresso* (Rome: Editori Riuniti, 1983), pp. 75–172, on p. 110.
65 Lussana, 'Il confronto con le socialdemocrazie', p. 482.
66 E. Berlinguer, *Austerità. Occasione per trasformare Italia. Le conclusioni al convegno degli intellettuali (Roma, 15-1-'77) e alla assemblea degli operai comunisti (Milano, 30-1-'77)* (Rome: Editori Riuniti, 1977), p. 13.
67 E. Berlinguer, 'Ruolo ed iniziativa del Pci per una nuova fase della lotta per il socialismo in Italia ed in Europa' (1982), in: P.C.I. *Socialismo rea e terza via*, pp. 11–44, on p. 26.
68 R. Dutschke, 'Subkultur und Partei (Fragen der Organisierung)' (1977), in: Dutschke, *Geschichte ist Machbar*, pp. 164–171, on p. 170.
69 S. Mende, *"Nichts recht, nichts links, sondern vorn". Eine Geschichte der Gründungsgrünen* (Munich: Oldenbourg Verlag, 2011), pp. 279–285; U. Wesel, *Die verspielte Revolution. 1968 und die Folgen* (Munich: Karl Blessing Verlag, 2002), p. 308; Hanshew, *Terror and Democracy in West Germany*, p. 240; Thomas, *Protest Movements in 1960s*, p. 201.
70 R. Dutschke, 'Kein Mensch ist austauschbar. Über Gewalt und Gegengewalt', in: Dutschke, *Mein langer Marsch*, pp. 97–106, on p. 104.
71 E.G. Frankland, 'Germany: The Rise, Fall and Recovery of *Die Grünen*', in: D. Richardson and C. Rootes eds., *The Green Challenge. The Development of Green Parties in Europe* (London: Routledge, 1995), pp. 17–32, on p. 17. See also: Hockenos, *Joschka Fischer and the Making of the Berlin Republic*.
72 H. Mewes, 'A brief history of the Green party', in: M. Mayer and J. Ely eds., *The German Greens* (Philadelphia: Temple University Press, 1998), pp. 29–48.
73 L. Klotzsch et al., 'What Has Happened to Green Principles in Electoral and Parliamentary Politics?', in: M. Mayer and J. Ely eds., *The German Greens* (Philadelphia: Temple University Press, 1998), pp. 97–127.

74 P. Kelly, 'Schwerter zu Pflugscharen—ohne Systemgrenze!', in: M. Coppik and P. Kelly eds., *Wohin den Wir. Texte aus der Bewegung* (Berlin: Oberbaumverlag, 1982), pp. 7–16. For a discussion of the greens as a branch of the social movements, see: F. Schieder, *Von der sozialen Bewegung zur Institution? Die Entstehung der Partei DIE GRÜNEN in den Jahren 1978 bis 1980. Argumenten, Entwicklungen und Strategien am Beispiel Bonn/Hannover/Osnabrück* (Münster: LIT Verlag, 1998).
75 Die Grünen, *Das Bundesprogramm* (1980), p. 5. Found on: https://www.boell.de/sites/default/files/assets/boell.de/images/download_de/publikationen/1980_001_Grundsatzprogramm_Die_Gruenen.pdf, accessed on 10 June 2015.
76 Mende, *"Nichts recht, nichts links, sondern vorn"*, pp. 460–467.
77 Die Grünen, *Das Bundesprogramm*, p. 5.
78 *Ibid.*
79 Die Grünen, *Das Bundesprogramm*, p. 5.
80 P. Kelly, *Um Hoffnung kämpfen. Gewaltfrei in eine grüne Zukunft* (Berlin: Lamuv Taschenbuch Verlag, 1983), pp. 20–21.
81 *Ibid.*, p. 21.
82 La Voie, *Elections bourgeoises ou action révolutionnaire* (1968), p. 7. Found on: http://edocs.lib.sfu.ca/projects/mai68/pdfs/POST_May_Perspectives.pdf, accessed on 4-11-2013.
83 B. Villalba, 'La genèse inachevée des Verts', *Vingtième Siècle. Revue d'histoire*, no. 53 (1997), pp. 85–97.
84 Gordon, 'A "Mediterranean New Left"?', pp. 312–313.
85 'M. Rocard, 'L'avenir de Mai 68' (1978), in: M. Rocard ed., *Parler vrai. Textes politiques* (Paris: Éditions de Seuil, 1978), pp. 97–101, on p. 99.
86 R. Drake, 'Catholics and the Italian Revolutionary Left of the 1960s', *The Catholic Historical Review*, vol. 94, no. 3 (2008), pp. 450–475, on p. 471. Calabresi was held responsible for the death of an innocent anarchist being held in custody on suspicion of involvement in the 1969 Piazza Fontana bombing.
87 Della Porta, *Social Movements, Political Violence and the State*, p. 92.
88 Drake, 'Catholics and the Italian Revolutionary Left', p. 474.
89 Bobbio, *Storia di Lotta continua*, p. 77.
90 'Sul partito, tattica e statuto', *Lotta Continua*, 11 January 1975, p. 2.
91 'Concluso il congresso nazionale', *Lotta Continua*, 14 January 1975, p. 4.
92 'Votare democrazia proletaria. Votare i candidati di Lotta continua', *Lotta Continua*, 20–21 June 1976, p. 2.
93 Bobbio, *Storia di Lotta continua*, pp. 163–168.
94 Democrazia Proletaria, *Costituente del Partito di Democrazia e Proletaria. Contribuiti alla preparazione dell'assemblea congressuale* (N.P., 1975), p. 17.
95 'Votare democrazia proletaria. Votare i candidati di Lotta continua', *Lotta Continua*, 20–21 June 1976, p. 2.
96 Quoted by: Bobbio, *Storia di Lotta continua*, p. 178.
97 Schönhoven, 'Aufbruch in die sozialliberale Ära', p. 137; Tolomelli, '1968: Formen der Interaktion zwischen Studenten- und Arbeiterbewegung', pp. 98–99; Koenen, *Das rote Jahrzehnt*, p. 203; Gordon, 'A "Mediterranean New Left"?', pp. 312–313; Bergounioux and Grunberg, *L'ambition et le remords*, p. 311.
98 La Voie, *Elections bourgeoises ou action révolutionnaire* (1968), found on: http://edocs.lib.sfu.ca/projects/mai68/pdfs/POST_May_Perspectives.pdf, accessed on 4-11-2013.
99 G. Viale, *Il Sessantotto. Tra rivoluzione e restaurazione* (Milan: Mazzotta Editore, 1978), p. 244.
100 Lumley, *States of Emergency*, p. 235.
101 Tolomelli, *Terrorismo e società*, p. 210; Tranfaglia, 'Parlamento, partiti e società civile nella crisi repubblicana', pp. 827–835.

102 Parti Socialiste and Parti Communiste Français, *Programme Commun du gouvernement*, pp. 143–149; PCF, *Projet de déclaration des libertés du Parti communiste français. Introduction de Georges Marchais* (Paris: l'Humanité, 1975), pp. 22–23; Courtois and Lazar, *Histoire du Parti communiste français*, pp. 356–386; Lazar, *Le communisme*, pp. 40–41.
103 G. Marchais, 'Première partie. La voix des communistes français', in: Marchais and Hourdin, *Après le 22ᵉ Congrès*, pp. 7–49, on p. 22.
104 Courtois and Lazar, *Histoire du Parti communiste français*, p. 355.
105 Knapp, *Parties and the Party System in France*, p. 104; Courtois and Lazar, *Histoire du Parti communiste français*, p. 358.
106 G. Ross, 'Party Decline and Changing Party Systems: France and the French Communist Party', *Comparative Studies*, vol. 25 (1992), pp. 43–61, on pp. 49–51; Lazar, *Le communisme*, pp, 128–135; Knapp, *Parties and the Parties in France*, pp. 104–105.
107 F. Mitterrand, *Ici et Maintenant. Conversations avec Guy Claisse* (Paris: Fayard, 1980), p. 44. See also: M. Winock, *La Gauche en France* (Paris: Perrin, 2006), p. 424.
108 D.S. Bell, *Parties and Democracy in France. Parties under Presidentialism* (Aldershot: Ashgate, 2000), p. 202.
109 M. Bernard, 'Les relations entre Valéry Giscard d'Estaing et la majorité (1974–1978)', in: S. Berstein, R. Rémond and J.-F. Sirinelli eds., *Les années Giscard. Institutions et pratiques politiques 1974–1978* (Paris: Fayard, 2003), pp. 191–207, on p. 191.
110 G. Dubois, 'La conception de la présidence de Valéry Giscard d'Estaing', in: Berstein, Rémond and Sirinelli eds., *Les années Giscard*, pp. 59–75.
111 Atkin, *The Fifth French Republic*, p. 123.
112 Mitterrand, '1974: Élection présidentielle', on p. 555.
113 Mitterrand, 'L'avènement du socialisme', p. 247.
114 *Ibid.*, p. 246.
115 *Ibid.*, p. 247.
116 F. Mitterrand, '110 Propositions pour la France' (1981), in: F. Mitterrand ed., *Politique II 1977–1981* (Paris: Fayard, 1981), pp. 305–324, on p. 311.
117 And the Front National's first major breakthrough, see: Vinen, 'The Fifth Republic as Parenthesis?', p. 95.
118 See, for instance: Bell, *François Mitterrand*, p. 44.
119 See, for instance: Bergounioux, 'Socialisme français et social-démocratie européenne', p. 101.
120 Atkin, *The Fifth French Republic*, pp. 139–144.
121 Berstein, *Histoire du Gaullisme*, p. 398.
122 J. Jennings, *Revolution and the Republic. A History of Political Thought in France since the Eighteenth Century* (Oxford: Oxford University Press, 2012), p. 568; Berstein, 'De la démocratie plébiscitaire au Gaullisme'; Hazareesingh, 'L'imaginaire républicaine en France'.
123 Hazareesingh, *In the Shadow of the General*, pp. 135–136.
124 Lupo, *Partito e antipartito*, p. 222.
125 Numbers pertain to the period from 1969 to1980; see: M. Galleni ed., *Rapporto sul terrorismo* (Milan: Rizzoli Editore, 1981) 49.
126 See, most notably: Pons, *Berlinguer e la fine del comunismo*.
127 E. Berlinguer, *L'Italia di oggi ha bisogno dei comunisti. Per essere governata, risanata, rigenerata. Il discorso di Enrico Berlinguer alla Camera dei Deputati, 20/2/1976* (Rome: Stabilimento grafico editoriale fratelli Spada, 1976), p. 5.
128 F. Lussana, 'Il confronto con le socialdemocrazie e la ricerca di un nuovo socialismo nell'ultimo Berlinguer', *Studi storici*, vol. 45, no. 2 (2004), pp. 461–488, on p. 470.

129 E. Berlinguer, 'Costruire un'Europa nuova' (1974), in: E. Berlinguer ed., *La "Questione Comunista" 1969–1976* (Rome: Editori Riuniti, 1976), pp. 675–682, on p. 678.
130 Vittoria, *Storia del PCI 1921–1991*, p. 134.
131 See, for instance: R. Rufilli, 'L'ultimo Moro: dalla crisi del centro-sinistra all'avvio della terza fase', in: Malgeri ed., *Storia della Democrazia Cristiana. Vol. IV*, pp. 317–334; Cotturi, 'Moro e la transizione interrotta', p. 497; Gualtieri, *L'Italia dal 1943 al 1992.*, p. 184.
132 A. Moro, 'Sviluppo democratico e presenza della DC (1976), in: A. Moro ed., *Scritti e discorsi Vol. VI 1974–1978* (Rome: Edizioni Cinque Lune, 1990), pp. 3469–3489, on p. 3488.
133 A. Moro, 'Un quadro politico da costruire' (1976), in: Moro, *Scritti e discorsi Vol. VI*, pp. 3491–3506, on p. 3506.
134 M. Rumor, 'Democrazia cristiana partito del cambiamento e della continuità' (1978), in: Rumor, *Discorsi*, pp. 431–439, on p. 434.
135 Gualtieri, *L'Italia dal 1943 al 1992*, pp. 184–198.
136 A. Giovagnoli, 'Democrazia Cristiana e terrorismo', in: V.V. Alberti ed., *La DC e il terrorismo nell'Italia degli anni di piombo* (Soveria Manelli: Rubbettino, 2008), pp. 19–31.
137 See also: Barbagallo, 'Enrico Berlinguer, il compromesso storico e l'alternativa democratica', p. 944.
138 P. Bufalini, *Terrorismo e democrazia. La relazione al Comitato Centrale del PCI 18 aprile 1978* (Rome: Editori Riuniti, 1978), p. 21.
139 F. Barbagallo, 'Il Pci dal sequestro di Moro alla morte di Berlinguer', *Studi storici*, vol. 42, no. 4 (2001), pp. 837–883, on p. 840.
140 Giovagnoli, *Il caso Moro*, p. 14.
141 Pons, *Berlinguer e la fine del comunismo*, p. 154.
142 Giovagnoli, *Il caso Moro*, p. 264.
143 PCI, 'Risoluzione della direzione del Pci' (1980), in: P.C.I. *Socialismo reale e terza via. Il dibattito sui fatti di Polonia nel Comitato centrale del P.c.i. I documenti sulla polémica con Pcus* (Rome: Editori Riuniti, 1982), pp. 235–245, on p. 236.
144 A. Occhetto, 'La Relazione di Achille Occhetto. Una Costituente per aprire una nuova prospettiva della sinistra', (1989), in: PCI, *Documenti per il congresso straordinario del PCI. Il Comitato Centrale della svolta. Roma 20–24 Novembre 1989* (Rome: L'Unità, 1989), pp. 3–25, on p. 6.
145 M.J. Bull, 'The Great Failure? The Democratic Party of the Left in Italy's Transition', in: Gundle and Parker eds., *The New Italian Republic*, pp. 159–172.
146 Ginsborg, *A History of Contemporary Italy*, p. 356.
147 P. Ignazi, 'Italy in the 1970s between Self-Expression and Organicism', in: A.C. Bull and A. Giorgio eds., *Speaking Out and Silencing. Society, Politics and Culture in the 1970s* (London: Legenda, 2006), pp. 10–29, on p. 11. For cooperation between DC and PCI elites in the 1980s, see also: C. Carboni, 'Elites and the Democratic Disease', in: A. Mammone and G.A. Veltri eds., *Italy Today. The Sick Man of Europe* (London: Routledge 2010), pp. 19–33.
148 Giovagnoli, *Il caso Moro*; Cotturi, 'Moro e la transizione interrotta'; Lupo, *Partito e antipartito*, pp. 257–266.
149 S. Hellman, 'Italian Communism in the First Republic', in: Gundle and Parker eds., *The New Italian Republic*, pp. 72–84, esp. pp. 80–81.
150 A.Rödder, 'Das "Modell Deutschland" zwischen Erfolgsgeschichte und Verfallsdiagnose', *Vierteljahrshefte für Zeitgeschichte*, vol. 54, no. 3 (2006), pp. 345–363.
151 Müller, *Another Country*, pp 60–61; A. Wirsching, *Abschied vom Provisorium 1982–1990* (Stuttgart: Deutsche Verlags-Anstalt, 2006), pp. 199–203.
152 Wesel, *Die verspielte Revolution*, p. 312.

153 SPD, *Grundsatzprogramm*; C.D.U. *Grundsatzprogramm*.
154 H. Kohl, 'Das Grundgesetz. Verfassung der Freiheit. Rede in der Frankfurter Paulskirche' (1974), in: Kohl, *Der Kurs der CDU*, pp. 68–77, on p. 69.
155 Brandt and Schmidt, *Theorie und Grundwerte*, p. 10.
156 A. Peyrefitte, *Le mal français* (Paris: Plon, 1976).
157 E. Rydgren, 'France: The Front National, Ethnonationalism and Populism', in: D. Albertazzi and D. McDonnel eds., *Twenty-first Century Populism: The Spectre for Western European Democracy* (Basingstoke: Palgrave Mcmillan, 2007), pp. 166–180, p. 174.
158 Broche, *Une histoire des antigaullismes*, p. 563.
159 Fieschi, *Fascism, Populism and the French Fifth Republic*, p. 187; Bell, *Parties and Democracy in France*, p. 127.
160 Berstein, *Histoire du Gaullisme*, pp. 420–421; Hanley, *Party, Society, Government. Republican Democracy in France*, ch. 7.
161 Winock, *La gauche en France*, p. 427.
162 Barre, *Réflexions pour demain*, p. 26.
163 Broche, *Une histoire des antigaullismes des origines à nos jours*, p. 560; Atkin, *The Fifth French Republic*, p. 179.
164 W. Northcutt, 'François Mitterrand and the Political Use of Symbols: The Construction of a Centrist Republic', *French Historical Studies*, vol. 17, no. 1 (1991), pp. 141–158, on p. 150.
165 Piccoli, 'Un grande partito di popolò', p. 75.
166 Democrazia Cristiana, *Un programma per l'Italia. Elezioni politiche 14–15 Giugno 1987* (Rome: Agi, 1987), p. 6.
167 S. Colarizi and M. Gervasoni, *La cruna dell'ago. Craxi, il partito socialista e la crisi della Repubblica* (Bari: Laterza, 2005), pp. 79–82. Degli'Innocenti, *Storia del PSI*, p. 444; Vittoria, *Storia del PCI*, p. 139.
168 E. Berlinguer, 'La crisi della politica di solidarietà' (1979), in: Berlinguer, *La crisi italiana* (Rome: l'Unità, 1985), pp. 125–129, on p. 126.
169 E. Berlinguer, *La nostra lotta dall'opposizione verso il governo* (Rome: Editori Riuniti, 1979), p. 59.
170 P.C.I., 'La proposta di alternative per il cambiamento', p. 128.
171 Tolomelli, *Terrorismo e società*, p. 282.
172 P. Grillo di Cortona, *Dalla Prima alla Seconda Repubblica. Il Cambiamento politico in Italia* (Rome: Carocci editore, 2007), p. 46.
173 R. Rossanda, *L'album di famiglia* (1978), http://www.archivio900.it/it/articoli/art.aspx?id=4048, accessed on 28 April 2014.
174 Movimento Sociale Italiano, 'Il programma del M.S.I. 1979. Camera, Senato, Europa', *Fondazione Ugo Spirito*, Rome, Fondo movimento sociale italiano. Busta 1. Materiale di propaganda elettorale 1948–1983.
175 M. Panella, 'L'unica opposizione', (1976), in: M. Pannella ed., *Scritti e discorsi 1959–1980* (Milan: Gammalibri, 1982), pp. 300–313, on p. 302.
176 M. Panella, 'Esarchia, Partito radicale, informazione' (1978) in: Pannella, *Scritti e discorsi*, pp. 458–462, on p. 458.
177 Ginsborg, *Italy and its Discontents*, p.174. See also: M. Tarchi, 'Italy: A Country of Many Populisms', in: Albertazzi and McDonnel, *Twenty First Century Populism*, pp. 84–99; Grillo Di Cortona, *Dalla Prima alla Seconda Repubblica*, pp. 60–61;
178 E. Cohen, 'L'ombre portée de Mai '68 en politique: démocratie et participation', *Vingtième siècle. Revue d'histoire*, vol. 98 (2009), pp. 19–28, on p. 24.
179 V. Giscard d'Estaing, *La démocratie française* (Paris: Fayard, 1976), p. 151.
180 See also: Berstein, *Histoire du Gaullisme*, pp. 422–424.
181 J. Chirac, 'L'action politique', in: J. Chirac ed., *Discours pour la France à l'heure du choix. La lueur de l'espérance. Réflexions du soir pour le matin* (Paris: Éditions Stock, 1978), pp. 27–31, on p. 28.

182 J. Chirac, 'Les Buts' (1976), in: Chirac, *Discours pour la France*, pp. 15–26.
183 Chirac, *La Bataille de France*, p. 19.
184 Bösch, 'Die Krise als Chance', esp. pp. 303–305. On the reform of the party, see also: Kleinman, *Geschichte der CDU*, pp. 423–425.
185 Granieri, 'Politics in C Minor', p. 31; Cole, 'Political Leadership in Western Europe: Helmut Kohl in Comparative Perspective', p. 123.
186 H. Kohl, 'Aufbruch in die Zukunft' (1973), in: H. Kohl ed., *Der Kurs der CDU* (Stuttgart: Deutsche Verlags-Anstalt GmbH, 1993), pp. 37–55, on p. 45.
187 CDU, *Grundsatzprogramm "Freiheit, Solidarität, Gerechtigkeit"* 26. Bundesparteitag 23.-25. Oktober 1978 Ludwigshafen (1978), p. 155. Found on: http://www.kas.de/upload/themen/programmatik_der_cdu/programme/1978_Ludwigshafen_Grundsatzprogramm-Freiheit-Solidaritaet-Ger.pdf, accessed on 9 June 2015.
188 Ginsborg, *Italy and its Discontents*, p. 121.
189 See, also: Scoppola, *La Repubblica dei partiti*, p. 423.
190 F. Piccoli, 'Un grande partito di popolo per una rinnovata iniziativa di pace, di libertà e di solidarietà sociale. Relazione del Segretario Politico al XV Congresso Nazionale' (1982), in: D.C., *Atti del 15 Congresso nazionale della Democrazia cristiana, Roma 2–5 Maggio 1982* (Rome: Edizione Cinque Lune, 1982), pp. 59–84, on p. 72.
191 Grillo di Cortona, *Dalla Prima alla Seconda Repubblica*, pp. 62–65; Cotturi, 'Moro e la transizione interrotta', p. 504; Paggi, 'Violenza e democrazia nella storia della Repubblica', p. 949.
192 A. Moro, 'Garanzia e limiti di una politica' (1978), in: Moro, *Scritti e discorsi. Vol.VI*, pp. 3781–3796, on p. 3785; p. 3794.
193 Lupo, *Partito e antipartito*, p. 9.
194 M. Capanna, *Monopoli, DC, Compromesso Storico* (Milan: Mazzotta editore, 1975), p. 257.
195 PCI, 'La proposta di alternative per il cambiamento', p. 126.
196 G. Napolitano, 'I problemi del partito nell'attuale fase politica' (1981), in: G. Napolitano and E. Berlinguer ed., *Partito di massa negli anni ottanta. I problemi del partito al comitato centrale del PCI 7–8 gennaio 1981* (Rome: Editori Riuniti, 1981), pp. 7–46, on p. 13.
197 Moro, *Per un'iniziativa politica*, p. 127. See also: Malgeri, *L'Italia democristiana*, p. 112.
198 C. De Mita, 'Per la democrazia nella trasformazione', (1982), in: D.C., *Atti del 15 Congresso nazionale*, pp. 832–882, on p. 862.
199 D. Hine, 'Italian political reform in comparative perspective', in: S. Gundle and S. Parker eds., *The New Italian Republic. From the Fall of the Berlin Wall to Berlusconi* (London: Routledge 1996), pp. 311–325.
200 S. Köppel, 'Italy's Constitutional Odyssey. Failed Attempts at Constitutional Reform in the 1980s and 1990s', in: L. Risso and M. Boria eds., *Politics and Culture in Post-War Italy* (Newcastle: Cambridge Scholars Press, 2006) 223–236.
201 Degli'Innocenti, *Storia del PSI*, p. 402; S. Colarizi and M. Gervasoni, *La cruna dell'ago. Craxi, il partito socialista e la crisi della repubblica* (Bari: Laterza, 2005).
202 Craxi, *L'alternativa dei socialisti*, p. 83.
203 Craxi, *Una responsabilità democratica*, p. 31.
204 See the contributions in: PSI, *Una costituzione per governare. La "grande riforma": proposta dai socialisti* (Venice: Marsilio editori, 1981).
205 Ginsborg, *Italy and its Discontents*, p.148.
206 De Mita, 'Per la democracia nella trasformazione', p. 846.
207 PCI, 'La proposta di alternative per il cambiamento', p. 127.

208 Colarizi and Gervasoni, *La cruna dell'ago*, p. 163. See also: Di Scala, *Renewing Italian Socialism*, p. 223; Ginsborg, *Italy and its Discontents*, p. 173.
209 Scoppola, *La repubblica dei partiti*, p. 430.
210 PCI, 'La proposta di alternative per il cambiamento', p. 136.
211 Craxi, *L'alternativa dei socialisti*, pp. 82–83.
212 P. Farneti, 'Il Sistema dei partiti dalla costituzione a oggi', in: G. Amato ed., *Attualità e attuazione della costituzione* (Bari: Laterza, 1979), pp. 3–15, pp. 9–11.
213 A. Forlani, 'Dichiarazione d'intenti politico-programmatici', (1982), in: D.C., *Atti del 15 Congresso nazionale*, pp. 818–823, on pp. 818–819.
214 Malgeri, *L'Italia democristiana*, p. 111.
215 Della Porta, *Social Movements, Political Violence and the State*, p. 33.

Conclusion

The atmosphere of crisis plaguing political debates today is related to the process through which political actors shaped their understanding of democracy in the first decades after the Second World War. This relationship between present and past connects the divergent historiographies of democracy since the *Tendenzwende* of the 1970s, in which scholars disagree on whether we can speak of a 'victory' by one model of democracy or a loss of consensus on the principles of democracy.[1] Understanding this nexus requires a long-term historical perspective.

The Second World War was a watershed in the history of democracy, and democracy indeed emerged 'transformed' from the struggle with fascism.[2] In the immediate aftermath of the war, all actors claimed to be democratic, even those who were reluctant to accept the new rules, because the democratic ideal received such overwhelming support from the political elites and became the dominant paradigm. Postwar democracy also saw the rise of new political parties with an inter-class appeal, most notably the Christian Democrats,[3] whereas the communists shed some of their pre-war militancy. The Italian and French communist parties tried to become 'new' parties that accepted the rules of political pluralism.[4] Yet these attempts to break with the weaknesses of interwar democracy could not conceal the fact that 'transforming democracy' was far from a consensual and harmonious enterprise. Various readings of the rise of fascism, combined with the mutual distrust instilled by the Cold War, led politicians to seek different avenues to 'transform' democracy; they were deeply divided on the question of capitalism, on how representative institutions should respond to popular sovereignty, and on the relationship between parties and democracy. So whereas there was nominally an agreement, expressed in postwar constitutions, that postwar democracies should unite social security with individual liberties and parliamentary control with a stable executive, there was no agreement at all on how these ideals should be achieved—and which ideal should take priority; these issues were a matter of intense dispute in the first fifteen years after the war.

The different ideas on how to arrive at shared democratic ideals ran roughly parallel with the divisions between the Left on the one hand and

Christian Democrats and Gaullists on the other. The most vocal supporters of popular sovereignty and civic participation were traditionally found on the Left.[5] The Left felt democracy should be representative but that a powerful parliament that represented the people need not be complemented by non-elected intermediate institutions. Conservatives were often much warier of popular sovereignty. They paid tribute to the notion that all state power derived from the people but argued at the same time that this power should be subject to strong checks and balances because the interwar years had shown how volatile the will of the people could be. Additionally, both the communist and the non-communist Left questioned—or, to be more precise, often flatly rejected—the relationship between democracy and capitalism. Indeed, to secure German democracy, Kurt Schumacher argued that it was his task to ensure the country would be 'in its economy socialist and in its politics democratic'.[6] The Christian Democrats were also committed to socioeconomic reforms, but they felt it was more democratic to restrict, rather than to expand, state power.[7] Democracy had to be both politically and economically 'liberal', meaning it had to be capitalist. The sweeping social reforms advocated by the Left required a measure of state intervention that Christian Democrats regarded as dangerously close to dictatorial. Indeed, as Adenauer remarked in reference to the SPD, '[E]verywhere, socialism . . . leads to a total state as it concentrates power in the hands of a few'.[8]

These ideological differences were reflected in Italy and West Germany's constitutions, which safeguarded the protection of individual liberties and provided for extensive socioeconomic reforms. In the long run, the left-wing opposition accused the Christian Democrats of breaching the spirit of the postwar settlement by neglecting to bring the full scope of constitutionally arranged socioeconomic reforms to fruition. But aside from these disputes over the constitution's interpretation, the very existence of these constitutions based on compromise between ideologically diverse factions contributed to the institutional resilience demonstrated by both Italy and West Germany. Indeed, the Left and Christian Democrats' shared allegiance to the constitution not only provided a lowest common denominator in West Germany but did so in Italy as well. There, the communists felt the Italian state had retained some of its fascist characteristics, but they took care not to let this criticism detract from their support for the constitution, which they continued to cherish.[9] From this perspective, the triumph of the French parties over De Gaulle in 1946 was a Pyrrhic victory as it did not foster a broad cross-party consensus on the political outline of postwar France. Instead, the chance to build a shared democratic framework failed to materialize, and institutional instability was the inevitable result.

These observations provide a paradoxical picture of democracy in the 1950s. With hindsight, democracy may have been much less stable than it appears to have been. Many politicians found it a problematic ideal, difficult to implement in practice and seemingly under constant threat by forces aiming to abuse or even overthrow the postwar settlement. Governments in all three states adapted the electoral system to their own advantage in the early 1950s, with the aim of 'protecting' or 'stabilizing' democracy. The exclusion of the Left from government in Italy and West Germany, and the antagonism between the Third Force and the Gaullists and communists in France, deprived all the postwar settlements of legitimacy. These settlements became the centre of a deeply ideological debate on what democracy was and what conditions it required. This not only casts doubt on the idea that there was a 'deep longing for normality' and a rejection of ideology in the wake of the war[10] but also on portrayals of the 1950s as the nexus of an 'exceptional period' in which leaders arrived at a single definition of democracy.[11]

The paradox is that the competing narratives defining democracy, as proposed by the major socialist, communist, Gaullist and Christian Democratic parties, and the heated debate these sparked, also contributed to democracy's deeper entrenchment. By continuously disputing democratic notions and using democratic principles to contest and establish political legitimacy, the various political actors kept each other in balance. There proved to be certain limits to the indeterminate range of meanings democracy could have, which also restricted the scope of action that political actors could claim to be democratic. This not only led to a vigorous debate on what counted as 'democratic', but more crucially it guaranteed a certain level of democratic accountability when matters got out of hand and new democratic structures were put to the test. This even holds true in the case of Italy, as evidenced by the annulment of the Scelba laws enacted by the DC in the 1950s, the motives for the PSI's break with the communists after 1956, and the government's legitimization of the neo-fascists in 1960—a move that badly backfired. The balance between various competing democratic paradigms was even evident in the most acute crises, such as in France in 1958, when an army coup seemed a real possibility. Not only was a coup averted, but even in the midst of the crisis the 'republican' parties were able to force De Gaulle to at least partially play by their rules and commit to parliamentary democratic principles. As a result, De Gaulle became the last prime minister of the Fourth Republic that he had always despised and even made an effort to present the Fifth Republic as a parliamentary regime.[12]

The fall of the Fourth Republic and the establishment of the Fifth was not an example of French exceptionalism; it conformed to a general trend in which stark postwar divisions were gradually bridged from the turn of the 1960s onwards. This trend in turn paved the way for coalition governments composed of forces that had previously denied each other's democratic credentials.[13] The Fifth Republic was presented as a compromise between a presidential and parliamentary regime and hence as the resolution of perpetual debates between executive and legislative conceptions of democracy.[14] This was typical of how paradigms of postwar democracy emerged, broadly endorsed by political elites and accelerated by rapid socioeconomic changes and diminishing Cold War tensions. In West Germany and Italy, the antagonism between left-wing opposition and Christian Democratic-led governments melted away partly because of economic growth that eased social inequalities and made the 1960s the finest hour of the Western European middle class[15] but also partly because the Christian Democrats had added social security and state intervention in the economy to their repertoire,[16] whereas socialists universally endorsed individual liberties. The clearest example of the interrelationship between these factors remains the long process of centre-Left coalition building in Italy, which coincided with the *boom economico* of 1958 to 1963.[17] However, it took more than a decade after the war's end to even begin this process, and its ultimate success cannot hide the deep tensions that marked the intervening years when the nature of democracy's postwar transformation—and in France, even the postwar constitution—were the topic of heated debate.

The turn of the 1960s marked the moment when the debate on democracy in Italy diverged ever more widely from France and West Germany. At that time, France and West Germany bridged the main divides that had typified the postwar period. The SPD and the Christian Democrats buried the hatchet on the relationship among democracy and the economy, foreign policy and civic participation, whereas the clashes between Gaullist and anti-Gaullists over the separation of powers lost their sharpest edges. In Italy, the two main rifts in the debate—between 'party' and 'anti-party' on the one hand and between communists and Christian Democrats on the other—remained unresolved in the early 1960s despite the formation of a DC–socialist coalition government and the first steps towards integrating the communists into the party system. Not only was rapprochement between the communists and Christian Democrats too piecemeal to bring about true reform of Italian democracy, but it even made matters worse by tightening the political parties' stranglehold on the political scene.

Italy's centre-Left coalition of the early 1960s can be evaluated from many perspectives; an angle frequently discussed is its failure to enact socioeconomic reforms.[18] However, the centre-Left stood at the cradle of the First Republic's later crisis in a much more fundamental sense.[19] As the 1960s wore on and mainstream political parties increasingly viewed alternative means of political participation as antagonistic to democracy, the centre-Left coalition reinforced the political elites' tendency to take a paternalistic stance towards ordinary citizens.[20] DC Party Secretary Mariano Rumor exemplified this in a speech to the DC party congress in 1967. He claimed that the central problem of Italian democracy was the lack of faith in the political party system, which had led to a gap between the *paese reale* and *paese legale*. He called upon political elites to combat this trend but said the real problem lay 'not in political institutions, but in how political parties are linked to society. We have to acknowledge that civic development has not kept pace with economic development. We are all responsible for this and in this regard everyone, the parties first and foremost, has to make a commitment'.[21] It was this patronizing stance towards civic involvement combined with institutional weakness that bred distrust among citizens and widened the gap between state and society.[22]

Even as the Italian debate took on a dramatic tone reflecting an ongoing crisis in the relationship between the state and citizens, a broader development was afoot in Italy too, whereby political elites were increasingly coalescing on the meaning of democracy. This coalescence first became visible at the turn of the 1960s in the marginalization of the political fringes, as Italy's MSI was permanently sidelined from government[23] and the Poujadists in France faded away with the fall of the Fourth Republic. There was an unmistakeable resistance to the growing uniformity in politics, as evidenced in the positions taken by the PSU, the PSIUP and political actors like Mitterrand and Mendès France and in the communists' resistance to 'bourgeois democracy', although the latter example was at best a formal stance. The growing consensus described here was certainly not as obvious to contemporaries as it appears in retrospect, but from a long-term perspective, it is clear that whatever resistance there was proved too weak to prevent the entrenchment of cross-ideological agreement on democracy.

Paradoxically, the trend towards consensus among political elites was buttressed by the disruptive events of 1968 and 1973. The extra-parliamentary protests of the late 1960s can be seen as a generational revolt, and the students' conceptions of democracy were in some respects a radical form of 'co-decision' as propagated by the Left after the war. But these protests were also undeniably 'a crisis of postwar political culture'. The protests were targeted at the very tendency of political elites to seek a uniform paradigm of democracy; protest leaders claimed that the traditional parties' political model was not democratic at all.[24] Indeed, as one German student noted at the time that what the students did was 'to turn the claim of democracy *against* the organized society'—the vision of democracy endorsed by the ruling Christian Democrats. The French and Italian variants of the protest movement did the same.[25] Despite these attacks, the main political parties closed ranks in their commitment to capitalist representative party democracy. The more radical the resistance to the political class became, the more determined the parties seemed to grow in their insistence that democracy was a matter for professional politicians only. This disparity was most glaring in Italy. This country had the most varied array of social movement activism, but comparatively speaking these movements had the least impact on political parties' notions of democracy.[26]

The economic downturn after 1973 helped foster a stronger consensus among political elites by upsetting the balance in the conceptual struggle between social equality and individual liberty. Politics veered to the right as virtually every party stressed individual liberty and regarded state intervention with increased suspicion.[27] Obviously, this consensus was partly due to the delegitimization of left-wing, Keynesian policies, regardless of whether these were part of the demise of social democracy.[28] But the decoupling of democracy from social equality was also evident in the way neo-Gaullists opportunistically alternated between liberal and state interventionist positions and in the makeover of Christian Democrats, who in West Germany became a typical centre-Right party in favour of small government[29] and in Italy ultimately disintegrated as a large part of their electoral base flocked to the 'business-firm party' *Forza Italia*.[30]

Although Keynesian politics lost its primacy, the change in the democratic paradigm after the 1973 oil crisis cannot be characterized as a complete overhaul. Some aspects of the new model were nothing new; wariness of state intervention as a threat to individual freedom and democracy had been a staple of the Christian Democrats' postwar ideological diet. Adenauer stated in 1948 that 'personal freedom is and remains the highest value of the people . . . when we refuse to accept a state that is too powerful and consequently an enemy of individuals, we also turn against, and will continue to turn against, *collectivism* in whatever form, because it is a bigger enemy of personal freedom than anything else'.[31] The economic downturn brought these dormant ideas to the surface, and the Left had little choice but to concur with the tendency to view the state with suspicion and to champion individual liberty. In short, the economic crisis upset the precarious balance between social equality and individual liberty that had been established in the debate on democracy during *les trente glorieuses*.

Whereas it should not be interpreted as a triumph or a sign of the postwar democratic model's unequivocal success, the unified political reaction to 1968 and 1973 firmly anchored the consensus between the main ideological currents on the meaning of democracy. In West Germany and France, the mainstream parties toned down their traditional differences concerning democracy, whereas in Italy these differences evaporated altogether when the First Republic fell in the early 1990s. The reasons for this radical change in Italy were manifold, and a few were linked to developments outside the 'republic of the parties', but most stemmed from the political elites' failure to adapt the principles of Italian democracy to changes in Italian society.[32] This has rekindled the discontent with the principles of postwar democracy that had died down under the First Republic.[33] The result is a never-ending debate in which the principles of Italian democracy are renegotiated and reconfigured, without any significant agreement on how democracy should be reformed. Assuming that disagreement on the renewal of political institutions is an intrinsic part of democratic debate, this might seem a positive development as the debate on democracy in Italy is much more vital and vibrant than elsewhere. In a more realistic light, however, this infinite debate testifies only to the gravity of the Italian crisis, which after the fall of the First Republic, is now fuelled by the failure to make good on the promises of a Second Republic.[34]

Although Italy stands out as a rather disheartening example, the country is still part of a general trend that provides increasing room to question the democratic substance of the current debate between the mainstream political parties, given its conformity and lack of reform mindedness.[35] In other words, the consensus among the traditional parties has opened up ideological space for new parties that fault political elites for their 'sameness' and their tendency to dismiss ideas from outside the political mainstream as anti-democratic. These criticisms contain a grain of truth in the sense that the 'rules of the game' are an important aspect, and perhaps even the most important aspect, of any political debate. These new voices are often labelled 'populist', mostly of a right-wing variety.[36] There is growing academic interest in them and their relationship with democracy. Many new studies describe how these parties juxtapose their commitment to the will of the people with what Jan-Werner Müller has called the 'constrained civilian democratic administrative statehood' of postwar liberal democracies.[37] Whereas this is doubtlessly one of their main characteristics, these assessments have so far been made mostly by political scientists rather than by historians, so it is still unclear where these parties stand on historical expressions of discontent towards the political elites' consensus on the meaning of democracy in postwar Europe.

It is hard to disagree with Müller's argument that the 'populist' concepts of alternative parties have not yet significantly affected the shape of political institutions, even if they are slowly whittling away at the principles that have underpinned these institutions.[38] Their politics are at times far from coherent, realistic, or desirable, but this should not stop historians from seeing them as the part of the 'struggle between contesting models of democracy, including ideologies of the left and right which one might not automatically associate with democracy'.[39] At the level of political rhetoric, the current debate shows many similarities with the way political actors at the height of the Cold War vilified each other for being anti-democrats who should be excluded from any kind of government. At the level of political policy, however, these similarities fade away. This is because the new parties' desire to transform democracy is not motivated by the faults of democracy in the interwar period but rather by the way postwar political elites have shaped the meaning of democracy since 1945. Hence, the new parties attack the core features of the democratic paradigm now shared by the main political parties. They question the principle of representation and party democracy, the distance between political elites and citizens, and the primacy of rule of law rather than popular sovereignty in democracy. As Dan Stone recently argued, these parties also accuse the political elites of giving economics priority over politics and hollowing out social security arrangements in the name of individual liberty.[40] In this sense, these new movements are not solely a sign of discontent with the consensus model but also an attempt to 're-ideologize' the debate on democracy and to reconfigure democracy's meaning.

In a long-term perspective, the history of democracy is indeed the history of competing democratic paradigms in which no end of ideology can ever be proclaimed. The meaning and principles of democracy were deeply contested throughout the postwar era, notwithstanding a broad common tribute to the democratic ideal and an increased consensus among the major political parties. If one strips this postwar debate down to its bare essence, the continuing attempts to reconfigure democracy's meaning actually emerge as one of its most distinctive characteristics, and the meaning of democracy simply boils down to the possibility of renegotiating the meaning of democracy. The attempt to continuously readjust has become obscured by growing agreement among political elites over the past several decades, although the resistance to this trend has demonstrated that democracy is a perpetual problem that requires ever-changing solutions and new ideas. Or, as the prominent Christian Democrat Guido Gonella remarked in the immediate aftermath of the Second World War, 'Democracy is not a virtue in itself, but it is the *possibility* of virtue'.[41]

Notes

1. Vinen, *History in Fragments*, p. 404, asserts that the consensus 'was even more secure from the 1970s onwards'. Müller contends that the challenges of 1968 and neoliberalism did not significantly affect the dominant understanding of democracy in Western Europe, which was exported to the East after 1989: Müller, *Contesting Democracy*, ch. 6. Cf: Stone, *Goodbye to All That?*; Conway. 'The Rise and Fall'.
2. Maier, 'Democracy after the French Revolution', p. 138; Dunn, *Setting the People Free*, p. 156; Mazower, *Dark Continent*, p. 287.
3. E. Lamberts, 'Christian Democrats and the Constitutional State in Western Europe 1945–1995', in: T. Kselman and J.A. Buttigieg eds., *European Christian Democracy. Historical Legacies and Comparative Perspectives* (Notre Dame: University of Notre Dame Press, 2003), pp. 121–137.
4. Judt, *Postwar*, p. 47.
5. Eley, *Forging Democracy*, pp. 5–7.
6. Schumacher, 'Aufgaben und Ziele der deutsche Sozialdemokratie', p. 86.
7. Conway, 'The Age of Christian Democracy'.
8. Adenauer, 'Wahlrede bei einer CDU/CSU Kundgebung am Heidelberger Scloβ', p. 147.
9. Paggi, 'Violenza e democrazia nella storia della repubblica', p. 951.
10. As argued by: Mazower, *Dark Continent*, p. 291.
11. Conway, 'The Rise and Fall', p. 88.
12. Berstein, *Histoire du Gaullisme*, pp. 216–217.
13. The establishment of the Fifth Republic was indeed seen as an attempt to establish consensus: Vinen, *History in Fragments*, p. 360. The governments led by De Gaulle in the period from 1958 to 1962 are said to have resembled governments of national unity, see: Berstein, *Histoire du Gaullisme*, p. 220.
14. Jennings, *Revolution and the Republic*, p. 568.
15. Conway, 'The Rise and Fall', pp. 80–81.
16. Kleinmann, *Geschichte der CDU*, p. 171; Roggi, 'L'impegno della Dc nella storia italiana', pp. 220–225.
17. Giovagnoli, *Il partito italiano*, p. 109.
18. Crainz, *Storia del miracolo italiano*, pp. 223 ff.
19. Tranfalgia, 'Parlamento, partiti e società civile', p. 827; Giovagnoli, *Il partito italiano*, p. 121; Orsina, 'The Republic after Berlusconi, p. 78.
20. Orsina, *Il Berlusconismo nella storia d'Italia*, ch. 2.

21 Rumor, 'Iniziativa dei democratici Cristiani per il rinnovamento dello Stato', p. 424.
22 Orsina, *Il Berlusconismo nella storia d'Italia*, ch. 2–3
23 Ferraresi, *Minacce alla democrazia*, p. 57.
24 Eley, *Forging Democracy*, p. 407.
25 Bergmann, Dutschke, Lefèvre and Rabehl, *Rebellion der Studenten*, p. 174. My emphasis.
26 Horn, *The Spirit of '68*, p. 233.
27 Berger, 'Democracy and Social Democracy', p. 29.
28 T. Judt, *Ill fares the land* (New York: Penguin Press, 2010).
29 Granieri, 'Politics in C Minor', p. 31.
30 F. Raniolo, 'Forza Italia: A Leader with a Party', *South European Society and Politics*, vol.11 no.3–4 (2006) pp. 439–455, p. 439.
31 Adenauer, 'Eine Hoffnung für Europa', p. 124.
32 G. Crainz, *Il paese reale. Dall'assassino di Moro all'Italia di oggi* (Rome: Donzelli editore, 2012), pp. 330–331.
33 Capozzi, 'La polemica antipartitocratica'; Orsina, *Il Berlusconismo nella storia d'Italia*.
34 M.J. Bull, 'The Italian Transition that Never Was', *Modern Italy*, vol. 17 no. 1 (2012), pp. 103–118
35 M. Lazar, 'Testing Italian Democracy', *Comparative European Politics*, vol. 11 no. 3 (2013), pp. 317–336.
36 Even though that is not necessarily the case, see for instance: F. Decker, 'Germany: Right Wing Populist Failures and Left-wing Successes', in: Albertazzi, *Twenty-first Century Populism*, pp. 119–134.
37 J.-W. Müller, 'Research Note: The Triumph of What (if Anything)? Rethinking Political Ideologies and Political Institutions in Twentieth Century Europe', *Journal of Political Ideologies*, vol. 14, no. 2 (2009), pp. 211–226, on p. 222. M. Canovan, 'Taking Politics to the People: Populism as the Ideology of Democracy', in Y. Mény and Y. Surel eds., *Democracies and the Populist Challenge* (Basingstoke: Palgrave McMillan, 2002), pp. 25–44; M. Canovan, 'Trust the People? Populism and the Two Faces of Democracy', *Political Studies*, vol. 47, no. 1 (1999), pp. 2–16.
38 Müller, 'Research note'.
39 Conway, 'The Rise and Fall of Europe's Democratic Age', p. 88.
40 Stone, *Goodbye to All of That*, ch. 5, ch. 7; C. Mudde, *Populist Radical Right Parties in Europe* (Cambridge: Cambridge University Press, 2012), ch. 6; P. Mair, 'Populist Democracy vs Party Democracy, in: Mény and Surel eds., *Democracies and the Populist Challenge*, pp. 81–98, on p. 91.
41 Gonella, 'La DC per la nuova costituzione', p. 503. Italics in original.

References

Primary Sources

Newspapers

Fronte dell'Uomo Qualunque
Lotta Continua

Archives

Archivio del Partito Comunista Italiano, Istituto Gramsci, Rome, Italy
Archivio del Movimento Sociale Italiano, Fondazione Ugo Spirito e Renzo di Felice, Rome, Italy
International Institute of Social History, Amsterdam, the Netherlands

Electronic sources

A New Form of Organization in the Factories. Retrieved from: http://edocs.lib.sfu.ca/projects/mai68/pdfs/A_New_Form_of_Organization_in_the_Factories.pdf. Accessed on 4-11-2013.

Adenauer, K., 'Rede zum Programm der CDU' (1946). Retrieved from: http://www.kas.de/upload/ACDP/CDU/Reden/1946-03-06-Rede-Neheim-Huesten.pdf. Accessed on 30 July 2014.

Barzel, R., 'Regierungsprogramm CDU 1972. Wir bauen der Fortschritt auf Stabilität' (1972). Retrieved from: http://www.kas.de/upload/ACDP/CDU/Programme_Bundestag/1972_Regierungsprogramm_Wir-bauen-den-Fortschritt-auf-Stabilitaet.pdf. Accessed on 13 November 2013.

CDU, *Kölner Leitsätze. Vorläufiger Entwurf zu einem Programm der Christlicher Demokraten Deutschlands* (1945), Retrieved from: http://www.kas.de/upload/bilder/cdu_goslar1950/koelner_leitsaetze.pdf. Accessed on 8 June 2015.

CDU, *Ahlener Programm der CDU für die Britische Zone* (1947). Retrieved from: http://www.kas.de/upload/themen/programmatik_der_cdu/programme/1947_Ahlener-Programm.pdf. Accessed on 25 April 2013.

CDU, *Hamburger Programm* (1953). Retrieved from: http://www.kas.de/upload/ACDP/CDU/Programme_Bundestag/1953_Hamburger-Programm.pdf. Accessed on 30 July 2015.

CDU, *Grundsatzprogramm "Freiheit, Solidarität, Gerechtigkeit" 26. Bundesparteitag 23.-25. Oktober 1978 Ludwigshafen* (1978). Retrieved from: http://www.kas.de/upload/themen/programmatik_der_cdu/programme/1978_Ludwigshafen_Grundsatzprogramm-Freiheit-Solidaritaet-Ger.pdf. Accessed on 9 June 2015.

Claris, P. and La Ruche Ouvrière, 'L'autogestion, l'état et la révolution'. *Supplément noir et rouge, no. 41* (1968). Retrieved from: http://edocs.lib.sfu.ca/cgi-bin/Mai68?Display=3485, Accessed on 5-11-2013.
Die Grünen, *Das Bundesprogramm* (1980). Retrieved from: https://www.boell.de/sites/default/files/assets/boell.de/images/download_de/publikationen/1980_001_Grundsatzprogramm_Die_Gruenen.pdf. Accessed on 10 June 2015.
Dutschke, R., Das Sich-Verweigern erfordert Guerilla-Mentalität (1967). Retrieved from: http://glasnost.de/hist/apo/67dutschke.html, Accessed on 5 November 2013.
FDP, *Bremerplatform* (1949). Retrieved from: http://ia700405.us.archive.org/10/items/BremerPlattform/1949_Bremer_Plattform.pdf. Accessed on 24 April 2013.
FDP, *Freiburger Thesen zur Gesellschaftspolitik der Freien Demokratischen Partei* (1971). Retrieved from: http://www.freiheit.org/files/288/1971_Freiburger_Thesen.pdf. Accessed on 7 November 2013.
La Voie, *Elections bourgeoises ou action révolutionnaire* (1968). Retrieved from: http://edocs.lib.sfu.ca/projects/mai68/pdfs/POST_May_Perspectives.pdf. Accessed on 4-11-2013.
Militants des comités d'action Sorbonne, Vincennes, Nanterre, *Apres mai 1968 les plans de la bourgeoisie et le mouvement révolutionnaire* (1969). Retrieved from: http://edocs.lib.sfu.ca/cgi-bin/Mai68?Display=1268, Accessed on 4-11-2013.
Mitterrand, F., *Réponse au discours d'investiture du général de Gaulle* (1958). Retrieved from: http://www2.assemblee-nationale.fr/decouvrir-l-assemblee/histoire/grands-moments-d-eloquence/francois-mitterrand-1958-reponse-au-discours-d-investiture-du-general-de-gaulle-1er-juin-1958, Accessed on 5 March 2015.
PSU, *Tribune Socialiste, no. 371* (1968). Retrieved from: http://edocs.lib.sfu.ca/cgi-bin/Mai68?Display=3385, Accessed on 30 June 2015.
Reynaud, P., *Débat de censure* (1962). Retrieved from: http://www2.assemblee-nationale.fr/decouvrir-l-assemblee/histoire/grands-moments-d-eloquence/paul-reynaud-georges-pompidou-1962-debat-de-censure-4-octobre-1962, Accessed on 10 June 2015.
Rossanda, R., *L'album di famiglia* (1978). Retrieved from: http://www.archivio900.it/it/articoli/art.aspx?id=4048, Accessed on 28 April2014.
Scheel, W., 'Zu den Notstandgesetze' (1968). Retrieved from: http://chronik.fnst.de/files/77/Scheel-Notstandgesetze_1.pdf. Accessed on 30 July 2015.
SDP, *Politische Leitsätze* (1946). Retrieved from: http://germanhistorydocs.ghisdc.org/pdf/deu/Parties%20WZ%202%20GER.pdf. Accessed on 24 April 2013.
SPD, *Wahlaufruf. Für ein freies Deutschland in einem neues Europa* (1949). Retrieved on: http://library.fes.de/spdpd/1949/490801-sondervers.pdf. Accessed on 18 August 2015.
SPD, *Grundsatzprogramm der Sozialdemokratische Partei Deutschlands* (1959) Retrieved on: http://library.fes.de/pdf-files/bibliothek/retro-scans/fa-57721.pdf. Accessed on 2 September 2015.
SPD, *Grundsatzprogramm der Sozialdemokratische Partei Deutschlands* (Berlin, 1989). Retrieved from: http://library.fes.de/pdf-files/bibliothek/retro-scans/fa90-00398.pdf. Accessed on 10 June 2015.

Published Sources

Adenauer, K., 'Die Demokratie ist für uns eine Weltanschauung: Grundsatzrede im Nordwestdeutschen Rundfunk über das Programm der CDU' (1946), in: Adenauer, *Die Demokratie ist für uns eine Weltanschauung*, pp. 1–9.
———, 'Rede in der Aula der Universität zu Köln' (1946), in: Adenauer, *Reden*, pp. 82–106.
———, 'Zeigt daβ Ihr auf dem Wege der politische Reife seid: Wahlkampfrede in Pulheim bei Köln' (1946), in: Adenauer, *Die Demokratie ist für uns eine Weltanschauung*, pp. 10–26.

———, 'Eine Hoffnung für Europa: Eröffnungsrede zum 2: Parteitag der CDU der Britischen Zone in Recklinghausen' (1948), in: Adenauer, *Reden*, pp. 122–131.
———, 'Erste Regierungserklärung von Bundeskanzler Adenauer' (1949), in: Adenauer, *Reden*, pp. 153–169.
———, 'Wahlrede bei einer CDU/CSU Kundgebung um Heidelberger Schloß' (1949), in: Adenauer, *Reden*, pp. 137–149.
———, 'Regierungserklärung vor dem Deutschen Bundestag' (1950), in: Adenauer, *Reden*, pp. 193–200.
———, 'Mitbestimmung' (1951), in: Adenauer, *Bundestagsreden*, pp. 79–83.
———, 'Ansprache vor dem Bundesparteiausschuß der CDU' (1952), in: Adenauer, *Reden*, pp. 263–280.
———, 'Wahlrede auf einer Großkundgebung in Regensburg' (1961), in: Adenauer, *Reden*, pp. 413–423.
———, 'Abschiedsansprache auf der Sondersitzung des Deutschen Bundestages' (1963), in: Adenauer, *Bundestagsreden*, pp. 453–456.
———, *Bundestagsreden* (Bonn: AZ Studio, 1972).
———, *Reden 1917-1967: Eine Auswahl* (Stuttgart: Deutsche Verlags-Anstalt, 1986).
———, *Die Demokratie ist für uns eine Weltanschauung. Reden und Gespräche 1946-1967* (Bonn: Konrad Adenauer Stiftung, 1998).
Aron, R., *Le grand schisme* (Paris: Gallimard, 1948).
Barre, R., *Une politique pour l'avenir* (Paris: Plon, 1981).
———, *La crise des politiques économiques et sociales et l'avenir des démocraties industrielles* (Rome: Banco di Roma, 1983).
———, *Réflexions pour demain* (Paris: Hachette, 1984).
Basso, L., 'Sul progetto di Costituzione della Repubblica' (1947), in: Basso, *In difesa della democrazia*, pp. 19–24.
———, *Due totalitarismi: Fascismo e democrazia cristiana* (Milan: Garzanti, 1951).
———, 'Sulla comunicazione del governo' (1963), in: Basso, *In difesa della democrazia*, pp. 98–107.
———, *In difesa della democrazia e della costituzione: Scritti scelti* (Milan: Edizioni punto rosso, 2009).
Bergmann, U., R. Dutschke, W. Lefèvre and B. Rabehl, *Rebellion der Studenten oder die neue Opposition* (Berlin: Rowolt, 1968).
Berlinguer, E., *Per un governo di svolta democratica: Il testo integrale del rapporto tenuto al XIII Congresso nazionale del Partito comunista italiano* (Rome: Editori Riuniti, 1972).
———, 'Riflessione sull'Italia dopo i fatti di Cile' (1973), in: E. Berlinguer, *La crisi italiana*, pp. 45–75.
———, 'Costruire un'Europa nuova' (1974), in: E. Berlinguer, *La "Questione Comunista" 1969-1976* (Rome: Editori Riuniti, 1976), pp. 675–682.
———, *L'Italia di oggi ha bisogno dei comunisti: Per essere governata, risanata, rigenerata: Il discorso di Enrico Berlinguer alla Camera dei Deputati, 20/2/1976* (Rome: Stabilimento grafico editoriale fratelli Spada, 1976).
———, *Austerità: Occasione per trasformare Italia: Le conclusioni al convegno degli intellettuali (Roma, 15-1-'77) e alla assemblea degli operai comunisti (Milano, 30-1-'77)* (Rome: Editori Riuniti, 1977).
———, 'La crisi della politica di solidarietà' (1979), in: Berlinguer, *La crisi italiana*, pp. 125–129.
———, *La nostra lotta dall'opposizione verso il governo* (Rome: Editori Riuniti, 1979).
———, 'Ruolo ed iniziativa del Pci per una nuova fase della lotta per il socialismo in Italia ed in Europa' (1982), in: P.C.I. *Socialismo reale e terza via*, pp. 11–44.
———, *La crisi italiana* (Editrice l'Unità, 1985).
Blum, L., 'Notes d'Allemagne (1943–1945)', in: Blum, *L'Œuvre de Léon Blum. V*, pp. 500–514.

———, 'La Constitution de 1946' (1946), in: Blum, *L'Œuvre de Léon Blum. VI*, pp. 295–332.

———, 'La démission du général De Gaulle et le gouvernement Félix Gouin' (1946), in: Blum, *L'Œuvre de Léon Blum. VI*, pp. 158–173.

———, 'Les problèmes constitutionnels' (1946), in: Blum, *L'Œuvre de Léon Blum. VI*, pp. 217–224.

———, 'L'intervention de De Gaulle et le referendum du 1946' (1946), in: Blum, *L'Œuvre de Léon Blum. VI*, pp. 305–319.

———, 'Motion pour un congrès extraordinaire de la S.F.I.O.' (1947), in: Blum, *L'œuvre de Léon Blum. VII*, pp. 109–113.

———, 'La formation de la double opposition' (1947), in: Blum, *L'œuvre de Léon Blum. VII*, pp. 395–415.

———, 'Communisme et Gaullisme' (1948), in: L. Blum, *L'œuvre de Léon Blum. VII*, pp. 239–244.

———, 'À la recherche d'une majorité' (1949), in: L. Blum, *L'œuvre de Léon Blum. VII*, pp. 252–262.

———, *L'œuvre de Léon Blum. V (1940–1945): Mémoires de la prison et le procès: À l'échelle humaine* (Paris: Éditions Albin Michel, 1955).

———, *L'œuvre de Léon Blum. VI (1947–1950): La fin des alliances, la troisième force, politique Européenne, pour la justice* (Paris, 1963).

———, *L'œuvre de Léon Blum. VII (1947–1950): La fin des alliances, la troisième force, politique Européenne, pour la justice* (Paris, 1963).

Bracher, K.D., 'Die zweite Demokratie in Deutschland—Strukturen und Probleme' (1962), in: R. Löwenthal ed., *Die Demokratie im Wandel der Geschichte* (Berlin: Colloquium Verlag, 1963), pp. 113–135.

Brandt, W., 'Zur Nachkriegspolitik der deutschen Sozialisten' (1944) in: W. Brandt, *Berliner Ausgabe: Band 2*, pp. 154–205.

———, 'Das Regierungsprogramm der SPD: Rede Willy Brandt SPD Kongress Bonn' (1961), in: W. Brandt, *Berliner Ausgabe: Band 4*, pp. 230–257.

———, 'Entscheidung für Deutschland' (1961), in: W. Brandt, *Berliner Ausgabe: Band 4*, pp. 257–264.

———, Artikel des Regierenden Bürgermeisters von Berlin und Vorsitzenden der SPD, Brandt, für Die Neue Gesellschaft' (1966), in: W. Brandt, *Berliner Ausgabe: Band 7*, pp. 94–106.

———, 'Aus der Rede der Bundesminister des Auswärtigen: Brandt, vor dem Deutschen Bundestag' (1968), in: W. Brandt, *Berliner Ausgabe: Band 7*, pp. 148–156.

———, 'Aus der Regierungserklärung des Bundeskanzlers Brandt vor dem Deutschen Bundestag' (1969), in: W. Brandt, *Berliner Ausgabe: Band 7*, pp. 218–224.

———, 'Politik in Deutschland—Wertvorstellungen unter Ideologieverdacht: Aus der Rede des Bundeskanzlers, Brandt, in der Evangelischen Akademie in Bad Segeberg' (1973), in: W. Brandt, *Berliner Ausgabe: Band 7*, pp. 444–456.

———, Perspektiven der neuen Mitten: Aus der Rede des Bundeskanzler, Brandt, anlässlich Der Verleihung des Theodor-Heuss-Preises in München' (1974), in: W. Brandt, *Berliner Ausgabe: Band 7*, pp. 480–490.

———, 'Aus der Erklärung von Parteivorstand, Parteirat und Kontrollkommission der SPD zur Bundeskonferenz in Recklinghausen 17 Februar 1975' (1975), in: W. Brandt, *Berliner Ausgabe: Band 5*, pp. 151–157.

———, *Berliner Ausgabe: Band 2: Zwei Vaterländer: Deutsch-Norweger im swedischen Exil—Rückkehr nach Deutschland 1940–1947* (Berlin: Willy Brandt Stiftung, 2000).

———, *Berliner Ausgabe: Band 4: Auf dem Weg nach vorn: Willy Brandt und die SPD 1947–1972* (Bonn: Verlag J.H.W. Dietz Nachfolger GmbH, 2000).

———, *Berliner Ausgabe: Band 7: Mehr Demokratie wagen: Innen- und Gesellschaftspolitik 1966–1974* (Bonn: Verlag J.H.W. Dietz Nachf, 2001).

———, *Berliner Ausgabe: Band 5: Die Partei der Freiheit: Willy Brandt und die SPD 1972–1992* (Bonn: Dietz Verlag, 2002).
Brandt, W. and H. Schmidt, *Theorie und Grundwerte: Weiterarbeiten am Modell Deutschland: Reden von Willy Brandt und Helmut Schmidt* (Bonn: SPD, 1976).
Bufalini, P., *Terrorismo e democrazia: La relazione al Comitato Centrale del PCI 18 aprile 1978* (Rome: Editori Riuniti, 1978).
Capanna, M., *Movimento Studentesco: Crescita politica e azione rivoluzionaria* (Milan: Sapere, 1968).
———, *Monopoli, DC, Compromesso Storico* (Milan: Mazzotta editore, 1975).
Capitant, R., 'La force du Gaullisme' (1961), in: R. Capitant, *Écrits politiques*, pp. 9–11.
———, 'Nécessité et légitimité du referendum' (1960), in: R. Capitant, *Écrits politiques*, pp. 65–67.
———, 'Réfutation du « non »' (1962), in: R. Capitant, *Écrits politiques*, pp. 151–160.
———, *Écrits politiques 1960–1970* (Paris: Flammarion, 1971).
Chirac, J., 'Les Buts' (1976), in: J. Chirac, *Discours pour la France*, pp. 15–26.
———, 'L'action politique' (1976), in: J. Chirac, *Discours pour la France*, pp. 27–31.
———, *La Bataille de France: Discours prononcée au Rassemblement du 11 Février 1978* (Paris: Création Publicité Impression, 1978).
———, *Discours pour la France à l'heure du choix: La lueur de l'espérance: Réflexion du soir pour le matin* (Paris: Éditions Stock, 1978).
Cohn-Bendit, D. and G. Cohn-Bendit, *Obsolete Communism: The Left-wing Alternative* (London: Penguin Books, 1969 [1968]).
Comité Général d'Étude, 'Le problème constitutionnel français' (1944), in: Michel and Mirkine-Geutzévitch eds., *Les Idées politiques et sociales de la Résistance*, pp. 287–297.
Cortese ed., *Il Movimento Studentesco: Storia e documenti 1968–1973* (Milan: Valentino Bompani, 1973).
Craxi, B., *Marxismo, Socialismo e Libertà: Discorso pronunciato a Trevieri il 4 Maggio 1977* (Roma: Biblioteca Rossa, 1977).
———, *L'alternativa dei socialisti: Il progetto del PSI presentato da Bettino Craxi* (Milan: Edizione Avanti, 1978).
———, *Una responsabilità democratica: Una prospettiva riformista per l'Italia che cambia: Relazione introduttiva al 44 Congresso, Rimini 31 marzo-5 aprile 1987* (Rome: Avanti, 1987).
DC, 'Linee di ricostruzione (redatto da De Gasperi, marzo 1943)', in: F. Malgeri ed., *Storia della Democrazia Cristiana*: Vol. I, pp. 377–379.
———, 'Idee ricostruttive della Democrazia Cristiana (Rome, 1943)', in: F. Malgeri ed., *Storia della Democrazia Cristiana*: Vol. I, pp. 389–393.
———, 'Il programma di Milano (1943)', in: F. Malgeri, ed., *Storia della Democrazia Cristiana: Vol. I*, pp. 396–398.
———, 'Il programma della Democrazia Cristiana (Vicenza, 1944)', in: F. Malgeri ed., *Storia della Democrazia Cristiana*: Vol. I, pp. 419–428.
———, '24–27 Aprile 1946: Roma: I Congresso Nazionale della DC: Il programma della DC per la nuova costituzione', in: A. Damiliano ed., *Atti e documenti della democrazia Cristiana 1943–1967. Vol I* (Rome: Edizione Cinque Lune, 1968), pp. 233–251.
———, 'L'appello al Paese per le elezioni politiche' (1948), in: F. Malgeri ed., *Storia della Democrazia Cristiana. Vol II*, pp. 442–443.
———, *I problemi dell'economia Italiana superamento della crisi e nuove prospettive di sviluppo sociale. Convegno nazionale di studi DC. Perugia, 9–12 Dicembre 1972. Vol 3. L'assemblea generale* (Rome: Edizione Cinque Lune, 1973).
———, *Per la società nuova. Un grande partito di popolo. Assemblea nazionale DC. Roma 25–30 Novembre 1981* (N.P. 1981), pp. 23–24.

———, *Un programma per l'Italia. Elezioni politiche 14–15 Giugno 1987* (Rome: Agi, 1987).
Debré, M., *La République et son pouvoir* (Paris: Nagel, 1950).
———, *Ces princes qui nous gouvernent* (Paris: Plon, 1957).
———, 'Construire enfin un régime parlementaire' (1958), in: M. Debré, *Refaire une démocratie*, pp. 15–35.
———, 'Pourquoi oui ?' (1958), in: M. Debré, *Refaire une démocratie*, pp. 73–79.
———, *Refaire une démocratie un état un pouvoir* (Paris: Plon, 1958).
Deist, H., *Wirtschaft von Morgen. Beiträge zur Wirtschaftspolitik der SPD* (Berlin: Dietz Verlag, 1959).
Democrazia Proletaria, *Costituente del Partito di Democrazia e Proletaria. Contribuiti alla preparazione dell'assemblea congressuale* (N.P., 1975).
Duclos, J., *L'avenir de la démocratie* (Paris: Éditions sociales, 1962).
———, *De Napoléon III à De Gaulle* (Paris: Éditions Sociales, 1964).
Dutschke, R., 'Demokratie, Universität und Gesellschaft' (1967), in: R. Dutschke, *Geschichte ist machbar*, pp. 61–75.
———, Professor Habermas, Ihr begriffsloser Objektivismus erschlägt das zu emanzipierende Subjekt!' (1967), in: R. Dutschke, *Geschichte ist machbar*, pp. 76–84.
———, 'Keiner Partei dürfen wir vertrauen' (1967), in: R. Dutschke, *Geschichte ist machbar*, pp. 86–88.
———, 'Subkultur und Partei (Fragen der Organisierung)' (1977), in: R. Dutschke, *Geschichte ist machbar*, pp. 164–171.
———, 'Unser Prozeß der Revolution wird ein sehr lange Marsch sein. Träume, Wünsche, Hoffnungen', in: R. Dutschke, *Mein langer Marsch*, pp. 11–29.
———, 'Kein Mensch ist austauschbar. Über Gewalt und Gegengewalt', in: R. Dutschke, *Mein langer Marsch*, pp. 97–106.
———, *Geschichte ist machbar. Texte über das herrschende Falsche und die Radikalität des Friedens* (Berlin: Klaus Wagenbach, 1980).
———, *Mein langer Marsch. Reden, Schriften und Tagebücher aus zwanzig Jahren* (Reinbek bei Hamburg: Rowolt Verlag, 1980)
Eichler, W., *Grundwerte und Grundforderungen im Godesberger Grundsatzprogramm der SPD* (Bonn: Vorstand der SPD, 1962).
Erhard, L., 'Marktwirtschaft im Streit der Meinungen' (1948), in: L. Erhard, *Gedanken aus fünf Jahrzehnten*, pp. 134–152.
———, 'Wahlaufruf zum ersten Bundestag' (1949), in: L. Erhard, *Gedanken aus fünf Jahrzehnten*, pp. 214–215.
———, 'Die Ziele des Gesetz gegen Wettbewerbsbeschränkungen' (1955), in: L. Erhard, *Deutsche Wirtschaftspolitik*, pp. 267–275.
———, *Wohlstand für Alle* (Düsseldorf: ECON Verlag, 1957).
———, 'Wohlstand für Alle' (1957), in: L. Erhard, *Wirken und Reden. 19 Reden aus die Jahre 1952–1965* (Ludwigsburg: Martin Hoch Druckerei, 1965), pp. 343–360.
———, 'Soziale Ordnung schafft Wohlstand und Sicherheit' (1961), in: L. Erhard, *Deutsche Wirtschaftspolitik*, pp. 567–587.
———, *Deutsche Wirtschaftspolitik: Der Weg der Sozialen Marktwirtschaft* (Düsseldorf: ECON Verlag, 1962).
———, 'Formierte Gesellschaft. Rede vor dem 13. Bundesparteitag der CDU' (1965), in: L. Erhard, *Gedanken aus fünf Jahrzehnten* (Düsseldorf: Ludwig Erhard Stiftung, 1988), pp. 915–931.
———, *Gedanken aus fünf Jahrzehnten* (Düsseldorf: Ludwig Erhard Stiftung, 1988).
Fabius, L., 'Moderniser et rassembler. Discours d'investiture' (1984), in: L. Fabius, *Le Cœur du Futur*, pp. 49–62.
———, 'L'impact des nationalisations' (1984), in: L. Fabius, *Le cœur du Futur*, pp. 209–211.
———, *Le Cœur du Futur* (Paris: Almann-Levy, 1985).

Fanfani, A., 'L'azione DC per le zone depresse' (1954), in: A. Fanfani, P. Campilli and E. Colombo, *La Democrazia cristiana per le zone depresse. Documenti* (Rome: Edizione Cinque Lune, 1954), pp. 9–21.

———, 'La D.C. di fronte al problema socialista. Relazione al Consiglio Nazionale della Democrazia Cristiana Vallombrosa' (1957), in: A. Fanfani, *Da Napoli a Firenze 1954–1959: Proposte per una politica di sviluppo democratico* (Rome: Garanzi editore, 1959), pp. 177–207.

———, *Centro-Sinistra '62* (Rome: Garzanti, 1962).

Farneti, P., 'Il Sistema dei partiti dalla costituzione a oggi', in: G. Amato ed., *Attualità e attuazione della costituzione* (Bari: Laterza, 1979), pp. 3–15.

Feenberg, A. and J. Freedman eds., *When Poetry Ruled the Streets. The French May Events of 1968. Part 2. Documents of the May Movement* (Albany: State of University of New York Press, 2001).

Forlani, A., 'Dichiarazione d'intenti politico-programmatici', (1982), in: D.C., *Atti del 15 Congresso nazionale della Democrazia cristiana, Roma 2–5 Maggio 1982* (Rome: Edizione Cinque Lune, 1982, pp. 818–823.

Fraenkel, E., *Die Repräsentative und die plebiszitäre Komponente im demokratischen Verfassungsstaat (*Tübingen: J.C.B. Mohr, 1958).

Gasperi, A., de, 'Il programma della Democrazia Cristiana' (1944), in: A. de Gasperi, *Scritti politici*, pp. 274–287.

———, 'La democrazia cristiana e il momento politico (1944)', in: F. Malgeri ed., *Storia della Democrazia Cristiana. Vol I*, pp. 453–462.

———, 'Le basi dello stato democratico e la battaglia di domani' (1945), in: F. Malgeri ed., *Storia della Democrazia Cristiana. Vol. I*, pp. 463–469.

———, Le ragioni del "governo di emergenza"'(1947), in: A. de Gasperi, *Scritti politici*, pp. 316-339.

———, 'Non serviamo l'America, non osteggiamo la Russia, difendiamo l'Italia' (1948), in: F. Malgeri ed., *Storia della Democrazia Cristiana. Vol II*, pp. 444–456.

———, 'Dopo l'attentato a Togliatti' (1948), in: A. de Gasperi, *Scritti politici*, pp. 339–343.

———, 'Costituzione e riforma elettorale' (1952), in: A. de Gasperi, *Scritti politici*, pp. 383–386.

———, 'La legge maggioritaria. La DC e la dottrina sociale cattolica' (1953), in: A. de Gasperi, *Scritti politici*, pp. 392–396.

———, Le ragioni di una politica anticomunista', (1951), in: A. de Gasperi, *Scritti politici*, pp. 365-370.

———, *Nella lotta per la democrazia* (Rome: Edizione Cinque Lune, 1954).

———, *Scritti politici di Alcide de Gasperi* (Milan: Feltrinelli, 1979).

Gaulle, C., de, 'Discours prononcé à l'assemblée consultative provisoire' (9 novembre 1944), in: C. de Gaulle, *Discours et Messages. Pendant la guerre*, pp. 471–474.

———, 'Discours prononcé à l'assemblée consultative' (1945), in: C. de Gaulle, *Discours et Messages. Pendant la guerre*, pp. 521–532.

———, 'Déclaration à l'assemblée constituante' (1945), in: C. de Gaulle, *Discours et Messages. Pendant la guerre*, pp. 661–664.

———, 'Discours radiodiffusé (12th July 1945)', in: C. de Gaulle, *Discours et Messages: Pendant la guerre*, pp. 581–585.

———, 'Discours prononcé à Bayeux' (1946), in: C. de Gaulle, *Discours et Messages: Dans l'attente*, pp. 5–11.

———, 'Discours prononcé à 'Épinal' (1946), C. de Gaulle, *Discours et Messages: Dans l'attente*, pp. 26–33.

———, 'Discours prononcé à Rennes' (1947), in: C. de Gaulle, *Discours et Messages: Dans l'attente*, pp. 97–104.

———, 'Déclaration' (1947), in: C. de Gaulle, *Discours et Messages: Dans l'attente*, pp. 109–110.

———, 'Discours prononcé à Vincennes' (1947), in: C. de Gaulle, *Discours et Messages: Dans l'attente*, pp. 122–128.

———, 'Allocution prononcée à la radiodiffusion française' (1951), in: C. de Gaulle, *Discours et Messages : Dans l'attente*, pp. 435–438.

———, 'Conférence de presse tenu à Palais d'Orsay' (1958), in: C. de Gaulle, *Discours et Messages : Avec le Renouveau*, pp. 4–10.

———, 'Allocution radiodiffusée et télévisé au palais d'Élysée' (1962), in: C. de Gaulle, *Discours et Messages : Pour l'effort*, pp. 20–24.

———, 'Allocution radiodiffusée et télévisé au palais d'Élysée 4 Octobre' (1962), in: C. de Gaulle, *Discours et Messages*, pp. 30–33.

———, 'Allocution radiodiffusée et télévisée prononcée au palais de l'Élysée (30 May 1968)', in: C. de Gaulle, *Discours et Messages: Vers le terme*, pp. 291–293.

———, 'Allocution radiodiffusée et télévisée prononcée au palais de l'Élysée (11 March 1969)', in: C. de Gaulle, *Discours et Messages : Vers le terme*, pp. 384–389.

———, *Discours et Messages : Pendant la guerre juin 1940-janvier 1946* (Paris: Plon, 1970).

———, *Discours et Messages : Dans l'attente 1946–1958* (Paris: Plon: 1970).

———, *Discours et Messages : Avec le Renouveau 1958–1962* (Paris: Plon, 1970).

———, *Discours et Messages : Pour l'effort. Aout 1962—Décembre 1965* (Paris: Plon, 1970).

———, *Discours et Messages : Vers le terme 1966–1969* (Paris: Plon, 1970).

Giscard d'Estaing, V., *La démocratie française* (Paris: Fayard, 1976).

Gonella, G., 'La DC per la nuova costituzione' (1946), in: F. Malgeri ed., *Storia della Democrazia Cristiana: Vol. I*, pp. 485–519.

———, *Fedeltà e coerenza* (Rome: Società nuova, 1963).

———, *L'apertura incondizionata* ([1962] Rome: Società nuova, 1963).

Grosser and J. Seifert eds., *Die Spiegel Affäre: Vol. I: Die Staatsmacht und ihre Kontrolle: Texte und Dokumente zur Zeitgeschichte* (Olten und Freiburg im Breisgau: Walter Verlag, 1966).

Heuss, T., *Die deutsche Nationalidee im Wandel der Geschichte* (Stuttgart: Mittelbach Verlag, 1946).

———, 'Das deutsche Schicksal und unsere Aufgabe' (1947), in: T. Heuss, *Politiker und Publizist: Aufsätze und Reden* (Tübingen: Wunderlich, 1984), pp. 337–346.

Iniziativa Democratica, 'Prospettiva' (1951), in: F. Malgeri ed., *Storia della Democrazia Cristiana: Vol II*, pp. 555–557.

Jaspers, K., 'Wahrheit, Freiheit und Friede' (1958), in: K. Jaspers, *Hoffnung und Sorge: Schriften zur deutsche Politik 1945–1965* (Munich: Piper, 1965), pp. 174–184.

———, *Freiheit und Wiedervereinigung: über Aufgabe deutscher Politik* (Munich: Piper, 1960).

KPD, *Aufruf zum des Zentralkomitees der KPD vom: 11 Juni 1945 an das Deutsche Volk zum Aufbau eines antifaschistisch-demokratischen Deutschland* (1945), in: M. Reimann ed., *Dokumente der Kommunistische Partei Deutschland 1945–1956* (Berlin: Dietz Verlag, 1965), pp. 1–8.

Kelly, P., 'Schwerter zu Pflugscharen—ohne Systemgrenze!', in: M. Coppik and P. Kelly eds., *Wohin den Wir: Texte aus der Bewegung* (Berlin: Oberbaumverlag, 1982), pp. 7–16.

———, *Um Hoffnung kämpfen: Gewaltfrei in eine grüne Zukunft* (Berlin: Lamuv Taschenbuch Verlag, 1983).

Kogon, E., 'Die Verhängnisvolle Vorsorge' (1968), in: E. Kogon et al., *Der totale Notstandstaat* (Frankfurt am Main: Stimme Verlag, 1968), pp. 3–9.

Kohl, H., *Zwischen Ideologie und Pragmatismus: Aspekte und Ansichten zu Grundfragen der Politik* (Stuttgart: Verlag Bonn Aktuell, 1973).

———, 'Aufbruch in die Zukunft' (1973), in: H. Kohl, *Der Kurs der CDU*, pp. 37–55.

———, 'Das Grundgesetz: Verfassung der Freiheit: Rede in der Frankfurter Paulskirche' (1974), in: H. Kohl, *Der Kurs der CDU*, pp. 68–77.

———, 'Handeln als Christliche Demokraten: Rede auf dem 31: Bundesparteitag der CDU in Köln' (1983), in: H. Kohl, *Der Kurs der CDU*, pp. 205–227.
———, 'Das Erbe Ludwig Erhards—Herausforderung an die Wirtschaftspolitik' (1987), in: H. Kohl, *Reden zu Fragen der Sozialen Marktwirtschaft* (Bonn: Presse und Informationsamt der Bundesregierung, 1990), pp. 7–26.
———, *Der Kurs der CDU* (Stuttgart: Deutsche Verlags-Anstalt GmbH, 1993).
'La nuova fase politica del movimento studentesco trentino' (1968), in: Movimento Studentesco, *Documenti della rivolta universitaria*, pp. 41–43.
Longo, L., *Democrazia borghese e democrazia popolare* (N.P, 1952).
Malgeri, F., ed., *Storia della Democrazia Cristiana: Vol. I Le origine: Dalla Resistenza alla Repubblica 1943-1948* (Rome: Edizione Cinque Lune, 1987).
———, *Storia della Democrazia Cristiana: Vol II. De Gasperi e l'età del centrismo 1948-1954* (Rome: Edizione Cinque Lune, 1987).
———, *Storia della Democrazia Cristiana Vol. III: Gli anni di transizione 1954–1962: Da Fanfani a Moro* (Rome: Edizione Cinque Lune, 1988).
———, *Storia della Democrazia cristiana: Vol. IV: Dal Centro-sinistra agli "anni di piombo" (1962-1978)* (Rome: Edizione Cinque Lune, 1989).
———, *Storia della Democrazia cristiana: Volume V: Dal Delitto Moro alla Segretaria Forlani 1979-1989* (Rome: Edizione Cinque Lune, 1989).
Malraux, A., 'Discours prononcé au parc des expositions' (1968), in: A. Malraux, *Essais: Œuvres Complètes VI* (Paris: Gallimard, 2010), pp. 512–517.
Marchais, G., *Préface : Programme Commun du gouvernement du Parti communiste français et du Parti socialiste (27 juin 1972)* (Paris: Éditions Sociales, 1972).
———, *Le Défi Démocratique* (Paris: Éditions Grasset & Fasquelle, 1973).
———, 'Première partie : La voix des communistes français', in: G. Marchais and G. Hourdin, *Après le 22ᵉ Congrès du P.C.F. Communistes et Chrétiens ou Communistes ou Chrétiens* (Paris: Desclée, 1976), pp. 7–49.
Mendès France, P., 'La crise de la démocratie' (1955), in: Mendès France, *Œuvres complètes : Vol. IV*, pp. 81–102.
———, 'La république' (1957), in: Mendès France, *Œuvres complètes : Vol. IV*, pp. 341–347.
———, 'Le rejet de la constitution de la Ve République' (1958), in: Mendès France, *Œuvres complètes : Vol. IV*, pp. 435–452.
———, 'L'investiture du Général de Gaulle' (1958), in: Mendès France, *Œuvres complètes : Vol. IV*, pp. 418–425.
———, 'Aucun démocratie est possible dans le mensonge' (1959), in: Mendès France, *Œuvres complètes : Vol. IV*, pp. 525–527.
———, 'Gaullisme, Mendèsisme et la Ve République' (1961), in: Mendès France, *Œuvres complètes : Vol. IV*, pp. 656–660.
———, 'La République moderne. Propositions' (1961), in: Mendès France, *Œuvres complètes : Vol. IV*, pp. 737–888.
———, La crise de Cuba et le Référendum sur l'élection du président de la République au suffrage universel' (1962), in: Mendès France, *Œuvres complètes : Vol. IV*, pp. 894–902.
———, *Œuvres complètes : Vol. IV : Pour une République moderne* (Paris: Gallimard, 1987).
———, *Œuvres Complètes : Vol. V : Préparer l'avenir 1963-1973* (Paris: Gallimard, 1989).
Michel, H. and B. Mirkine-Guetzévitch eds., *Les Idées politiques et sociales de la Résistance* (Paris: Presses Universitaires de France, 1954).
Mita, C., de, 'Per la democrazia nella trasformazione', (1982), in: D.C., *Atti del 15 Congresso nazionale*, pp. 832–882.
Mitterrand, F., *Le Coup d'État permanent* (Paris: Julliard, 1984 [1964]).
———, 'Mai 68 et ses conséquences' (1968), in: F. Mitterrand, *Politique*, pp. 478–507.

———, 'Discours au Congrès de l'unité des socialistes : Épinay, 13 Juin 1971', in: M. Ouraoui ed., *Les Grands Discours socialistes français du XXe siècle* (Paris: Bibliothèque Complexe, 2007), pp. 142-161.
———, *La Rose au poing* (Paris: Flammarion, 1973).
———,'1974: les élections presidentielles et ses consequences', in: F. Mitterrand, *Politique*, pp. 555-571.
———, *Politique* (Paris: Fayard, 1977).
———, *Ici et Maintenant : Conversations avec Guy Claisse* (Paris: Fayard, 1980).
———,'110 Propositions pour la France', in: F. Mitterrand, *Politique II 1977–1981* (Paris: Fayard, 1981), pp. 305-324.
Mollet, G., 'Démocratie et révolution' (1946), in: G. Mollet, *Textes choisis*, pp. 44-47.
———, *Nous travaillons pour une bonne cause* (Arras: Société d'éditions du Pas-de-Calais, 1949).
———, 'Participation au gouvernement de Mendès France ?' (1954), in: G. Mollet, *Textes choisis*, pp. 83-94.
———, *13 mai 1958–13 mai 1962* (Paris: Plon, 1962).
———, *Textes choisis : Le socialiste et le républicain 1945–1975* (Paris: Bruno Leprince Éditeur, 1995).
Moro, A., 'La politica dell'uomo qualunque' (1945), in: A. Moro *Scritti e discorsi: I*, pp. 254-255.
———, 'Tre pilastri della democrazia' (1947), in: A. Moro *Scritti e discorsi: I*, pp. 453-463.
———, 'Il congresso di Firenze' (1959), in: A. Moro, *Scritti e discorsi: II*, pp. 637-718.
———, 'Le ragioni delle convergenze parallele' (1960), in: A. Moro, *Scritti e discorsi: II*, pp. 794-813.
———, 'La relazione di Moro' (1962), in: Democrazia Cristiana, *Consiglio Nazionale D.C. 10–11-12 Novembre 1962* (Rome: Documenti SES Cenrale, 1962), pp. 49-50.
———, 'Il partito e le scelte di fondo della politica nazionale' (1962), in: F. Malgeri ed., *Storia della Democrazia Cristiana Vol. III*, pp. 473-559.
———, 'Il patto di Centro-Sinistra' (1963), in: A. Moro, *Scritti e discorsi: II*, pp. 1351-1374.
———, Il terzo governo Moro' (1966), in: A. Moro, *Scritti e discorsi: IV*, pp. 2006-2045.
———, 'Il X Congresso Nazionale della DC' (1967), in: A. Moro, *Scritti e discorsi: IV*, pp. 2437-2465.
———, 'Invita alla partecipazione' (1968), in: A. Moro, *Scritti e discorsi: IV*, pp. 2498-2507.
———, 'Sviluppo democratico e presenza della DC (1976), in: A. Moro, *Scritti e discorsi: IV*, pp. 3469-3489.
———, *Per una iniziativa politica della Democrazia cristiana* (Rome: Agenzia Progetto, 1973).
———, 'Un quadro politico da costruire' (1976), in: A. Moro, *Scritti e discorsi: IV*, pp. 3491-3506.
———, 'Garanzia e limiti di una politica' (1978), in: A. Moro, *Scritti e discorsi: IV*, pp. 3781-3796.
———, *Scritti e discorsi: Volume I 1940–1947* (Rome: Edizione Cinque Lune, 1982).
———, *Scritti e discorsi: Volume II 1951–1963* (Rome: Edizioni Cinque Lune, 1982).
———, *Scritti e discorsi: Volume IV 1966–1968* (Rome: Edizione Cinque Lune, 1987).
Mouvement Républicain Populaire, *Le M.R.P. parti de la Quatrième République* (N.P., 1946).
Movimento Studentesco, *Documenti della rivolta universitaria* (Bari: Laterza, 1968).
———, *La situazione attuale e i compiti politici del Movimento Studentesco* (Milan: Sapere Edizioni, 1969).
———, 'La DC, partito della borghesia' (1972), in: Cortese ed., *Il Movimento Studentesco*, pp. 39-42.

———, 'La fascistizzazione dello Stato' (1974), in: Cortese ed., *Il Movimento Studentesco*, pp. 121–123.

'Mozione di 26 Febbraio: Firenze', in: Movimento Studentesco, *Documenti della rivolta niversitaria* (Bari: Laterza, 1968), pp. 362–363.

Napolitano, G., 'I problemi del partito nell'attuale fase politica' (1981), in: G. Napolitano and E. Berlinguer, *Partito di massa negli anni ottanta: I problemi del partito al comitato centrale del PCI 7–8 gennaio 1981* (Rome: Editori Riuniti, 1981), pp. 7–46.

Nenni, P., *Che cosa vuole il Partito Socialista? Discorso pronunciato alla Sala Roma di Napoli il 3 Settembre 1944* (Roma: Consiglio Nazionale del PSI, 1944).

———, *Legge truffa e costituzione: Ragioni dell'ostruzionismo socialista* (Milan: Avanti, 1953).

———, *Dialogo con la sinistra cattolica* (Milan: Avanti, 1954).

———, 'Relazione di Pietro Nenni al 31 Congresso' (1955), in: P.S.I. *31 Congresso Nazionale del Partito socialista italiano*, pp. 37–89.

———, 'I "vergognosi fatti" del rapporto segreto di Krusciov' (1956), in: P. Nenni, *Le prospettive del socialismo dopo la destalinizzazione* (Turin: Einaudi, 1962), pp. 33–51.

———, 'Al 32 Congresso' (1957), in: P. Nenni, *Il socialismo nella democrazia*, pp. 5–44.

———, 'Al 33 Congresso' (1959), in: P. Nenni, *Il socialismo nella democrazia*, pp. 49–82.

———, 'L'avventura di destra dell'estate '60 stroncata dalla sollevazione della coscienza antifascista della nazione' (1960), in: P. Nenni, *La battaglia socialista per la svolta a sinistra nelle terza legislatura 1958–1963* (Milan: Avanti, 1963), pp. 45–80.

———, 'Al 35 Congresso: Il primo governo Moro' (1963), in: P. Nenni, *Il socialismo nella democrazia*, pp. 243–276.

———, 'La relazione di Pietro Nenni' (1963), in: P.S.I., *Il 35 Congresso Nazionale, Rome 25–29 Ottobre 1963: Resoconto integrale con una Appendice di documenti precongressuali* (Milan: Avanti, 1964), pp. 27–74.

———, *Il socialismo nella democrazia: Realtà e presente* (Florence: Valecchi Editore, 1966).

Nous Sommes en Marche, 'The Amnesty of the Blinded Eyes' (1968), in: Feenberg and Freedman eds., *When Poetry Ruled the Streets*, pp. 81–86.

Ollenhauer, E., 'Voraussetzungen der Demokratie' (1949), in: E. Ollenhauer, *Reden und Aufsätze*, pp. 182–194.

———, 'Bericht über die bisherige Tätigkeit der sozialdemokratische Bundestagfraktion', in: SPD, *Es gibt nur eine Wahrheit: Kurt Schumacher und Erich Ollenhauer auf dem Hamburger Parteitag der Sozialdemokratischen Partei Deutschlands im mai 1950* (Bonn: Vorstand der SPD, 1950), pp. 32–48.

———, 'Es geht um mehr als Divisionen' (1952), in: Ollenhauer, *Reden und Aufsätze*, pp. 195-205.

———, 'Gemeinschaft der Freien und Gleichen' (1952), in: Ollenhauer, *Reden und Aufsätze*, pp. 215–241.

———, 'Das Grundsatzprogramm der SPD: Der Vorsitze der SPD Erich Ollenhauer auf dem Außenorderntliche Parteitrag in Bad Godesberg: 13.-15. November 1959', in: S. Miller ed., *Die SPD vor und nach Godesberg* (Bonn: Verlag Neue Gesellschaft, 1975), pp. 110–116.

———, 'Zum Godesberger Grundsatzprogramm' (1959), in: Ollenhauer, *Reden und Aufsätze*, pp. 275–306.

———, *Reden und Aufsätze* (Hannover: Dietz Verlag, 1964).

Onori, F., *Democrazia progressiva* (Rome: l'Unità, 1945).

———, *Projet de déclaration des libertés du Parti communiste français: Introduction de Georges Marchais* (Paris: l'Humanité, 1975).

PCI, *Risoluzioni e decisioni del VII Congresso nazionale del Partito comunista italiano: Roma 3–8 aprile 1951* (Rome: l'Unità, 1951).

———, 'Risoluzione della direzione del Pci' (1980), in: P.C.I. *Socialismo reale e terza via*, pp. 235–245.

180 References

———, 'La proposta di alternative per il cambiamento: Documento politico con gli emendamenti approvati dal XVI Congresso' (1983), in: E. Berlinguer, *Economia, stato, pace: l'iniziativa e le proposte del PCI: Rapporto, conclusioni e documento politico del XVI Congresso* (Rome: Editori Riuniti, 1983), pp. 75–172.

———, *Socialismo reale e terza via: Il dibattito sui fatti di Polonia nel Comitato centrale del P.c.i. I documenti sulla polémica con Pcus* (Rome: Editori Riuniti, 1982).

———, *Il PCI e la svolta di '56* (Rome: Rinascità, 1986).

PSI, *31 Congresso Nazionale del Partito socialista italiano: Nel decennale della Liberazione, unità del popolo per restaurare la democrazia nello Stato, nelle fabbriche, nelle campagne* (Milan: Avanti, 1955).

———, *Convegno sulle Partecipazioni Statali: Atti e documenti, Roma, 3–4 maggio 1959* (Milan: Avanti, 1960).

———, *Una costituzione per governare: La "grande riforma": proposta dai socialisti* (Venezia: Marsillo editore, 1981).

———, *Governare il cambiamento: Intervento alla conferenza di Rimini 4 aprile 1982* (Rome: Sezione propaganda e sezione del P.S.I., 1982).

PSIUP, *1 Congresso Nazionale: Per la pace e la libertà contro l'imperialismo, per il socialismo contro lo sfruttamento e il potere del capitalismo, rafforziamo nelle lotta l'unità dei lavoratori* (Rome, 1965).

PSIUP, *Tesi approvati del 2 Congresso'*, in: PSIUP, *2 Congresso Nazionale del PSIUP: Unità della sinistra per una alternative al centrosinistra e per un nuovo internazionalismo proletario: Napoli 18–21 dicembre 1969* (Rome, 1969), pp. 7–39.

PSU, 'Les 17 thèses du P.S.U. Adoptées au Congrès du Dijon mars 1969' (1969), in: Rocard, *Le P.S.U. et l'avenir de la France*, pp. 123–183.

Panella, M., 'L'unica opposizione', (1976), in: M. Pannella, *Scritti e discorsi*, pp. 300–313.

———, 'Esarchia, Partito radicale, informazione' (1978) in: M. Pannella, *Scritti e discorsi*, pp. 458–462.

———, *Scritti e discorsi 1959–1980* (Milan: Gammalibri, 1982).

Parri, F., 'Per la chiarezza democratica' (1946), in: F. Parri, *Scritti 1915–1975* (Milan: Feltrinelli, 1976), pp. 207–221.

Parti Socialiste and Parti Communiste Français, *Programme Commun du gouvernement du Parti communiste français et du Parti socialiste (27 juin 1972)* (Paris: Éditions Sociales, 1972).

Peyrefitte, A., *Le mal français* (Paris: Plon, 1976).

Piccoli, F., 'Idee, struttura e iniziative della Democrazia cristiana per il rinnovamento delle Istituzioni nell'attuazione della Costituzione e nello sviluppo della società nazionale' (1969), in: F. Malgeri ed., *Storia della Democrazia cristiana: Vol. IV*, pp. 457–506.

———, *Un grande partito di popolo per una rinnovata iniziativa di pace, di libertà e di solidarità sociale: Relazione del Segretario Politico al XV Congresso Nazionale'* (1982), in: D.C., *Atti del 15 Congresso nazionale della Democrazia cristiana, Roma 2–5 Maggio 1982* (Rome: Edizione Cinque Lune, 1982), pp. 59–84.

Poujade, P., *J'ai choisis le combat* (Saint Cère: Société Générale des Éditions et des publications, 1955).

Résistance, 'Des partis, oui, mais d'autres' (1943), in: Michel and Mirkine-Geutzévitch eds., *Les Idées politiques et sociales de la Résistance*, pp. 115–116.

Rocard, M., *Le P.S.U. et l'avenir socialiste de la France* (Paris: Éditions du Seuil, 1969).

———, 'L'avenir de Mai 68' (1978), in: M. Rocard, *Parler vrai : Textes politiques* (Paris: Éditions de Seuil, 1978), pp. 97–101.

———, 'La pensée socialiste est en crise' (1979), in: M. Rocard, *A l'épreuve des faits*, pp. 21–31.

———, 'La redécouverte de l'individu' (1985), in: M. Rocard, *A l'épreuve des faits*, pp. 203–205.

———, 'Nous avons changé, osons le dire' (1985), in: M. Rocard, *A l'épreuve des faits*, pp. 37–49.

———, Rocard, *A l'épreuve des faits : Textes politiques 1979–1985* (Paris: Seuil, 1986).
Rossanda, R., *L'anno degli studenti* (Bari: De Donato editore, 1968).
Rumor, M., 'Una forza popolare' (1952), in: F. Malgeri ed., *Storia della Democrazia Cristiana: Vol II*, pp. 558–559.
Rumor, M., 'Iniziativa dei democratici Cristiani per il rinnovamento dello Stato per lo sviluppo della democrazia per la libertà e per la pace' (1967), in: F. Malgeri ed., *Storia della Democrazia Cristiana: Vol. IV*, pp. 423–466.
———, 'La Democrazia cristiana raccoglie le sfide del futuro', (1968), in: M. Rumor, *Discorsi*, pp. 372–381.
———, 'Democrazia cristiana partito del cambiamento e della continuità' (1978), in: M. Rumor, *Discorsi*, pp. 431–439.
———, *Discorsi sulla Democrazia cristiana* (Milan: Franco Angelli, 2010).
Saragat, G., Il discorso di Firenze' (1946), in: G. Saragat, *Quaranta anni di lotta per la democrazia*, pp. 285–316.
———, 'La restaurazione dei valori democratici' (1960), in: G. Saragat, *Quaranta anni di lotta per la democrazia*, pp. 536–543.
———, *Quaranta anni di lotta per la democrazia.Scritti e discorsi 1925–1965* (Rome: U. Mursia, 1966).
Scelba, M., *Solidarietà nazionale e coscienza democratica* (Rome, 1950).
Schauer, H. ed., 'Schlußerklärung des Kuratoriums "Notstand der Demokratie" zm Kongreß', in: H. Schauer ed., *Notstand der Demokratie: Referate, Diskussionsbeiträge und Materialien von Kongreß am 30. Oktober 1966* (Frankfurt am Main, 1966), pp. 209–211, at pp. 209–210.
Scheel, W., 'Zum geistigen Standort der Liberalen in dieser Zeit', in: W. Scheel et al., *Formeln deutscher Politik: Sechs Praktiker und Theoretiker stellen sich* (Munich: Bechtle Verlag, 1965), pp. 15–50.
———, 'Opposition: Kritik und Kontrolle', *Liberal*, vol. 11 (1967), pp. 806–809.
Schmid, C., 'Weg und Ziel der Sozialdemokratie' (1945), in: C. Schmid, *Politik als geistige Aufgabe: Gesammelte Werkte I* (Munich: Scherz Verlag 1973), pp. 12–33.
———, 'Der ideologische Standort der deutschen Sozialismus in der Gegenwart' (1958), in: C. Schmid, *Politik und Geist* (Stuttgart: Ernst Klett Verlag, 1961), pp. 245–278.
Schmidt, H., 'Für eine Politik der Vernunft' (1973), in: H. Schmidt, *Auf dem Fundament des Godesberger Programms* (Bonn: Verlag Neue Gesellschaft, 1973), pp. 9–34.
Schumacher, K., 'Konsequenzen deutscher Politik' (1945), in: K. Schumacher, *Turmwächter der Demokratie: II*, pp. 25–50.
———, 'Aufgaben und Ziele der deutsche Sozialdemokratie' (1946), in: K. Schumacher, *Turmwächter der Demokratie: II*, pp.75–101.
———, 'Die Wandlungen um den Klassenkampf' (1946), in: K. Schumacher, *Turmwächter der Demokratie: II*, pp. 292–298.
———, Kontinentale Demokratie' (1946), in: K. Schumacher, *Turmwächter der Demokratie: II*, pp. 410–423.
———, Sozialismus—Eine Gegenwartsaufgabe' (1947), in: K. Schumacher, *Turmwächter der Demokratie: II*, pp. 102–108.
———, 'Von der Freiheit zur sozialen Gerechtigkeit' (1948), in: K. Schumacher, *Turmwächter der Demokratie: II*, pp. 111–138.
———, 'Demokratie und Sozialismus' (1948), in: K. Schumacher, *Turmwächter der Demokratie: II*, pp. 51–74.
———, 'Die Aufgabe der Opposition' (1949), in: K. Schumacher, *Turmwächter der Demokratie: II*, pp. 166–185.
———, 'Das Volk soll entscheiden! Für die deutsche Gleichberechtigung' (1950), in: K. Schumacher, *Reden—Schriften—Korrespondenzen*, pp. 863–882.
———, 'Der Parteitag der SPD vom 21 bis 25 Mai 1950 in Hamburg. Grundsatzreferat Schumachers: Die Sozialdemokratie im Kampf um Deutschland und Europa' (1950), in: K. Schumacher, *Reden—Schriften—Korrespondenzen*, pp. 746–780.

———, 'Um die Lebensnotwendigkeit des Volkes' (1950), in: K. Schumacher, *Turmwächter der Demokratie: II*, pp. 186–220.

———, 'Gesellschaftsumbau—ein Nationale Aufgabe' (1951), in: K. Schumacher, *Turmwächter der Demokratie: II*, pp. 249–281.

———, *Turmwächter der Demokratie: Ein Lebensbild von Kurt Schumacher: II: Reden und Schriften* (Berlin: GMBH Verlags, 1953).

———, *Reden—Schriften—Korrespondenzen 1945–1952* (Bonn: Dietz Verlag, 1985).

Sozialistische Reichspartei, 'Aktionsprogramm Sozialistische Reichspartei' (1951), in: O.K. Flechtheim ed., *Dokumente zur parteipolitische Entwicklung in Deutschland seit 1945: Vol. 2* (Berlin: Verlag Dr. Herbert Wendler & Co, 1963), pp. 489–493.

Strauß, F.J., 'Strauß erklärt Wirtschaftsleben für nicht demokratisierbar' (1968), in: F.J. Strauß, *Das Konzept der deutschen Rechten*, pp. 39–40.

———, 'Über die APO' (1968), in: F.J. Strauß, *Das Konzept der deutschen Rechten*, pp. 43–48.

———, 'Freiheit oder Abhängigkeit?' (1974), in: F.J. Strauß, *Signale*, pp. 147–150.

———, 'Die Zeit der Entscheidung ist da' (1977), in: F.J. Strauß, *Signale*, pp. 201–208.

———, *Deutschland deine Zukunft* (Stuttgart: Seewald Verlag, 1975).

———, *Das Konzept der deutschen Rechten: Aus Reden und Schriften des F.J. Strauß* (Cologne: Pahl Rugenstein Verlag, 1971).

———, *Signale: Beiträge zur deutschen Politik 1969–1978* (Munich: Verlag Bayernkurier, 1978).

Sturzo, L., 'Partitocrazia e Parlamento' (1950), in: L. Sturzo, *Opera omnia di Luigi Sturzo: Seconda serie: Saggi—Discorsi—Articoli: Volume 11: Politica di questi anni: Consensi e critiche (1950–1951)* (Rome: Istituto Luigi Sturzo, 1966), pp. 254–258.

———, 'Partiti e partitocrazia' (1951), in: L. Sturzo, *Opera omnia di Luigi Sturzo: Seconda serie: Saggi—Discorsi—Articoli: Volume 12: Politica di questi anni: Consensi e critiche (1951–1953)* (Rome: Istituto Luigi Sturzo, 1966), pp. 39–43.

———, 'Democrazia e partitocrazia' (1954), in: L. Sturzo, *Opera omnia di Luigi Sturzo: Seconda serie: Saggi—Discorsi—Articoli: Volume 13: Politica di questi anni: Consensi e critiche (1954–1956)* (Rome: Istituto Luigi Sturzo, 1966), pp. 30–35.

Tambroni, F., *Un governo amministrativo: Discorsi pronunciato dal 4 aprile al 14 luglio 1960* (Rome: Editrice les problèmes de l'Europe, 1960).

Thorez, M., 'Une politique française : Renaissance—démocratie—unité : Rapport au Xe congrès du Parti communiste français' (1945), in: M. Thorez, *Une politique du grandeur française* (Paris: Editions Sociales Paris, 1945), pp. 263–366.

———, 'Le combat pour l'unité' (1947), in: M. Thorez, *Ouvres Choisies en trois volumes : II 1938–1950* (Paris: Éditions sociales, 1965), pp. 476–491.

———, 'Quelques questions capitales posées au XXe Congrès du Parti Communiste de l'Union Soviétique' (1956), in: M. Thorez, *Œuvres choisis en trois volumes : III*, pp. 45–70.

———, 'Intervention au comité central d'Arcueil' (1956), in: M. Thorez, *Ouvres Choisies en trois volumes : III*, pp. 71–93.

———, 'Discours Clôture au Comité Central d'Ivry (1958), in: M. Thorez, *Œuvres choisis en trois volumes : III*, pp. 94–119.

———, 'Intervention au Comité Central de Bezons' (1962), in: M. Thorez, *Œuvres choisis en trois volumes : III*, pp. 243–256.

———, 'Unité pour la démocratie, pour le socialisme' (1964), in: M. Thorez, *Œuvres choisis en trois volumes : III*, pp. 316–331.

———, *Œuvres choisis en trois volumes : III 1953–1964* (Paris: Editons sociales, 1965).

Togliatti, P., *Avanti verso la democrazia: Discorso pronunciato 24 settembre 1944* (Rome: l'Unità, 1944).

———, *La nostra lotta per la democrazia e per il socialismo: discorso pronunciato alla Conferenza nazionale d'organizzazione, Firenze 10 gennaio* (Rome: UESISA, 1947).
———, *Per l'unità di tutto il popolo contro il governo della discordia* (Rome: Superstampa, 1947).
———, *Tre minacce alla democrazia Italiana: Rapporto al 6 Congresso del PCI* (Rome: Centro diffuso Stampa del PCI, 1948).
———, 'Il rapporto al VIII Congresso' (1956), in: P.C.I., *Il PCI e la svolta di '56*, pp. 49–100.
———, 'Elementi per una dichiarazione programmatica del P.C.I.' (1956), in: P.C.I., *Il PCI e la svolta di '56*, pp. 113–141.
———, 'Linea democratica e prospettiva rivoluzionaria' (1961), in: Togliatti, *Democrazia e socialismo*, pp. 15–20.
———, 'A proposito di socialismo e democrazia' (1961), in: Togliatti, *Democrazia e socialismo*, pp. 21–50.
———, Togliatti, *Democrazia e socialismo: Da l'Unità e la Rinascita: Febbraio—Aprile 1961* (Rome: Partito Comunista Italiano, 1961).
———, 'Rilancio della DC', (1964), in: Togliatti, *Opere VI*, pp. 759–761.
———, 'Le strade del partito socialista' (1963), in: Togliatti, *Opere VI*, pp. 740–743.
———, *Opere VI 1956–1964* (Rome: Editori Riuniti, 1984).
Various authors, 'The Revolutionary Action Committee of the Sorbonne' (1968), in: Feenberg and Freedman eds., *When Poetry Ruled the Streets*, pp. 152–168.
Viale, G., 'Cinquanta giorni di lotta alla FIAT' (1969), in: Viale, *S'avanza uno strano soldato*, pp. 49–58.
———, 'La Rivoluzione culturale nelle fabbriche italiane' (1969), in: Viale, *S'avanza uno strano soldato*, pp. 59–67.
———, *S'avanza uno strano soldato* (Rome: Edizioni di Lotta Continua, 1973).
———, *Il Sessantotto: Tra rivoluzione e restaurazione* (Milan: Mazzotta Editore, 1978).
Vogel, H.-J., 'Politischer Ausblick' (1984), in: A. Möller ed., *Wirtschaftspolitik in den 80er Jahren* (Bonn: Verlag Neue Gesellschaft, 1984), pp. 210–215.
Wehner, H., 'Außenpolitische Lage: Aussprache über die Regierungserklärung zur außenpolitische Lage' (1960), in: H. Wehner, *Bundestagsreden* (Bonn: AZ Studio, 1970), pp. 197–215.
Wehner, H., 'Demokratie und Landesverteidigung: Diskussionsbeitrag vor dem Godesberger Parteitag der SPD' (1959), in: H. Wehner, *Wandel und Bewährung. Ausgewählte Reden und Schriften 1930–1975* Frankfurt am Main: Ullstein Verlag, 1976), pp. 217–218.

Secondary Literature

Agosti, A., 'Il Partito comunista italiano e la svolta del 1947', *Studi Storici*, vol. 31, no. 1 (1990), pp. 53–88.
———, 'Partito Nuovo e democrazia progressiva nell'elaborazione dei comunisti', in: C. Franceschini, S. Guerrierie and G. Monina eds., *Le idee costituzionali della resistenza: Atti del Convegno di studi Roma 19, 20 e 21 ottobre 1995* (Rome: Presidenza del Consiglio dei ministri, 1995), pp. 235–248.
Agulhon, M., 'De Gaulle et l'histoire de France', *Vingtième Siècle. Revue d'histoire*, vol. 53, no. 1 (1997), pp. 3–12.
Alatri, P., 'Luigi Sturzo a cento anni della nascita', *Studi storici*, vol. 13, no. 1 (1972), pp. 199–215.
Alibert-Fabre, V., 'La pensée constitutionnelle du général de Gaulle à « l'épreuve des circonstances »', *Revue française de science politique*, vol. 40, no. 5 (1990), pp. 699–713.

Alleman, F.R., *Bonn ist nicht Weimar* (Cologne: Kiepenheurer & Witsch, 1956).
Allum, P., 'The Changing Face of Christian Democracy', in: C. Duggan and C. Wagstaff eds., *Italy and the Cold War: Politics, Culture, Society* (Oxford: Berg, 1995), pp. 117–130.
Atkin, N., *The Fifth French Republic* (Basingstoke: Palgrave McMillan, 2005).
Avagliano, L., 'Democrazia cristiana e politiche economiche', in: E. Lamberts ed., *Christian Democracy in the European Union 1945–1995: Proceedings of the Leuven Colloquium* (Leuven: Leuven University Press, 1997), pp. 363–368.
Barbagallo, F., 'Classe, nazione, democrazia: La sinistra in Italia dal 1944 al 1956', *Studi Storici*, vol. 33, no. 2/3 (1992), pp. 479–498, at p. 492.
———, *Dal '43 a '48: La formazione dell'Italia democratica* (Rome: l'Unità/Einaudi, 1996).
———, 'Il Pci dal sequestro di Moro alla morte di Berlinguer', *Studi storici*, vol. 42, no. 4 (2001), pp. 837–883.
———, 'Enrico Berlinguer, il compromesso storico e l'alternativa democratica', *Studi Storici*, vol. 45, no. 4 (2004), pp. 939–949.
Bauerkämper, A., 'The Twisted Road to Democracy as a Quest for Security: Germany in the Twentieth Century', *German History*, vol. 32, no. 3 (2014), pp. 431–455.
Becker, W., 'Der Einfluß der Unionsparteien auf der politische Ordnung der Bundesrepublik Deutschland', in: E. Lamberts ed., *Christian Democracy in the European Union 1945–1995: Proceedings of the Leuven Colloquium* (Leuven: Leuven University Press, 1997), pp. 224–241.
Bedeschi, G., *La prima repubblica (1946–1993): Storia di una democrazia difficile* (Rome: Rubettino editore, 2013).
Bell, D.S., *Parties and Democracy in France: Parties under Presidentialism* (Aldershot: Ashgate, 2000).
———, *Francois Mitterrand: A Political Biography* (Cambridge: Polity Press, 2005).
Berger, S., 'Democracy and Social Democracy', *European History Quarterly*, vol. 32, no. 1 (2002), pp. 13–37.
———, 'Communism, Social Democracy and the Democracy Gap', *Socialist History*, vol. 27 (2005), pp. 1–20.
———, 'A Return to the National Paradigm? National History Writing in Germany, Italy, France, and Britain from 1945 to the Present', *The Journal of Modern History*, vol. 77, no. 3 (2005), pp. 629–678.
Bergounioux, A. and G. Grunberg, *Le long remords du pouvoir : Le Parti socialiste français 1905–1992* (Paris: Fayard, 1992).
———, *L'ambition et le remords : Les socialistes français et le pouvoir (1905–2005)* (Paris: Fayard, 2005).
Bernard, M., 'Les relations entre Valéry Giscard d'Estaing et la majorité (1974–1978)', in: S. Berstein, R. Rémond and J.-F. Sirinelli eds., *Les années Giscard : Institutions et pratiques politiques 1974–1978* (Paris: Fayard, 2003), pp. 191–207.
Berstein, S., *The Republic of De Gaulle* (Cambridge: Cambridge University Press, 1993).
———, 'De Gaulle and Gaullism in the Fifth Republic', in: H. Hough and J. Horne ed., *De Gaulle and Twentieth Century France* (London: Hodder Education Publishers, 1995), pp. 109–123.
———, 'The Crisis of the Left and the Renaissance of the Republican Model 1981–1995', in: M. MacLean ed., *The Mitterrand Years: Legacy and Evaluation* (Basingstoke: Palgrave McMillan, 1998), pp. 46–65.
———, 'La modèle républicaine: une modèle politique syncrétique', in: S. Berstein ed., *Les cultures politiques en France* (Paris: Éditions du Seuil, 1999), pp. 119–151.
———, 'De la démocratie plébiscitaire au Gaullisme: naissance d'une nouvelle culture politique républicain', in: Berstein ed., *Les cultures politiques en France*, pp. 153–187.
———, *Histoire du Gaullisme* (Paris: Perrin, 2001).

Bobbio, L., *Storia di Lotta continua* (Milan: Feltrinelli, 1988).
———, *Die Adenauer-CDU: Gründung, Aufstieg und Krise eine Erfolgspartei 1945–1969* (Munich: Deutsche Verlags-Anstalt, 2001).
Bouvier, B.W., *Zwischen Godesberg und Großer Koalition: Der Weg der SPD in die Regierungsverantwortung: Außen, Sicherheits- und Deutschlandpolitische Umorientierung und gesellschaftliche Öffnung der SPD 1960–1966* (Bonn: Diez Verlag, 1990).
Bracke, M., *Which Détente? Whose Socialism? West European Communism and the Czechoslovak Crisis* (Budapest: Central European University Press, 2007).
Brandt, P. 'Germany after 1945: Revolution by Defeat?', in: R. Rürup ed., *The Problem of Revolution in Germany 1789–1989* (Oxford: Berg, 2002), pp. 129–160.
Brauntahl, G., 'Opposition in the Kohl Era: The SPD and the Left', in: C. Clemens and W.A. Paterson eds., *The Kohl Chancellorship* (London: Port Class, 1998), pp. 143–162.
Broche, F., *Une histoire des antigaullismes des origines à nos jours* (Paris: Bartillat, 2007).
Brouard, S., 'The Politics of Constitutional Veto in France: Constitutional Council, Legislative Majority and Electoral Competition', *West European Politics*, vol. 32, no. 2 (2009), pp. 384–403.
Buchanan, T., 'Anti-fascism and Democracy in the 1930s', *European History Quarterly*, vol. 32, no. 1 (2002), pp. 39–57.
Buchanan, T., and M. Conway, 'The Politics of Democracy in Twentieth Century Europe: Introduction', *European History Quarterly*, vol. 32, no. 1 (2002), pp. 5–12;
Bull, M.J., 'The great failure? The Democratic Party of the Left in Italy's Transition', in: S. Gundle and S. Parker eds., *The New Italian Republic: From the Fall of the Berlin Wall to Berlusconi* (London: Routledge, 1996), pp. 159–172.
———, 'The Italian Transition that Never Was', *Modern Italy*, vol. I7, no. 1 (2012), pp. 103-118.
Callot, E.F., *Le mouvement républicain populaire : Un parti politique de la démocratie chrétienne en France: Origine, structure, doctrine, programme et action politique* (Paris: Éditions Marcel Rivière, 1978).
Campanini, C., 'I programmi del partito democratico cristiana', in: F. Malgeri ed., *Storia della Democrazia Cristiana: Vol. I 1943–1948: Le origini: La DC dalla resistenza alla repubblica* (Rome: Edizione Cinque Lune, 1987), pp. 205–229.
Canovan, M., 'Trust the People? Populism and the Two Faces of Democracy', *Political Studies*, vol. 47, no. 1 (1999), pp. 2–16.
———, 'Taking Politics to the People: Populism as the Ideology of Democracy', in Y. Mény and Y. Surel eds., *Democracies and the Populist Challenge* (Basingstoke: Palgrave McMillan, 2002), pp. 25–44.
Capozzi, E., 'La polemica antipartitocratica', in: G. Orsina ed., *Storia delle destra nell'Italia repubblicana* (Soveria Mannelli: Rubbettino editore, 2009), pp. 179–206.
Carboni, C., 'Elites and the Democratic Disease', in: A. Mammone and G.A.Veltri eds., *Italy Today: The Sick Man of Europe* (London: Routledge 2010), pp. 19–33.
Castellani, P., 'La Democrazia cristiana dal Centro-sinistra al delitto Moro (1962–1978), in: F. Malgeri ed., *Storia della Democrazia cristiana: IV: Dal Centro-sinistra agli "anni di piombo" (1962–1978)* (Rome: Edizione Cinque Lune, 1989), pp. 3–118.
Cavedon, R., 'Cronaca politica di un decennio: la DC dal delitto Moro alla segretaria Forlani' (1979–1989), in: F. Malgeri ed., *Storia della Democrazia cristiana: Volume V. Dal Delitto Moro alla Segretaria Forlani 1979–1989* (Rome: Edizione Cinque Lune, 1989), pp. 3–31.
Chafer, T. and E. Godin eds., *The End of the French Exception? Decline and Revival of the French Model* (Basingstoke: Palgrave McMillan, 2010).

Charlot, J., *Le gaullisme d'opposition 1946-1958 : Histoire du gaullisme* (Paris: Fayard,1983).
Chiarini, R., 'La fortuna del gollismo in Italia: L'attacco della destra alla "Repubblica dei partiti"', *Storia Contemporanea*, vol. 23, no. 3 (1992), pp. 385–424.
Cohen, E., 'L'ombre portée de Mai '68 en politique: démocratie et participation', *Vingtième siècle : Revue d'histoire*, vol. 98 (2009), pp. 19–28.
Colarizi, S. and M. Gervasoni, *La cruna dell'ago: Craxi, il partito socialista e la crisi della Repubblica* (Bari: Laterza, 2005).
Cole, A., 'Political Leadership in Western Europe: Helmut Kohl in Comparative Perspective', in: C. Clemens and W.A. Paterson eds., *The Kohl Chancellorship* (London: Port Class, 1998), pp. 120–142.
Conwans, J., 'French Public Opinion and the Founding of the Fourth Republic', *French Historical Studies*, vol. 17, no. 1 (1991), pp. 62–95.
Conway, M., 'Democracy in Postwar Europe: The Triumph of a Political Model', *European History Quarterly*, vol. 32, no. 1 (2002), pp. 59–84.
———, 'The Age of Christian Democracy: The Frontiers of Success and Failure', in: T. Kselman and J.A. Buttigieg eds., *European Christian Democracy: Historical Legacies and Comparative Perspectives* (Notre Dame: University of Notre Dame Press, 2003), pp. 43–67.
———, 'The Rise and Fall of Europe's Democratic Age 1945–1973', *Contemporary European History*, vol. 13, no. 1 (2004), pp. 67–88.
Conway, M. and V. Depkat, 'Towards a European History of the Discourse of Democracy: Discussing Democracy in Western Europe, 1945–60', in: M. Conway and K.K. Patel eds., *Europeanization in the Twentieth Century: Historical Approaches* (Basingstoke: Palgrave McMillan, 2010), pp. 132–156.
Conze, W., H. Maier, C. Meier and H.L. Reimann, 'Demokratie', in: O. Brunner, W. Conze and R. Koselleck eds., *Geschichtliche Grundbegriffe* (7 vols., Stuttgart, 1972–1992), I, pp. 821–899.
Cooke, P., *Luglio 1960: Tambroni e la repressione fallita* (Milan: Teti editore, 2000).
Corduwener, P., 'Democracy as a Contested Concept in Postwar Western Europe: A Comparative Study of Political Debates in France, West Germany and Italy', *Historical Journal*, vol. 59, no. 1, pp. 197–220.
Cotturi, G., 'Moro e la transizione interrotta', *Studi Storici*, vol. 37, no. 2 (1996), pp. 489–511.
Courtois, S. and M. Lazar, *Histoire du Parti communiste français* (Paris: Presses universitaires de France, 1995).
Coutier, P., *La Quatrième République* (Paris: Presses Universitaires de France, 1986).
Crainz, G., *Il paese mancato: Dal miracolo eocnomico agli anni ottanta* (Rome: Donzelli editore, 2003).
———, *Storia del miracolo italiano: Cultura, identità e trasformazioni fra anni cinquanta e sessanta* (Rome: Donzelli editore, 2004).
———, *Il paese reale: Dall'assassino di Moro all'Italia di oggi* (Rome: Donzelli editore, 2012).
Crozier, M., S.P. Huntington, and J. Watanuki, *The Crisis of Democracy: What's Troubling the Trilateral Countries?* (New York: New York University Press, 1975).
D'Abzac-Épezy, C. et al., *Charles de Gaulle et le Rassemblement du Peuple Français 1947–1955* (Paris: Colin, 1998).
Dahl, R.A., *Democracy and Its Critics* (New Haven: Yale University Press, 1989).
Dalton, R.J. and M. Kuechler, 'The Challenge of New Movements' in: R.J. Dalton and M. Kuechler eds., *Challenging the Political Order: New Social and Political Movements in Western Democracies* (Cambridge: Cambridge University Press, 1990), pp. 3–20.
Decker, F., 'Germany: Right Wing Populist Failures and Left-wing Successes', in: D. Albertazzi and D. McDonnel eds., *Twenty-first Century Populism: The Spectre for Western European Democracy* (Basingstoke: Palgrave McMillan, 2007), pp. 119–134.

Degli'Innocenti, M., *Storia del PSI: Vol. III Dal dopoguerra a oggi* (Bari: Laterza, 1993).
Della Porta, D., *Social Movements, Political Violence and the State: A Comparative Analysis of Italy and Germany* (Cambridge: Cambridge University Press, 1995).
Dittberner, J., 'FDP—Partei der Zweiten Wahl: Ein Beitrag zur Geschichte der liberalen Partei und ihrer Funktionen im Pateiensystem der Bundesrepublik' (Opladen: Westdeuscher Verlag, 1987), pp. 14–39.
Dormois, J.P., *The French Economy in the Twentieth Century* (Cambridge: Cambridge University Press, 2004).
Drake, R., 'Catholics and the Italian Revolutionary Left of the 1960s', *The Catholic Historical Review*, vol. 94, no. 3 (2008), pp. 450–475.
Dreyfus, M., *Le PCF : Crises et dissidences* (Brussels: Éditions complexes, 1990).
Drummond, G.D., *The German Social Democrats in Opposition 1949–1960: The Case against Rearmament* (Norman: University of Oklahoma Press, 1982).
Dubois, G., 'La conception de la présidence de Valéry Giscard d'Estaing', in: S. Berstein, R. Rémond and J.-F. Sirinelli eds., *Les années Giscard : Institutions et pratiques politiques 1974–1978* (Paris: Fayard, 2003), pp. 59–75.
Dumoulin, M., 'The Socio-economic Impact of Christian Democracy in Western Europe', in: E. Lamberts ed., *Christian Democracy in the European Union* (Leuven: Leuven University Press, 1997), pp. 369–374.
Dunn, J., *Setting the People Free: The Story of Democracy* (London: Atlantic, 2005).
Dutton, D.V., *Origins of the French Welfare State: The Struggle for Social Reform in France 1914–1947* (Cambridge: Cambridge University Press, 2002).
Eichengreen, J.B., *The European Economy since 1945: Coordinated Capitalism* (New Jersey: Princeton University Press, 2007).
Eley, G., 'Legacies of Antifascism: Constructing Democracy in Postwar Europe', *New German Critique*, vol. 67 (1996), pp. 73–100.
———, *Forging Democracy: A History of the Left in Europe 1850–2000* (Oxford: Oxford University Press, 2000).
Evans, M., *Algeria: France's Undeclared War* (Oxford: Oxford University Press, 2012).
Facon, P., *La IVe République : De la libération au 13 Mai* (Paris: Pygmalion, 1997).
Feldkamp, M.F., *Der Parlamentarische Rat 1948–1949: Die Entstehung des Grundgesetz* (Göttingen: Vandenhoeck & Ruprecht, 1998).
Ferrara, M., 'The South European Countries', in: F. Castles et al. eds., *The Oxford Handbook of the Welfare State* (Oxford: Oxford University Press, 2010), pp. 616–629, at p. 620.
Ferraresi, F., *Minacce alla democrazia: La destra radicale e la strategia di tensione in Italia nel dopoguerra* (Milan: Feltrinelli, 1995).
———, *Threats to Democracy: The Radical Right in Italy after the War* (New Jersey: Princeton University Press, 1996).
Fieschi, C., *Fascism, Populism and the French Fifth Republic: In the Shadow of Democracy* (Manchester: Manchester University Press, 2004).
Forlenza, R., 'A Party for the *Mezzogiorno*: The Christian Democratic Party, Agrarian Reform and the Government of Italy', *Contemporary European History*, vol. 19, no. 4 (2010), pp. 331–349.
Forner, S.A., 'Das Sprachrohr keiner Besatzungsmacht oder Partei: Deutsche Publizisten, die Vereinigten Staaten und die demokratische Erneuerung in Westdeutschland, 1945–1949', in: A. Bauerkämper, K.H. Jarausch and M.M. Payk eds., *Demokratiewunder: Transatlantische Mittler und die kulturelle Öffnung Westdeutschlands, 1945–1970* (Göttingen, 2005), pp. 159–189;
Forner, S.A., *German Intellectuals and the Challenge of Democratic Renewal: Culture and Politics after 1945* (Cambridge: Cambridge University Press, 2014).
Frankland, E.G., 'Germany: The Rise, Fall and Recovery of *Die Grünen*', in: D. Richardson and C. Rootes eds., *The Green Challenge: The Development of Green Parties in Europe* (London: Routledge, 1995), pp. 17–32.

Galleni, M. ed., *Rapporto sul terrorismo* (Milan: Rizzoli Editore, 1981).

Galli, G., *Il bipartismo imperfetto: comunisti e democristiani in Italia* (Bologna: Il Mulino, 1966).

———, *Storia del PCI: Il partito comunista italiano: Livorno 1921—Rimini 1991* (Rome: Kaos editore, 1993).

———, *Storia della DC 1943-1993: Mezzo secolo della Democrazia cristiana* (Rome: Kaos editore, 2007).

Gallie, W.B., 'Essentially Contested Concepts', *Proceedings of the Aristotelian Society*, vol. 56 (1955-1956), pp. 167-198.

Gassert, P., 'Narratives of Democratization: 1968 in Postwar Europe', in: M. Klimke and J. Scharloth eds., *1968 in Europe: A History of Protest and Activism, 1957-1977* (Basingstoke: Palgrave MacMillan, 2008), pp. 307-324 at p. 315.

Gervasoni, M., *Storia d'Italia degli anni ottanta: Quando eravamo moderni* (Venice: Marsilio editore, 2010).

Giachetti, D., *L'autunno caldo* (Rome: Ediessi, 2013).

Gilcher-Holety, I., 'France', in: M. Klimke and J. Scharloth eds., *1968 in Europe: A History of Protest and Activism, 1957-1977* (Basingstoke: Palgrave MacMillan, 2008), pp. 111-123.

Gildea, R., *Children of the Revolution: The French 1799-1914* (Boston: Harvard University Press, 2010).

Ginsborg, P., *A History of Contemporary Italy: Society and Politics 1943-1980* (London: Penguin Press, 2003).

———, *Italy and its Discontents: Civil Society, Family, State, 1980-2001* (New York: Penguin, 2003).

Giovagnoli, A., *Il partito italiano: La Democrazia cristiana dal 1942 al 1994* (Bari: Laterza, 1996).

———, *Il caso Moro: Una tragedia repubblicana* (Bologna: Il Mulino, 2005).

———, 'Democrazia Cristiana e terrorismo', in: V.V. Alberti ed., *La DC e il terrorismo nell'Italia degli anni di piombo* (Rome: Rubbettino, 2008), pp. 19-31.

Glossner, G.L., *The Making of the German Post-War Economy: Political Communication and Public Reception of the Social Market Economy after World War II* (London: I.B. Tauris Publishers, 2010).

Gordon, D.A., 'A "Mediterranean New Left"? Comparing and Contrasting the French PSU and the Italian PSIUP', *Contemporary European History*, vol. 19, no. 4 (2010), pp. 309-330.

Görtemacher, M., *Geschichte der Bundesrepublik: Von Gründung bis zum Gegenwart* (Munich, C.H. Beck Verlag, 1999).

Gosewinkel, D., 'Zwischen Diktatur und Demokratie: Wirtschaftliches Planungsdenken in Deutschland und Frankreich: Vom Ersten Weltkrieg bis zur Mitte der 1970er Jahre', *Geschichte und Gesellschaft*, vol. 34, no. 3, (2008), pp. 327-359.

Granieri, R.J., 'Politics in C Minor: The CDU/CSU between Germany and Europe since the Secular Sixties', *Central European History*, vol. 42, no. 1 (2009), pp. 1-32.

Grillo di Cortona, P., *Dalla Prima alla Seconda Repubblica: Il Cambiamento politico in Italia* (Rome: Carocci editore, 2007).

Guarltieri, R., *L'Italia dal 1943 al 1992: DC e PCI nella storia della Repubblica* (Rome: Carocci editore, 2006).

Guerrieri, S., 'Le idee costituzionali del Pcf e del Pci all'indomani della Liberazione', *Studi Storici*, vol. 36, no. 3 (1995), pp. 863-882.

Gundle, S., 'The Rise and Fall of Craxi's Socialist Party', in: S. Gundle and S. Parker eds., *The New Italian Republic: From the Fall of the Berlin Wall to Berlusconi* (London: Routledge 1996), pp. 85-98.

Gunter, R. and L. Diamond, 'Types and Functions of Parties', in: R. Gunter and L. Diamond eds., *Political Parties and Democracy* (Baltimore: John Hopkins University Press, 2001), pp. 3-39.

Haan, I, de., 'The Western European Welfare State beyond Christian and Social Democratic Ideology', in: D. Stone ed., *The Oxford Handbook of Postwar European History* (Oxford: Oxford University Press, 2012), pp. 299–318.

Hanagan, M., 'Changing Margins in Post-war European Politics', in: R. Wakeman ed., *Themes in Modern European History since 1945* (London/New York: Routledge, 2003), pp. 120–141.

Hanley, D., *Party, Society, Government: Republican Democracy in France* (Oxford: Berghahn Books, 2002).

Hansen, H., *Die Sozialistische Reichspartei: Aufstieg und Scheitern einer rechtsextremen Partei* (Düsseldorf: Droste Verlag, 2007).

Hanshew, K., *Terror and Democracy in West Germany* (Cambridge: Cambridge University Press, 2012).

Hayward, J., 'Moins d'État or Mieux d'État: the French Response to the Neo-liberal Challenge', in: M. MacLean ed., *The Mitterrand Years: Legacy and Evaluation* (Basingstoke: Palgrave McMillan, 1998), pp. 23–35.

Hazareesingh, S., 'Bonapartism as the Progenitor of Democracy. The Paradoxical Case of the French Second Empire', in P. Baehr en M. Richter eds., *Dictatorship in History. Bonapartism, Caesarism, and Totalitarianism* (Cambridge: Cambridge University Press 2004), pp. 129–152.

———, 'L'imaginaire républicain en France, de la Révolution française à Charles de Gaulle', *Revue historique*, no. 659 (2011), pp. 637–654.

———, *In the Shadow of the General. Modern France and the Myth of De Gaulle* (Oxford: Oxford University Press, 2012).

Hellman, S., 'Italian Communism in the First Republic', in: S. Gundle and S. Parker eds., *The New Italian Republic: From the Fall of the Berlin Wall to Berlusconi* (London: Routledge 1996), pp. 72–84.

Hewlett, N., *Democracy in Modern France* (London: Bloomsbury Publishing, 2005).

Hine, D., 'Italian political reform in comparative perspective', in: S. Gundle and S. Parker eds., *The New Italian Republic: From the Fall of the Berlin Wall to Berlusconi* (London: Routledge 1996), pp. 311–325.

Höbel, A., 'Il Pci di Longo e il '68 studentesco',*Studi Storici*, vol. 45, no. 2 (2004), pp. 419–459.

Hockenos, P., *Joschka Fischer and the Making of the Berlin Republic: An Alternative History of Post-war Germany* (Oxford: Oxford University Press, 2006).

Hodge, C.C., 'The Long Fifties: The Politics of Socialist Programmatic Revision in Britain, France and Germany',*Contemporary European History*, vol. 2, no. 1 (1993), pp. 17–34.

Hoeres, P., 'Von der "Tendenzwende" zur "geistig-moralischen Wende". Konstruktion und Kritik konservativer Signaturen in den 1970er und 1980er Jahren', *Vierteljahrshefte für Zeitgeschichte*, vol. 61, no. 1 (2013), pp. 93–119.

Horn, G.R., *The Spirit of 1968: Rebellion in Europe and North America 1956–1976* (Oxford: Oxford University Press, 2007).

Horne, J., 'The Transformation of Society', in J. McMillan ed., *Modern France 1880–2002* (Oxford: Oxford University Press, 2003), pp. 127–149.

Ignazi, P., *Il polo escluso: Profilo storico del Movimento Sociale Italiano* (Bologna: Il Mulino, 1989).

———, *Postfascisti? Dal Movimento sociale italiano ad Alleanza nazionale* (Bologna: Il Mulino, 1994).

———, 'Italy in the 1970s between Self-Expression and Organicism', in: A.C. Bull and A. Giorgio eds., *Speaking Out and Silencing: Society, Politics and Culture in the 1970s* (London: Legenda, 2006), pp. 10–29.

Imbriani, A.M., *Vento del Sud. Moderati, Reazionari, Qualunquisti 1943–1948* (Bologna: Il Mulino, 1996).

Jackson, J., 'General De Gaulle and his Enemies: Anti-Gaullism in France since 1940', *Transactions of the Royal Historical Society*, vol. 9 (1999), pp. 43–65.

Jarausch, K., *Die Umkehr: Deutsche Wandlungen 1945–1995* (Munich: Deutsche Verlags- Anstalt, 2004).

Jennings, J., *Revolution and the Republic: A History of Political Thought in France since the Eighteenth Century* (Oxford: Oxford University Press, 2012).

Judt, T., *Postwar: A History of Europe since 1945* (London: Heinemann, 2005).

———, *Ill fares the Land* (New York: Penguin Press, 2010).

Kaelbe, H., *The 1970s in Europe: A Period of Disillusionment or Promise?* (London: German Historical Institute, 2009).

Kappenküper, U., 'Zwischen "Sammlungsbewegung" und "Volkspartei": Die CDU 1945-1969', in: M. Gehler, W. Kaiser and H. Wohnout eds., *Christdemokratie in Europa in 20: Jahrhundert* (Vienna: Böhlau Verlag, 2001), pp. 385–398.

Kirchner, E.J. and D. Broughton, 'The FDP in the Federal Republic of Germany: The Requirements of Survival and Success', in: E.J. Kirchner ed., *Liberal Parties in Western Europe* (Cambridge: Cambridge University Press, 1988), pp. 62–92.

Kleinmann, H-O., *Geschichte der CDU: 1945–1982* (Stuttgart: Deutsche Verlags-Anstalt, 1993).

Klimke, M., 'West Germany', in: M. Klimke and J. Scharloth eds., *1968 in Europe: A History of Protest and Activism, 1957–1977* (Basingstoke: Palgrave MacMillan, 2008), pp. 97–110.

Klotzsch, L. et al., 'What Has Happened to Green Principles in Electoral and Parliamentary Politics?', in: M. Mayer and J. Ely eds., *The German Greens* (Philadelphia: Temple University Press, 1998), pp. 97–127.

Knapp, A., *Parties and the Party System in France: A Disconnected Democracy?* (Basingstoke: Palgrave Macmillan, 2004).

Koenen, G., *Das rote Jahrzehnt. Unsere kleine deutsche Kulturrevolution, 1967–1977* (Cologne: Kiepenheuer & Witsch, 2001).

Köppel, S., 'Italy's Constitutional Odyssey: Failed Attempts at Constitutional Reform in the 1980s and 1990s', in: L. Risso and M. Boria eds., *Politics and Culture in Post-war Italy* (Newcastle: Cambridge Scholars Press, 2006), pp. 223–236.

Kuisel, R.F., *Capitalism and the State in Modern France* (Cambridge: Cambridge University Press, 1981).

Kurz, J. and M. Tolomelli, 'Italy', in: M. Klimke and J. Scharloth eds., *1968 in Europe: A History of Protest and Activism, 1957–1977* (Basingstoke: Palgrave MacMillan, 2008) pp. 83–96.

Lafon, F., 'Structures idéologiques et nécessités pratiques au congrès de la S.F.I.O. en 1946', *Revue d'histoire moderne et contemporaine*, vol. 36, no. 4 (1989), pp. 672–694.

Lamberts, E., 'Christian Democrats and the Constitutional State in Western Europe 1945–1995', in: T. Kselman and J.A. Buttigieg eds., *European Christian Democracy: Historical Legacies and Comparative Perspectives* (Notre Dame: University of Notre Dame Press, 2003), pp. 121–137.

Lazar., M., 'Forte e fragile, immuable et changeante . . . La culture politique communiste', in: S. Berstein ed., *Les cultures politiques en France* (Paris: Éditions du Seuil, 1999), pp. 227–257.

———, *Le communisme, une passion française* (Paris: Perrin, 2002).

———, 'La gauche e la défi des changements dans les années 1970–80 : Les cas français et italien, *Journal of Modern European History*, vol. 9, no. 2 (2011), pp. 241–262.

———, 'Testing Italian democracy', *Comparative European Politics*, vol. 11, no. 3 (2013), pp. 317–336.

Lijphart, A., 'Comparative Politics and the Comparative Method', *The American Political Science Review*, vol. 65, no. 3 (1971), pp. 682–693.

Loewenstein, K., 'Militant democracy and fundamental rights I', *The American Political Science Review*, vol. 31, no. 3 (1937), pp. 417–432.
——, 'Militant democracy and fundamental rights II', *The American Political Science Review*, vol. 31, no. 4 (1937), pp. 638–658.
Lomartire, C.M., *Il Qualunquista: Guglielmo Giannini e l'antipolitica* (Milan: Mondadori, 2008).
Loreto, P., di, *Togliatti e la "Doppiezza": Il PCI tra democrazia e insurrezione: 1944–1949* (Bologna: Il Mulino, 1991).
Lösche, P. and F. Walter, *Die SPD: Klassenpartei—Volkspartei—Quotenpartei: Zur Entwicklung der Sozialdemokratie von Weimar bis zur deutschen Vereinigung* (Darmstadt: Wissenschaftliche Buchgesellschaft, 1992).
Lowe, K., *Savage Continent: Europe in the Aftermath of World War II* (New York: St. Martin's Press, 2012).
Lumley, R., *States of Emergency: Cultures of Revolt in Italy 1968–1978* (London: Verso, 1990).
Lupo, S., *Partito e antipartito: Una storia politica della prima repubblica (1946–1978)* (Rome: Donzelli editore, 2004).
Lussana, F., 'Il confronto con le socialdemocrazie e la ricerca di un nuovo socialismo nell'ultimo Berlinguer', *Studi storici*, vol. 45, no. 2 (2004), pp. 461–488.
Maier, C.S., 'Democracy since the French Revolution', in: J. Dunn ed., *Democracy: The Unfinished Journey 508 BC-1993 AD* (Oxford: Oxford University Press, 1992), pp. 125–152.
Mair, P., 'Populist Democracy vs Party Democracy, in: Mény and Surel eds., *Democracies and the Populist Challenge*, pp. 81–98, at p. 91.
Major, P., *The Death of the KPD: Communism and Anti-Communism in West Germany 1945–1956* (Oxford: Clarendon Press, 1997).
Malgeri, F., *L'Italia democristiana: Uomini e idee dal cattolicismo democratico nell'Italia repubblicana (1943–1993)* (Rome: Gangemi editore, 2004).
Mayeur, J.-M., 'La Démocratie d'inspiration Chrétienne en France', in: E. Lamberts ed., *Christian Democracy in the European Union 1945–1995: Proceedings of the Leuven Colloquium* (Leuven: Leuven University Press, 1997), pp. 79–92.
Mazower, M., *Dark Continent: Europe's Twentieth Century* (London: Lane/Penguin Press, 1998).
McCarthy, P., *The Crisis of the Italian State: From the Origins of the Cold War to the Fall of Berlusconi and Beyond* (Basingstoke: Palgrave McMillan, 1997).
Mende, S., *"Nichts recht, nichts links, sondern vorn": Eine Geschichte der Gründungsgrünen* (Munich: Oldenbourg Verlag, 2011), pp. 279–285.
Mény, Y. and Y. Surel eds., *Democracies and the Populist Challenge* (Basingstoke: Palgrave McMillan, 2002).
Metzler, G., 'Am Ende aller Krisen? Politisches Denken und Handeln in der Bundesrepublik in der sechziger Jahre', *Historisches Zeitschrift*, vol. 275 (2002), pp. 57–103.
Mewes, H., 'A Brief History of the Green Party', in: M. Mayer and J. Ely eds., *The German Greens* (Philadelphia: Temple University Press, 1998), pp. 29–48.
Mitchell, M., 'Materialism and Secularism: CDU Politicians and National Socialism, 1945–1949', *The Journal of Modern History*, vol. 67, no. 2 (1995), pp. 278–308.
Moreau, J., 'Le congrès d'Épinay-sur-Seine du parti socialiste', *Vingtième siècle : Revue d'histoire*, vol. 65, no. 1 (2000), pp. 81–96.
Mudde, C., *Populist Radical Right Parties in Europe* (Cambridge: Cambridge University Press, 2012).
Mudde, C. and C.R. Kaltwasser eds., *Populism in Europe and the Americas: Threat or Corrective to Democracy?* (Cambridge: Cambridge University Press, 2013).
Müller, J.W., *Another Country. German Intellectuals, Unification and National Identity* (New Haven: Yale University Press, 2000).

———, 'Research Note: The Triumph of What (if Anything)? Rethinking Political Ideologies and Political Institutions in Twentieth Century Europe, *Journal of Political Ideologies*, vol. 14, no. 2 (2009), pp. 211–226.

———, 'European Intellectual History as Contemporary History', *Journal of Contemporary History*, vol. 46, no. 3 (2011), pp. 574–590.

———, *Contesting Democracy: Political Thought in Twentieth Century Europe* (New Haven: Yale University Press, 2011).

Nencioni, T., 'Tra neutralismo e atlantismo: La politica internazionale del Partito socialista italiano 1956–1966', *Italia Contemporanea*, vol. 260 (2010), pp. 438–470.

Nicholls, A.J., *The Bonn Republic: West German Democracy 1945–1990* (London and New York: Longman, 1997).

Nonn, C., 'Das Godesberger Programm und die Krise des Ruhrbergbaus: Zum Wandel der deutschen Sozialdemokratie von Ollenhauer zu Brandt', *Vierteljahrshefte für Zeitgeschichte*, 50 (2002), pp. 71–97.

Nord, P., *France's New Deal. From the Thirties to the Postwar Era* (New Jersey: Princeton University Press, 2010).

Northcutt, W., 'François Mitterrand and the Political Use of Symbols: The Construction of a Centrist Republic', *French Historical Studies*, vol. 17, no. 1 (1991), pp. 141–158.

Nullmeier, F. and F.-X. Kaufmann, 'Post-war Welfare State Development', in: F. Castles et al. eds., *The Oxford Handbook of the Welfare State* (Oxford: Oxford University Press, 2010), pp. 81–101.

Orlow, D., 'Delayed Reaction: Democracy, Nationalism and the SPD 1945–1966', *German Studies Review*, vol. 16, no. 1 (1997), pp. 77–102.

Orsina, G., 'The Republic after Berlusconi: Some Reflections on Historiography, Politics and the Political Use of History in Post-1994 Italy', *Modern Italy*, vol. 15, no. 1 (2010), pp. 77–92.

———, "L'antipolitica dei moderati: dal qualunquismo al berlusconismo', *Ventunesimo secolo*, vol. 30, no. 1 (2013), pp. 91–111.

———, *Il Berlusconismo nella storia d'Italia* (Venice: Marsilo editore, 2013).

Otto, V., *Das Staatsverständnis des Parlamentarischen Rates: Ein Beitrag zur Entstehungsgeschichte des Grundgesetzes für die Bundesrepublik Deutschland* (Düsseldorf: Rheinisch-Bergische Druckerei und Verlagsgesellschaft, 1971).

Padgett, S., 'The Chancellor and his Party', in: S. Padgett ed., *Adenauer to Kohl: The Development of the German Chancellorship* (London: Hurst, 1994), pp. 44–77.

Paggi, L., 'Violenza e democrazia nella storia delle Repubblica', *Studi storici*, vol. 39, no. 4 (1998), pp. 935–952.

Parr, S.J. and R. Putnam eds., *Disaffected Democracies: What's Troubling the Trilateral Countries?* (New Jersey: Princeton University Press, 2000).

Pelinka, A., 'Die Christdemokraten als europäische Parteifamilie', in: M. Gehler, W. Kaiser and W. Wohnout eds., *Christdemokraten in Europa in 20: Jahrhundert* (Vienna: Böhlau Verlag, 2001), pp. 537–555.

Pero, del, M., 'The United States and "Psychological Warfare" in Italy, 1948–1955', *Journal of American History*, vol. 87, no. 4 (2001), pp. 1304–1334.

Plattner, M.F., 'The Democratic Moment', *Journal of Democracy*, vol. 2, no. 4 (1991), pp. 34–46.

Piretti, M.S., 'Continuità e rottura alla nascita del sistema dei partiti', in: C. Franceschini, S. Guerrieri and G. Monina eds., *Le idee costituzionali della resistenza: Atti del Convegno di studi Roma 19, 20 e 21 ottobre 1995* (Rome: Presidenza del Consiglio dei ministri, 1995), pp. 206–212.

Pons, S., *L'impossibile egemonia: L'USSR, il PCI e le origine della guerra fredda (1943–1947)* (Rome: Carocci editore, 1999).

———, *Berlinguer e la fine del comunismo* (Turin: Einaudi editore, 2006).

Posner, R.A., *The Crisis of Capitalist Democracy* (Boston: Harvard University Press, 2010).

Pritchard, G., 'Schwarzenberg 1945: Antifascists and the Third Way in German Politics', *European History Quarterly*, vol. 35, no. 4 (2005), pp. 499–522.
Pulzer, P., *German Politics 1945–1995* (Oxford: Oxford University Press, 1995).
Radi, L., *Tambroni trent'anni dopo: La nascita del centro-sinistra* (Bologna: Il Mulino, 1990).
Raniolo, F., 'Forza Italia: A Leader with a Party', *South European Society and Politics*, vol. 11, no. 3–4 (2006) pp. 439–455.
Rioux, J.P., 'De Gaulle in Waiting', in: H. Hough and J. Horne ed., *De Gaulle and Twentieth Century France* (London: Hodder Education Publishers, 1995), pp. 35–49.
——, *La France de la Quatrième République : 2 : L'expansion et l'impuissance 1952–1958* (Paris: Éditions du Seuil, 1983).
——, *The Fourth Republic 1944–1958* (Cambridge: Cambridge University Press, 1987).
Rödder, A., 'Das "Modell Deutschland" zwischen Erfolgsgeschichte und Verfallsdiagnose', *Vierteljahrshefte für Zeitgeschichte*, vol. 54, no. 3 (2006), pp. 345–363.
Rogers, D.E., 'Transforming the German Party System: The United States and the Origins of Political Moderation 1945–1949', *Journal of Modern History*, vol. 65, no. 3 (1993), pp. 512–541.
Roggi, P., 'L'impegno della Dc nell'economia durante gli ultimi quarant'anni', in: F. Malgeri, ed., *Storia della Democrazia cristiana: Vol. IV: Dal Centro-sinistra agli "anni di piombo" (1962–1978)* (Rome: Edizione Cinque Lune, 1989), pp. 197–246.
Rosanvallon, P., *Le modèle politique français : La société civile contre le jacobinisme de 1789 à nos jours* (Paris: Seuil, 2006).
Roseman, M., 'Restoration and Stability: The Creation of a Stable Democracy in the Federal Republic of Germany', in: J. Garrard, V. Tolz and R. White eds., *European Democratization since 1800* (Basingstoke: Palgrave Macmillan, 1999), pp. 141–160.
Ross, G., 'Party Decline and Changing Party Systems: France and the French Communist Party', *Comparative Studies*, vol. 25 (1992), pp. 43–61.
Rufilli, R., 'L'ultimo Moro: dalla crisi del centro-sinistra all'avvio della terza fase', in: F. Malgeri ed., *Storia della Democrazia cristiana: IV: Dal Centro-sinistra agli "anni di piombo" (1962–1978)* (Rome: Edizione Cinque Lune, 1989), pp. 317–334.
Rupieper, H.J., 'Peacemaking with Germany. Grundlinien amerikanischer Demokratisierungspolitik 1945–1954', in: A. Bauerkämper, K.H. Jarausch and M.M. Payk eds., *Demokratiewunder: Transatlantische Mittler und die kulturelle Öffnung Westdeutschlands, 1945–1970* (Göttingen, 2005), pp. 41–56.
Rydgren, E., 'France: The Front National, Ethnonationalism and Populism', in: D. Albertazzi and D. McDonnel eds., *Twenty-first Century Populism: The Spectre for Western European Democracy* (Basingstoke: Palgrave McMillan, 2007), pp. 166–180.
Salvati, M., 'Il partito nell'elaborazione dei socialisti', in: C. Franceschini, S. Guerrieri and G. Monina eds., *Le idee costituzionali della resistenza: Atti del Convegno di studi Roma 19, 20 e 21 ottobre 1995* (Rome: Presidenza del Consiglio dei ministri, 1995), pp. 249–267.
Santamaria, Y., *Le parti de l'ennemi ? Le parti communiste française dans la lutte pour la paix (1947–1958)* (Paris: Armand Colin, 2006).
Sassoon, D., 'Politics', in: M. Fulbrook ed., *Europe since 1945* (Oxford: Oxford University Press, 2001), pp. 14–52.
——, 'The Rise and Fall of West European Communism 1939–48', *Contemporary European History*, vol. 1, no. 2 (1992), pp. 139–169.
——, *One Hundred Years of Socialism: The West European Left in the Twentieth Century* (London: Tauris Publishers, 1996).
Scala, R, di., *Renewing Italian Socialism: Nenni to Craxi* (Oxford: Oxford University Press, 1988).

Scarpari, G., *La Democrazia cristiana e le leggi eccezionali 1950–1953* (Milan: Feltrinelli, 1977).
Schieder, F., *Von der sozialen Bewegung zur Institution? Die Entstehung der Partei DIE GRÜNEN in den Jahren 1978 bis 1980: Argumenten, Entwicklungen und Strategien am Beispiel Bonn/Hannover/Osnabrück* (Münster: LIT Verlag, 1998).
Schmidtke, M.A., 'Reform, Revolte oder Revolution? Der Sozialistische Deutsche Studentenbund (SDS) und die Students for a Democratic Society (SDS), 1960–1970, *Geschichte und Gesellschaft*, vol. I7 (1998), pp. 188–206.
Schönhoven, K., 'Aufbruch in die sozialliberale Ära. Zur Bedeutung der 60er Jahre in der Geschichte der Bundesrepublik', *Geschichte und Gesellschaft*, vol. 25, no. 1 (1999), pp. 123–145.
———, *Wendejahre. Die Sozialdemokratie in der Zeit der Große Koalition, 1966–1969* (Bonn: Dietz Verlag, 2004).
Schot, H., *Die Formierte Gesellschaft und das deutsche Gemeinschaftswerk: Zwei gesellschaftspolitische Konzepte Ludwig Erhards* (Doct. Dissertation, Bonn, 1981).
Scilanga, G., *Le Due Italie dalla Resistenza alla Repubblica* (Bari: Laterza, 2010).
Scoppola, P., *La democrazia cristiana in Italia dal 1943 al 1947* (Milan: Dott. A. Giuffrè editore, 1975).
———, *La repubblica dei partiti: Evoluzione e crisi di un sistema politico* (Bologna: IlMulino, 1997).
Sirinelli, J.-F., *Mai 68 : L'événement Janus* (Paris: Fayard, 2008).
Sontheimer, K., *So war Deutschland nie: Anmerkungen zur politischen Kultur der Bundesrepublik* (Munich: C.H. Beck, 1990).
———, 'Intellectuals in the Political Life of the Federal Republic of Germany', in R. Pommerin ed., *Culture in the Federal Republic of Germany, 1945–1995* (Oxford: Berg, 1996), pp. 75–92.
———, *Die Adenauer Ära: Grundlegung der Bundesrepublik* (München: Deutscher Taschenbuch Verlag, 2003).
Souillac, R., *Le mouvement Poujade : De la défense professionnelle au populisme nationale (1953–1962)* (Paris: Sciences-Po Presses, 2007).
Spicka, M.E., *Selling the Economic Miracle: Economic Reconstruction and Politics in West Germany 1949–1957* (Oxford: Berghahn Books, 2007).
Spotts, F. and T. Wieser, *Italy: A Difficult Democracy: A Survey of Italian Politics* (Cambridge: Cambridge University Press, 1987).
Stegmann, F.J., 'Sozio-ökonomische Vorstellungen der Unionsparteien CDU/CSU', in: E. Lamberts ed., *Christian Democracy in the European Union 1945–1995: Proceedings of the Leuven Colloquium* (Leuven: Leuven University Press, 1997), pp. 295–312.
Stone, D., *Goodbye to All of That? A Story of Europe since 1945* (Oxford: Oxford University Press, 2014).
Tarchi, M., 'Italy: A Country of Many Populisms', in: D. Albertazzi and D. McDonnel eds., *Twenty-first Century Populism: The Spectre for Western European Democracy* (Basingstoke: Palgrave McMillan, 2007), pp. 84–99.
Tarchi, M., *L'Italia populista: Da qualunquismo ai girotondi* (Bologna: Il Mulino, 2003).
Thomas, N., *Protest Movements in the 1960s in West Germany: A Social History of Dissent and Democracy* (Oxford: Berg, 2003).
Thum, H., *Mitbestimmung in der Montanindustrie: Der Mythos vom Sieg der Gewerkschaften* (Stuttgart: Deutsche Verlagsanstalt, 1982).
Tolomelli, M., '1968: Formen der Interaktion zwischen Studenten und Arbeiterbewegung In Italien und der Bundesrepublik', *Geschichte und Gesellschaft*, vol. 17 (1998), pp. 82–100.
———, *Terrorismo e società: Il pubblico dibattito in Italia e Germania negli anni Settanta* (Bologna: Il Mulino, 2006).
Tracol, M., *Changer le travail pour changer la vie? Genèse des lois Auroux, 1981–1982* (Paris: L'Harmattan, 2009).

Traldi, F., 'Il Psi di fronte ad Bad Godesberg', *Ventunesimo secolo*, vol. 8, no. 18 (2009), pp. 137–161.
Tramontin, S., 'La Democrazia cristiana dalla Resistenza alla Repubblica', in: F. Malgeri ed., *Storia della Democrazia Cristiana: Vol. I 1943–1948: Le origini: La DC dalla resistenza alla repubblica* (Rome: Edizione Cinque Lune, 1987), pp. 13–177.
Tranfaglia, N., *Il labirinto italiano: Il fascismo, l'antifascismo, gli storici* (Florence: La nuova editrice, 1989).
———, 'Socialisti e comunisti nell'Italia repubblicana: Un dialogo sempre difficile', *Studi Storici*, vol. 33, no. 2/3 (1992), pp. 499–511.
———, 'Parlamento, partiti e società civile nella crisi repubblicana', *Studi storici*, vol. 42, no. 4 (2001), pp. 827–835.
Ullrich, S., *Der Weimar-Komplex: Das Scheitern der ersten deutschen Demokratie und die politische Kultur in der frühen Bundesrepublik* (Göttingen: Wallstein Verlag, 2009).
Ventresca, R., *From Fascism to Democracy: Culture and Politics in the Italian Election of 1948* (Toronto: Toronto University Press, 2004).
———, 'Mussolini's Ghost: Italy's Duce in History and Memory', *History and Memory*, vol. 18, no. 1 (2006), pp. 86–119.
Villalba, B., 'La genèse inachevée des Verts', *Vingtième Siècle : Revue d'histoire*, no. 53 (1997), pp. 85–97.
Vinen, R., *France 1934–1970* (Basingstoke: Palgrave McMillan, 1996).
———, 'The Fifth Republic as Parenthesis? Politics since 1945', in: J. McMillan ed., *Modern France 1880–2002* (Oxford: Oxford University Press, 2003), pp. 74–102.
———, *History in Fragments: Europe Twentieth Century* (London: Verso, 2005).
Vittoria, A., *Storia del PCI 1921–1991* (Rome: Carocci editore, 2006).
Wesel, U., *Die verspielte Revolution: 1968 und die Folgen* (Munich: Karl Blessing Verlag, 2002).
Winkler, H.A., *Germany: The Long Road West* (2 vols., Oxford: Oxford University Press, 2006).
Winock, M., *La Gauche en France* (Paris: Perrin, 2006).
———, Le parti socialiste dans le système politique français : Rupture et intégration', *Vingtième Siècle. Revue d'histoire*, no. 96 (2007), pp. 11–21.
Wirsching, A., *Abschied vom Provisorium 1982–1990* (Stuttgart: Deutsche Verlags-Anstalt, 2006).
Wolfrum, E., *Die geglückte Demokratie: Geschichte der Bundesrepublik Deutschland von ihren Anfang bis zur Gegenwart* (Bonn: Bundeszentrale für Politische Bildung, 2007).
Wolgast, E., *Die Wahrnehmung des Dritten Reiches in der unmittelbaren Nachkriegszeit (1945–1946)* (Heidelberg: Universitätsverlag Winter, 2001).
Wünsche, H.F., *Ludwig Erhards Konzept der Sozialen Marktwirtschaft. Erläuterungen und Interpretationen auf der Grundlage von wissenschaftlichen Schriften Erhards* (Freiburg, 1985).

Index

Adenauer, Konrad 12, 17, 18, 22, 27–9, 39, 41, 47, 49, 51, 52, 54, 58, 69–70, 74–5, 161, 165
Algerian War 51, 56, 58, 65, 78, 79, 81, 83, 85
Allies 5, 12

Barre, Raymond 128, 130, 144
Barzel, Rainer 107
Basic Law 15, 30–1, 50, 54
Basso, Lelio 19, 23, 27, 55, 77, 97–8
Bayeux programme 20, 22, 56, 79, 81, 108
Berliner Programme 131
Berlinguer, Enrico 113–14, 132, 136, 140–1, 143, 145, 148
Blum, Léon 14, 18, 21, 23, 26, 28, 43
Brandt, Willy 16, 19, 69, 74, 98, 109–10, 115, 131

Capanna, Mario 104, 148
Capitant, René 80, 83
CDU: and postwar reform 13, 20, 24, 27, 29; in the 1950s 40–2, 46, 51–4; and changes in the 1960s 65, 68–70, 72–5, 86, 95, 97; and reaction to '68, 100, 107–8, 115; after 1973 127, 144, 147
centre-left coalition in Italy 65–6, 71–2 76–8, 86, 95–9, 108, 145, 163
Chirac, Jacques 128, 138, 144–7
cohabitation 145
Cohn-Bendit, Daniel 100, 102–4
Comitato di Liberazione Nazionale 11–12, 21
Common Man's Front 12, 21–2, 30
Common Programme between PCF and PS 111–12, 115, 138

constitutional court: in Germany 5, 50, 52, 54; in Italy 25, 53, 55
Craxi, Bettino 129, 145, 148–9

DC: in the 1950s: 40–2, 44, 45, 51, 53, 55, 58; and changes of the 1960s 65, 67–8, 70–8, 86; and historic compromise (*see* historic compromise); and postwar reform 15–16, 18, 20, 23–5, 29–30; and reaction to 1968 101, 108, 115; and reaction to economic crisis in the 1970s 126–7, 132; in the 1980s 145–8, 150
Debré, Michel 48–9, 79–81
De Gasperi, Alcide 15, 28, 41, 44, 51, 53–5, 70
De Gaulle, Charles 5, 6, 11, 14, 16, 20–1, 24–5, 28, 31, 39, 42–3, 48, 56–7, 65, 78–86, 95–7, 100, 107–8, 111–12, 115, 138, 161–2
Deist, Heinrich 66
Democrazia Proletaria 136
Der Spiegel Affair 74
Dutschke, Rudi 100–6, 133

Eichler, Willi 66–7
emergency laws 97, 100, 115
Épinay Congress 111, 130, 137, 139
Erhard, Ludwig 27, 41, 45, 69, 74, 97, 127
eurocommunism 142
extra-parliamentary Left 7, 87, 94, 99, 101–10, 112–16, 133–5, 137–8, 148, 164

Fabius, Laurent 130
Fanfani, Amintore 45, 71–2, 77

fascism 2, 4, 16, 21, 22, 24, 39, 42, 44, 46, 49, 55, 67, 70, 73, 77, 81, 86, 160
FDP 70, 73–4, 95, 97, 99, 109–10, 131
Ferruccio Parri 13
Fifth Republic 5, 65, 78, 80–2, 84–6, 95, 97, 100, 108, 111–12, 115, 137–40, 143–5, 147, 162
Forlani, Arnaldo 126, 150
Forza Italia 165
Fourth Republic 5, 14, 21, 31, 39, 40, 42–4, 48, 51, 55–8, 65, 78–81, 84, 86–7, 162, 164
Freiburger Thesen 110
Front National 6, 144, 150

Gallie, Walter Bryce 2
Gaullists 5, 7, 13, 16–18, 20, 23–5, 28, 31
Giscard d'Estaing, Valéry 128, 138–40, 146
Godesberger Programme 66–9, 86–7, 131
Gonella, Guido 24, 70, 77, 167
Grand Coalition 65, 70, 86, 95, 97, 100, 102
Green Party in West Germany 133–6, 144, 150

Heuss, Theodor 11, 17
historic compromise 113, 137, 142–3, 146, 148
Hitler, Adolf 13, 17, 100
Hot Autumn 1969 103, 105, 113
Hungarian Uprising 58, 67, 73, 76, 82, 86

Jaspers, Karl 51, 75

Kelly, Petra 134
Keynesianism 44, 68, 73, 95, 124, 126, 128, 164–5
Kohl, Helmut 107, 127, 147
KPD 13–14, 52

Lega Nord 146
Les Verts 135
Liberal Italy 15, 17
Lotta Continua 101, 103, 105–6, 135–7

Marchais, Georges 111–12
Mendès France, Pierre 50, 58, 79, 81–3, 95–6, 164

militant democracy 17, 22, 52
Mita, Ciriaco, de 148–9
Mitterrand, François 79, 81, 95–6, 111–12, 115, 125, 128, 130, 139–40, 143–5, 164
Mollet, Guy 26, 44, 50, 56, 79, 81, 84–5, 115
Moro, Aldo 4, 22, 24, 71–2, 75, 85, 99, 107–9, 114, 141, 143, 148
Moscow *see* Soviet Union
Movimento Studentesco 101, 104–5
MRP 24, 47, 55, 57
MSI 12, 21, 50, 58, 70–1, 73, 77, 146, 164
Müller, Jan-Werner 2, 166
Mussolini, Benito 4, 55

Napolitano, Giorgio 148
Nazism 14, 29, 41–2, 97
Nenni, Pietro 14, 26, 46, 56, 66–8, 70–2, 75, 77, 85

Ochetto, Achille 142
Oil Crisis 124–5, 131, 165
Ollenhauer, Erich 51, 54, 66–7

Parliamentary Council 15, 18
PCF 19, 23, 26, 43, 56–7, 82, 84, 109, 111–12, 115, 132, 138, 142
PCI: in the 1950s: 41–2, 44, 47, 53, 54; and changes of the 1960s 67, 70–1, 74, 76, 78, 86–7, 96, 98; and 'democratic turn' 113–16; and economic reforms in the 1970s 132; and historic compromise *see* historic compromise; and party reform in the 1970s and 1980s 140–1, 145–6, 149; and postwar reform 13, 20, 23, 25, 29; and reaction to '68 101, 108, 112
pentapartito 145
Piccoli, Flaminio 108, 145
Pompidou, Georges 108, 138–9
Popular Front in Italy 13, 40, 42, 58
populism 6, 166
Poujadism 50, 57, 164
Prague Spring 111
PS 111, 112, 115, 130, 133, 138
PSI: in the 1950s: 41–2, 44, 47, 54; and crisis of Italian democracy in the 1970s and 1980s 143; and postwar reform 17, 29; and reaction to oil crisis 129–30; and reform in the 1960s 65–74, 76–7, 85, 87

PSIUP 77, 95, 97–9, 101, 110, 114, 164
PSU 96–9, 101, 106, 110, 114, 135, 164

Radical Party in France 50
Radical Party in Italy 146
referenda: in France 18, 23, 43, 79–84 108; in Italian constitution 30, 53
regional reform in Italy 53, 72, 78
Rocard, Michel 106, 130–1, 135, 137
Rosanvallon, Pierre 5
Rossanda, Rossana 112, 146
RPF 42, 53, 56
Rumor, Mariano 51, 99, 108, 141, 163

Saragat, Giuseppe 13, 26, 70, 73
Scelba, Mario 46, 53, 55, 58, 162
Scheel, Walter 95, 97
Schmid, Carlo 19, 21, 85
Schmidt, Helmut 115, 127, 131
Schumacher, Kurt 12–14, 16, 19, 25–6, 29, 42, 46, 51, 54, 161
Scoppola, Pietro 149
SFIO 14, 26, 29, 43–4, 49, 55, 57, 86–7
Socialist Reichs Party 50
Socialist Student Union 106, 134
social market economy 3, 25, 41–2, 44–5, 97, 127, 131
Sofri, Adriano 135–6

Soviet Union 11, 20, 40, 42, 52, 67–8, 73, 76, 78, 86, 101, 109, 111, 113, 138, 141–2
SPD: and economic reform after 1973 129, 131; and postwar reform 12–13, 15–16, 19–20, 22, 24, 26–7, 29–30; in the 1950s 39–42, 44–7, 51–2, 54–5; and reaction to '68 100, 103, 109–110, 112, 115, 133, 137; and reform around 1960 66–70, 72–5, 85–7, 95–8
Stalin, Joseph 41, 56, 58, 65, 67, 82
Strauss, Franz Josef 75, 107, 127
Sturzo, Luigi 49

Tambroni, Fernando 70–1, 73, 75
technocrats 94–5, 97, 99–101, 103, 130
terrorism 116, 124, 133, 143, 146
Third Force 40, 43, 56, 162
Third Republic 14, 16–18, 40, 48
Thorez, Maurice 11, 17–19, 25, 56, 82–3, 96
Togliatti, Palmiro 13, 20, 23, 30, 42, 43, 53, 55, 70, 76, 113, 146

Vecchietti, Tullio 95
Viale, Guido 101, 102, 105–6, 136–7
Vogel, Hans-Jochen 131

Weimar Republic 14, 21, 42